Sex and the Cinema

UNIVERSITY OF CHICHESTER

Sex and the Cinema

Tanya Krzywinska

WALLFLOWER PRESS

LONDON & NEW YORK

First published in Great Britain in 2006 by
Wallflower Press
6a Middleton Place, Langham Street, London W1W 7TE
www.wallflowerpress.co.uk

A catalogue for this book is available from the British Library

ISBN 1-904764-73-8 (pbk)
ISBN 1-904764-74-6 (hbk)

Book design by Elsa Mathern

Printed by Replika Press Pvt Ltd., India

Contents

Acknowledgements

Thanks to Yoram Allon for asking me to write this book; Brunel University for giving me the time I needed to finish writing it; Michele Aaron, Leon Hunt, Geoff King, Caroline Ruddell, Mary Richards and Nina Taunton for their generosity and helpful suggestions; Ken Stone, Judy Homer and Viv Atkins for their encouragement; David Bessell for sustenance and patience; *World of Warcraft* and my guildies for downtime fun; and Imogen Watson for more than I am able to say.

$\mathscr{I}$ntroduction

$\mathscr{R}$omantic intimacies. The supple ripple of satin lingerie. A sculpted bare torso. A hand brushing a naked thigh. Furtive sex in a seedy hotel room. Passion in the embrace of nature. From the sanctioned to the forbidden, the suggestive to the blatant, evocations of the sexual have saturated cinema with a heady distillation of fleshly passions. Whether laced in the rapturous rhetorics of romance or seeking to pack a harder erotic punch, sex has provided cinema with one of its major attractions. Sex and sexuality in the cinema are shaped by a wide variety of factors, some formal or generic, some relating to the institutions that regulate what is allowed to be seen and not seen, and others grounded in the more general configurations of the socio-historical context in which a film is produced and consumed. Sex can be used to spice up a weak storyline, as noted by Linda Ruth Williams (2002: 478), or build characterisation. It may provide an important aspect of a narrative, a subtext, undercurrent, or motivational force. Some aspect of sexual desire and sexuality has a presence across the entire range of cinema, most obviously in films that focus on sex itself such as *Secrets of a Chambermaid* (1997), a soft-core film expressly designed to titillate. But the presence of sex is also found in more mainstream films where it is not so overtly central, as with the melodramatic and adulterous kiss in the wave-surge in *From Here to Eternity* (1953) set against the backdrop of the events of Pear Harbour, the 'will-they-or-wont-they' relationship between the central protagonists in the high-fantasy 'PG'-rated anime *Princess Mononoke* (*Mononoke-hime*, 1997), in the way that Brad Pitt's body is shot to express the desires of one of the protagonists, functioning as an articulation of the male body as erotic object of the gaze, in the female buddy movie *Thelma and Louise* (1991), and the more subtly portrayed submissive sexual desire of the male protagonist in the film noir *Out of the Past* (aka *Build My Gallows High*, 1947). Despite differences in form, uses and intent, whether sold directly as a sex film or couched in the generic trappings of romance, art cinema, comedy, crime, tragedy, high fantasy or melodrama, sex and sexuality have proved a primary means to sell films to potential audiences throughout cinema history.

Sex and cinema have a very intimate, special and sometimes stormy relationship. Subject to regulation and censorship, yet often articulating diverse fantasies, the portrayal of sex and sexuality in cinema runs the gamut between raw transgressive acts and idealistic notions of sex as an expression of romantic love. Sex has perhaps caused more controversy than any other aspect of cinema and is subject to competing claims that range between the extremes of libertarianism and conservativism. Cinema is intended mainly for a mass audience and it therefore operates in full view of the public sphere. Sexual acts are meant conventionally to be closeted in the private domain so their public presence has tended to solicit intense debate hinging on what constitutes public morality. Unlike radio or the written word, cinema shows rather than tells. This has an impact on the way that sex and sexuality are mediated by film, tailored to fit with the particular contours of the medium, as well as the capacity of the camera to manufacture that which might ordinarily be, or perhaps imagined to be, hidden from view. Many films from across the range trade precisely on such a seductive promise. Robert Kolker claims that 'film and the erotic are linked in some of the earliest images we have' (1999: 18). Evidence for his assertion is found with the Edison Company's *The Kiss* (1896). The allure of the sexual has been integral to the appeal of cinema ever since.

The spectacle of cinematic sex is often intended to produce strong reactions, with controversy proving to be an excellent marketing tool. Many films, from *The Kiss* to *9 Songs* (2004), have traded on the conflicts that inevitably arise when entertainment and moral values clash. It is clear from the ubiquitous presence of sex in cinema that it has a strong seductive power and it may well provide images and ideas that affect our own expectations and fantasies about sex, sexuality and desire. Representations of sex and sexuality in cinema have therefore been regarded as having the potential to destabilise dominant mores about sex and desire. As such, cinematic sex is subject to the scrutiny of vested interests, beyond the average cinema-goer. At times these are able to influence what is considered acceptable for public consumption. However, throughout cinema's existence stakeholders have disagreed over what they consider the role and impact of cinema to be in society and what should be sanctioned against. The history of sex in the cinema is therefore informed in often dynamic ways by struggles between competing investments.

The major aim of this study is to identify and analyse the impact of the most significant factors that shape representations of sex and sexuality in English-speaking cinema. Sex in cinema is framed and contextualised by a dizzying number of factors, however. Some of these factors are formal and media-specific while others are institutional and conceptual. All of these are related in some way to the broader socio-cultural arena, which in itself is composed of competing trends with concomitant pressures and contentions. These ebb and flow in time accord with the rhythms of dominant and emergent forces, narrative trends and social concerns. Sex and sexuality in the cinema are tightly bound to these ever-shifting contours. In looking across the history of sex and sexuality in the cinema we shall see that the definition and understanding of concepts as varied as good taste, civilisation, perversion, pleasure, morality, shame, love and obscenity are all subject to reinterpretation and change. Some concepts and the issues appended to them fade from view while others arise. Others have acquired radically different meanings; some moving away from the margins, their places taken by other incarnations. In exploring the factors that shape the cinematic representation of sex and sexuality it is possible to build a picture of the way that the various facets of such representations are keyed into and fashioned by broader contexts.

Existing works on this much discussed subject tend to focus on particular aspects of sex in the cinema. Censorship, gender, sexuality, issues of sexual identity and definitions of pornography are common topics. Others focus in on a particular era, genre or methodological approach to the topic. By contrast, *Sex and the Cinema* takes a broader approach and addresses the ways in which sex and sexuality – the one does not come without the other – are mediated by the particularities of cinema. It is inevitable that through the process of selecting examples for inclusion in the book that certain trends, films and national cinemas are absent. Examples are drawn from across a fairly wide spectrum, however. These have often been chosen because they represent key trends, issues or conventions in the portrayal of sex in cinema. I have selected examples of soft-core, hard-core, art films that focus expressly on sex, as well as using examples of films that are more focused on sexuality, some of which are filtered through the conventions of genres, including horror, romance and melodrama. I have sought to use films that are fairly easily obtainable on video or DVD and have used mainly, but not exclusively, English-language films. A range of historical eras, cinemas and genres are represented and I have included films from Europe and Asia where they prove influential on English-language films or where they illustrate a point of cultural or formal difference.

This book is designed to provide an academic, yet accessible, cultural archaeology of the representation of sex in cinema. In order to examine the factors that contribute to representations of sex and desire, the book has two parts. Part I, 'Defining Sex in Cinema: Form and Frameworks', maps out the various institutional and industrial forces that each play their hand in the way that sex appears in cinema. An analysis of the relationships between form, context and knowledge frameworks provides a basis from which to move to an examination of common conventions used in the representation of sex and common narrative types.

This is followed by an account of the impact of censorship and regulation on the way that sex appears in both legitimate and illegitimate cinema. Part II, 'Themes of Transgression', focuses in on a selected number of themes that are encoded as in some way transgressive: adultery, bestiality, incest, bondage, domination, sado-masochism and real sex. Each of the sections devoted to these themes draw on a range of films from various genres and cinematic traditions. The conditions that permit the exhibition of sexually transgressive themes such as these are linked to what is culturally sanctioned at any given juncture; often 'art' values are employed as a means of rendering the unconscionable suitable for consumption as entertainment. As we shall see, under the aegis of transgression, psychoanalytic theories of sexuality and the psyche often make an appearance at a thematic level. The practice of couching sex in such rhetoric works for the industry, acting as something of a strange attractor for prospective audiences, yet, as will become plain, the rhetorics of transgression employed in the representation of sex take many different forms and have a range of implications and intentions.[1]

Although this study is not designed to be a chronology of sex in cinema, it nevertheless seeks as one of its goals to demonstrate how the representation of sex in cinema is subject to historical, cultural and stylistic change. Because of its particular aims, this book does not make use of a single methodological approach. Instead it is organised around a number of frameworks, trends, issues, themes and approaches that present themselves as significant in the representation of sex in cinema and which typify the influence of certain ideas about sexuality that have emerged in a broader context. As we will see, cinematic sex is intricately interwoven into a matrix of industrial, economic, social and cultural factors. Within and between these, various competing claims are often in evidence. The amalgam of perspectives on the representation of sex in cinema taken by this study is designed to acknowledge and analyse the diverse range of forces, frameworks and factors that shape those representations.

Defining Sex in Cinema: Forms and Frameworks

Forms and Contexts

*R*eactions to watching cinematic sex are highly variable. It might be found exciting, banal, outmoded, ridiculous, erotic, or even dull. It might provoke lust, disgust, laughter, pity, or embarrassment. Yet no matter how instances of on-screen sex are experienced by individual viewers they are always tailored to fit the commercial and formal particularities of cinema. Cinema mediates sex and sexuality to serve its very specific purposes and values.[2] Aspects of sex that we encounter on screen may well relate in some way to our own lives, fantasies, prurient curiosities and experiences; if they did not then cinematic sex would not attract our interest. While the constructed nature of sex in cinema is obvious when we regard films as industrial or commercial products, its mediated nature is perhaps less blatant when we are captivated by intimate, erotic or even alarming actions on screen or faced with a film that wants us to believe that what we are watching is real. It is worthwhile being sceptical about any putative dividing line between the constructed, the natural and the real, particularly as sex and sexuality in life are themselves performative, grounded in the imagination, often staged and involving role-play and fantasy. Yet that which is designed for cinema – whether 'real' in some sense or not – is a commercial product, and a product that is designed to pull, tease and please a certain pre-defined target audience.

Cinematic sex, in whatever guise, is squeezed into shape by the exertion of various forces. These can be divided into the following: aesthetic and formal; industrial and market-based; institutional, discursive and socio-cultural-historical. It is the effect of these forces on the representation of sex and sexuality that this book is concerned with. Each belong to a particular domain, yet they are often intimately connected. Formal frameworks established and used in cinema might make a film aesthetically or stylistically interesting but they also operate to some degree, and in different ways depending on the type of film, as a form of marketing device. 'Art' films, for example, often flaunt experimental formal techniques that break with established practice in order to attract a particular, identifiable, niche audience.

The shaping forces of the formal and the industrial also operate within the larger framework of the socio-historical context in which a film is produced and consumed.

It is fairly easy to identify different formal devices used in the representation of sex in cinema and it is also relatively straightforward to analyse the type of markets that a film is aimed at. By contrast a socio-cultural-historical context is not an easy thing to grasp. It is not really an object, an event or a phenomenon. It has no definitive edges, temporally or spatially. At any given moment its fabric is composed of everything that makes up human life: the personal – thoughts, enthusiasms, events, experiences, memories – are nested within the collective and institutional shapers of life – law, national and local government policy, marriage, gender, language, media. Even the phrase itself seems beguilingly tidy and tends to obscure the gross complexity of diverse, multi-dimensional and shifting current and counter-currents of which socio-historical contexts are composed. Cultural historians or theorists look for patterns and trends within this intricate fabric; some look to institutional factors for indications of what characterises that context, or they may choose to focus on more localised and/or personal experiences. It is, however, unlikely that even the most diligent of analysts will ever gain more than an impression or partial view of a given social-historical context. Reductionism is not easily avoided, as the pressure to 'make sense' of a social-cultural context can produce over-simplification.

So far the forces that shape cinematic sex have been lightly sketched, to be filled in with greater detail in what follows, but a further dimension is so far missing that will prove to be important to this book. It might seem that I am delaying getting to the 'meat' of sex in the cinema but as this is, after all, an academic book it is important to outline the theoretical and contextual frameworks that prove influential in the way that cinema mediates sex. Cinema has often been regarded as a mirror held up to culture; it is certainly the case that within its frame issues of concern and collective fantasies about sex and sexuality are played with and played out. But cinema is also an active cultural and social institution. It does not simply reflect; it also plays a role in defining what is of collective concern. Cinema has, at times and in conjunction with other factors, contributed to shaping the meanings and values placed on sex and sexuality.

The formal features of a given film play perhaps the most overtly evident role in the way that cinematic sex and sexual themes acquire their shape and meaning. Story, editing, acting, visual style, music and sound all contribute to this. Take narrative, for example. Narrative is defined here as the way in which a story is realised by a film. In governing the placement of events within the trajectory of a story, narrative supplies the context through which an event, including sexualised events, makes sense. In the supernatural thriller *Don't Look Now* (1973) a fairly explicit, solitary sex scene appears around halfway through the film. It is quite a long scene in which a couple move from gentle foreplay through the intensity of orgasm to the post-'good sex' afterglow effect. The scene certainly won the film some notoriety mainly because of its naturalistic acting styles, the apparent authenticity of which is supported by hand-held camera work. The scene does not appear in real-time, a device that is most often found in films designed solely around showing 'real' sex (a characteristic that defines hard-core). Instead a montage of images of the couple undertaking various sexual activities build sequentially and are interleaved with cutaways that project forwards a short time to the characters dressing for an evening out, during which they are clearly shown as being affected, positively, by their earlier passion. What is important here is that the sex scene is actively contextualised both by narrative and the formal strategies in play. It is keyed into the contextual fabric of the couple's lives, something underpinned by the use of cutaways that punctuate the sex scene. The fact that the couple have sex at all is further linked to a chain of events. Not long before the scene in question, one of the characters is affected very deeply by an encounter with a strange woman and it is the effect of this event that promotes, to some degree, the sex that follows. Within the recent past the couple's small daughter drowned in their garden pond. Grief has subsequently burdened both characters and we learn later that the child's mother has been unable to work and is reliant on sedatives. These cues suggest that sex between the couple has ceased. While working in Venice, the couple encounter a pair of middle-aged women, one of whom is both blind and a seer (a psychic). She explains to the mother that she sees their dead child sitting happily between the couple, adding some detail that convinces the mother that what is said is true. After recovering from the initial shock, the debilitating grip of grief loosens, and as a result the intimate pleasures of sex are once again possible. The events that lead up to and frame the sex scene build particularities of situation and characterisation that then imbue that scene with an emotionally complex colouring. The leading melody of the scene, indicated by their pleasure, tenderness and their broad smiles, is joy, which contrasts strongly with the sombre tones of grief that otherwise characterise the film. In addition, the fact that their relationship has survived tragedy and that moments of joy are once more experienced makes the husband's violent death at the end of the film all the more distressing.

All these features hinge around the relationship of the sex scene to the narrative that contextualises it. Narrative supplies the framing logic for stylistic and other aesthetic devices that are used in the film. The washed-out, November-ish, colour palette adds to the sense of a world drained by grief of joy and meaning, a device that connects the external world to the subjective experience of the couple. The naturalistic acting, complemented by location shooting, enhances the sense that the characters should be regarded as real, emotionally complex, people. The sex scene itself does not appear to be carefully staged and lit to idealise the actors' bodies as occurs in many other films and emotion is given equal importance to the physical, a factor that is underpinned by the way the scene is structured by editing, where cross-cutting between the couple having sex to them dressing afterwards keeps the emotional and narrative context of the scene present in the viewer's mind. The editing translates into cinematic terms the way that this sexual act is interwoven into the couple's lives.

Many fictional feature films aim at attracting the widest possible audience and configure narrative using familiar conventions to allow the audience to focus on the flow of a story rather than on the mechanics of filmmaking. Within such typical 'illusionist' formulations, cinematic sex is most frequently presented as, in some way, believable, understandable in relation to situation and integral to the story (elsewhere sex might be more obviously 'posed' for the camera as is sometimes the case in hard-core sex films or in certain self-referential art or exploitation films[3]). Within many mainstream films narrative functions as one of a range of devices that hide the staged and simulated nature of mediated sex from view. The cloaking of the seams that might betray the artifice of a film and its sexual components is also achieved in most narrative-based fictional films by stitching acting, style, sound and mise-en-scène to the logical precedent set by the narrative, as we have seen in the case of Don't Look Now.

Genre-based films use predefined patterns to provide a framework within which various formal strategies might fit in a unified manner. The particular blend of these components gives specific shape to the representation of sex and sexuality. A romantic comedy, for example, is likely to have a narrative that is guided by a progression towards the union, or re-union, of a couple in love. It is likely to have a lightness of touch, capturing perhaps the dizziness of love. This may well be reflected in the particular style of music used, the acting-styles, costume design, setting and lighting. Within this generic context, sexual attraction and foreplay are located as a courtship game. Most of these accoutrements are present in the romantic comedy Pillow Talk (1959), starring Rock Hudson and Doris Day. The film includes exuberant and more reflective songs, in musical styles popular at the time, a particularly bright colour palette, and builds a story around a misunderstanding between the pair that defers the sexual union of the couple. That union is only achieved – and permitted by the female character – at the end of the film, once the pair marry. Given that the film was made for a non-restricted audience the act of coitus is only hinted at, indicated by the images used in the closing credits where two pillows are seen side by side on which 'The End' is written, on top of and between which a smaller pink pillow appears, bearing the words 'not quite', followed by a blue and then another pink one bearing the same words. The film makes its dramatic and comic capital out of the couple's differing sexual moralities, a difference that needs to be levelled out for romance to ensue (a common feature of romantic comedies). As with many Hollywood films of the 1950s there is a great deal of (pillow) talk about sex, but this is not matched by what is seen.

The particular set of formal devices used in a given film often cue spectators into regarding events and characters in certain ways. These cues often produce what is sometimes referred to by cultural theorists as a preferred or intended reading. This process of cueing constitutes one of the ways in which cinema can be said to operate as an active social institution, although such cognitive manipulation is certainly not specific to cinema. Because films often seek to steer a spectator's emotional reactions and the meanings that they are likely to read off the textual surface of a film in particular ways, it is common to find the imprint of particular moral agendas (generally, but for the purposes of this book the focus will fall on those relating to sex and sexuality). These may be personal to a filmmaker, but in many cases they are also geared around the type of audience a film is designed for, and often take into account regulatory factors that might define the make-up of an audience for a given film. In many films from across the history of cinema, particularly in American and European cinemas, a kind of moral double-dealing about sex and sexual themes is in evidence. Messages about what constitutes 'good' sexual morality are often present, commonly in the form of some kind of punishment for wrongdoing, but these may well be out-weighed by the excitement produced in watching that which is deemed elicit or transgressive. Commercial gain has often promoted films that present heavy-handed moral messages in a cynical way precisely to capitalise on the display of such transgressions. Accusations of such were, for example, levelled by contemporaries at the biblical and historical epics of Cecil B. DeMille, which often displayed 'unchristian' sexual acts and desires (of which more later).

Mainly because of the commercial, market-driven framework within which cinema often operates, the representation of sex and sexual themes often adopts conventionalised patterns in formal, moral and communicative terms. Narrative and genre type play a key role in creating such regularities that are connected to, sometimes set against, dominant moral paradigms prevalent in given time and culture. Along with others, Rick Altman (1984) argues that the formal patterns used in cinema generate meaning, and this can be understood through a combination of semiotics and cognitive psychology. The basic premise of semiotics is that signs carry conventionalised meanings that we learn. This approach dovetails quite neatly with some aspects of cognitive psychology, first developed by Jean Piaget, a psychologist interested in how humans acquire and develop knowledge. In Piaget's terms a schema describes a kind of pattern or framework that functions to organise thought. Fundamental to cognition is the propensity to look for these patterns. The presence of certain signs in the perceptual field and presented within a certain context will throw into a gear a set of expectations and conjectures. To illustrate, in cinematic terms: a mid-shot of long legs in fish-net stockings and black high-heeled shoes seen against a leopard-skin print chair may well cue a viewer into categorising those legs as belonging to a prostitute. David Bordwell states that 'the sensory data of the film at hand furnish the material out of which inferential processes of perception and cognition build meaning' (1991: 3). While all meaning is contingent, conventional and culturally grounded, viewers are active in this process of conjecture, always working, to some degree or other, to fit what they see and hear into a frame of reference. Film plays often with such expectations, perhaps as the camera cuts to a long shot we find that those legs in fact belong to a man in drag or a girl in fancy dress, if so then the viewer is likely to respond by accommodating this new information into a revised schema.

As a system of communication, film constantly makes use of familiar patterns or schemas. As a show rather than tell medium, film uses visual and auditory cues that invoke various conventional meanings, often as a kind of shorthand. The use of familiar inference-soliciting paradigms channel to a certain extent the way the viewer is likely to regard what they see, a factor that has an ideological dimension, particularly when a certain way of seeing things is presented as morally right. And it is also the case that the inferences that a film invites the audience to make through its formal features may conflict with those that arise from alternative schematic frameworks. For example a new piece of information might alter the way a film is read, as when the 'intended' meanings of *Pillow Talk* might be altered or seen in a different light with the knowledge that Rock Hudson was gay.

The way in which formal and broader contextual frameworks interlock to shape the way that sex is represented, schematised and afforded meaning can be illustrated by a brief consideration of 'noir' thrillers produced in Hollywood during the 1940s and early 1950s. Many noir narratives are set in contemporary urban America and focus on the effects of social malaise and corruption. 'Decent' moral values are under siege, which critics Sylvia Harvey (1978) and Frank Krutnik (1991) have argued arose from the 'uncertainties and confusions' (Krutnik 1991: 61) of the postwar period. Central to all this insecurity in most noirs is sex, which becomes highly polarised in accordance with a range of cinematic, entertainment, social and moral values. Sanctioned/legitimised sex is confined to the marital bedroom; it comes in crisp white cotton and its respectable status means it is also hidden from the public gaze. This is *good* sex in moral terms, but its absence from the screen, which keeps its status virtual and virtuous, suggests that it is not regarded as good morally to look at others having sex. In contrast to the codes of sexual decency at work in the films is the allure of that which is apparently outside the moral order. Sheathed in black satin and carrying a .45, this sex is seductive, dangerous and duplicitous. This polar organisation of noir sex is built into the formal strategies used in the film and illustrates quite neatly the way that the audiences are cued into making inferences about sexual morality and gender. The plots of both *Out of the Past* and *Double Indemnity* (1944), for example, pivot on the seductive allure of two sexual sirens who lure into treacherous waters men who have lost their authority and meandered away from the safety of moral certainty.

Many critics have often focused on the gender stakes in play in noir. Krutnik claims, for example, that 'noir femmes fatales tend to be women who seek to advance themselves by manipulating their sexual allure and controlling its value' (1991: 63) and that noir men are very likely to allow themselves to be seduced by such women. He brings these seductions back to the social context of postwar America: there is an 'erosion of confidence in the structuring mechanisms of masculine identity and the masculine role' (1991: 64). *Double Indemnity* and *Out of the Past* certainly seem to support these claims. The two femmes fatales of the films, Phyllis Dietrichsen (Barbara Stanwyck) and Kathie Moffat (Jane Greer) respectively, actively use their sexuality to gain power, a feature that is often claimed of more recent 'post-feminist' representations, and their double-dealing undermines the authority and confidence of the two main male protagonists. But as Krutnik rightly goes on to say, noir did not simply reflect social context but instead 'the generic spectrum of the noir "tough" thriller become institutionalised as the principle vehicle for the articulation of ambivalence and negativity' (1991: 61). Not all Hollywood films from this era dwelt on such issues nor did they all polarise sex so extremely. The specific generic features of the noir thriller acts as a schema that actively shapes the representation of sex and sexuality. Many of the formal devices that characterise noir carry codes that encourage audiences to make inferences about the moral status of characters.

The suspect morality and perfidious duplicity of both Phyllis and Kathie are aptly realised through the stylistic particularity of noir lighting. At certain moments of plot 'realisation' or 'discovery' these femmes fatales are lit by high-contrast low-key lights that throw strong dark shadows over parts of their faces. By contrast, the morally wholesome women of the films, those whose desires conform to family, marriage and subordination to men and who do not present a danger to the established gendered order, are lit with low-contrast, high-key lights, so few shadows are created (they, after all, have no discomforting ulterior motives to hide). The use of illumination and darkness accords with a moral order that is constructed through conventional concepts of good and evil (albeit that in noir this is translated into 'human' rather than metaphysical terms). The lighting code discloses the otherwise hidden state of being of the women in these films, leaving the audience in no doubt what the source of the trouble is in the case of the predatory femme fatale. What the lighting scheme asks the audience to surmise is that these women may be beautiful, but beauty does not necessarily mean moral 'goodness'. And, in order to fit with the regulatory code that stipulated that wrong-doing must be seen to be punished, the perfidy of the women is revealed and they are punished (Phyllis is shot by the man she has duped and Kathie dies in a car crash caused through a self-destructive act of desperation and selfishness). Part of the sexual-moral dimension of noir is therefore carried in the *mise-en-scène*, aspects of which are likely to induce audience members to infer certain meanings. Such inferences are also supported by the co-presence of narratives typically centred on alienation and the social impact of amorality or immorality. While these provide dramatic interest they also raised issues that resonate with publicly aired fears about the problems of contemporary society, and particularly the fear that sexual immorality was linked to crime.

Industrial and commercial contexts also have a role to play in shaping cinematic sex. Genre, for example, operates as a formal feature of cinema but it is also used to define the target audience for a given film. Whether noir, romantic comedy or supernatural thriller, genre has an important function in shaping the way that sex is portrayed and the type of meanings it is likely to carry or encourage an audience to infer. Individual generic formulations and their concomitant visual styles create different modes with which to approach sexual subjects. Horror films tend to mediate sex in a way quite different from romantic comedies, for example, and each has a distinctive set of narrative possibilities open to them, which are aimed at a specific market segment. Potential box-office appeal is often a leading concern for the film industry that keys into genre formulations and the particular approach taken to the representation of sex and sexuality. Marketing a film begins before it is even made and involves a calculated prediction about what audiences expect, or are likely to want to see. This may involve the use of particular directors or stars to aid the process of genre or non-genre film branding, important as a means of creating audience recognition.

Different genres and styles can be seen as a way of segmenting and manipulating the market. To explore some of the implications of the division of the market into different sectors it is useful to compare films made for the mainstream market and those that take a more explicit approach to sex.

Big-budget mainstream films made for the widest audience base are often those that have fairly mild sexual content so that they can gain the lucrative 'PG' or '12' grading; as a result sex is often coded in such a way that innuendos or sexual suggestiveness pass over the heads of minors, providing a kind of dual address. 'U' certificate films often attract smaller audiences than 'PG', '15' and '12' certificate films, which Linda Ruth Williams suggests is because 'U' certificate films are regarded as not being stimulating enough for older audiences.[4] Films that portray more explicit sex are likely to receive a classification that limits their potential audience. In an effort to manage this, big-budget films with more explicit sexual scenes therefore tend to have stars or directors that are likely to help pull in the adult market. Stanley Kubrick's *Eyes Wide Shut* (1999) is a good example of a film focused on sex and sexual desire that has a well-known director *and* high-profile stars. Independently-produced films are often made on lower budgets and therefore require less return. In some cases the independent sector provides new directors with the opportunity to make their names and allows them to tackle subjects related to sex and sexuality that are perhaps less likely to attract a broader mainstream audience; Spike Jonze's *Being John Malkovich* (1999) is a good example. At the other end of the scale are hard-core sex films.[5] These are designed to target a very specific niche market (and they divide down further into subgenres that cater for specific interests). In order to distinguish themselves from other types of film and other types of films focused on sex, say soft-core of the type that are legally shown on British pay-per-view television or exploitation movies, hard-core sex films adopt a particular set of conventions and formulas for presenting sex on screen. These govern the ways in which the films are specifically marketed and exhibited, a factor that prevails, at least in some Western countries, now as much as when the first 'smoker' or 'stag' reels were made in the first decades of the twentieth century.[6] The specificity of hard-core's approach to representing sex has set a benchmark that, even now in the age of increasingly niched media, divides the marketplace for sex-based films.

However, in the world of cinema boundaries between films targeted for particular market sectors are liable to movement; this too is often driven by commercial interests. Although the distinction between hard-core and 'legitimate' cinemas has persisted for over a century, a number of recent films seeking more mainstream distribution for strong sexual themes, such as *Romance* (1999) or *Baise-moi* (2001), utilise some conventions that hitherto had only been used in hard-core, but these are somewhat limited and framed rather differently than they might be in hard-core. The traditional distinctions between hard-core and mainstream are diminishing somewhat therefore, yet before we jump to the conclusion that hard-core no longer operates as a primary driver in the segmentation of the market, it should be noted that there are still conditions that apply to the adoption of hard-core conventions in most Western countries and that this process of exchange between regulated, less regulated and non-regulated cinemas is not a totally new phenomenon (see Part II, 'Real Sex', for further discussion).

A significant trend in the history of sex in English-language cinema is that which blossomed in mainstream Hollywood cinema of the 1950s. Films such as *A Streetcar Named Desire* (1951), *Baby Doll* (1956), *Cat on a Hot Tin Roof* (1958) and *Written on the Wind* (1958) were made specifically for an adult audience.[7] The industry took advantage of the relaxation of regulation in the US to include more explicit references to sex and sexual desires than had appeared in mainstream Hollywood-based film since the stricter implementation of the Production Code in 1934. The production of such films represents a strategic move on the part of the ailing American film industry to lure audiences back to the cinemas and away from family-oriented television. The trend also responded to the financial success of foreign imports, particularly ...*And God Created Woman* (*Et Dieu ... créa la femme*, 1956), a film that brought 'sex kitten' Brigitte Bardot to widespread attention. In these 'adult melodramas', as Barbara Klinger calls them (1994: 37–41), sex was strategically deployed to mark a distinction between competing media. The lure of erotic sensationalism – hitherto more commonly used to market exploitation films that were less stringently regulated than mainstream cinema, which was unseen in post-1934 American mainstream cinema – became a primary selling technique. Hollywood's move into more overt sexual realms can therefore be linked to a crisis in the film industry, which went hand in hand with a shift in regulatory and censorship protocols. The use of sexual sensationalism to sell such films, which like many exploitation films of the era have far less sexual content than their advertising suggests, can be seen in the posters created for *Cat on a Hot Tin Roof*. One poster proclaimed the film as having 'all the shock and fervour of Tennessee Williams' scorchingly outspoken play'. As seen in the reproduction opposite, the visual rhetoric used in the poster is informed by a strong sexual current: Elizabeth Taylor, as Maggie the Cat, invites the viewer into the bedroom, even onto the bed, with her seductive look.

The strategic placement of sexual material within the context of more traditional melodramatic forms was instrumental to the acceptance of such films by the mainstream industry. Further, many of these films are cinematic remakes of plays that had already been seen on Broadway, and the name of Tennessee Williams, the author of many of these plays-to-films, lent the films a certain artistic gravitas and a pre-sold reputation for quality. Unlike Britain, America did not have a ratings system; as a result these films could be seen potentially by any age group (the 'X' rating did not appear in the US until 1968). The films had to handle their relatively risqué themes in a carefully choreographed manner, therefore. As such, a psychological line of approach to sex was taken that was couched within the established and industrially legitimated language of melodrama, providing thereby a convenient way of dealing with sexual themes in a visually non-explicit way. Many of these 'adult' films, *Cat on a Hot Tin Roof* included, deal with the emotional effects of 'impotency' and 'nymphomania', thereby reflecting the popular adoption of certain ideas and concepts that were part

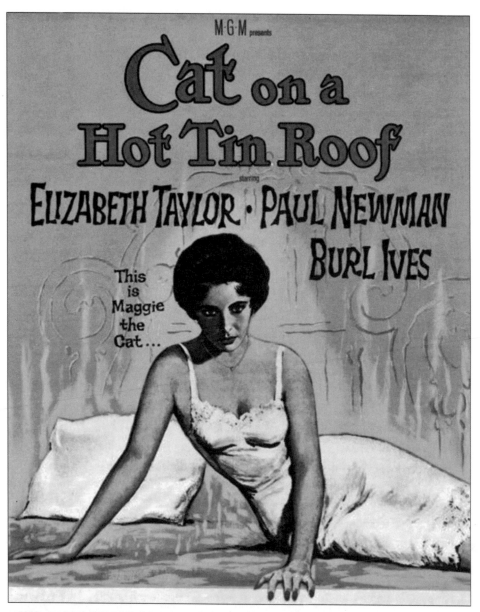

Maggie the Cat (Elizabeth Taylor) entices viewers with her seductive gaze, in a publicity poster for *Cat on a Hot Tin Roof* (1958)

of sexological discourse to speak of contemporary sexuality and norms (sexology and its influence on sex in cinema is discussed in more detail below).

As well as demonstrating that sexual content was used to rescue contemporary Hollywood from a downturn in cinema attendance, these adult melodramas also demonstrate a further definitional framework that plays a key role in the shaping of sex in cinema: this is institutional context of the regulation of cinematic content. The regulatory bodies of a given location and period play an important role in determining what is deemed as acceptable for public consumption. As Tom Dewe Mathews (1994) and Eric Schaefer (1999) have noted, the regulation of sex in mainstream film has tended to promote an excluded niche cinema that actively entices curious audiences with the lure of the *outré* (of which more later). Commercial pressures within mainstream cinema can prompt filmmakers and producers to look to excluded cinemas to promote renewed interest in mainstream products. This means that at certain junctures in the history of cinema the lines between the legitimate cinema and the excluded or fringe cinemas become blurred. Such is the case with adult melodramas of the 1950s, where aspects of exploitation cinema were adopted within a particular type of mainstream film and within certain parameters. A similar exchange occurred during the 1970s when elements of soft-core sex films were adopted into mainstream films that focused on sexual initiation themes. In these cases it is only certain elements that are drawn from the more *outré* cinemas, and these elements are framed by the use of forms established within the 'legitimate' cinema. It is tempting to think this process of adoption and accommodation are indicative of an increasingly liberal approach to the representation of sex in the media, and there might be a grain in truth in this, but generally the primary driver for these developments is a commercial imperative that arises, at least in part, from changes in media technology (television in the 1950s; video in the 1970s, and satellite and internet in the 1990s).

Demonstrating the way that formal features, industry and institution link to the broader cultural context is perhaps hampered by the fact that films are never a simple reflection of the socio-historical context in which they are produced, as stated earlier. Instead, and because of their remit to entertain, films effect a form of mediation or refraction of prevalent socio-historical factors. It is all too easy to make generalised and over-simplified connections between history (usually defined in terms of events that have an impact on a society: war, suffrage, changes in political policy) and a given film. A good example of this is 'decadism', in which it is often assumed that a decade, the 1940s say, is a kind of self-contained unit that is different quantifiably to the 1930s or 1950s. It is also reductive to assume that a given period is unified in terms of experience and culture. At a local level, individual experience is diverse. Social position, familial relationships, gender, age, ethnicity, religious belief, economic circumstance, temperament, taste and access to knowledge are all factors that impact on identity, interpretation and experience. Despite the problems these diverse circumstances make for a coherent understanding, historical contexts are of chief importance in the consideration of how sex in cinema has been shaped. Genres and narrative types do at least to some extent shift their contours in accordance with changes in industrial, institutional and socio-historical milieu.

As much of cinema is designed for a mass audience, it tends to speak for and to the majority. Cinema may not speak precisely of and to the experience of the individual, but its potential for popularity depends on connecting in some way to the experience of the majority. Necessary cautions duly noted, social-historical contexts are shaped by dominant ideas that relate to a lesser or greater extent to the majority experience of living in that context. These ideas are often constituted of dominant notions of the 'ideal' and the 'normal' and these define in a relational way what is considered to be aberrational or transgressive. Even if films do not reflect directly the social order, all films make use of such ideas (whether as critique or not). Cinema can and often does operate as a kind of social leveller by enticing viewers from diverse backgrounds to inhabit the particular moral perspective at work in a given film, and this is part of the way that cinema operates in some cases to reinforce particular 'norms'. The ways that an individual film frames its notions of virtue and vice are therefore deeply embedded in the types of knowledge systems that operate in a given social and historical context.

Knowledge Frameworks

$\mathcal{T}$he contours of a socio-historical context are shaped, at least in part, through ideas that have general currency at a given time. A term often used by cultural and social theorists to help in the process of understanding the way that such ideas are produced and disseminated is 'discourse'. Susan Hayward defines discourse as more than simply 'speech', rather a way of referring to 'the social process of making sense of and reproducing reality, and thereby of fixing meanings' (2000: 87). Various discourses originating from a wide range of sources inform the way that sex and sexuality are generally understood. Over the last 150 years, social science (anthropology, sociology and psychology) and social engineering (government policy, regulatory bodies, reformist groups seeking to change cultural practices) have played significant roles in shaping popular understandings of sex and sexuality. Religious traditions and aesthetic practices have also played their part in the way sex is framed, understood and represented. What is understood by sex and sexuality, indeed the way they are defined and even experienced, is the product of the discursive frameworks that are active within a socio-historical context. Because the knowledge that these different frameworks produce comes from different perspectives it is inevitable that conflicts arise. They are often contingent, inter-relate at certain points, at times dialectically, and each evolves in relation to changes in values, fitness of purpose, or in relation to new scientific data.

Charting the meanings and nature of human sexuality has preoccupied numerous philosophers, social scientists, medical professionals, psychologists, various therapists and cultural theorists. Such work has often been done under the protective umbrella of academic institutions and may not, therefore, fully represent the more general way that sex is thought about and treated in a given society. Working within different methodological disciplines and conceptual modules, academic-based studies of sex and sexuality have in some cases provided paradigms that shape attitudes to and the meanings and values of sex and sexuality. Certain 'powerful' names – Sigmund Freud, Richard Krafft-Ebing, Alfred Kinsey and Michel Foucault for instance – are regarded as having provoked shifts in the conceptual paradigms that determine how sex and sexuality are regarded or, as in Foucault's case, in revealing certain foundation-setting 'myths' in the history of sex. The invocation of such names may, at times, be somewhat misleading: individuals' names are often used simply as shorthand ways of expressing shifts that, in fact, occur in a far broader social arena. Shifts in the ways that sex is thought about and given meaning are more likely to be reflected in, rather than motivated initially by, key works of figures deemed significant. Often a more circular motion of exchange takes place. Theorists develop concepts and ideas that articulate what they see as occurring in human relations; some of these concepts find their way, often in simplified and remediated form, into the popular arena (through magazines, news, film, television).[8] At this point they may become used more commonly to explain or define an aspect of sexuality, which can work to fix our view of that practice.

The particular approach taken to sexuality in a film is, as we have already seen, based on assumptions about the views of a film's potential audience. When normative views of sexuality are challenged in films it is related as much to what the intended audience is perceived as wanting to see than to broader cultural conceptions of what sexuality is. Direct challenges to normative ideas of sex and gender identity are rarely found in Hollywood blockbusters. Instead they are more likely to appear in films targeted at young and/or sophisticated audiences, as with films such as *Romance* or *The Brandon Teena Story* (1998), or in films targeted at niche audiences as with New Queer Cinema (as termed by B. Ruby Rich in 1992).[9] It is necessary therefore to address the ways in which discourse from the intellectual sphere enters into popular arenas if we are to understand how theory-based ideas inform the meanings that are assigned to sex in cinema.

Sigmund Freud (1856–1939) is a name that commonly appears in relation to a shift in the way that sexuality is regarded. Various cultural commentators have claimed that Freud changed the way that sex is thought about. Domna C. Stanton (1992), for instance, asserts that Freud catalysed an important alteration in the way that Western culture regards sexuality. Freud's concepts have made a significant contribution to way that sex and sexuality is understood and they have made a strong contribution to the way that sex and sexuality is presented in cinema. Yet the fact that concepts like Freudian slips, the unconscious and repression found a footing in popular consciousness must mean that they serve to articulate issues that were more generally of concern or interest (indeed, theories of sexuality in general seemed to have popular caché in the twentieth century). The presence of Freudian concepts in cinema arose partly from the popularity of psychoanalytic therapies amongst the American glitterati and partly because of the dramatic potential of concepts like the unconscious and the return of the repressed, which prove so useful to genres such as horror and melodrama (see section entitled 'return of the repressed' in the chapter on 'Narrative Forms', below).

Many academics regard Freud's work as institutionalising the view that sex and sexual desire are constructed socially, therefore subject to historical change rather that than innate and universal. In other words the history of sex, according to Freud, is the history of social relations. Sex and the sexual body are produced and channelled through the specific organisation of discourse and social relations. Taking Freud's blueprint a stage further, Thomas Laqueur states that the socio-sexual body is produced by 'social thuggery that takes a polymorphously perverse infant and bullies it into a heterosexual man or woman' (1990: 240). He also argues that Freud was aware of 'the painful processes through which body parts are sorted out and come to represent the most telling of differences' (1990: 241), which refers to the way that gender attributes are imposed on the child, based on the way that bodily differences are categorised and assigned meanings in the social. This view of monogamous heterosexuality and gender as something forced on us through socialisation differs significantly from dominant notions where they are regarded, often, as 'natural'.

Importantly for this study of sex in cinema, Freud argued that social forces work to repress certain behaviours that do not accord with the figuring and concomitant expectations of gender and sexuality. As a result of such repression certain sexual fantasies and desires of a transgressive nature arise, providing a central plank of Freudian psychoanalysis. The effect of these repressions, and the return of what has apparently been repressed, can work to undermine our sense of personal autonomy, causing conflicts and tensions for an individual. The notion that human sexuality and gender are battlegrounds, subject to repression and potentially to transgression was something of a gift to cinema. Within Freud's model, sex is the great unknown, the 'other within', a trope that invests sex with treachery and makes our own desires seem deeply mysterious; as we have seen noir thrillers trade precisely on these grounds. The 'other within' has proved an extremely attractive concept for makers of fiction and has informed the narratives, or been present as a sub-text, of many films from both inside and outside Hollywood. Films from diverse styles, genres and national cinemas, including melodrama, comedy, horror, surrealism and art cinema, have been stoked by the enigmatic, dramatic and sensationalist potential of the repressed and its return. It is therefore quite clear that Freudian views of sex and sexuality as forced social constructions and constituted of competing desires have had a strong impact in both theoretical and popular entertainment arenas (narrative forms based on the return of the repressed are discussed later in Part I and the 'transgressive' qualities of the trope are discussed in Part II). But it is nonetheless the case that, despite the fact that Freud's ideas have become popularised in a general sense, sexuality is still taken to mean *heterosexuality* and that it, like gender, is considered innate rather than culturally and hegemonically constructed. This paradigm, what some critics have termed the 'heterosexual matrix', underpins a polarisation of sex, sexuality and gender into that which is considered 'normal' and that considered 'perverse' or 'against nature', an inherently transgression-laden structure that appears with a range of different intentions in cinema.

Alongside psychoanalysis, sexology has also made a notable contribution to the contours that define popular understandings of sex and sexuality. Sexological work, such as

Krafft-Ebing's *Psychopathia Sexualis*, published in 1886, and Alfred Kinsey's publication of interviews with a range of people about their sexual practices, published in 1948 and 1953, have helped consolidate a 'vocabulary' of sexual practices that is commonly used in subsequent popular discourse. The vocabulary used in sexology to categorise and name various sexual practises has also proved instrumental in defining what are commonly thought of as 'perversions' and sexual aberrations. Early sexological works sought to divide sexual acts and desires into discrete categories, sometimes inventing names for certain 'perversions' of sexual desire and practice. These terms made their way into popular discourse, and are even included within Hollywood's Production Code of the 1930s and 1940s, which used sexologically identified 'perversions' in its prescriptions on what was deemed acceptable for mass consumption. The exploitation and hard-core sector have also drawn on sexological case studies to market and categorise their films: sado-masochism, for instance, is a neologism of two separate words glued together by Krafft-Ebing (see Part II, 'Bondage, Domination and Sado-Masochism'). The effect of sexological publications, which in some cases become mainstream bestsellers, was to consolidate an ideologically informed rhetoric of sex and sexuality. Certain acts and desires became pathologised and aberrational through the authority of (pseudo-)science. Cinema has often exploited such categories, sometimes using them to create sensationalist thrills, to endorse such ideological pathologisation or, more rarely, to challenge distinctions between so called normal and aberrational sexuality.

By providing vocabularies and paradigms for understanding sex and sexuality, both Freudian psychoanalysis and sexology have had prime roles to play in the way that Western societies have come to regard human sexuality. While aspects of psychoanalysis and sexology are now in question, the legacy of these knowledge systems persist in the way that sex and sexuality is assigned meaning and value, evidence of which can be found in many cinematic representations of sex. Although such discourses on sex have proved influential, they do not stand alone or uncontested, however, and they compete with alternative discourses from other arenas.

Neither sexology nor psychoanalysis has an expressly stated political agenda in the way that they describe, conceive and theorise sex (although there are underlying rhetorical agendas and such works have often been put to political and ideological use). Throughout the twentieth century reformists have played, or tried to play, a significant role in shaping the meaning of sex. Although various reformist groups have diverse aims, they each endeavoured to make changes in the socio-sexual order. Some, such as the Catholic League of Decency active in the US throughout much of the twentieth century, or Mary Whitehouse's Festival of Light which achieved a high media profile in the UK in the 1970s, advocate sanctions against representing or practising what they regard as anti-Christian, anti-family 'vice' or 'perversion'. These groups often regarded popular film (designed for mass consumption) as a principal means of communicating virtue and setting moral example. While not all reformist agendas are alike, reformists have often regarded film as having didactic potential. One of cinema's great ironies is that the reformist use of film to convey knowledge to the public in the 'sex hygiene' films of the 1920s were repackaged within the salacious context of exploitation cinema (see Schaefer 1999: 165–216). Lobbyist groups have at times been successful in altering the regulation of sex in cinema, including shifting the institutional boundaries that define the difference between legitimate and illegitimate cinemas. Certain filmmakers have also trodden the reformist path, albeit from very different perspectives. D. W. Griffith, for example, used film to convey his own personal reformist moral message, explored in more detail below.

'Civilisation' is also a concept that plays a constitutional role in Western knowledge systems and provides one of the foundations on which sex and sexuality as social constructs in the West rest. It is a concept that is nested into a number of knowledge systems, some of which stretch back into early history, and it has mutated in accord with various discursive paradigms. 'Discourse analysis', an approach grounded in the work of Foucault, provides a means by which the impact of the concept of civilisation on the way that sex and sexuality is conceived can be analysed, with its variant incarnations and norm-producing effects. Civilisation rests on the notion that there is a distinction between 'superior' refined societies, with complex social institutions, and 'inferior' tribal societies, or, still further down the food chain, the animal world (*civis* in Latin means 'citizen' or 'townsman'). Civilisation is a word conceived, therefore, to support hierarchal and nationalistic discourse. Filtered through various subsequent discursive mutations, as well as through the values and formal particularities of cinema, the civilisation/barbarian and civilisation/animal binaries can often be seen in play in the representation of sex and sexuality. In many films dramatic tension is provided by the presence of sexual desires (bestial, perverse, amoral) that do not accord with dominant notions of civilised conduct (a topic tackled in detail below in consideration of 'return of the repressed' narratives and in Part II, 'The Beast Within').

A brief excursion into the nineteenth century will also help to contextualise the way sex is understood in the West and how such understanding informs cinematic representations. Many of the ideas about sex that took root at that time arise in cinema and they also prove important to the development of sexology and psychoanalysis. During the nineteenth century, hierarchal uses of the concept of 'civilisation' were consolidated through Charles Darwin's theory of evolution and, working in tandem, these concepts provided archaeological, historical and scientific underpinning for hierarchal views of ethnicity, nationality and class. Sex was firmly implicated in this. Unfettered sexuality was regarded by many in polite and reformist society, often hypocritically, as a sign of 'degeneration' into the primitive (links to Freudian notions of repression of uncivilised behaviours are clear), as opposed to simply sin as it was in Medieval Europe. Hence the patenting of various contraptions designed to prevent masturbation. Sexual 'degeneracy' was juxtaposed with an ideal view of 'civilised' society as sexually contingent, monogamous and geared to work, rather than to pleasure. Working under the rubric of 'civilisation', science, reformism, religion and evolutionary theory supported colonial and missionary endeavours abroad as well as increasing social management of those at home. This alliance invoked the authority of the Bible to present marriage as the ideal context for sex with the main goal of producing and rearing children needed for industrial work, and enabled a division of labour that served industry.

The promotion of marriage as the correct civilised forum for sex was a key means of managing working-class life, safeguarding vested interests by stabilising sex and gender roles. Georges Bataille has written: 'Pleasure is so close to ruinous waste that we refer to the moment of climax as the "little death". Consequently anything that suggests erotic excess always implies disorder' (1987: 170). Bataille links sexual 'puritanism' to the particular needs of industrial society, in which pleasure is seen as a waste of workers' energies and he argues that this economic motive is the basis for marriage and its concomitant organisational effect on sexual morality. The rhetoric of shame found in the biblical notion of The Fall,[10] combined with evolutionary theory, promoted the idea that sexual licentiousness was decadent regression in the case of the upper classes, or primitive and base in the case of the working class or other(ed) cultures. However, despite the repressive intent of such rhetoric, it was also the case that there was a thriving sex industry, aimed particularly at middle-class men (prostitution in particular, but also photographic and written pornography). Various feminist critics have argued that there was a deep division in way that middle-class men of the era saw women – as either goddesses or whores. This may be overstated; even Queen Victoria wrote in her diary about the pleasures of sex with Albert. Yet perhaps the more prudish prescriptions on sexuality stoked the allure of a forbidden and othered sensuality, something that has proved of value in the representation and marketing of sex in cinema.

The evolutionary/civilisation combination also carries with it an invidious racial/racist hierarchy. Black cultures are deemed inferior and primitive, often seen as being in need of white authority and civilisation. The legacy of an equation between sexuality and primitivism is often apparent in representations of black people in cinema. Donald Bogle has written at length about this trope, in particular the stereotype of what he calls 'the black buck', 'big baadddd niggers, over-sexed and savage, violent and frenzied as they lust for white flesh' (1991: 13). D. W. Griffith's *The Birth of a Nation* (1915) is an early and extreme example. The film sets out to show white men that white women must be protected from the brute animal sexuality of black men. As Bogle has said, 'Griffith played on the myth of the Negro's high-powered sexuality, then articulated the great white fear that every black longs for a white woman … Griffith played hard on the bestiality of his black villainous bucks and used it to arouse hatred' (1991: 13–14). What we see here is how the concept of civilisation supports both race and class hierarchies, which in turn serve to provide the discursive 'policing' of sexual behaviours and morality. The mobilisation of the civilised/uncivilised binary at work in the meanings assigned to sex has, and continues to have, presence in film.

While 'civilisation' has come to be regarded in more relative and sceptical terms, and the use of evolution to prove the validity of social hierarchy may now appear to belong to the 'bad' past, the effects of such ideas nonetheless still inform the way in which sex and sexuality are regarded. In general, attitudes to sex and its representations may have become more 'liberal', yet the civilised/uncivilised paradigm continues to play an influential role, albeit in revised forms. It can be seen operating in a range of films and is built into certain generic vocabularies. In 'gross-out' comedies, for example, the source of comedy is often to be found in the way in which a character has failed to become 'socialised' (civilised). Geoff King (2002) argues that gross-out frequently leans on a notion of regression, a term that is not too far removed from evolutionary 'degeneration'. Another example is provided within a horror and fairytale context in which sexual desire is linked literally to animal transformation with films such as *Cat People* (1942; 1982), *The Company of Wolves* (1984), *Wolf* (1992), *Ginger Snaps* (2001) or evoked more subtly as in the characterisation of Bob, the incestuous, werewolf-like alter-ego of Laura Palmer's father in *Twin Peaks: Fire Walk with Me* (1992) (see Part II 'The Beast Within' for more on these films). The regressive connection between sex and animals is also apparent in the title of *Sexy Beast* (2000) and in the flirtatious, sexually frustrated, central character of *Cat on a Hot Tin Roof* nicknamed Maggie the Cat.

All these examples trade on the notion that 'civilisation' depends on the successful repression of certain 'instinctual' behaviours, an idea that draws on mythology, aspects of Christianity, Darwinism, psychoanalysis and certain types of reformism. Filtered through Medievalist notions of sin, as well as the nineteenth-century knowledge systems covered above, sex, at least the *wrong* type of sex, at the wrong time or in the wrong place, is laced in the rhetorics of regression, shame and transgression. As a rather perverse effect of this, sex accrues a fabulous, marketable, obscene (as in offensive to modesty) and erotic dimension that would, perhaps, otherwise be missing. It is ironic that these dominant discursive frameworks, which often operate to police sex and sexuality, have rendered sex and sexual desire into easily exploitable transgressive terms. Sex in cinema is frequently linked to primitivism – the uncivilised, unruly unconscious desire, obscenity, regression and degeneration – the value of which is that it endows sex with a compelling vitality as well as providing a resonant source of narrative disruption. As I will demonstrate in Part II of this book, rhetorics of transgression have furnished cinema with material for fuelling narratives and for attracting audiences, as well as producing, in many cases, a tangle of rhetorical contradictions. In using discourse analysis to focus on concepts like civilisation and transgression, it is possible to see how cinematic sex draws on a complex mix of ideas that are filtered to suit the particular agendas of medium and its commercial/market context.

Other approaches to the analysis of sex in cinema have sought to demonstrate how the representation of sex and sexuality are grounded in knowledge systems and social practices that privilege one group over others. Marxist frameworks applied to the analysis of film focus on political economy, and it is often argued that mainstream films popularise and naturalise exploitation and commodification. Cinematic representations of sex are clearly implicated. Feminist approaches to film are largely reformist in intention; feminist critiques of cinema often focus on the ways that women in particular are represented in film. They are concerned with demonstrating that many films carry and reinforce rhetorics of gender that underpin inequality between men and women, a line of argument that came to prominence in the mid-1970s with Molly Haskell's analysis of cinematic representations of women in *From Reverence to Rape* (1987), first published in 1975, and Laura Mulvey's influential essay, 'Visual Pleasure and Narrative Cinema' (1975). Mulvey's psychoanalytically-informed work sought to demonstrate that the cinematic forms developed in classical Hollywood cinema presented women as sexual objects for the male gaze. Her work has had a significant impact on the way that representations of gender and sex are regarded and analysed in film studies, although her arguments have been strongly contested. Many critics of her work have argued that the way that she conceives of identification is over-simplified, or that she sidelines the fact that men are also often set up as erotic objects of the cinematic gaze.

As well as providing a framework for thinking about the way that sex appears in cinema, feminism has also informed cinematic content; sometimes loosely, sometimes more coherently. Many films focus on the 'battle of the sexes', which has provided a theme around which to construct narrative conflict, dramatic and sexual tension. This spans across a number of genres and periods, including early short films such as *Milling the Militants* (1913), a comedy in which a man oppressed by his suffragette wife fantasises various humiliations for such women. Many melodramas, film noirs, romantic comedies, art films and blockbusters, such as *Thelma and Louise* – a film that reworks the male buddy movie to create a kind of Hollywoodised feminist film – have taken up the gender conflict theme. The sheer mass of films that foreground gender conflict, in whatever guise and often in a sexualised way, indicates that the meanings of gender and investments in various configurations of gender and sexual difference are central to the life experiences of the cinema-going audience. Feminist ideas have played a key role in the theorisation of representations of gender, sexuality and sex, as well as the erotic dimension of spectatorship where women are regarded as the object of the gaze. Feminist ideas have also, to some extent, shaped the textual practices of certain filmmakers such those deployed in films made by female directors such Sally Potter, Chantal Ackerman, Suzanne Pitt and Jane Campion.

Queer theory-based approaches to film that arose during the 1980s sought to look awry at the ways in which mainstream cinema reinforced heterosexuality as a norm. It aimed to establish a model of sexuality, gender and desire that is inherently fluid and is less inclined to fix these into definitive and normative categories. The use of the term 'queer' itself is indicative of a process of seeing and desiring differently; the pejorative use of the term is ironised and remoulded through a celebration of the difference of sexual identity and desire that it marks. As Teresa de Lauretis has argued, queer theory sought to overturn rigid definitions of sexual and gender identity (1991: v). Alongside the trendification and raised profile of 'queer' culture in the 1980s, aspects of queer theory also became a source of ideas for the group of films known collectively as New Queer Cinema. *Swoon* (1992), for example, reworked Hitchcock's *Rope* (1948) to make homosexual desire more overt than in the original and to make 'queer' excitingly and transgressively stylish. Following the theory, New Queer Cinema endeavoured to promote a more heterogeneous view of masculinity, which not only undermined hegemonic and very narrow notions of ideal masculinity but also sought to overturn the negative, diffused, disavowed or denied representations of ho-

mosexuality in dominant cinemas (and elsewhere) by making it the central focus of attention. An alternative model of the cinematic 'gaze' also features, one that accommodates the
possibility that erotic investments could be made between rather than across genders.[12]

Queer theory also highlights the activity of reading known as 'against-the-grain'. This
is an important concept in general terms as it demonstrates that the interpretation of film
content is an active experience on the part of the viewer. In the context of queer theory, against-the-grain reading arises out of 'a struggle or negotiation between competing
frames of reference, motivation and experience' (Gledhill 1992b: 120) and has the aim of
disrupting and undermining the dominant 'heteronormative' ideologies that are so often
naturalised rhetorically within film. An example of such subversive tactics of interpretation
can be seen in Paul Burston's somewhat mischievous 'queer' reading of *Top Gun* (1986). As a
mainstream action movie starring big guns Tom Cruise and Val Kilmer, it was intended to be
read as a testosterone-induced celebration of 'ideal' heterosexual masculine values. Burston
reads the film through his experience of being a gay man and thereby replaces the homosocial with the homosexual and the homoerotic. Scenes of men playing together, playing
volleyball or general 'horsing around' are read by Burston as charged with homoeroticism.
This reading is made possible through the presence of certain signifiers probably intended
to indicate 'macho' competition and physical strength, as is the case in the beach volleyball
sequence. As much of this sequence is in slow-motion the audience is encouraged to look
at the half-naked, muscled bodies of the men playing the game which is accompanied by
a soundtrack entitled 'Playing with Boys'. In addition, character dialogue is also often wide
open for a queer reading, typified by the speech of one character who insists, 'I want some
butt, and I want it now' (1995: 117–20). Burston goes on to say that 'the pleasures of such
readings are simple: what better revenge on a culture which seeks to exclude you…', but
also suggests that such readings should not preclude support of more 'openly queer cultural production' (1995: 120). What his reading demonstrates is that, as he says, 'cultural texts
do not have single meanings' (ibid.). The frame of reference he, as a gay man, brings to the
film alters the meaning of what is signified in sexual terms. As well as providing a useful foil
to dominant conceptions of gender, sex, desire and sexuality, Burston's against-the-grain
reading demonstrates that the meanings associated with sex in cinema are actively constructed through a variety of cognitive, experiential and knowledge schemas or frameworks
that interface between text and reader.

Sex and the Cinema

Formal Conventions of Cinematic Sex

$\mathcal{R}$epresentations of sex in cinema have taken a vast array of textual forms, a factor which presents a problem for a book such as this that seeks to map such broad terrain. Sex is the primary focus of genres such as soft-core and hard-core and each has an established set of conventions used in the depiction of sexual activity designed to attract particular target markets. It has already been noted that some of these conventions have at various points in time found their way into mainstream and art films. Sex and sexuality also appear in a more general way across most genres and styles. It is therefore difficult to make the case that sex in cinema is guided by a particular aim, mode or form (as with comedy or tragedy for instance). It should also be noted that sex in cinema is not simply an issue of formal content as the erotic dimensions of fantasy and desire also play a significant role in the way that spectators are sold films and the way they are engaged with. Potential audiences are often lured by the prospect of seeing certain stars in an erotic context and the reception of a film can be based on the solicitation of sexual or erotic investments on the part of the viewer. For example, the presence of an admired star might attract a viewer to watch a film in a genre that is not of immediate interest. Cinematic representations of sex and sexuality are subject to some very different types of moods, aesthetic forms and strategic narrative intent, yet it is possible to identify certain patterns, conventions and trends. Before going on to identify and explore the effects of genre, style, themes, narrative and textual devices on the representation of sex, it is useful to consider in more detail the way that the form of cinema itself has a significant role to play in the shaping of representations of sex.

One of the distinctive formal issues presented by cinematic sex is born of the specific nature of cinematic form. Cinema relies on a combination of visual and auditory devices to entertain and captivate audiences. It seems obvious to say that audiences are spectators of what is presented; some consideration of this factor is important as it is part of the specific nature of cinema that a story unfolds without direct intervention on the part of the viewer (even if we might imagine or wish to do so). This is why some theorists have emphasised the role played by voyeurism in the pleasure of watching of a film. This does not mean that watching a movie is a form of cold observation, however, as there are many ways in which viewers can become intellectually, emotionally, even sexually engaged (boredom or disbelief might be experienced, yet even these are forms of emotional engagement). In the main, cinema trades precisely on its ability to involve and engage us with a story and characters; in this sense it is an affect-driven medium. For many film historians the history of cinema lies precisely in the development of techniques to facilitate greater spectator involvement. Most mainstream films, as well as many others, deploy continuity devices to enable audiences to focus on character and action rather than on form or production, for example. The aim of such continuity tactics is to encourage viewers to develop empathy with characters and the situations that they are faced with and aid in the process of suspension of disbelief. Soliciting emotional engagement is important to making a fictional narrative construct engrossing and believable in some way (no matter how outlandish the story or situation might be). Such involvement is, for many films, a prerequisite for audiences to be able to regard sex as part of a story. The 'continuity' approach to filmmaking does, however, raise some very interesting issues about what is constituted as 'valuable' in moral, aesthetic and institutional terms, and it is here that we are brought to the fraught debate of what constitutes *pornography*.

One way that cinematic pornography has been defined and separated from other film-based representations of sex lies in the extent to which a film makes scenes of sexual activity a part of a general storyline (this is often less ambiguous than defining pornographic films in terms of whether the sex is 'simulated' or 'acted'). Said in this way, it would appear that it is simply a matter of a formal and aesthetic distinction with no moral judgement attached (this 'aesthetic' approach is often used by regulators to skirt the moral implications of their judgements). The pejorative use of the 'pornography' label is often used to suggest that a film has no redeeming narrative or artistic value and is only preoccupied with exploiting the commercial gains of salacious content. By contrast, it is often the case that the shortened term 'porn' is used more affectionately by those who enjoy watching sex films. Whatever view one has of explicit sex films, it is nonetheless the case that like mainstream cinema even the most pared-down hard-core film is dependent on the use of established formal cinematic devices to facilitate the viewer's entry into the onscreen space, an aspect often sidelined by critics who argue loudly and in a generalised way for increased censorship of sexually explicit material.

The presentation of sex in mainstream cinema is often exhibited in conventionalised ways, which are wrought in terms of style, genre conventions and target audience. Many of the conventions used to represent sex in cinema are governed, at least in part, by the need to translate the very tactile experience of sex into an audiovisual medium. Certain themes, conventions and stylistic devices have been reiterated so regularly that they have come to provide powerful shorthand ways of invoking fairly complex ideas. Such devices may provide ways and means of suggesting sex without actually showing it. These devices can also be linked to the demands made on films that seek a broad audience, which must accord with the various classification criteria employed by regulatory bodies at a given time, such as the British Board of Film Classification or national equivalents.

One such device that has widespread use, to the extent that is has become something of a cliché, is the ellipsis. A typical scenario is to build towards a sexual event and then, at the point it becomes fairly obvious what will occur, the scene fades to black. Alternatively a cutaway shot might be used to present an event that occurs at the same time elsewhere, returning to the original scene at a later point. Elliptical edits may well be book-ended with various indicators to help manage what the viewer infers has happened in that offscreen time. The fact that viewers understand what is happening in these jumps in time works with their knowledge of cinema. A useful example is provided by *Out of the Past*, a film made when sexual imagery in American legitimate cinema was tightly regulated. As the illicit couple make for the bedroom to consummate their affair, the camera pans away from them back towards the front door which has been blown open by a tropical storm. The only lamp left on in the room is blown over and darkness falls. The strong wind provides a diegetic justification for a fade to black that signals an ellipse in time. The ellipse allows the film to suggest rather than show sex (necessary under the controls over sexual content at the time the film was made). While such controls might be seen as a constraint on artistic freedom, the resulting work-arounds contribute to the development of a pronounced cinematic style that is dripping with suggestive symbolism of the type that enrich so many melodramas and noirs made during the 1940s in Hollywood. The storm in *Out of the Past*, to which our gaze is drawn, evokes intense passion and foreshadows turmoil, and the fade to black which follows expresses in cinematic and symbolic terms the main character's fall from moral grace. The ellipse, as it is staged in this film, has, therefore, an important role in urging the viewer to actively read the cinematic 'signs'; the viewer is invited by those signs to infer intense sexual passion and imagine what it is that might be going on in the off-screen room. As such, one of the strengths of the ellipse is that it allows the viewer to project into the gap their own personally tailored fantasy.

There are many other ways of suggesting that sex has taken place without showing it. In *Now, Voyager* (1942), for example, the couple who have been kept apart by his unhappy marriage stand on a balcony, he lights two cigarettes and passes one to her. This act seems very intimate, as the cigarette goes from his mouth to hers, something that might regarded as a post-coital act. It is never clear that sex has taken place, however, but this neat little device suggests it has. The exchange stands in for the missing sexual event, an event that explains the bond between the couple, reinforced perhaps by the fact that cigarettes were an illicit pleasure for the main character when she was living under the rule of her overbearing mother. Elsewhere in the film, and earlier in the female protagonist's life, a passionate sexual encounter is actually interrupted by the intrusive and controlling mother-figure; well-timed interruption is another common device used in film, where it is often used to create narrative and dramatic tension (as occurs in many films focused on adultery), as well as evading potential censorship.

In *Raiders of the Lost Ark* (1981), a rather different type of interruption device is used. Around two-thirds into the film, as the couple reach the apparent safety of a sea-going ship, the potential moment to act on the obvious sexual spark between them occurs at last. Marion (Karen Allen) has just been given a glamorous satin nightdress, and enters the cabin in which Indiana Jones (Harrison Ford) lies on a bunk taking stock of his many wounds. She begins to kiss his wounds better, moving closer progressively towards his mouth, but Jones is so tired from his vigorous exploits that he falls sound asleep. This is a neat comic device that has multiple functions: it postpones the consummation of their romance and keeps sexual tension in play; sex is kept safely offscreen, necessary because the film is targeted at an audience that will include children (the film has a 'PG' rating in the UK and US), while at the same time 'winking' at an informed adult audience about the sexual desire that underpins the couple's rather fraught relationship; in kissing Indiana's wounds, Marion does what most mothers would do when their child scrapes a knee or bruises an elbow, a factor that may help make sense of the scene to younger children.

Another blocking device used in films to enable sex or nakedness to be shown in less explicit ways is the use of visual barriers. Physical barriers such as legs or arms, strategically-placed props or clothing keep genitals and breasts out of sight (a convention treated comically to demonstrate the contortional absurdity of such censorship effects in an independent gay short film entitled *What Can I do With a Male Nude* (1975)). Often such barriers or strategic framing permits simulated sex to imply that penetration is taking place. In *Don't Look Now*, for example, the pivotal and transformational sex scene is carefully arranged to keep the inferred genital contact out of the frame. Yet the positions taken by the characters and their movements lead the audience to believe that genital contact is taking place. Similar strategies are often used by producers of explicit sex films where two versions of a film are made; one shows penetration and genital contact and one where these are kept out of frame (genital close-ups, for example, can be left out in the edit process). 'Masked' versions of hard-core films made for the soft-core market can make it difficult for censors to judge whether real sex is taking place or not (even if offscreen). Such films work the rules of the regulation system to maximise their potential market. It could be argued that regulatory rules, which outlaw the display of the mechanics of sex – what is, after all, a common activity – actively promote an unregulated underground market.

These are just a few of the numerous inventive devices that have been used throughout the history of cinema to suggest, rather than show, sex. The onscreen kiss is often acceptable as an indicator of love or passion; perhaps the kiss invokes romance more effectively and provides just enough information to spark viewer-generated fantasy for some viewers than is the case with the fleshly presence of 'vulgar, groaning fornication' (Žižek 1991: 110). Nonetheless the coyness within which sex is so often treated in mainstream cinema constructs more fleshly encounters as taboo, giving them an edge that adds up to greater sensationalist impact. Managing the presentation of sex through suggestion and interruption lends it a mysterious transgressive caché, but it is this reticence to deal with sex explicitly that some films use to sell themselves by claiming that they reveal more than their predecessors dared, as is the case with hard-core and exploitation, as well as more legitimated examples such as *Cat on a Hot Tin Roof* or *Baise-moi*.

Cinematic sex is figured through a host of formal and aesthetic rhetorics: two that are commonly in play in the representation of sex in cinema are idealism and realism. These are powerful agents that shape the way that sex, sexuality and desire appear in cinema and they have the power to both construct and challenge the normative. While these concepts operate in some ways as opposites, they can and regularly do appear in conjunction in a given film. The lines between them are not always clearly drawn, making for some interesting problems and tensions in the representation of sex in cinema.

Idealisms: perfect sex

Idealism underlies the representation of cinematic sex in several dimensions, including narrative, theme, ideology and style. By virtue of its thematic emphasis on the joy of being in love, traditional romance is perhaps the most obviously idealistic, in sexual terms, of all film genres. Romance often frames sex in the normative terms of ideologies of ideal heterosexual love and courtship. These aspects are reflected in the trajectory of the narrative and in the stylistic and thematic treatment of sex. It is also common for such films to take place in attractive settings that provide visual spectacle and underscore the escapist fantasy-led agenda of the genre. *Roman Holiday* (1953), *Titanic* (1997) and *Moulin Rouge* (2001) are good examples of romance-based films in which the ideal nature of a central courtship is supported by a glamorous location: gloriously sunny 1950s Rome in the former, the decadence and overt theatrical spectacle of *fin de siecle* Paris in *Moulin Rouge* and the opulence of the Edwardian-era ship-board interiors in *Titanic*. Richard Dyer has argued that Hollywood entertainment rests on providing a respite from the drab weariness of daily life by providing sounds and images that are suffused with exuberance, intensity and abundance (1992: 20–1). The appealing settings used in these films are visual metaphors for the pleasures of romantic dalliance as a sensual 'holiday' from the tedium of everyday routine, but also from emotional and sexual confusion, dissatisfaction or complexity.

The narrative arcs of these three mainstream romances are geared around the union of a complementary couple, who represent the romantic ideal (the idealised complementary couple are not limited to romance, however, and such is the importance of the 'proper couple' format in the history of sex in cinema that it will be returned to later). Obstacles are set up that defer the sexual consummation of the romance. As well as lending a necessary dramatic dimension, the struggle to achieve union places even greater value on the relationship, reinforcing its ideal status. Unlike most upbeat romantic comedies, *Titanic* and *Moulin Rouge* add a 'weepie' dimension through the death of Jack (Leonardo di Caprio) and

Satine (Nicole Kidman) towards the end of the films. While there is no happy ending, Jack and Satine's deaths are designed to elevate the romance to the very loftiest podium of the ideal. Loss of passion through familiarity, domestic hardship, class or lifestyle differences that may have ensued if the couples had gone to marry are transcended through death; romantic love, which will inevitably evolve into something else, is preserved in aspic. The ordinary, cooler business of domestic life that we all know is kept offscreen.

Lust too, it seems, is anathema to romance; the two are often kept firmly apart structurally and thematically. The construction of the romantic ideal in cinematic romances frequently entails that lust and enjoyment of sex for its own sake is confined to villains or antagonists. In both *Titanic* and *Moulin Rouge* lust combines with moral decadence to define the gothic villain of the piece who, in both cases, seeks to prevent the ideal, complementary couple from being together and who desires to possess the woman on his own terms (in the case of the latter for 'perverse' sexual ends). The presence of the lustful villain in these films inversely reinforces normative notions of ideal sex as the preserve of romantic love, with its qualities of mutuality and complementarity. In general, traditional romance-based films tend to steer clear of direct representations of sex, preferring instead to invoke it through tacit references, interrupted trysts or symbolic acts. The passionate screen kiss is generally the closest that many romances come to showing sex; even this is left out in many Hollywood films from the classical era. There is, for example, no consummatory kiss or romantic clinch in the archetypal romantic comedy *Bringing Up Baby* (1938)). Reflecting shifts in regulation, in *Titanic* there are a few sex scenes. These are shot using conventions that are more commonly associated with soft-core erotic films, particularly the use of soft focus to give a flattering diffused glow to the image of trysting bodies. Context dictates meaning, however. In soft-core the use of soft focus visually articulates the glow of erotic sensuality, whereas in the context of *Titanic* it signifies the idealistic aura of romantic love. Both instances speak of something ideal, but they are somewhat different. Soft focus unites couples in the visual field, making them seem to meld together slightly. In soft-core this is a mode of signalling perfectly absorbing sex; in romance it contributes to the coding of a relationship as 'right and proper' – fated. In *Titanic*, the complementary nature of the couple is so powerful that it transcends their class differences.

In most romances the constitution of the ideal is highly normative. Romantic love is mainly the preserve of young, white attractive men and women, although gay romances like *Love and Death on Long Island* (1997) seek to recoup the format from the hetero-normative and there are a few examples of romances where the complementary couple are differently raced such *A Bronx Tale* (1993). Romances between older people are less prevalent perhaps because, logically, they are more likely to be mired in domestic entanglements – older people have 'histories' that produce emotional and familial baggage that might detract from representing romance as ideal (*The Bridges of Madison County* (1995) is a fairly rare exception, discussed in Part II, 'Adultery: Domestic Transgressions'). Young romance is, it seems, the primary convention signifing hope and idealism. Within most romance films sex is deferred until the conditions are 'right', and on the whole it is hinted at but not shown explicitly. Under the conditions outlined above, which operate in concert as a kind of protective magic circle, sex becomes more than a physical and emotional experience. It is not lust, fornication or illicit, but sublime and transcendent – ideal. The strategies used to present and lend meanings to sex in these films that aim to appeal to a wide audience have a number of attributes that consolidate and preserve the idealistic framework of romance. Any explicit sexual imagery is kept offscreen, and sexual passion is often indicated metonymically by a kiss or a body-entwining clinch. The absence of direct representations of sex places greater emphasis on the emotional rather than the physical register, the latter recast in the antithetical domain of lust. Such deft management of the conditions of sex reserves its place as the apotheosis of love. Importantly for the ability of the romance genre to involve its viewers, its elliptical format leaves room for viewers to fantasise about what sex between the couple might be like, and thereby its idealistic nature is, potentially at least, kept intact.

Such idealistic representations of sex are not the sole preserve of the romance genre, however. Soft-core sex films designed for mainstream consumption, and beginning with those made in the 1970s, also often present sex in melodious, idealised visual tones. The gauzy soft-focus visual style of *Bilitis* (1977), for example, tallies with an impossibly idealised take on the sexual initiation of a young girl or woman (a common theme almost always idealised in soft-core, discussed in more detail below). Even the bondage and domination film *The Story of O* (*Histoire d'O*, 1975), which focuses on the initiation of a woman into the intense pleasures of sexual submission, is mostly shot in soft focus. In conjunction with fairytale settings, the film has a dreamy quality. This approach lends the film's more violent scenes visual sensuality, rather than brutal realism. It also ties into the film's attempt to capture the imaginary nature of sexual fantasy, where what would, in reality, be deeply unpleasant becomes in the world of make-believe the source of sensual pleasure. In keeping with its soft-core aesthetic, *The Story of O* deals with the erotics of submission in a highly idealised way in aesthetic and narrative terms, and, at the end of the film, O (Corinne Clery) finds sexual and intellectual satisfaction when she establishes a partnership with a dominant man who loves, respects and tests her sexually. In this sense the film is an idealistic romantic love story, where the complementarity of the couple lies primarily in their interlocking sexual predilections.

Other films that are not straightforwardly idealised romantic fantasies may also deploy aspects of idealised sex, but often what seems to be ideal sexually becomes its opposite, a dramatic device that is used often in thriller and horror films. In *Fatal Attraction* (1987), for example, an extramarital 'affair' appears at first as an idealised erotic dalliance until the jilted female protagonist begins to persecute the male protagonist and his family. Rendered within the generic conventions of horror, the moral message is made clear: an escapist, extramarital sexual fling has horrific repercussions, which Susan Faludi (1992) sees as expressing a backlash against feminist gains. *Cat People* (1982) presents an idealised and quite tender sexual initiation scene, lit beautifully to accentuate Nastassja Kinski's supple body. Soon after sex has taken place she transforms into a panther, able and poised to rip her tender lover apart (she does not; love prevails just in time on her animal mind). Such beauty-turns-beast transformations are quite common in horror- and fantasy-based films, as with the beautiful witch who, when she reaches orgasm, becomes a lethal flying fireball in *Conan the Barbarian* (1982). An apparently ideal sexual encounter is apt therefore in some genres to become the source of danger. This also turns out to be the case in the Mexican-beach love affair between Kathie Moffat (Jane Greer) and her dupe, Jeff Markham (Robert Mitchum) in *Out of the Past*.

The duplicitous ideal provides the fuel for many narratives, creating the type of transgressions and dramatic tensions deemed to lure audiences, but are often given a moral lesson-style rider. Jeff Markham, for example, was weak in giving in to Kathie's spider-woman charms when she walks back into his, now settled and decent, life. The punishment for Kathie's romantic duplicity and Jeff's complicity through inaction ('Baby, I don't care') is their death. The principle of 'what looks and feels good may in fact be bad' operates in numerous noirs, horrors and melodramas. In other contexts the duplicitous or impossible ideal may provide a means of exploring the dividing line between fantasy and reality, as in *Eyes Wide Shut*, or, as a means of questioning attitudes to marriage, sexual desire and sexuality as in …*And God Created Woman*.

Like many romance-based films, *Roman Holiday*, *Moulin Rouge* and *Titanic* complement glamorous locations with glamorous stars in the central romantic roles. Linking physical beauty to romantic love provides another means by which romance-based films enter the ideological and normative terrain of ideal sex, desire and sexuality. Cinema's ability to foreground and accentuate ideal sex and create idealised sexual bodies is in part constitutional of its norm-producing potential. It has a taste-setting function in making certain looks fashionable and erotically charged. Not only are certain physical features valued more highly than others (some shift quite rapidly over time, whereas others, such as youth and facial symmetry, seem more deeply rooted), there is also often a connection between physical appearance and a character's 'soul'.[13] This is part of the way that cinema uses visual signs to code character and their sexuality. Frequently such associational logic is used to yoke physical beauty of a certain kind to sexual moral alignment. Often this works in conjunction with the coding of clothing and acting, neatly illustrated by the two female protagonists of the action-adventure film *Brotherhood of the Wolf* (*Le Pacte de Loups*, 2001), which is set in eighteenth-century provincial France.

Sylvia (Monica Bellucci) has dark eyes and hair, her eyes are quite small, often narrowed as if scheming, she has a husky voice and foreign accent (Italian rather than French as with the other characters) and her breasts are prominently full. Marianne (Émilie Dequenne) has a round face, lighter hair, large light-coloured eyes, a slighter body and a wide smile. Sylvia first dresses in black lace (she is also shown nude), her face is often veiled, her movements and speech are slow and languorously seductive. Marianne wears a more diverse range of richly-coloured clothes, some of which are like those of a boy, she moves quickly and speaks impetuously. Sylvia not only uses sex for pleasure and power, she is highly morally ambiguous, saving the hero for her own pleasure. Marianne is a plucky, virgin 'princess', the love of the hero's life and is morally upright both sexually and in her dealings with the world. She looks much younger than Sylvia and her demeanour and face is more open. The cleanly-divided moral world of much mainstream cinema, where appearance corresponds with sexual moral standing, is in itself highly idealistic and frequently shapes the meaning of sex. In *Brotherhood of the Wolf*, sex with the morally ambiguous exotic woman is an amusing dalliance for the hero, whereas romantic love and courtship, which, if less erotically charged perhaps, carries greater affective weight in the film than the former.

The cinematic drive to maximise beauty is born in part of the need for cinema to arrest the gaze and conjure erotic desire, in the service of which impossibly ideal bodies are manufactured. Along with all the other accoutrements in play to help create the illusion of the ideal body (make-up, high heels or other elevation devices, steroids, silicone, nip/tuck), strategically placed and hued lighting can help to hide blemishes, accentuate musculature, sculpt inviting curves and hollows. Golden, glowing bodies, shot through filters and gauze, that appear across a variety of genres and cinema types follow the 'glamour' techniques used to film female stars in classical Hollywood. It is the allure of the ideal sexual body that underpins the star system. Offered up as objects for the gaze (male or female), stars who are signified as ideal in some way act potentially as triggers for romantic and sexual fantasy and are often marketed as such. Dirk Bogarde and Rock Hudson, for example, were sold by cinema and women's magazines in the 1950s as 'eligible bachelors', inviting readers to fantasise becoming their partners. Stars are less 'groomed' now in terms of lifestyle than was the case in classical Hollywood, but they are still proffered as idealised objects of desire worthy of pin-up adoration and marketed often to a particular audience. Looking around our staff office there are posters of Johnny Depp and Viggo Mortensen, for example, both stars marketed as 'thinking-girls' pin-ups. Stars are often used to brand a film, as trailers and posters often testify, and as commodities they are frequently represented in their best and most appealing light. It is not simply a star's face and personality that attracts attention, a body part or bodily characteristic may become an important part of a star's 'meaning' in the public domain and help to turn their bodies into cinema-friendly spectacle: long legs (Betty Grable, Nicole Kidman), large breasts (Marilyn Monroe, Pamela Anderson), muscles (Marlon Brando, Arnold Schwarzenegger), a swaggering walk (Errol Flynnl, John Wayne), full lips (Brigitte Bardot, Angelina Jolie), and so on. These provide examples of the way that the bodies of stars have been emphasised and sold as ideal sexually – often in conjunction with other attributes – to create a marketable, idealised difference from other stars.

Cinema's investment in ideal sexual bodies is interestingly illustrated by the use of body doubles for sex or nude scenes. Examples include replacing Catherine Deneuve's body in a shower scene in *The Hunger* (1983) (she was in her forties when the film was shot), the replacement of Britt Ekland's body by another's when seen nude from behind in *The Wicker Man* (1973) (she was, it is said, in the early stages of pregnancy at the time), and the 'bottom' double used by the lead female in *Preaching to the Perverted* (1997). Body doubles are not always used simply because of modesty or not having the required ideal body: the time-equals-dollar factor is significant. Yet in most cases the drive to create the impression of physical perfection is at work. In addition, the body double allows a star's body to remain a mystery and may in some cases preserve the star's status as 'respectable' or modest (thereby making a further claim in a different way on the ideal). Commenting on the subjective and political effect of using of a 'breasts' double in *Demolition Man* (1993), Sandra Bullock has said 'there was the virtual reality sex scene ... and they wanted to see breasts. Obviously mine didn't stand up to the task so they got other breasts. I said, "At least let me pick them out, so I can be in charge of my own boobs".[14] Knowing this somehow makes her more 'human', more likeable and perhaps easier to identify with, an actor doing her job rather than an embodiment of the impossibly ideal. But, in the same article, John Travolta's comments demonstrate that an ideal body is, however, required if a star is to retain their screen appeal: 'If it's a nude scene and you're not in the shape you want ... you use a double'.[15]

A star, as opposed to an actor, is a mythical figure who, it seems, must represent physical-sexual qualities deemed ideal and that audiences are thought to admire, covet or regard as erotic. This is why the star system deployed in cinemas that place emphasis on glamour can be seen to serve the purposes of consumer culture. The rise of the Hollywood star goes hand-in-hand with the use of stars to advertise glamorous products. Sarah Michele Gellar has appeared in television adverts for Maybelline's make-up brand, for instance. She follows in the promotional footsteps of many female film stars of the past, a trend pursued and consolidated by Max Factor in 1930s and 1940s. There is an interesting dual approach here: the 'sexy' star is deployed as an ideal figure, yet they require some help from the product. They are therefore presented as being both like us and not like us: an ambiguity that serves to wed the ideal, normative creating values of film to the machinations of consumer culture. The implication being that if a star-endorsed product is purchased, the consumer will almost magically be afforded the ideal and idealised sex appeal of the star.

Where does this notion of identification with the ideal come from, in theoretical terms? In seeking to understand our relationships with others, psychoanalysis provides a rhetorical vocabulary through which this idea is formulated. The psychoanalytic term 'ego-ideal' expresses that which an individual adopts as a model to aspire to (see Freud, 'On Narcissism: An Introduction' (1991a)). The 'ego-ideal' plays an important role in the way that people become socialised and relate to the world around them. Parents are often adopted as the first ego-ideals but as the child's contact with the world broadens other attributes belonging to other people are likely to be adopted as ego-ideals. This involves an imaginary identification with the attribute, deemed sexually attractive or otherwise, that is aspired to, but because what we aspire to be is often impossible to achieve in reality, it can also create a sense of loss or anxiety, which might prove motivational or to be debilitating. It could be argued that cinema and consumerism exploit a fundamental gap between reality and what we aspire to, and perhaps the model helps to explain the persistent popularity of always-triumphant heroes and heroines in popular culture. The same principle applies to the draw of the sexually-alluring body, which cinema would have us believe opens doors on to pleasure, happiness, sexual plenitude and even power. Cinematic ideals often do seem designed to temporarily fill the gap of lack with identifications with fantasy figures and circumstances, yet these might also prove in the longer term to widen that gap. While the psychoanalytic understanding of identification with the ideal proves fruitful, it should also be remembered that the ideals of cinema are in themselves social and rhetorical constructs, created to give pleasure; they carry with them a range of values that are often in themselves ideals centred on sexual and gender performance that are impossible to achieve.

The ideal in cinema is not simply present to promote viewers' aspirations and anxieties, it is also important in terms of style, dramatic tension, censorship and the politics of gender and the gaze. The combination of sex, romance and beautiful bodies couched primarily in idealistic aesthetic terms have often provided cinema with a way of escaping censorship; a way of making sex into 'art' and thereby evading accusations of judicial obscenity. Cinema has often had recourse to such a strategic marriage of sex and aesthetic beauty, a precedent set in painting and sculpture, but despite this sex is likely to be related to different forms of transgression, conflict and blockage mainly because the simply ideal has little dramatic potential. *Stealing Beauty* (1996) provides a useful example. Following the narrative path trodden by earlier soft-core sex films, the film focuses on the 'natural' allure of a young girl's awakening sexuality. However, the emphasis, as signalled by the title, is on 'stealing' Lucy's (Liv Tyler) beauty, which goes beyond surface appearance as it also refers to her burgeoning sexuality. The entire story arc builds towards Lucy losing her virginity. Her beauty and sexuality are made available to the gaze and sexual investments of both the filmmaker and viewers. While in many films the pleasures of voyeurism are masked and/or disavowed, they are foregrounded here, creating, potentially, an extra sense of intimacy for the viewer with Lucy. The viewer, of whatever gender, is actively invited to contemplate under the protective kudos of aesthetically inviting art cinema the flowering and deflowering of a highly idealised young woman. Lucy is heterosexual, interested in all the men she mets (she is looking for her father as well as a lover) and she is photographed to emphasis her beauty, even at one point posing for an artist with one of her breasts exposed (who it turns out is in fact her father). As a well-made character she has her reasons, but she is clearly designed to be consumed as 'art' by all comers.

In other films there is often an attempt to draw a line between voyeurism as a sexual perversion, embodied by a pathologised character, and the voyeurism of the viewer (although in films such as *Rear Window* (1954) or *Peeping Tom* (1959) the distinction is deliberately blurred so that viewer becomes discomforted by their own urge to look). What insists on this line-drawing is a rather prudish, but nonetheless pervasive, assumption that 'decent folk' ideally would not undertake to have sex in public nor would they want to watch other people have sex (at least not without the anonymity afforded by the mediation of the camera). Hence the erotic pleasures of looking, which are impressed with a perverse coding, are

Art object: Lucy (Liv Tyler) posing for an artist in *Stealing Beauty* (1996)

authorised in some instances by devices such as the presence of onscreen audiences or a character with whom the viewer is invited to identify (safety afforded by the presence of other consenting and appreciative others perhaps). While Western society might consider itself generally liberal about sex, it is still the case that sex should, ideally, be kept private and intimate. This is grounded in the sex-in-the-context-of-romance equation that operates normatively as the sexual ideal. When an actor takes part in a sex scene in a film they are, in a sense, committing a form of transgression by making sex public, and the viewer too, by virtue of being a viewer, becomes complicit in that transgression. Idealised beauty can, in part, ameliorate this act by sanctioning the gaze because beauty as an ideal is coded to be looked at in art and elsewhere. By the same logic the elevating presence of ideal beauty attenuates the audience's 'perverse' voyeuristic activity in watching filmed sex. This is the way that ideal beauty is 'stolen' in *Stealing Beauty*.

As has already been noted, adult melodramas of 1950s Hollywood explored the social and psychological tensions around sexuality. Adult melodramas were produced in conjunction with the weakening of industry-based regulation rulings on the representation of sex in the US which in part enabled Hollywood to compete with more risqué 'foreign' films, such as …*And God Created Woman*, that were proving popular at the box-office. A common strategy in such films was to present a character, played by a known star, who has to deal with the problems that ensue from the experience of insistent sexual desires. Although melodrama has been defined in many ways, it is commonly understood by most as the type of film that focuses intensively on the emotional register of interpersonal and familial relations. In contrast to contemporary romantic comedies such as *Pillow Talk*, where sex is talked about but kept offscreen to uphold the ideal notion that sex should be an expression of love, private and intimate, the focus of 1950s family melodramas is the failure of the ideal. Within this context sex and sexual desire become problematic and disruptive. …*And God Created Woman* typifies the trend.

Juliete Hardy (Brigitte Bardot) embodies the cliché of innocent sexuality. She is a creature of nature, wilful, yet gentle, and ignites passion in the men she meets. This unwitting power stems from her ideal and idealised beauty, yet it causes pain and strife to her and others. She is not a scheming urban 'vamp' or a wicked seductress of the type seen in noirs or in earlier films, such as those played by Theda Bara. Instead Juliete is a free spirit, her bare feet and Dionysiac dancing to African rhythms links her to primitive, 'pagan passions' (a description used in the voiceover of the American trailer for the film). Yet she cannot attain the man she desires so strongly and the practicalities of her life lead her to marry the younger brother of the man she truly loves, leaving her to cope with the difference between her ideal object of desire and reality. Like the barefoot witch Gillian (Kim Novak) in the near contemporary *Bell, Book and Candle* (1958), Juliete has to relinquish her 'wild' ideals to be able to conform to the very different – idealised – behaviour required to make herself into a good wife. Juliete knows and takes pleasure in the power afforded to her through her attraction to men, yet she nonetheless retains an air of child-like naïveté. She regularly appears nude, or in a state of partial undress – although she is framed so as not to reveal genitals or give a complete view of her breasts. As it is contextualised within the film, nudity serves to demonstrate an idealised, untamed 'naturalness', providing a Rousseauesque critique of social repression filtered through the super-innocence of nudie-cutie pin-ups. Here nudity is not linked to shame as it is in the Bible, yet her ideal form causes (diegetic) problems. Bardot's 'natural' nudity also marks her out as the (ideal) object of both the onscreen and offscreen gaze. The conflicts that Juliete experiences between differing ideals are never fully resolved at the end of the film. By contrast, and under the aegis of the fantasy-romance genre, a far greater sense of resolution is achieved in *Bell, Book and Candle*. With some regret, Gillian seems relatively happy with the exchange of her witchy-wildness for love and marriage. Although Juliete is seen hand-in-hand with her jilted husband at the end of the film, there is still a sense that she will continue to be lead by her passions, as she had been before. Her past behaviour cues the assumption that she is simply, and understandably, looking for comfort at that juncture, but that will not be sufficient as time goes by.

Both …*And God Created Woman* and *Bell, Book and Candle* show women who are struggling with conflicting ideals. To find acceptance they must conform to a set of ideals that suppresses aspects of their characters. In both films, to become an ideal, successful wife (and mother) and enter into domestic service comes at a heavy cost. Juliete had little choice; if she had not married she would have been placed in a children's home until she came of

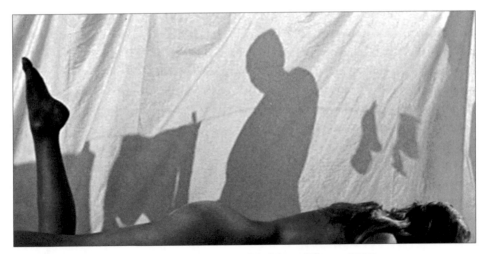

Juliete (Brigitte Bardot) in her 'natural' state in ...*And God Created Woman* (1956)

age at 21. But for Gillian it was a choice; romantic love was the pay-off. The situation seems to beg viewers to ask if that pay-off is too costly.

Like ...*And God Created Woman*, Hollywood melodramas such as *From Here to Eternity*, *Cat on a Hot Tin Roof*, *A Streetcar Named Desire*, *Baby Doll* and *Written on the Wind* do not provide idealised anodyne romantic resolutions that contain and channel sexual desire within the safe confines of a solid, complementary marriage. These films tend to present sexual desire as disturbing and dangerous, out of step with both the desire of the other and the constraints made on desire in the context of conventionalised social mores and family life. Sex and desire are therefore less idealistically rendered than in some other genres: both are full of pain, problems, tensions and irreconcilable power relations. These problems are, however, often cranked-up to hyper-proportions, to the extent that they are now regarded by some as camp. And, importantly, even if these films uncover the problems of sex, desire and family life, they still work, inversely, to affirm normative ideals, especially as often the cause of narrative tension is that the married couple do not conform in some way to the ideal status of complementarity.

In a broad cultural sense, the ideals of a given time and context are not always complementary. Often they conflict and confuse. Ideals might express the unachievable, the sublime and they may support insidious and harmful ideologies. For all this, the ideal, in whatever rhetorical guise, serves cinema well and plays an important role in shaping the representation of sex and sexuality. Ideals regularly generate narrative, are taken up thematically, and work through representational schemes. Ideal sex in cinema is cast between two poles: the first is found in the way that romance and sex are paired; its naughty twin, found in many films that focus directly on sex, is perfectly absorbing 'pornutopian' sex. Sitting between the two are films where the ideal romantic context for sex acts as a benchmark against which a drama of dysfunctionality plays out. This is evident even in the apparently non-romantic and 'feminist' *Romance*, a film that hinges on the female protagonist's quest for a relationship that is both loving and passionately sexual. The cinematic need for dramatic tension means that the ideal is problematised on a regular basis; the way that this is achieved is dependent on institutional regulation and industrial factors such as presenting stars as objects of desire. Cinema's demand for narrative disruption and for visual spectacle often means that the invocation of the ideal is often couched within the dangers of thrilling and transgressive seduction or that it remains an unachieved goal (as in 1950s Hollywood adult melodramas). The ideal therefore often goes hand in hand with danger, transgression and peril (physical or moral), and this is not simply confined to genres such as the horror film or the thriller. One of the main arguments of this book is that because of its need for narrative disruption and spectacle, cinema has a significant investment in representing sex as excitingly transgressive and dangerous. The ideal in its many forms therefore has an ambiguous and conflict-generating status in most films. While in some the ideal sexual-romantic relationship is served up to audiences as a dream of achieving the plenitude and richness missing in real life, in others it is also often a lure, a trap woven out of unwholesome, wild sexual fantasies into which the hapless fall. Perhaps such dramatic twists are intended to act as a warning to viewers about becoming too captivated by the rich and impossible sexual fantasies paraded on the silver screen.

Realisms: imperfect sex

Alongside idealism, various forms of realism play an important role in the cinematic mediation of sex and sexuality. Realism and idealism can be regarded as diametrically opposed, but frequently they have a systemic and contingent relationship; often the one depends on the other for its meaning. Broadly, there are three types of realism that imprint strongly on cinematic sex: that which focuses directly on the 'realities' of sex and sexuality as a social problem, the logic of which dictates acting style, theme, narrative and setting; the second focuses on the psychological and affective realities of sex and sexuality, and these might appear in a more fantastic, overblown or more obviously artificial context; the last is the use of certain sexual acts or indicators of arousal to guarantee that the sex seen on screen is 'real'. Some films mix together these types, perhaps most obviously in those that fall under the aegis of art cinema: *Summer with Monika* (*Sommaren med Monika*, 1953), *Betty Blue* (*37°2 le matin*, 1986) and *Virgin* (*36 fillette*, 1988), for example. In many films that deploy realist aesthetics, love and romance are often either absent (as is also the case with most hard-core films) or they operate as unattainable ideals that ultimately cause pain. Most fiction-based films combine aspects of realism with fantasy and the ideal in some way, thereby reflecting the subjective nature of sexual desire. Often this mix produces the type of tensions that might be called 'melodramatic'. In the particular context of hard-core, real sex is expected, and this is coded in certain ways, but in the majority of hard-core, the real of sex is balanced with other factors that are clearly the stuff of sexual fantasy. In recent years films like *Baise-*

moi, for instance, deploy images more commonly seen in hard-core. In combining these with rawer and more disturbing images, such as rape, the viewer's experience that what they are watching should be taken as real, at least within the frame of representation, is consolidated.

A key motive behind the use of realism, either in terms of a documentary-style aesthetic or psychological realism, is to show that sex is a physical and problematic business. Realism is often used in films that focus on sex in the light of problems originating within the social order, and, in some cases, facilitate the demonstration of the effects of a hierarchical differentiation in the exercise of power. In some genres, such as melodrama, aspects of realism may be employed to highlight the difficult relationship between the ideals of romantic fantasy and the harsh realities of sex and sexual relationships. Realist representations have often been subject to closer censorship than more idealistic representations, partly because they are less inclined to provide imaginary and ideologically safe solutions to real social problems or because of rules that regulate the presentation of authentic sex in the public domain.

Pre-Code American cinema and European cinema of the 1920s and 1930s was often in the business of addressing the social and personal effects of pre-marital sex, with films often termed 'fallen women' movies.[16] In D. W. Griffith's version of *Way Down East* (1920), poor country-cousin Anna (Lillian Gish) believes she is married to the man of her dreams. When she tells him she is pregnant, he informs her that their marriage was a staged hoax and leaves. She is left with no money or support. Life becomes hard, her baby dies in her arms and she is destitute, hounded out of rented accommodation and work for being an unmarried mother. Gish's innocent, open face increases the pathos of the scenario. The effects of her sexual pleasure may be melodramatically overblown, but the frame of melodrama enables the raw realities of sex outside of marriage to be explored at an emotional and social level (the acting style in the film may seem overwrought to us now, but at the time it was considered to be understated). Granted Griffith had his own idealist agenda to pedal about the need to respect the innocence and frailties of 'woman', but nonetheless the film uses sentimentality and melodrama to represent the emotional and social effect of sexual transgression on women at that time. As Nicholas A. Vardac has said, Griffith 'developed the realistic capacities of the medium to serve in the exploitation of his romantic conceptions' (1991: 360).

Way Down East uses big-budget spectacular effects (the infamous ice-flow sequence, for example) and melodramatic tension to purvey a reformist agenda and, therefore, carries an idealistic notion of how society should operate. In its sympathetic focus on the plight of an unmarried mother, *Way Down East* demonstrates the profound effects of the then real social stigmas on illegitimacy and pre-marital sex that affected many women at that time, illustrated by the historical and horrifying fact that some unmarried mothers were incarcerated in insane asylums in Britain. Griffith's earlier film *Intolerance: Love's Struggle Through the Ages* (1916) uses a documentary-style aesthetic combined with melodrama to convey the harsh realities of life in urban America in the 'Mother and the Law' episode. In one scene a women's child is taken from her by a group of 'do-gooding' women who wrongly believe the mother is a drunk. This represents an attack on what Griffith sees as middle-class reformists meddling in working-class lives. The events of *Way Down East* and *Intolerance* may seem highblown to audiences today, but, as Scott Simmon has said, *Intolerance* 'transmute(s) into the stark morality of melodrama certain crisis points in rapidly evolving American society' (1993: 139).

Melodramatic modes combined with what can be thought of as a realist approach have often been used in cinema to explore the effects of sex and sexual desire, heightening emotions certainly, but nevertheless providing an expressive form through which the psychological economics of sexual relations can be explored. Christine Gledhill argues that melodrama provides 'an aesthetic apprehension of reality that could manage the enormous social changes accompanying the secularisation and industrialisation of the Western world' (1992a: 131). And, further, she suggests that Hollywood cinema meshes together 'the melodramatic and the realistic – the metaphoric and the referential, the social and the psychological' (1992a: 165). A pertinent example is Max Ophüls' *Letter from an Unknown Woman* (1948), in which a girl (Joan Fontaine) falls in love with a musician (Louis Jourdan), and, despite several affairs with him throughout their lives, he never recognises her as the same woman. During one of these she becomes pregnant, he learns this only after she and the child are dead, through the eponymous letter. The cinematic style and setting of the film are 'romantic', but the story is not. As the film progresses her firm romantic belief that he will finally recognise her is gradually undermined, and she realises that her view of him was a fantasy that bears no relation to actuality. The trajectory from romantic illusion to disillusion, pain and death underscores the film's ironic take on romance. This is no Griffithian morality tale; instead it is a sophisticated engagement with the mismatch between the ideal and the real. Here melodrama and psychological realism meet. The social and emotional consequences of obsessive romantic fantasy that have real effects on the protagonists' lives are primed to deliver a high-impact melodramatic experience. Through its focus on psychology and emotional affect, the film is able to speak to audiences about the gulf between reality and the ideal. The film also offers a sophisticated reflexive comment on the way that Hollywood cinema and the star system rely on eliciting imaginary romances with distant and idealised movie stars. The reflexive take on the impact of cinema on the sexual imagination of young women is also something that appears more blatantly in the less baroque and more realist context of *Summer with Monika*.

Sex in art cinema is framed by various realist modalities. Some films deploy realist aesthetics whereas others use more stylised, expressionistic and allegorical forms to reveal the emotional, experiential and social realities of sex and sexuality. Pier Paolo Pasolini's *Arabian Nights* (*Il fiore delle mille e una notte*, 1974) lies somewhere between these two forms. Taking a series of nested, episodic fantasy tales about sexual couplings, the film uses natural light, location shooting (North Africa mainly) and, in some cases, non-professional actors to present fairytale fantasy in a realistic way. The driving idea behind the film is the joyful 'naturalness' of sex relationships between people of whatever gender and age, even if some end in psychological pain and physical violence. Unlike many other films focused on sex, there is no direct thematic or narrative use of shame or repression (such films are discussed below). In this fairytale world sex is essential to human life, abundant and transient. Bodies are naked rather than nude – they are not adorned in the usual conventional softening gauzes or contour-enhancing lighting commonly found in art-stylised soft-core of that era. Male and female genitals are shown, yet not in close-up or specially foregrounded, as is characteristic of hard-core and soft-core. Intercourse between men and women in the film involves no frenetic pumping action, just gentle movements – not very realistic perhaps, but this adds to the general picture of innocent, shameless sex. Same-sex desire, female interest in sex, and group sex are not couched in overtly transgressive rhetoric: all the sexual acts shown are mutually desired and enjoyed by participants. These textual factors create the sense that sex is an ingenuous expression of life and the source of joy and pleasure. In many ways the film's view of sex is idyllic because it is thematically free of the rhetoric of sexual shame.

The search for his abducted lover, Aziza (Tessa Bouché), undertaken by Aziz (Ninetto Davali), links each of the film's nested stories. Although this complementary couple are deeply in love they do not stop having sex with other people when they are apart. In this film sex is about pleasure, embracing the sensuous experiences offered by life rather than anchored in love and marriage. Youthful bodies are certainly of central importance; their presence contributes to the pre-lapsarian atmosphere, but these are not the idealised manicured bodies of those we might expect in Hollywood films. All the film's characters, no matter what gender, age or ethnicity, are active sexual beings. The film's realist aesthetic combines with an adult fairytale to demonstrate an idealistic view of sex unconstrained by social taboo and regulation. By contrast *Last Tango in Paris* (*Ultimo tango a Parigi*, 1972) uses a realist aesthetic in a very different way, and unlike *Arabian Nights*, repression and shame are central to its realist erotic agenda.

Last Tango in Paris has been described as a hybrid film that embraces Hollywood forms as well as European art cinema. The film charts the 'deterioration' (Lev 2000: 79) of a romance that starts with anonymous sex in an empty apartment. It is an open essay on the realities, emotional highs and lows of a sexual relationship, and focuses on what Bernardo Bertolucci, the director, has called 'the present of fucking' (cited in Mellen 1974: 131). The intention to capture the suspension of time in the act of sex operates, as Joan Mellen says, as 'a pure cinematic moment of authenticity beside which every other experience in the film is derivative' (1974: 142). The central theme of the film is the search for authentic experience that is masked by the affectations and taboos of bourgeois life. Sex is the primary route to existential authenticity. The present of fucking is further underpinned by improvised speeches, method acting, and the way in which Marlon Brando stitches truths about his own life and role as an aging man into his performance (Brando is trained in the Method acting style, which seeks to build realistic psychological and even physiological elements into a performance). However, sex does not prove to be the universal panacea for healing the distortions inflicted by social conditioning. Instead, it remains as a moment of respite in which authenticity is only fleetingly achieved. As with Ophüls' melodramas (and indeed in the work of psychoanalyst Jacques Lacan), sex and romance is flawed because it resides mostly in fantasy and, despite the idealistic optimism of the Hollywood romance, we never truly know the other: herein lies one aspect of the film's psychological realism, which is combined with the location of the film in the 'here and now' of the time the film was made. Many other art movies, such as *Romance*, *Summer with Monika* and *Ai No Corrida* (*Empire of the Senses*, 1976) for example, inhabit similar territory. These films are deeply pessimistic about the possibility of achieving a reciprocal rich and lasting sexual relationship, a theme that works in tandem with a realist aesthetic and the here-and-now locations that allow sex and desire to be seen within a broader social context. Such pessimism, alongside psychological realism, is at odds with the rosy picture of love present in many light Hollywood romances. And, it also contrasts with the less idealistic but life-enhancing view of sex and inter-couple relations that features in *Don't Look Now* (albeit that this serves relationally to inflate the tragic/horror elements of the film).

Sexual themes in art cinema often carry intellectual and/or psychological dimensions to differentiate them from other forms of sex-based cinema. *Last Tango in Paris*, *Ai No Corrida* and *Romance* gained notoriety for their explicit treatment of sex (which helped boost box-office returns). To some extent the explicitness of each film is sanctioned because the films do intellectual or philosophic work, notably around Lacan's psychoanalytic observation of the impossibility of a truly complementary 'sexual relation'.[17] (The qualifications that authorise sexual explicitness in art cinema are explored in greater detail in Part II, 'Real Sex'.) Bertolucci has spoken of the centrality of psychoanalysis to his life and cinema (see Mellen 1974: 136). As such *Last Tango in Paris* laces its explicit images with psychoanalytic concepts that are used to theorise the construction of adult sexuality, such as unconscious fantasy, repression and the Oedipus complex. Key to the attraction of an art cinema audience as well as informing the psychological realism of these films is the notion that sex provides a potential liberation from everyday repressions, rituals and family ties. But none of the couples in *Romance*, *Last Tango in Paris* or *Ai No Corrida* fully achieve release and each film ends with the death of the male partner at the hands of the female protagonists (even if for different reasons). The realist aesthetic of these films lies, at least in part, in the way that they seek to engage viewers' interest with the real and knotty complexities of desire. In so doing these films expose the illusionary and anaesthetic properties of anodyne cinematic romances. While they have complex psychological dimensions, some use is also made of the rhetoric of authentic sex, as developed within the context of hard-core, with which to lure audience attention.

In Britain, in particular, *Romance* pushed the boundaries of cinema censorship because it uses certain images that are common to hard-core (hitherto excised from films seeking British Board of Film Classification certification outside the 'R18' category).[18] *Romance* uses images that speak of the materiality of the sexual body: erect penises, penetration and the graphic and close-up depiction of a child being born. Each of these real, rather than simulated, acts lends the film a greater air of visceral authenticity. But despite such strategies the film is not made in the conventional mode of hard-core. Instead, it focuses intently on the subjective experiences of Marie (Caroline Ducey), the central protagonist. Through a combination of direct speech and dialogue she contemplates the construction of masculine desire, particularly in terms of the operation of the Madonna/whore binary,[19] which is clearly at work in the way that her husband treats her – particularly his disdain for her interest in sex. This duality which Marie sees in her husband and all men (Marie is speaking for the director/writer Catherine Breillat it seems) is typified graphically in a fantasy scene where a number of women are laid on tables in a circular room. The women's lower bodies are separated by a wall from their upper bodies. While heads and torsos are located in a clean white room brightly lit, with their lovers stroking their faces, their lower bodies are in a darkened and dirty space, their legs dangling down, where they are inspected and fucked by a group of large men. In voiceover, as if she were speaking to her lover, Marie states 'you can't have a face when a cunt tags along'. In expressing the subjective reality Marie experiences, the film makes its intervention into sexual politics. The sentiments of the scene echo certain feminist critiques of patriarchal culture and analysis of the representation of women in cinema (Molly Haskell's *From Reverence to Rape* in particular), that argue that heterosexual men view women either as sexual objects (whore) or de-sexualised objects of worship (Madonna/mother). The scene also illustrates the film's core distinction from hard-core convention. The film makes use of graphic sexual imagery which carry a realist caché because the acts depicted are not simulated, but unlike hard-core these are designed to address real-life problems, tensions and conflicts of interest that arise in relation to sex, including gender politics and the complexities of interpersonal relations.

Romance may not be 'feminist' in a classical sense; there are no 'solutions' presented here. Instead the pleasures on offer are revenge – although the killing of the father of her child could be said to stand for the death of patriarchy – and the portrayal of a woman who is a complex sexual subject and who is in search of sexual romance on her own terms. Like *Ai No Corrida* and *Last Tango in Paris*, the film deals with the intersection of conflicting pressures: fantasy, sexual needs and desires, and social reality. What these films have in common are narratives that focus, in terms of psychological realism, on the lack of true romance and complementary sexual relations, and their broadly realist representations of sex are framed by this theme.

The type of realism used in these films is markedly different from the form of politically informed social realism deployed in films that follow the path taken by British television play *Cathy Come Home* (1966) and, more recently, *Vera Drake* (2004). Social realism deals with sex, more likely its consequences, in terms of the inequalities in the social order. Such films often aim to make inequalities clear as a counter move to the escapist fantasies of Hollywood-style films. Often these films are set in urban locations that are far from glamorous or picturesque – backstreets, tenement blocks, run-down housing estates. Unlike the gritty working-class reality of social realism found, for example, in *Intimacy* (2001) and *Vera Drake*, *Romance*, *Ai No Corrida* and *Last Tango in Paris* utilise art-house conventions that are most apparent visually in their carefully choreographed colour palettes. White and beige predominate in *Romance*, signifying the; passionless, clean and narcissistic order of Marie's husband's life. This is juxtaposed with the red and black used in the apartment of middle-aged and tender Robert (François Berléand), who helps realise Marie's exploration of her more *outré* sexual fantasies. The apartment in *Last Tango in Paris* is flooded with golden light, signifying the outside-of-time aspect of the sexual encounters that occur there. With an emphasis on beauty the film contrasts very strongly in stylistic terms with those films that utilise the aesthetics of social realism; the room in which the adulterous couple have sex in *Intimacy* for example, is the front room of a shared and ill-kept house. It is harshly lit and full of debris – empty beer cans, records, ashtrays. In this film sex happens in the midst of the everyday banal rather than outside it. *Romance*, *Ai No Corrida* and *Last Tango in Paris* draw on the values of art cinema in their use of classical forms of composition, their contemplation of the human condition and their markedly beautiful colour schemes. These afford the films a certain status that enables them to circumvent the censorship that their authentically coded sexual content might solicit, and differentiate the films from the raw visual style more common to social realist-based films or some forms of hard-core. Thereby realism operates in the representation of sex in different ways, according to the aesthetic framework, genre or style, and the target market identified for a given film.

Hard-core makes its entry into the domain of realism mainly through its promise to portray authentic rather than simulated sex. Psychological and social realism are absent,

Paul (Marlon Brando) and Jeanne (Maria Schneider) wrapped together in post-coital glow in *Last Tango in Paris* (1972)

however. Such films rely on coding certain sexual activities as indicative of 'authentic' sex to create a marketable difference from soft-core and mainstream sex films; these include penetration of various kinds, erection, the visible presence of bodily fluids (mainly, but not exclusively, what is termed either the 'money shot' or the 'cum shot'). Recent films, such as *The Idiots* (*Idioterne*, 1998), *Romance* and *Baise-moi*, are beginning, to some extent, to blur the boundaries between simulated sex and authentic sex as they deploy some, admittedly fairly limited, representations of penetrative sex.[20] While hard-core is defined by the presence of penetrative sex, we ignore at our peril the genre's wide diversity of narrative types, intertextual references and target markets. Hard-core ranges from slick and narrative-heavy productions, typified by Michael Ninn's *Latex* (1995), through to low-budget parodies of Hollywood productions, such as *Rambone the Destroyer* (1985), to rough and edgy fly-on-the-wall-type videos, typified by no-budget *Punky Girls* (c. 1995). The latter is perhaps closest to the grainy video-based forms that have a realist currency in contemporary media and various sexual activities carried out by the two women who feature in the film provide transgressive spectacle.[21]

In most hard-core films there is often a rather thin line between the realism provided by the presence of real sexual acts and the grotesque. The overt focus on various body fluids, poses designed to enable camera access to the mechanics of sex, women who appear to be in a perpetual state of orgasm, bad acting and poor dubbing; hard-core sex can easily become a bizarre novelty (something some films seek to capitalise on). These features can, however, be regarded as reclaiming base sexual matters for comedy, parody or even in some cases noted for their ability to provide viewers' with a visceral jolt. Despite the way that various aspects of hard-core create a sense of transparency and immediacy, it is nonetheless a highly escapist, fantasy-based and idealistic genre. In almost all hard-core films, sexual satisfaction is shown to be achieved by all participants. It comes with no psychological problems or hang-ups to get in the way of sexual plenitude. *Latex* is a rare exception, and comes from an inventive filmmaker with a budget. Unlike most hard-core, *Latex* has a narrative, and it is based on the psychological problems experienced by John Doe who can 'see' the sexual fantasies of everyone he meets. This provides the premise for various types of sexual encounters that are evenly spaced out through the film (episodic structure is ubiquitous in hard-core). More generally, there is no such thing as 'no' in hard-core, it is governed by the pleasure principle; despite its particular claims on realism, this is what makes it a 'pornutopian' genre.

It should now be clear that the modal qualities of idealism and realism are rarely mutually exclusive and the two often intersect, either through a relative difference deployed in a given film to create visual and narrative tension, or because realism is framed by an idealistic impetus (to expose gender inequality, for example). While the thematic and/or stylistic aspects of idealism and realism have a strong influence over the meanings assigned to sex in cinema, they also interlink with other formal factors, particularly in relation to the shaping attributes of narrative and generic patterns, the subject of the next chapter.

Narrative Formulas

As we have already seen, narrative plays an important role in shaping the meaning of sex as it provides, amongst other things, a context that affects character function and actions. While narrative can take potentially many different forms, it often keys into genre-based thematic patterns. Narrative and genre forms may evolve into certain common patterns, but they also respond and adapt to changes in regulation and culturally specific pressure points. This chapter maps some of the chief types of narrative formations that frequently appear in films that are concerned with sex and/or sexual desire. It is not, and cannot be, an exhaustive list but certain types that have been commonly used in cinema, or that have proved influential or significant in some way, are identified.

Proper/improper couples

One of the basic building blocks of narrative in general terms is the use of obstacles to prevent a protagonist from achieving their goal. This device is found in the earliest known stories, including Homer's *The Odyssey* (c. 800 BCE), and other myths and fairytales. It is extremely common to find that in romance-focused films the moment when a couple cement their relationship sexually is deferred until the end of the film; this is not the case in hard-core where narrative is often of little importance and sex rather than romance is the focus. Delay does help, however, to keep sexual tension in play, but provides a structure and focus very different to that found in the more episodic forms found in hard-core or the escalation formula of increasingly more intense or *outré* sexual acts often found in soft-core (as is typified by *Secrets of a Chambermaid*). This structure appears across a number of genres including romance, melodrama, action/adventure, comedy, musicals, thrillers and teen movies, and is also present in a slightly distorted way in some art films (as is the case with *The Piano Teacher* (*Le Pianiste*, 2000)). The trajectory of such narratives involves a series of blocks on a 'properly' matched couple getting together, either sexually or in marriage. Different genres lend this formulation a particular slant, and the types of blockages may depend on the specific milieu and stock situations created and used by a given genre. Within the action/adventure generic context of *Raiders of the Lost Ark*, for example, the central couple have to overcome a barrage of archaeological traps, Nazis, and the tensions that arise from an earlier break-up before romantic and sexual union becomes possible. Perhaps in an effort to address its adult, rather than child, audience, the film encourages viewers to desire that union because the couple are so well matched in a range of ways. The stalling narrative formula has proved a staple of Hollywood throughout its classical period, and is perhaps most common in 'comedies of the sexes'. An indicative example is found in *Pillow Talk*. Like many mainstream classical Hollywood films the story focuses on courtship and a negotiated romantic surrender on the part of a woman. In such films an ideology of requited romantic love is deployed, the realisation of which is often deferred through blocking events or characters, misunderstanding or misinterpreted behaviours (a formula used in many of Shakespeare's comedies). From the melodramatic milieu of *Way Down East* through to more recent romantic films such as *You've Got Mail* (1998), this narrative building block has structured countless films, lending mild suspense, creating comic and melodramatic scenarios and cueing viewers into desiring a satisfying resolution.

The stalling device is an important component of a common narrative formation that can be termed the 'proper/improper couple' scenario. Again this is a format that has a long pedigree, appearing in Greek myths and Shakespeare's *Midsummer Night's Dream*, for example. Often an improper, or badly-matched, couple is juxtaposed against or intertwined with a proper, well-matched, couple; the mixing of the two lends dramatic tension and operates within the classic narrative formula of overcoming obstacles towards a happy ending. In more downbeat films, particularly melodramas and thrillers, the effects of mismatched relationships provide dramatic interest and may be used to create a morality tale. Unlike romantic comedies, it is rare for these films to end with the promise of a sexually united, happy couple. The 'wrong couple' formula ranges across cinema history; although perhaps most common in melodrama, it does appear in other modes, styles and genres where it is given a relevant flavour. Shifts in social mores also mean that the specific nature of the couple's incompatibility is diversely rendered.

Class difference constructs an insurmountable barrier between the married couple in the maternal melodrama *Stella Dallas* (1937). Both age and class difference puts pressure on the romantic relationship in *All That Heaven Allows* (1955). The couple are complementary as far as the film is concerned, but is 'wrong' in the view of most of the other characters in the film. Middle-class and middle-aged Carrie (Jane Wyman) falls for her young gardener, Ron (Rock Hudson), much to the chagrin of her peers and children. While the folk at the country club gossip about Carrie and snub her, it is her children that are instrumental in forcing Carrie to give up her liaison with Ron; they buy her a television set as a substitute. But when Ron becomes paralysed in an accident, Carrie's priorities become clear and becomes his nurse, but in so doing she takes on a role more akin to that of Ron's mother than lover. Until the age, class and experientially mismatched couple in *Rebecca* (1940) become more 'equal', towards the end of the film, their relationship is fraught with problems. In each of these examples dramatic tension is lent by the marriage or liaison of a mismatched couple, it is only if some kind of change is made to the situation that the couple become compatible. What constitutes 'compatible' is keyed into the social, cultural and and regulatory milieu in which a given film was made. Some films seek to overturn prejudices, providing drama, yet showing that certain values are under pressure. Many films operate on the like-meets-like compatibility stake, as in *Raiders of the Lost Ark* where the couple are adventurous, independent and resourceful.

The proper/improper-couple narrative often has recourse to the historical past to present obstacles to romance that would not perhaps prevail in the more liberal context of late twentieth- and early twenty-first-century culture. The aim of films like *Titanic* and *Moulin Rouge*, for example, is to allow viewers to bask in the pleasures of romance, special effects and period features. Such narratives also lend a positive, if ideologically loaded, value to supposed shifts in attitudes to class, race and gender hierarchy. *Titanic*, for example, makes use of the social hierarchy and the concomitant etiquette rituals of the Edwardian upper class to lend the central romance greater transgressive, and dramatic, weight. In *Titanic* and *Moulin Rouge*, the moral incompatibility between the mismatched couples underscores the 'right' fit between the proper couples. In both of these films the romantic female leads are coupled with improper partners, who are made in the mode of gothic aristocratic villains. With his black hair, cold expression and aristocratic snobbery Cal Hockley (Billy Zane) in *Titanic* is clearly not correctly matched with Rose (Kate Winslet) and her more liberal sensibilities. Similarly *Moulin Rouge*'s Duke of Monroth (Richard Roxburgh) is also a powerful aristocrat whose designs on Satine (Nicole Kidman) threaten the 'true romance' between her and the poetic Christian (Ewan McGregor). In accordance with the more playful and overtly anachronistic aspect of *Moulin Rouge*, Monroth is a completely unbelievable figure, derived from the gothic Grand Guignol (complete with gothic castle and suitably wicked desires). These cold-hearted villains represent anti-romantic, anti-human forces. Their antipathetic presence provides the means by which the films purvey in dramatic terms the 'value' of sex as an expression of love, and their negative attributes enable the films to present romantic love as an equalising, life-affirming apotheosis of human experience that transcends material gain.

In general the value of combining love and passion is paramount in much of cinema, thereby proper couples are able to overcome the majority of obstacles that arise (excluding the death of a partner, although there are some notable exceptions). Such couples are even able to overcome those obstacles that spring from their own differences: divorce (*The Philadelphia Story* (1940)); race (*A Bronx Tale*; *Fear Eats the Soul* (*Angst Essen Seele Auf*, 1974)); class (*All That Heaven Allows*, *Pretty Woman* (1990)); age (*Fear Eats the Soul*, *An American in Paris* (1951)); temperament and magic use (*Bell, Book and Candle*; *I Married a Witch* (1942));

class/occupation (*Rear Window*); rival factions (*West Side Story* (1961), *Romeo + Juliet* (1996)); supernatural class (*Underworld* (2003)); human/supernatural divide (*Dracula* (1992)). In all these films we are invited to consider the couples in question as 'proper couples'. There are many types of difference that do not appear in the proper-couple corral, however: cross-race pairings are fairly rare, as are certain types of age differences, there a few same-sex complementary couples in mainstream cinema and morally divergent couples are rare. More recently there have appeared some playful exceptions to the rule. The romantic relationship between Bill (John Carradine) and Beatrix Kiddo (Uma Thurman) in the *Kill Bill* films (2003; 2004) sits somewhere between proper/improper, for example. They are a proper couple in the sense that they are well-matched, yet because of the bloody vendetta between them the finale does not resolve into union. Instead, Beatrix is reunited with her daughter and Bill is killed by Beatrix's gentle yet deadly five-fingers-of-death touch. The tease in the last section of the film is that it looks as if they will reconcile in conventional romantic terms. She discovers the child that she thought Bill had killed is alive and looked after by him, but unlike the usual process of reconciliation, here the deeds of the past, the pain directly and indirectly that she suffered by his hands, cannot be transcended.

In teen-comedy movies *American Pie* (1999) and *American Pie 2* (2001), what starts out as couple incompatibility rests in one case on the difference between the ideals of adolescent sexual fantasy and the 'real' of an authentic relationship, yet in traditional comedy mode a 'right', if quirky, couple is eventually established. *Go Fish* (1994) also centralises the proper-couple theme within a lesbian context and charts Ely's (V. S. Brodie) search for and eventual discovery of a compatible romantic partner. Melodramas tend to focus on the psychological impact of an incompatible relationship; examples include one member of the couple being overly ambitious (as in *Bringing Up Baby*, *Imitation of Life* (1934; 1959) and *Mildred Pierce* (1945)) or mismatched in terms of sexual appetite or sexual sensibility (*Cat on a Hot Tin Roof*, *Romance*). Couple incompatibility raises its head in a more fantastical way in the Japanese horror film *Hellish Love* (*Seidan botan-dôrô*, 1972). The proper couple are clearly romantically and sexually matched at the start of the film, yet when the female partner returns in fleshly form from an early grave to have sex with her lover, he makes every effort to reject her advances. Towards the end of the film he is killed by her amorous attentions and the two are united in the spirit world – a sort of happy ending based on the achievement of mortal equality. The horror genre frame lends a spooky necrophiliac twist to the proper-couple format. Love returns from beyond the veil of death, a trope developed by gothic writers such as Edgar Allen Poe and reproduced in Roger Corman's versions of his stories such as *The Fall of the House of Usher* (1960) and *The Tomb of Ligeia* (1965). While these films are presented with a deadly seriousness, a comic approach is taken in *Evil Dead II* (1987); girlfriend turns to amorous but literally man-eating *girlfiend* when she returns from the dead as a zombie.

The proper-couple format is also an important feature of science fiction films, which are often viewed as being perhaps one of the least 'romantic' genres, concerned as it often is with space travel, action/adventure and science-technology-based themes. *Forbidden Planet* (1956), *Solaris* (*Solyaris*, 1972), *Blade Runner* (1982), *Flash Gordon* (1982), *Starship Troopers* (1997), *The Matrix* (1999) and *Solaris* (2003) each carry a proper-couple narrative component, even if, in some cases, these are not absolutely central to the main narrative. In science fiction-based cinema (as we have also noted of films such as *Titanic* and *Moulin Rouge*) romantic involvement is often used to indicate 'humanity' – emotional, vulnerable and in need of sexual and emotional companionship. A common structural feature of science fiction is the juxtaposition of the rational with the irrational. Often the rational is presented as stifling the human, with all its idiosyncracies and imperfections. In *Demolition Man* sex, swearing, non-educational play, and eating spicy food are regarded as irrational, going against the greater social good, and are outlawed. In many science fiction films, social engineering, science and technology lead to the regimentation of human life or the type of exploitation seen in the diegetic world created by the *Matrix* franchise, where humans act as batteries to fuel machines. The irrationality of emotions and hope for a better future signify the human, to which sex and romantic love become intrinsic. The proper-couple dimension, which looks to the future and the preservation of the 'human', serves these thematic concerns well. Its presence also serves to make science fiction potentially more appealing to a female audience with a preference for stories focused on interpersonal relationships.

As well as being in love, the proper couple are frequently matched in physical terms (the idealism of which is as discussed above). The frequent use of close-ups to consolidate a romance in a kiss, for example, places even greater attention on appearance, and it seems that film producers believe that the couple must be desirable if the audience is to identify and empathise with them. By contrast many hard-core films deliberately eschew any sense of romance or the complementary physical attributes of the 'proper couple' format. Lust-driven sexual physicality is hard-core's characteristic mode. In many such films made during the 1970s and 1980s, this preoccupation is often underscored by a common scenario in which good-looking youthful women have sex with fat, hairy and frankly ugly middle-aged men (it is far less common the other way around, however, although as hard-core has become an established industry and distribution networks widened it is now the case that many different 'curiosities' are catered for). This is perhaps testimony to the audience type – middle-aged men – that were believed to be the most likely group to purchase and view such films. Physical complementarity is by no means as central to explicit material as it is in mainstream cinema, even though there is a growth in 'mom and pop' style of hard-core that draws on the Hollywood conventions designed to extend the market of such films by addressing the sexual interests of a female and 'couple' audience. One of the primary drivers of hard-core is the fantasy that any man can have any woman he wants without incurring moral, social or other forms of repercussion; complementarity is based purely on the keying together of anatomical parts. Hard-core uses its largely anti-romantic stance to support and market its status as an obscene (not in the prejorative sense, but as a powerful attractor) and transgressive form. In comparing the improper couplings found in many hard-core films with the proper couple narratives of romance-based films it is possible to see how the latter constructs rhetorically a very idealised view of sexual desire.

What is common to the proper/improper couple format is the general principle that the romantic couple are matched equally and complementarily. The constitution of equality changes over time of course, and sometimes, as in *Pillow Talk*, concessions on the part of the characters may be required if the couple is to find a complementary basis for the romance to work. Even in films that address the melodramatic romance from a non-traditional perspective often refer back to the romantic proper couple format. Rainer Werner Fassbinder's *Fear Eats the Soul*, a reworking of Douglas Sirk's Hollywood-produced adult-melodrama *All That Heaven Allows*, provides an indicative example. A middle-aged white German and rather plump woman strikes up a somewhat unlikely romance with a sleek-bodied younger Moroccan man. Ultimately age, class and racial differences work against the successful continuation of the relationship. The film works with the romance myth in that most viewers are encouraged to hope that prejudices are overcome to enable the relationship to continue (the ambiguous ending keeps that hope alive). While certain differences can be overcome, it is more generally the case that class or social status, age, moral and physical compatibility are essential ingredients for the achievement of proper couple status. This is neatly illustrated in the anti-Cinderella story of *Roman Holiday*, where a princess's (Audrey Hepburn) illicit day trip into ordinary life and romance is curtailed because of her commitment to duty. That she does not pursue her love of an American journalist (Gregory Peck) is built on the principle that their relationship could never be equal: her commitment to duty is framed as a noble realisation of the reality of social hierarchy. The film therefore carries a clear message that 'fantasy' must be distinguished from social reality, a warning perhaps to cinema-goers who place too much emotional investment in idealised romance.

The 'fallen woman' film is yet another flavour of the proper/improper couple narrative formula and is specific to a certain era of filmmaking, as indicated by the strong biblical resonance of the subgenre's title. These often feature a failed romance, a proper couple that have somehow been parted, as in *The Sin of Madelon Claudet* (1931), or a naïve woman seduced into an improper liaison, as in *Way Down East*. A woman is usually duped by a man into a sexual encounter outside marriage, the product of which is an illegitimate child. *Letter from an Unknown Woman*, *Madame X* (1937) (filmed previously in 1916, 1920 and 1929) and *Waterloo Bridge* (1940) (a play previously filmed in 1931) each use variations on this narrative format. The rendering of this formula is very dependent on the proscriptions of the Production Code, which meant that the 'fallen woman' must be punished for her actions (even if she was a victim rather than a bad girl). This meant that the happy 'proper couple' ending of *Way Down East* was not available to filmmakers working under the constraints of the Production Code (which similarly applied to films made outside Hollywood but seeking a place in the American market). In *Way Down East* Anna is able to marry her beau with the blessings of his parents once it is proved that her earlier pregnancy – the child rather conveniently dies early in the film – resulted from her being duped by a wily philanderer; under the Code no such ending was permitted. Made under the auspices of the Production Code *Letter from an Unknown Woman* and the 1940 version of *Waterloo Bridge* entailed that the death of the unmarried mother (and her child) was a formal necessity. The combination of the cultural context in which these films were made, the Code and the melodramatic register of fallen woman narratives render pre-martial sex, whether with a suitable partner or not, a perilous activity that has socially treacherous ramifications.

The 'fallen woman' film has pretty much died out in Hollywood and Europe, a response to changing attitudes to sex, marriage and gender role, although some period-based films do still employ the notion of a fallen or ruined woman in keeping with the period setting (*Dangerous Liaisons* (1988) is a good, if slightly perverse, example). Reflecting the continued investment in the social importance of marriage the format is still common, however, in 'Bollywood' films set in the present era and there have been a number of remakes of made-under-the-Code Hollywood melodramas.

Men too are often the subject of being duped by ambitious, mischievous or perverse women, providing another variation on the improper couple narrative theme. Two Pre-Code Hollywood films, both starring 'new woman' Jean Harlow, have different takes on the 'duped man' theme. In *Platinum Blonde* (1931) Harlow plays a rich socialite who marries a working-class writer. Deemed 'cinderella man' by his peers, he is a kept man, a gender rever-sal on the pygmalion theme. In this tale of different class values, he has no control over his wife, and eventually leaves her for a girl who will keep house for him. *Red-Headed Woman* (1932) is also a class difference-based improper couple tale. Harlow seduces her married boss, he divorces his same-class wife, marries Red, she squanders his money, blots his social reputation with her *outré* ways and has an affair with the chauffeur (who mirrors her class and morality). Sexual seduction is not, therefore, confined to wolfish men and in the main it is power that the seductress seeks to achieve. Mae West's early cinematic roles in films such as *She Done Him Wrong* (1933) are rather different in that she seeks sexual pleasure rather than seeking to climb the social ladder. In *Out of the Past* Jeff Markham does not stick with the good woman with whom he could potentially set up a proper family; instead he is lured by his femme fatale ex-girlfriend into a web of deceit and crime. His inability to resist her charms and hold a firm moral line leads to his demasculinisation in traditional terms. The danger of being seduced is tuned to even greater cruelty in *Scarlet Street* (1945). While it is desire that drives Jane Greer, Jean Harlow and Mae West's characters, here both the middle-aged man and the object of his desire are manipulated by the woman's violent and exploitative boyfriend.

More recently, the 'duped man' theme has crossed into new territory. *Angels and Insects* (1995) is a British/American co-production based on a short story by A. S. Byatt set in the nineteenth century. The film bears all the accoutrements of the heritage movie yet includes a perverse and challenging twist, that is in part indebted to the success of *The Piano* (1993). The central middle-class protagonist falls for the beautiful daughter of his aristocratic mentor. They marry and many children are born, each looking uncannily like their mother. The twist in the tale is that these children are the product of a prolonged incestuous sister/brother relationship. This constitutes an interesting contortion on the proper/improper couple format. While we are encouraged to have some sympathy for the 'duped man', particularly as the brother is something of a gothic aristocratic brute villain, the film gives the sister a strong speech in which she justifies her behaviour and is not about to give it up. The fact that the brother and sister are more appropriately matched in terms of class, taste, morality and sexual appetite problematises and ironises the familiar concept of the proper/improper couple format. In sharp contrast to the deep shock of the duped man caused by the masculinity-shrinking revelation of incest in *Angels and Insects* is the comic reaction of the sexually 'used' male teenager in *American Pie* ('I've been used – cool'). There is no angst about masculine control or paternity here, only relief that he has finally got laid, and, as it transpires, this impromptu pairing becomes the proper couple in the sequel.

As typified by films discussed above, the improper couple scenario is regularly linked to the normalisation of gender roles. The improperly gendered and improper couple of *Out of the Past* end up dead, which, while conforming to the rules laid down by the Production Code, and purveying a conservative moral message, nonetheless invokes an exciting and dramatic transgressive allure (key to the attractions of noir and thrillers). Within the cultural context in which they were made, the proper/improper couple narrative becomes a means by which to express concerns about the changing roles of women (often prompted by economic shifts). Where cinematic women seek to gain power through seduction they are construed as crossing both class and gender lines. In many ways the new women, bad girls of classical Hollywood, act as 'frontierswomen'. Their *outré* ways carve out what might retrospectively be seen as models for post-feminist mappings of desire and sexual power. But before we offer unqualified praise for these representations of women it should also be noted that Hollywood's bad girls are used to reaffirm traditional gender boundaries and conservative patterns of morality; providing an example of the way in which cinema serves up sexual transgression only to censure it.

While the proper/improper couple formula is absolutely central to romance-based genres, it also appears in other generic and non-generic contexts. It underlies the 'fallen woman' morality tales as well as the more sex-positive forms of soft-core and mainstream cinema, from *Emmanuelle* (1974) to *American Pie*. In the main, the proper couple narrative relies strongly on the idea that the couple are matched not only in terms of sexual attraction but in relation to class and other aspects of social status (with some leeway for love to conquer and overcome relatively small differences). While aspects of idealism and utopianism are present, the proper/improper couple format also has a norm-setting function. Courtship ritual, partnership (marriage in earlier films), mutual compatibility and respect, frame and constrain sex and sexual attraction. These are taken in many films as if they are fundamental to building a long-lasting and meaningful relationship. This is as true of more recent films as older ones and can be seen in films such as *Amelie* (2001), a non-genre film that plays with the proper couple format by making the female protagonist complicit with the stalling of the central romance.

The proper/improper couple structure thus provides a powerful role in the shaping of sex and sexuality in cinema. Of all narrative formations it is the most ubiquitous device in cinema; it is present in most genres, cuts across different national cinemas, and has a strong presence across cinema's history. There are, however, a number of narrative types that diverge from the proper/improper couple structure. These illustrate the ways in which choice of narrative form can be used to express different philosophical or moral perspectives on love, romance, sexuality and sex.

Circuits of desire

The narrative of Max Ophüls' version of Arthur Schnitzler's play *Der Reigen* from 1903, entitled *La Ronde* (1950), is structured as a circular daisy chain, as the name suggests. This form is relatively uncommon in cinema yet what makes it pertinent here is that it has been used to present sex and desire in a very different manner from that which appears in many of the proper couple, stalled romance films discussed above (particularly those made in classical Hollywood). Set in Vienna of 1900, *La Ronde* is composed of a linked succession of casual sexual encounters, ten in total (this format is one that is often found in hard-core but the film is a comment on the nature of sexual desire and relationships rather than focused on sexual acts). One partner from each episodic sexual encounter goes on to partner temporarily another, who then moves on to another, until the last character forms a liaison with one of the characters from the very first liaison. Each tryst provides a duet that contributes to the overall dance of desire that both drives and provides the framing structure of the film. Every encounter is overseen by an intriguing male narrator figure, who is located mostly outside the main world of the film and is often pictured in proximity to a steam-powered carousel. He seems to feed off the sexual energies of the other characters and has the ability to lubricate their path to the sexual consummation of their liaisons. In one case, this occurs when a young man has achieved his goal of seducing an older married woman, but is unable to act on his desire. This scene is cross-cut with a temporary breakdown of the carousel, once the narrator fixes the mechanical problem the young man is able to proceed.

On the surface the film appears frothy, playful and superficial, signalled by the focus on seduction, transient liaisons, art nouveau-style *mise-en-scène*, comic moments and the fluid spiralling camera work. But, underlying this lightness is the more musty flavour of melancholy that arises from the film's engagement with the complex vicissitudes of sexual desire. In contrast to the proper/improper-couple narrative structure or the rise and fall structure that is often seen in American films that enables sexual transgression to be punished, and in which marriage and monogamy are normalised, *La Ronde* has no inherent denouncement of extra-marital sex as immoral. While sex in classical Hollywood was governed by a 'moral occult' (a hidden moral code that dictated events) that operated to punish sexual conduct that did not fit the edicts of the Production Code, in this film no one is punished by a moral occult of the film just for acting on their desire – in fact the diegetic moral occult impels characters to act on their desire. The brief sexual encounters are presented as delightful diversions but each encounter has little meaning beyond the pursuit of sexual gratification; no-one gets married, and unlike the 'fallen woman' film the repercussions of sex are not the focus of this film. The encounters are not cost free, however; sometimes they are painful for the participants. A creeping despondency comes with watching this transitory cycle of sexual dalliance. But, what is intriguing and fresh about the film, born of its structure, is that sex is not fixed or defined as any one thing: sometimes it is raw, tawdry and businesslike, while at others it is romantic and tender.

With his top hat, the narrator (Anton Walbrook) – billed as 'Raconteur' – is presented as the ringmaster of this circle of seduction.[22] His role is to promote sexual dalliance and ward off potential obstacles to the affairs. This represents a significant departure from the generic placement of tension-inducing blocks on sex and/or romance that drive the narratives of many of the films that have been discussed in the previous section. The narrator can easily be construed as a director, setting up and orchestrating fleeting liaisons between actors. At one point in the film he is seen snipping at a length of film, a reflexive gesture that works alongside the diegetic division between the 'real world' of the film and the behind-the-scenes space occupied by the narrator and from which the audience is addressed directly. It has also been noted that the film-snipping sequence was Ophüls' comment on the censorship he felt the film would receive outside France. The film's structure works to highlight artifice, and provides a fitting *mise-en-scène* for the performative role-playing that is an intrinsic part of sexual conduct. Critics have read the play and the film in terms of the spread of sexually-transmitted diseases, but there is no substantive reference to this (the film is a long way off the format of 'sexual hygiene' films found in early exploitation cinema). This is just one possible inference and one that is based on reading in absent repercussions. While there is a memetic (viral) quality to the film's circular form, its main function is to express the transient and playful nature of sexual desire as a kind of whirling waltz that demonically and inexorably drives the 'dancers' to act in pursuit, for whatever reason, of sensuous pleasures. Because the film was made in France, which at that time enforced film monogamy less rigorously than the US, Ophüls was able to use the circular form to tackle the theme of 'promiscuous' desire and the pleasures of sex in a non-judgemental way that would not have been possible in the US under the Production Code (the film was banned in the US and received an 'X' certificate with cuts in the UK in 1951[23]).

In certain ways *La Ronde* bears a structural resemblance to many hard-core films. Like *La Ronde*, many hard-core films centralise a series of episodic sexual encounters that are presented in a non-judgemental way with an emphasis on sexual gratification in casual scenarios. *La Ronde* does not detail the nature of its sexual encounters in the way that hard-core does, yet the form and subject matter are similar. As Linda Williams points out, hard-core's narrative form has a link with that of the musical in that the narrative is shaped by each of the 'numbers' performed (1990: 130). The numbers or encounters each have a 'conflict-resolving function or [act as an] expression of ultimate satisfaction' (1990: 133). The same can be said of *La Ronde*, in which the smaller components are part of a greater whole. The difference is that most contemporary musicals end with the establishment of a stable heterosexual relationship, sexual desire is sublimated into song/dance and channelled ideologically into marriage, whereas in *La Ronde*, by virtue of its perfect circular form, this is not the case. In *La Ronde* desire itself – as if it were an entity born of interpersonal interaction – acts as a form of 'passed-along-song' moving from couple to couple and working in unison with the circular form.

The film's conception of desire resembles that taken in the work of certain postmodern and psychoanalytic thinkers who conceptualise it as a form of energy that constantly reshapes and invests itself in multiple and conflicting forms, acting as a psychical 'engine' that grows from interpersonal relations and which inflects every aspect of human existence.[24] *Arabian Nights* also uses a circular, daisy-chain form and mirrors the libertarian, pleasure-driven, approach to sex and desire taken in *La Ronde*. In many hard-core films, as well as *La Ronde* and *Arabian Nights*, the episodic form is used in conjunction with a realist aesthetic interleaved with aspects of fantasy, rendering the putative line between the two blurred. These films differ from most hard-core films in that they are more knowingly concerned with cinematic form and make sophisticated play with narrative and reshape it to present a different view of sex from that which appears in Hollywood. Their respective use of a circular and episodic narrative form, in conjunction with the combination of fantasy and realism, are used to achieve a meditation on what is seen as the implacable, opaque and fluid complexity of libidinal desire.

Aspects of *La Ronde*'s form and focus, as well as more specific stylistic and cinematic features, appear in Stanley Kubrick's *Eyes Wide Shut* (both are based on literary works by Schnitzler). Although *Eyes Wide Shut* is not fully circular in structure, its narrative is constructed from a network of doublings, connections and interwoven events, thereby taking a formal cue from the art nouveau decorative form of flowing interknotted curlicues. These convoluted patternings dovetail with the film's elegant interlacing of desire with fantasy and reality. Subtle allusions to *La Ronde*, and other films directed by Ophüls, are found in the way that desire shapes fantasy and reality, in the use of fluid spiralling camera movement, in the prominent presence of Christmas fairy lights (which appear in Ophüls' *The Reckless Moment* (1949)) that signal magic and enchantment couched in a consumerist context, in the art nouveau-style *mise-en-scène* (consisting of elaborate convoluted shapes such as spiral staircases, décor and furniture style that belong to the *fin de siecle* period of *La Ronde*), and in the use of the waltz form (the dance and music). These intertextual reflections resonate with and frame the film's focus on the metamorphic convolutions of sexual desire that disrupt any firm distinction between objective and subjective spheres.

Eyes Wide Shut is laced with extra-marital seductions, flirtations and exotic-erotic encounters, each of which are never consummated except in fantasy, but nonetheless shape profoundly the film's diegetic world and the central character's relations with it (accordingly the two are largely synonymous). The moral occult of this film works overtly to protect the central character, Bill Hartford (Tom Cruise), from breaking the seal of his monogamous marriage, at least physically, and thereby preventing him from contracting the HIV virus. Bill's close but deferred encounters of a sexual kind are linked to his fall from a position of authority and autonomy into uncertainty and confusion facilitated by conflicting desires and the subjectively refracted, and obscured, desires of others. Something said, heard or seen, which carries the weight of desire beyond its ostensible meaning, sparks a chain of consequential and interdependent thoughts, fantasies and actions. In *La Ronde* the carousel operates as an energised metaphor for desire that is conceived as dependent on the continued connection between each of the couples to keep it turning, and is, therefore, more than the sum of those relations. *Eyes Wide Shut* also conceives of desire as relational, demonic and transiently affective. In both films it is desire (conceived on psychoanalytic lines) that fuels the circuitous unresolved narrative form that is essentially composed of a set of linked and increasingly convoluted detours.

The desire-circuit of *Eyes Wide Shut* starts with a lavish party with the central couple each engaged in a flirtation. These events prompt Alice (Nicole Kidman) to tell the all too self-assured Bill, her husband, her fantasy of having casual sex with a sailor. She does this in what appears to be an effort to undermine his surety about both her fidelity and his narcissistic view that, unlike men, women seek sex within a context of security and commitment. Soon after, an opportunity presents itself in which he can retaliate by acting out, potentially in reality, what she merely imagined. This appears to be born of a desire to re-establish an active, masculine and sexually-confident position. Although he does not take advantage of the situation, this is the first of a number of potential, yet always interrupted, sexual close encounters.

These coincidences interlace with a chance encounter with an old friend at the opening party, who inadvertently gives him the password (significantly *fidelio* (fidelity)) to gain entry into a masked sexual ritual held in a large baroque house. Bill is soon found to be an intruder and is rescued from an unknown fate – death is hinted at – by a masked woman. She appears to be the woman who he had treated for a near overdose at the opening party. She declares to the masked assembled group that she promises to make a sacrifice to save him. The next day he learns that she died that night of a drug overdose, which Bill believes is related to her promise. There is no revelation of the 'truth' behind these events, however, and on visiting Ziegler (Sydney Pollack), the wealthy host of the opening party and who is present at the second, Bill is warned to drop his enquiries into the woman's death. Ziegler offers Bill some very ambiguous and unconvincing explanations about what transpired: he claims it was simply coincidence that the masked woman died of an overdose that night and that she was just there to get her 'brains fucked out'. Bill is unconvinced and fears he has become embroiled in a high-level conspiracy, supported by the fact that he believes he is being followed.

Ritual sex as erotic spectacle in *Eyes Wide Shut* (1999)

The stylised artifice of the sex ritual/orgy scene, plus the contrived path that leads Bill to it, raises questions as to its 'real' status. With its spectacular naked women, robed men and women, baroque masks and opulent location, the scene resembles that which might be expected of a gothic-informed tradition of European erotic-occult fantasy fiction (such as the work of de Sade, *The Story of O* or even the black magic novels of Dennis Wheatley). Bill is told that the participants in the orgy are the most powerful people in the land and the implication is that this club is akin to or even an analogue of the Skull and Bones Society (to which many of the most powerful Americans belong). The theatrical combination of conspiracy with the accoutrements of ritual magic and sex seem tailored specifically to fit (the) Bill. Indeed it is the overtly transgressive connotation of this mannered orgy that sells the scenario to Bill (as much as to potential viewers in search of prurient thrills). The scene seems addressed directly to Bill; he is caught by the 'father' of the club for looking at what is forbidden to him, is subject to the desire of the group and only rescued by the woman whom he saved at an earlier party. The whole scene revolves around him and it has all the qualities of a masochist-style fantasy built from a patchwork of clichés. Is it Bill's fantasy? Like the viewer, Bill is caught up in a web of cinematic and enigmatic insistences, designed to intrigue and invite interpretation, and unlike most mainstream films there is no built-in narrative closure or assurances about what is real and what is not.

Ostensibly *Eyes Wide Shut* is a meditation on the difficulties of managing desire in a mo-nogamous relationship, yet it also spirals beyond this into the strange realm of desire and sexual fantasy. The complex structure and the world the film presents is never locked into a stable state, there is no resolution, no redemption – only an endless set of doublings, mirrorings and refractions and counter refractions. Desire is circulated, interrupted and re-routed, re-invested, transitory and elusive. It does not 'belong' to anyone; it is autonomous, other and disruptive, inflecting all it touches. It has no fixed or inherent meaning. While *Eyes Wide Shut* does not trace a full circle, its entire form, as with *La Ronde*, is used to invoke an image of sexual desire as convoluted, mysterious, endless and endlessly deferred. Circuitous form has appeared in other films that focus on the strangeness of sexual desire, including *Conspirators of Pleasure* (*Spiklenci Slasti*, 1996), where it is used to present a view of desire that shapes itself in accordance with the 'other' and that the other is in itself the product of the imagination, *ad infinitum*. The form does not lend itself to the more idealised and stable configurations of sexual relations that tend to promote the meaning of sex as an expression of love and tenderness in a stable partnership (whether this is in romance-oriented films or thrillers and noirs that frequently carry such values in their presentation of their opposite). Rather the circuitious formal structures used in these films reflect the thematic focus on sexual desire and as such these films undertake an aesthetically ambitious and intellectually complex view of sexual desire and relationships.

Sexual initiation and self-discovery

The 1970s saw the introduction into mainstream cinema of a group of soft-core sex films which drew on the already well-established sexual initiation narrative format to focus on women who embark on journeys of sexual self-discovery. Before the 1970s a range of European films had focused on the initiation of young women into sexuality; these include *Erotika* (*Erotikon*, 1929), *Maidens in Uniform* (*Mädchen in Uniform*, 1931) and *Ecstasy* (*Extase*, 1932/33). For the central character of *Maidens in Uniform* it was a painful affair, based on her love for a female teacher. In *Ecstasy*, however, the sensuous pleasures of sex prevail, as its title suggests. Sexual initiation narratives focus more intently on the sexual body than do romance-based genres, yet aspects of the sexual initiation narrative format are common in mainstream films, often appearing in conjunction with other thematic issues. In *American Pie* and *Mermaids* (1990), for example, sexual initiation constitutes an important aspect of growing up, but is seen in the broader context of teenage life and the protagonists' relation to the adult world. Sexual initiation narratives often cut across genres, most commonly in melodrama and comedy. These generic contexts affect the approach taken to the subject matter and have a bearing on the representation of gender. It has become a fairly well-established convention that when a man or boy is the subject of a sexual initiation narrative it is often framed as comedy, as with *American Pie*, *Confessions of a Window Cleaner* (1974) and the college geeks sequence in hard-core porn film *New Wave Hookers* (1985). When a woman or girl is the main protagonist, as in *Mermaids*, *Emmanuelle* and *Bilitis*, even where the format is framed by a soft-core 'porn' agenda, there is pronounced leaning towards the register of psychological melodrama. And, it is to soft-core melodramas of sexual self-discovery we now turn.[25]

While sexual initiation films had previously been the preserve of European and exploitation film, a shift occurred in cultural and institutional registers that enabled the format to enter into the mainstream. The introduction of the sexual self-discovery dimension to the initiation format was based on a hybrid between 'porn' and psychological melodrama. This particular combination led to films that differed from hard-core and that keyed into a broader context in which women were encouraged by the popular media to consider their own sexual needs. *Emmanuelle* provided the blueprint for the sexual self-discovery narrative format, sparking a cycle of soft-core films designed for mainstream distribution. Due to its somewhat risqué, yet timely, sexual self-discovery theme and 'pretty' art-cinema aesthetic the film was a commercial success (there are currently nine films in the franchise). As a result it was adopted, in slightly altered contexts, in *Bilitis* and *The Story of O*, and it has, as Linda Ruth Williams notes (2005: 391), continued to inform films that focus on women's sexuality, as with *Virgin*, *Romance* and *9½ Weeks* (1986).

In *Emmanuelle*, *The Story of O* and *Bilitis*, the central female character embarks on a journey of sexual self-discovery and development (ironic perhaps as the use of 'pornography' has often been linked, by therapists mainly, to arrested sexual development). These particular journeys are realised through lush art-cinema-style photography and *mise-en-scène*; soft-focus lenses, carefully staged sets, dreamy music and glamorous locations each contribute to the melodious aura of idyllic fantasy. Sex is graceful, often perfectly complementary (even if the participants are not matched conventionally) and visually rich, providing a significant contrast to the raw see-all-the-details glare of low-budget hard-core sex films. The quality production values of these soft-core films were designed to reposition sex-based films and broaden their potential market. In mixing elements of legitimate cinema (melodrama for example) with elements derived from hard-core, a dual gender market was actively sought. While there is a clear investment in the creation of visual pleasure, narrative tension is introduced through aspects that are more familiar to melodrama and the woman's film. The market advantage of including such legitimised formal elements is that it made the films more commercially and culturally acceptable (much like the strategy used by the 'adult melodramas' of the 1950s such as *Cat on a Hot Tin Roof*, discussed above). This is achieved, in part, by the way that these films contextualise sex in terms of the subjective dynamics of interpersonal relationships, an aspect that we have seen in films from a range of genres. It is, however, the focus on interpersonal relationships and the psychology of the protagonist that helps to differentiate these films from hard-core offerings. The sexual self-discovery film mixes the sensuous with the emotional: difficult choices often have to be made, a range of psychological and physical challenges are posed, as are changes to identity and role.

Sexual initiation and self-discovery narratives privilege the transition from innocence to experience. And as befits melodrama, experience comes with much soul searching, conflicting emotions, tears and joy. In *The Story of O* and *Emmanuelle* the self-discovery narrative trajectory is governed by the central female character's engagement with increasingly intense and challenging sexual acts. The former is based on O's (Corinne Clery) exploration of sexual submission. Emmanuelle (Sylvia Kristel) seeks sexual enlightenment through a range of erotic adventures. Sex is connected in both films to existential matters. O and Emmanuelle learn to expand their field of sexual experience outside of love and marriage. This carries with it risks, although not the same types of risks as incurred by sexually adventurous female characters in Hollywood under the Production Code. The risk element of these journeys of sexual self-discovery is based on the personal challenge of overcoming certain psychological, physical and social barriers, which once achieved leads in both cases to a greater self-confidence and awareness, rather than physical death or imprisonment.

In order to enrich and lend greater symbolic resonance to the form, and perhaps to enhance their status as 'art', these journeys have a quasi-mystical transcendental aspect. In *Emmanuelle*, set in Bangkok, there are numerous references to Tantric conceptions of sacred sex. In *The Story of O*, the regime at the Chateau is like that of a religious order. O is awoken at night to be beaten, must be silent at all times and her daily routine is entirely proscribed. Cut off from the world and its rhythms, O experiences a sense of timelessness and at one point the narrator tells us that O 'wondered why her terror was so delicious'; this is the type of transformational experience that is associated with mysticism. *Bilitis* also uses the initiation format to explore quite complex issues of sexual identity. The central character is younger than Emmanuelle and O; Bilitis (Patti D'Arbanville) is a sexually inquisitive teenager who experiences sex with men through the mediation of women. The film raises questions for both the viewer and Bilitis as to whether she is a lesbian or if her attraction to the glamorous Melissa (Mona Kristensen) is just a transitional 'stage' en route to heterosexuality. What typifies the self-discovery format is the sense of a multileveled, developmental journey into inter-subjective, as well as sensual, realms; a mixture that derives from the hybrid nature of the sexual initiation and self-discovery format.

Most sexual self-discovery films from the 1970s borrow certain structural elements from hard-core; sexual scenes are presented that have a certain discrete and structural integrity and which focus on a particular 'type' of sex: lesbian sex, voyeurism, fellatio, stranger sex, for example. Yet the particular narrative trajectory that characterises sexual initiation and self-discovery films lends a strong unifying thread that contextualises these scenes. And the fact that these films, often by virtue of the fact that they are structured around the experience of a central female protagonist, invoke issues about the meanings of gender and sexual identity and the subjective effects of transformation and emotional change, creates strong associations with art cinema, melodrama and the women's film. Thereby the initiation and sexual self-discovery narrative format allows the films to make a commercially more inclusive departure from the more risqué, episodic and emotionally disjunctive characteristics of hard-core. Given the soft-core context of these films, there is no explicit representation of penetration, as with hard-core; instead the acts depicted are designed to evade censorship and retain an air of erotic exoticism and fantasy rather than raw realism or clinical anatomical detail. The sexual initiation form gives a narrative context to the sexual events and, to some extent, the form also carries aspects of fairytale (as with the medieval-style costumes and chateau in *The Story of O*), the inclusion of which enables the films to better target a female audience. The women protagonists do not seek marriage, however, but fully sexual, sensual 'womanhood'; thereby components of traditional fairytales, which in themselves often carried sexual initiation elements, are tailored to fit the sexual self-discovery narrative format.

While these films intend to arouse the viewer of whatever gender sexually, they are also more than this by virtue of their particular hybrid form. The sexual initiation format facilitates the depiction of women as sexual subjects rather than simply objects of desire, although the women are invariably desired as objects by men and women in the films. Some feminist critics, such as Kaja Silverman (1992) have questioned the validity of this reading, especially in relation to the submissive focus of *The Story of O*. Silverman argues that O's desires are entirely manufactured in response to male desires. However, the initiation and self-discovery format provides the films with a structure that is inherently geared towards achieving a state of sexual self-determination, which in *The Story of O* means embracing the challenge of sexual submission. Susan Sontag argues that the female protagonists of these films are endowed with psychology, which sits in sharp contrast with the bone-bare anatomical ciphers of womanhood that are characteristic of hard-core (1983: 209). Given that the films use a narrative form to present progressively actively-desiring, non-monogamous, sexual women, who are not femme fatales nor presented as immoral or fallen, the sexual self-discovery narrative represents a significant shift in the traditional renditions of female desire in mainstream film.

While some earlier melodramas and women's films do address women's sexual desire (as with *La Ronde*, *Letter from an Unknown Woman*, *Stella Dallas*, *The Scarlet Empress* (1934) and *Lola Montès* (1955)), they tend to do so without focusing very intently on the experience of sex itself. The 1970s sexual self-discovery cycle places far greater emphasis on this and it is central to their narratives. So what has changed to facilitate the introduction of the sexual self-discovery form in mainstream adult cinema? The form certainly reflects the greater general prominence of a discourse of sexual fulfilment within British and American culture. As Jeffrey Weeks has stated, 'by the 1970s explicit sexuality (at least of a heterosexual sort) pervaded the social consciousness from newsstands to television, from private clubs to theatres and cinemas, from advertising billboards to streetlife' (1985: 25). This resulted from a combination of cultural factors, including greater leisure time and the growth of consumer culture (which plays a role in the commodification of sex), a rise in divorce rates, sexological texts reaching a mass audience on the self-improvement ticket, liberal feminism, the relaxation of general censorship, and the widespread availability of the contraceptive pill. Each of these contribute to what dissenters called the 'permissive' society and in conjunction with this sexual liberalisation, the line between soft-core and mainstream became increasingly blurred.

Male sexual initiation films are far less concerned with the emotional aspects of sexual initiation, replacing melodrama with the generic attributes of comedy. Leon Hunt sees the use of farce, slapstick and innuendo in *Confession of a Window Cleaner* as important to the acceptance of soft-core into the mainstream film industry (1998: 114). This argument could be broadened to include *Confession of a Window Cleaner* in a more general contemporary trend of sexual initiation and self-discovery films that in drawing on established generic attributes rendered the thematic focus on sex more suitable for mainstream consumption. The form and themes of *Emmanuelle*, *Bilitis* and *The Story of O* also coincide with a contemporary movement in which women are targeted as potential consumers for sex-related literature, promoting what Weeks calls the 'sexualisation of the female body' (1985: 26). These were often 'how to'-type manuals and articles with an emphasis on achieving orgasm and were on sale in mainstream outlets. Examples include *She* (a British-based women's magazine), *Forum* (a text-based magazine published by Penthouse) and the publication of Anaïs Nin's collection of short stories, *Delta of Venus* in 1978. Another important publication to reach the mainstream market was *The Joy of Sex* from 1972, which could be purchased from high street bookstores in Britain and the US. It stated that 'finding out someone else's needs and your own, and how to express them in bed, is not only interesting and educative but rewarding, and what sexual love is about'. This sums up effectively the new, therapeutically and commercially legitimised self-help approach to achieving sexual fulfilment. The sexual initiation and self-discovery form of *Emmanuelle*, *Bilitis* and *The Story of O* is best seen within the context of sexual self-help manuals and the mainstream commercialisation of sex, which frequently exhorted women to discover their supposedly undeveloped sexual potential. Women's aspirational magazines, such as *She* and *Vogue*, frequently linked glamorous, aestheticised lifestyles with sexual sophistication (making them a form of fantasy literature for most readers). In relation to which, it is useful to note that these films' directors, Just Jaeckin and David Hamilton, were both otherwise employed as fashion photographers. Glamorous photographs appear in all the films. O is employed as a fashion photographer, and in two different scenes in *Emmanuelle* women's magazines are very noticeably placed. In one scene a young woman masturbates with an open magazine balanced on her leg in which a full-page picture of Paul Newman appears, demonstrating the point that the films tie into a context in which women are seen as the new consumers of sexualised material. In another scene, a couple have sex over a dining room table on which an open magazine is positioned so that the title of article, 'Help is on its Way', is clearly seen, and in which context it can be interpreted as a sexual self-help article.

Surprising though it might seem, *Deep Throat* (1972) also works with the sexual self-discovery format, based as it is on the implausible premise that the protagonist's clitoris is located in her throat, a factor that she discovers is the reason why she has not been achieving orgasm during vaginal sex. The source of female orgasm was a favourite topic of self-help literature and comes out of psychoanalytic work based on the apparent difference between a vaginal and clitoral orgasm (the former being designated the 'mature' form by Freud, who as a heterosexual man may have had some personal investment in this classification). Echoes of this are present in *Deep Throat*. The film is more explicit, less 'romantic' and has less 'classy' production values than the other European sexual initiation and self-discovery films mentioned above. It could be argued that the film is geared more towards a male audience, partly because of its more realist style, which resembles that often seen in hard-core, and the centrality of fellatio, a sexual act that plays a very small role in the other European-based films. The 'self-discovery' aspect of *Deep Throat* is made in the light of a male fantasy in a more obvious way than the other films.

In all these films women's sexual self-discovery provides the narrative thread. With the partial exception of *Deep Throat*, the format is linked to the emotional register of melodrama and designed to appeal to the pro-sex *She*-reading female audience. The characteristics of the sexual self-discovery narrative form, with its complex storylines and focus on sex as central to subjectivity, all couched in carefully choreographed aspirational set design, provided the films with a certain aesthetic legitimisation that inoculated them against potential obscenity charges. Thereby they evaded, to an extent, traditional legalistic interpretations of pornography as that which is without artistic merit, while, at the same time, the overt presence of sex, often motivated by female desire, lent the films a certain risqué sexual attraction designed to appeal to men as well as to the new commercially recognised female audience.

The combination of generic hybridity with the sexual initiation and self-discovery narrative meant that more traditional pleasures were mixed with new ones. Rather than melodramas in which the woman retains the moral high ground in the face of male lust (as in *Dragonwyck* (1946) or *Blanche Fury* (1947) for example), or films that essentially promote marriage and monogamy, these films sold themselves on their sexual sophistication. In line with the 'brave new sexual world' tagline, contested on moral and social grounds by the New Right, the central premise of the films is that the old taboos that fettered women's sexuality and desire should be discarded. Perhaps more problematically for certain feminist critics the narratives tended to suggest that 'women's liberation' is entirely dependent on being beautiful and becoming sexually adventurous. What the sexual initiation and self-discovery form tends to disavow is the contemporary struggle for equal rights in both workplace and home. Perhaps such struggles do not belong in overt ways within the hazy-sensuous context of erotic fantasy. Yet the fact that these are mediated fantasies loaded with consumerist values and conceiving equality solely in sexual terms, should not be ignored. That is not to say that fantasy is a form that has no potential to envision new futures and identities, however. For some women these films provide a much-needed positive view of sexual fantasy itself, and offer an opportunity for vicarious experiences of sexual possibilities that are perhaps impossible in the real world. This might include the promise of 'no-repercussions'-sexual flings, sex without worries about contraception, menstruation or demanding

narrative formulas

children, sex undertaken for pleasure and thrill rather than obligation or routine, and these films may well have introduced some women to forms of sex they had not before considered. Above all these films link the growth of self-confidence and self-knowledge to sexual experience, in ways not apparent in previous cinemas.

The Story of O is the most challenging of all the films discussed here because of O being whipped, branded and passed on from one man to another (all of which she consents to). Perhaps because of these eroticised violations, and out of all the films discussed here, the film marks the diegesis strongly as fantasy, which is clearly signalled by the two different beginnings and endings. It is also clear that we are meant to regard the film's fantasy as having a female author due to the presence of a female narrator. She begins the film by stating 'One day O's lover…'. All these films have some female authorship, either in writing the screenplay or in the authorship of the novellas on which the films were based. The protagonists are each in their way sexual adventurers, frontierswomen who dare to break the old sex and gender codes and who gain self-assurance from their experiences. The context of sexual initiation and self-discovery means that they are not presented as simply notching up lays, as so often happens in male-based sexual initiation films. While for some feminist critics the sole focus on sexual desire does not represent a radical enough departure from other norm-creating representations of women, yet for others the films opened doors hitherto firmly shut by a variety of institutional and social taboos.

Sexual initiation and self-discovery films are very different in terms of their moral take on sex from, for instance, the fallen woman film or proper-couple romances. Rather than warning against sexual exploration, the emphasis is on sex as a vital and challenging part of life

O (Corinne Clery) is laced tight as part of her training as submissive in *The Story of O* (1975)

that should not be repressed or contained. Taking their cue from erotic fiction, such as the writings of Anaïs Nin, soft-core sexual self-discovery films often provide(d) receptive women with pro-sex texts that presented a different view of women's sexuality than the 'bad girl' representations of sexual women seen in noirs and melodramas made in Hollywood, as well as offering films that eschewed the type of rawness of hard-core or the 'damaged goods' narratives of exploitation films. Sexual initiation and self-discovery narratives are therefore strongly linked to changes in sexual mores. While certain feminist critics have proposed that such films are the product of male sexual fantasy, this has to be considered against the fact that these particular films are built on the premise that women have choices about their sexual identity and that they are positively desiring beings. Unlike the proper-couple narrative format, the sexual self-discovery narrative form is inherently pro-sex, anti-monogamy and not exclusively heterosexual. Sex is seen as essential to the human experience, and these films seek to act as an aid to enflame the sexual desire of both men and women. The sexual initiation and self-discovery format therefore represents a counter-weight to sex as a source of moral shame that informed many earlier mainstream melodramas. More recently films such as Catherine Breillat's *Virgin, Romance* and *Á ma soeur!* (2001) made use of the female sexual initiation and self-discovery form to explore issues of gender, identity, power and pleasure. These films are perhaps less dreamily utopian and often more explicit than those of the 1970s, yet there are many similarities (one of the reasons for which might be that Breillat wrote the screenplay for *Bilitis*). As we have seen, the sexual inititation and self-discovery narrative form and generic hybridity of *Emmanuelle, Bilitis* and *The Story of O* blur the line between mainstream cinema and soft-core. *Romance* uses the sexual self-discovery form and generic hybridity to evince a similar textual and institutional transgression, but, in this case, blurs the distinction between legitimate cinema and hard-core.

Return of the repressed

A narrative form that shapes the representation and meaning of sex and sexuality in a significant way and that has a major presence in cinema is based around the effects of that which has been 'repressed' by an individual or the social order. When the repressed returns it creates a disruption that drives the trajectory and logic of a story. The 'return of the repressed' narrative form has a special relationship with issues of sex, censorship (in its broadest sense) and morality, and, as such, often links through its rhetorical frame to the pressures and tensions that are present in the social order. Such narratives express the effects of psychological and/or social constraints on sexual desire – and its gendered forms – in often sensationalist ways and to create maximum dramatic tension. As such, 'return of the repressed' narratives often represent sexual material through rhetorics of transgression (the topic of Part II of this book) which operate in films that focus on sex as well as those focused more intently on the psychological aspects of sexuality and desires. Both capitalise often on the notion that desire and sexuality are duplictious and dangerous.

The underlying premise of this narrative form relates to a more general theoretical view, derived mainly from psychoanalysis, that to become a properly functioning member of the social order individuals must suppress certain fears, desires, fantasies or behaviours that would be disruptive to that social order.[26] As many critics have noted, the use of the concept of the repressed in cinema as a means of structuring narrative can be said to draw on the way in which the norms of dominant ideologies, gender role for example, become internalised through the processes of socialisation. Society demands that certain pleasures, urges and immediate gratification are given over; to become a 'subject' in the social order means conforming to certain rules, and whatever the particular nature of these rules, they are ideological and normative. Within the context of cinema, these rules create their own monsters. For example, the ideology of the good, nurturing mothering means there must be a defining binary inverse form – the bad, selfish mother. 'Return of the repressed' narratives, in whatever guise, express in a particular fictional form the effects of social and ideological processes on the individual. Often these narratives are propped up by the very concepts that define 'civilisation'. That which is repressed is often rendered as the 'uncivilised'; if the bonds of repression are broken then that which returns threatens the psychological unity of characters and the unity of the (diegetic) social order. To be 'civilised' means adopting certain norms, moral and gendered values and attributes, as discussed earlier. 'Return of the repressed' narratives work with the destablisation of certain norms, which provides narrative disruption requisite to the construction of dramatic tension, but frequently, and particularly in mainstream films, a resolution ensues as a means of creating closure, and as such repression and the normative are reinstated.

I have sketched out what characterises and underlies this narrative form, but it is also important to note that there is a significant difference between interpreting the events of a film in the light of psychoanalytic ideas and claiming that the return of the repressed is a distinctive (indeed common) narrative form. In some films the return of repressed sexual desires are dealt with overtly and provide narrative structure, as with *Dr Jekyll and Mr Hyde* (1931). In other films the return of the repressed is articulated less overtly, the sexual is diverted into other arenas, but nonetheless can be interpreted as acting as a narrative driver as, for example, with *Alien* (1979). In yet another, smaller, set of films the return of the repressed can be read as providing the source of narrative enigma, but its presence is not clearly signalled, as is the case with *Dr Jekyll and Mr Hyde*. This is the case in many of David Lynch's films. In *Twin Peaks: Fire Walk with Me*, for example, the character Bob (Frank Silva) is deeply enigmatic and puzzling, but the narrative logic of his presence becomes clear if he is seen as an archetypal manifestation of repressed primal instincts and under whose influence Leland Palmer (Ray Wise) commits incest and murder (of which more later in Part II, 'Family Relations: Incest in the Cinema'). Critics using psychoanalytic concepts have also been inclined to read the return of the repressed into many other types of films and at various levels; this is a rather different approach to the claim that the narratives of some films are structured according to the operation of the return of the repressed. However, in the case of *Twin Peaks: Fire Walk with Me*, a film that invites spectators to read meaning into its enigma-rich text, the line between what is essentially an interpretative frame and what is actually present in the text itself is quite obscure. This is perhaps testimony to the fact that psychoanalytic conceptions of repression and the return of the repressed have become part of more general and populist understandings of social constraint (and I would claim that cinema has played its part in this).

Quite a number of film academics, including Robin Wood, Barbara Creed and Carol J. Clover, have focused on the way that return of the repressed narratives in the horror genre provide an overt or implicit critique of the status quo. While some films that follow the classic narrative pattern of disruption and resolution end with the containment of the return of the repressed, others do not and considerable critical attention is assigned to the political and ideological status of how the repressed and its return are dealt with in a given film. Certain theoretical perspectives that are applied to cinema have an investment in seeing return of the repressed narratives as expressions of the pressures placed on sexuality and sexual desire by the social order. Psychoanalytic-based approaches to film studies, which draw on Freud's theory that repression is central to the formation of the socialised subject, are inclined to read the pleasures of cinema as deriving from the vicarious experience of repressed sexual material. This methodological, and interpretative, approach views repression as integral to our place in the social order (whatever that 'order' might be). As such psychoanalytic approaches to cinema are paradigmatically disposed to reading return of the repressed narratives as a kind of catharsis, providing a safety valve through which *outré* sexual fantasies, desires and instincts can be exorcised harmlessly by virtue of the protective circle of fiction. Marxist-based readings by contrast are more inclined to argue that the safety valve of fiction operates ideologically as a means of circumventing any real political action to change the system. Here return of the repressed narratives are seen as symptomatic of the way that the dominant social order suppresses certain radical and disruptive behaviours, points of views or experiences, even as they might be used to diagnose the operation of repressive power. Both approaches are co-opted by many theorists to foreground the way in which the dominant gender and sexual order creates its own repressions and concomitant returns. As such return of the repressed narratives, even where the potential threat is contained, can be mobilised as a means of critiquing the injustices, contradictions and hypocrisies of that order.

The return of the repressed narrative form has a presence across a number of genres – melodrama and comedy for instance, and non-genre films – but its most visceral and overt articulation is found in the often maligned and until recently critically ignored horror genre. As Clover has said 'to a remarkable extent, horror has come to seem not only the form that most obviously trades in the repressed, but is itself the repressed of mainstream filmmaking' (1992: 20). Within horror, it is usually a monster of some description that embodies the return of the repressed. And, importantly for this study, the monster often presents a violent threat to 'civilisation' and often in an overtly or implicitly sexualised way.

Long before Freud coined the phrase 'the return of the repressed' (less alliterative in the original German *wiederkehr des verdrängten*) , Matthew Lewis' gothic novel *The Monk* (1796) employed a narrative that is fuelled by the horrific effects of the suppression of sexual desires and urges. Much like later horror films, the novel sought to provide sensationalist thrills by portraying unconscionable sexualised acts (murder, incest, necrophilia, matricide, rape) that are attributed by the novel to the repressions of sexual desire demanded by the medieval church. In many respects *The Monk* is the archetypal return of the repressed narrative. As well as making the disturbing effects of the return of that which has been repressed central to its narrative, the novel was subject to authorial, self-imposed, censorship (as a form of repression) prompted by the threat of juridical prosecution: in later editions Lewis eliminated references to 'physical love or desire' and excised a brutal incestuous rape (see Clemens 1999: 63). The themes of what we might now call using the rhetoric of psychoanalysis the return of the repressed narrative form developed and deployed by gothic novels were themselves seen, even in some cases by sympathetic critics, as having the capability to corrupt certain readers. The return of the repressed narrative form itself was therefore considered dangerous because it exposed to consciousness desires that were considered better left buried. In so doing the form has the capacity to demonstrate in both an imaginary and real context the effects repression.

The Monk is built around the premise that the excessive repression of sexual desire brought about by cloistered life leaves the eponymous monk ill-equipped to deal with sexual temptation: 'Ambrosio was yet to learn, that to an heart unacquainted with her, Vice is ever most dangerous when lurking behind the Mask of Virtue' (Lewis cited in Clemens 1999: 69). *The Monk* is saturated in perversion and is laden with what are meant to be regarded as unnatural and supernatural events, as is the case with many gothic fictions. The irrational and atavistic rhetoric of the gothic novel arose, in what has been interpreted, as a counter-voice to the sterile rationalism of the Enlightenment, which claimed to potentially unveil every riddle of the physical universe. With the return of the repressed as constituting its blood and bones, the gothic novel provided a vehicle used by some to express all manner of repressions that originated from social institutions and inequalities. As a result the gothic genre can easily be regarded as itself a return of the repressed, looking as it did to the buried archaic past with its supernatural and hubristic worldview through which to critique and punish contemporary double standards in exhilarating, sometimes spine-chilling, ways. As Valdine Clemens argues, the gothic expresses conflicts between 'public values' of the social order and 'private impulses' in terms of sexual desire and morality (1999: 50). In using sexual repression and its violent return as the basis from which to create and structure stories that sought to solicit heightened emotional responses, the gothic novel provided a formal, sensation-laden blueprint for certain cinemas (and may even have influenced Freud's own writing and thinking, as indicated by his use of the gothic story 'The Sandman' in his paper on 'The "Uncanny"' (1919) – which locates the disturbing qualities of the tale in the return of the repression).

The use of the return of the repressed as a narrative structure within a gothic horror context has an exemplary incarnation in cinematic versions of *The Strange Case of Dr Jekyll and Mr Hyde*, a Victorian gothic novel written by Robert Louis Stevenson and published in 1886. The story builds on Matthew 'Monk' Lewis' return of the repressed gothic legacy but is located within the (then) contemporary era rather than the medieval. Making use of a dual personality trope that is common in gothic fiction, Stevenson aimed to expose the hypocrisies and dual standards of middle-class Victorian behaviours and values. It was not simply, as with some later film versions, a case of good Jekyll versus bad Hyde. Jekyll is deeply implicated in the particular evils of his monstrous double. Stevenson was at pains to comment that 'the Hyprocrite let out the beast of Hyde' (cited in Frayling 1996: 173). Clemens throws more light on such hypocrisies by explaining that prostitution was a thriving business and the subject of much public debate during the Victorian era (1999: 123). She claims that Hyde

> belongs to the 'night-side' of London life with which many Victorian men were actually quite familiar. However monstrous he may seem, he is the shadow self not only of Jekyll, but of Victorian society in general … Jekyll, whose repressed sexuality erupts in sadism and brutality and ends in his own self-destruction, epitomises a collective sense of guilt and concomitant anxiety about the 'reinvasion of darkness' into the comfortable, privileged lives of the ascendant professional and merchant classes of English society. (1999: 129)

As used by Stevenson, the return of the repressed is manifest in the regressive and violent Hyde and he can be regarded as the product of a sexual economy that arises out of particular imbalances and dual standards at work in the ordering of class and gender in late Victorian Britain. Yet this narrative form carries its own duality: it provides a means to critique moral hypocrisy while at the same time invoking the sensationalist qualities of freedom from moral restraints. As such, the moral ambiguity of the form and this particular story proved popular with filmmakers seeking to please punters and regulators. Many versions of the Stevenson novel have appeared, with several variations on the theme (www.imdb.com lists 38 films bearing variations on the title *Dr Jekyll and Mr Hyde*, starting from 1908). Rouben Mamoulian's 1931 version, along with *Mary Reilly* (1996) – a more recent version of Stevenson's tale – are used here to illustrate how the narrative form of the return of the sexual repressed has been tailored to suit the specificities of the medium of cinema. A comparison of the two films also serves as a means of demonstrating how the return of the repressed narrative form has been adapted in response to socio-cultural changes.

Mamoulian's *Dr Jekyll and Mr Hyde* and *Mary Reilly* frame their narratives in terms of psychoanalytic understandings of the return of the repressed in which the effects of sexual repression and oppression are central. This is most overtly apparent in the 1931 version in which science combines with sexual wish-fulfilment. The key role played by sexual repression in the film is promoted and facilitated by the introduction of a romance into the tale. The novel itself had no romantic element and its introduction here can be linked to the general strategy used by the makers of American horror films of the 1930s to appeal to both a male and female audience (see Berenstein 1996). Jekyll (Frederic March) is presented as young man who has had a measure of scientific success yet is thwarted in his desire to make a hasty marriage to the upper-class woman he loves and deeply desires. The woman's father, a pillar of Victorian values, is the obstacle to the marriage and insists that Jekyll must show 'decent' restraint and patience before the wedding can take place. Hyde appears at precisely the moment that Jekyll's fiancée is taken away on holiday by her father. Hyde magnifies and perversely acts out the desires that Jekyll had to repress. Given that the fiancée is safely out of reach, the object of Hyde's attention is Ivy Pearson (Miriam Hopkins), in an all but name a prostitute, who Jekyll had earlier rescued from a violent street scuffle. As Jekyll puts the apparently injured Ivy to bed she attempts to seduce him by undressing provocatively in front of him, which he resists. The image of her swinging a bared leg over the side of her bed and saying 'come back soon' lingers in Jekyll's mind, signified by a very long dissolve in which Jekyll walks with a friend overlaid by the image of the near-naked Ivy (excised in the US on the stricter implementation of the Production Code in 1934; all Ivy's scenes, with the exception of her murder, were scrubbed out by the BBFC in Britain (see Mathews 1994: 78); see also more on such censorship in the next chapter). After his chemical transformation, Hyde returns to Ivy's house, enslaves and terrorises her, leaving whip marks on her body, and eventually he strangles her, while aping the words spoken to her by 'Gentleman' Jekyll, Ivy's name for her rescuer, and only then does she realise they are the same man. Sexual restraint is clearly shown to be the cause of the return of the repressed, and leads to Ivy's implied rape and explicit violent death.

The figure of Hyde in this film is based on a particular rendition of the return of the repressed: regression. Hyde resembles the 'missing link': part ape, part Neanderthal. His movements are jerky and uncoordinated, and his animal-like agility is demonstrated as he swings on or leaps over objects. The prosthetic makeup emphasises his ape-like countenance, with a low sloping brow, coarse hair and wide nostrils. Even his speech becomes more gutteral. Cinematic effects realise the transformation as a form of evolutionary regression. Darwin's theory of evolution combines with a Freudian-style emphasis on the return of repressed, unrestrained sexual instincts. This particular articulation of the return of the repressed has been read usefully in terms of the context of the 1930s and the socio-economic divisions that were deepened by the Depression. As Annalee Newitz has said, Jekyll's contact with the 'lower' classes was not experienced as 'a new sense of community and social awareness, [instead] Hyde forces Jekyll to perform criminal, even primitive, acts already associated with proletarian culture' (1995: 12). Virginia Wexman Wright argues that Hyde's atavistic form expresses an underlying white fear of black male sexuality (1988: 288). This film realises the repressed as the other. This other is the by-product of civilisation, its 'flip-side', and the film purveys a liberal message that unnecessary stifling of sexual desire leads to an eruption of that which has been repressed. Hyde's monstrosity expresses cultural turbulence around the very definition of 'civilisation' and the film seeks to set up a clear definition of what is not 'civilised' and what might cause this. It is in that very definition that Hyde's true monstrosity lies; his form and behaviour articulate the way that 'civilisation' has been used to create hierarchies out of racial and class-based differences.

Elaine Showalter (1992) points out that the major emotional relationship in Stevenson's novel was between two men (Jekyll and his older mentor). As already stated, the heterosexual romance was a Hollywood addition likely to have been considered as a means of improving the commercial viability of the film. This romance and, importantly, the deferral of sexual union, are central to the narrative and thematic concerns of Mamoulian's film because it plays a significant role in explaining the psychological impetus behind Jekyll's transformation into Hyde. Showalter argues that the replacement of the male relationship of the novel with a heterosexual one in many of the films based on the novel is itself a symptom of repression. The repression of homosexuality in whatever form certainly has wider currency in classical Hollywood cinema and comes under the category of perversion in the Production Code (meaning that any positive representations of homosexuality were forbidden). Homosexual desire is, however, present in *Dr Jekyll and Sister Hyde* (1971), made in the more liberal regulatory context of the 1970s, where homosexuality is mixed with transvestism and transgenderism, a combination that shrieks sensationalism (as indicated by the film's tagline: 'The sexual transformation of a man into a woman will actually take place before your very eyes!'), and is therefore rather different from the emotional bond exhibited between the two male characters in the novel. Jekyll (Ralph Bates) is again a young male scientist but Hyde (Martine Bewick) is a beautiful but deeply immoral woman, who kills to collect the female hormones needed to create her. Jekyll must suppress the woman within if he is to marry his fiancée. Hyde meanwhile flirts with the fiancée's brother. Rather than accepting the woman within, Jekyll eventually commits suicide, as much to kill her as himself. It does not take too much of a wild leap of interpretation to read the film as an allegory for the way that repression is the product of social forces at work to police and ensure proper gender alignment. The return of the repressed narrative, even when based on one particular story, can therefore be turned to fit various agendas and invoke a variety of sensationalist transgressions.

Mamoulian's *Dr Jekyll and Mr Hyde* converts the complexities of Stevenson's novel into a clear-cut liberal message: Hyde's sexual sadism is the product of too stringent and unnecessary demands on Jekyll's sexual desires. With his vitality and 'modern' values, Jekyll may well have represented to a contemporary audience a more general dissatisfaction with outmoded 'Victorian' values that seemed to constrain 'true' romance, which, as the narrative form suggests, if not relaxed, would produce an atavistic return of the repressed. Added to this is a further dimension that links to anxieties around science and the socio-cultural context in which the film was made. Instead of a Faustian pact drawn up with the pleasure-loving devil to gain sexual wishes, the pact here is with amoral science, which becomes the new black magic and provides the key to the door that imprisons the id (the psychoanalytic term for the unknown, uncontrollable forces of the psyche and the repository of repressed sexual desires). In this case science and its untoward regressive effects could be read in the more general terms of modernity, particularly its potentially de-civilising attributes including alienation and the loss of humanistic values in favour of mass production. In the gloom of the deepening economic depression that gripped the United States in the 1930s, the life-enhancing promise of science and modernity looked increasingly empty and with various vice scares and the unpopularity of the prohibition on alcohol (repealed in 1933), there was perhaps a general sense that the conditions were right for the return of the repressed on a social scale. In this context Jekyll's transformation into Hyde appears as an allegory of the failure of the American dream.

David J. Skal suggests that mainstream fictions often attempt to reconcile apparently contradictory factors in an imaginary way. He argues that the 'mad scientist' figure, beloved of horror and science fiction, creates a bridge between science and the supernatural, and 'brings to science passion, drama, catharsis' (1998: 315). A further advantage of Skal's view is that it alerts us to the way that cinematic form makes capital out of the different intentions and aims of co-existing discursive-ideological agendas: through the mad scientist figure, science becomes co-opted in accordance with the generic demands of the horror film. *Dr Jekyll and Mr Hyde* links sex to science, providing thereby the source of the return of the repressed (a trope that occurs in many later films and particularly in science fiction horror hybrids). In using special effects, such as the clever use of make-up to seamlessly turn man into monster, split-screens and long dissolves, the film utilises the full potential of the specific qualities of cinema to present the return of the repressed as thrilling visually and dramatically. In yoking together sex and science the film carries with it various anxieties and social tensions, which are never fully resolved and, as we have seen, are available for a range of interpretations and investments.

Mary Reilly makes more subtle use of the return of the repressed narrative form within which sexuality and sexual desire is rendered as highly complex, disturbing and subversive. What the film adds to previous versions is that it plays strongly on the idea that repressed material has a collective, interpersonal dimension. While Hyde still represents that which is repressed in Jekyll (both played by John Malkovich), the central figure of Jekyll's maid, Mary Reilly (Julia Roberts), is also subject to the workings of her own repressed sexuality, which echo and interlock with those of Jekyll/Hyde. As a child, Mary was abused by her father, and while she can recount being locked under the stairs by him with a rat that scarred her arms and neck, she cannot fully recall, until later on in the film, his sexual abuse of her. As Hyde begins to dominate Jekyll and meets Mary regularly, often seeking her out to both shock and confide in her, she experiences him as both obscene and fascinating. This is partly due to his charming yet brutally frank manner, but also because Hyde adopts intentionally the characteristics of Mary's father, whom she had spoken of to Jekyll (motivating a number of flashback sequences in which the father appears). Hyde has her father's odd shuffling gate, repeats similar phrases ('now look what you made me do') and even leaves a disembowelled rat at the scene of a gory murder of a prostitute (which he knows Mary will see). It is never made clear whether his killing a rat, standing in for the one who scarred her, is a sign of his sympathy for her, or as a sadistic reminder of her pain and trauma. Given Hyde's perverse ambiguity, it is perhaps best interpreted as a little of both. Hyde's actions are clearly addressed to Mary and she responds to them in contradictory ways. In one scene Mary dreams she is once again a small girl about to be sexually abused by her drunken father (what she had repressed comes back to her in a dream). She runs screaming from the house, an action that is interlaced through cross-cutting with images of Hyde knocking to the ground a small girl in the street (the latter is a scene that appeared in Stevenson's novel in which a child prostitute is 'trampled' by Hyde). This editing regime establishes a close affinity between the two characters. In another dream sequence, Hyde appears on Mary's bed, much as an incubus or vampire, and begins to lick her bared back. She apparently awakens in horror, at which point he says, gently, 'I thought you invited me', to which she replies 'I did', and then awakens truly in even greater horror at her own complicity. It is implied that in some way she feels she invited her father's sexual and sadistic abuse and this is echoed in her contradictory relationship with Hyde.

Hyde speaks and acts through Mary's repressed memories and desires. This creates for her an inner conflict that correlates in less literal terms with the splitting of Jekyll and Hyde. Through the split nature of these characters the return of the repressed form is used to speak of sexual desire as something over which we have little conscious control, an agent that makes use of what is most feared. As played by Malkovich (and playing on his role as sexual manipulator in *Dangerous Liaisons*), Hyde is rendered as a dangerous yet compelling, vital and physically and sexually attractive character. Making Hyde attractive is important if the audience is to empathise or indeed identify with Mary's conflicting emotions and desires. In some respects *Mary Reilly* takes on elements of the beauty and the beast fairytale, as is also the case with Francis Ford Coppola's *Dracula* (1992) and for the same reasons. The abject loathsomeness of the novels' monsters is significantly ameliorated in these two films by the humanising effect of Beauty's emotional connection with them, the fact that they adopt, at certain times, a physically attractive form and that both are psychologically complex. As well as introducing female desire into the mix, these factors help promote greater audience sympathy for the 'monsters' and prevents them from being regarded simply as easily dismissable incarnations of metaphysical 'evil'. Unlike the case with less complex horror movie monsters, the introduction of romantic pathos and psychological complexity into the return of the repressed narrative may prompt viewers to reflect on the ways that they too might have experienced sexual desires as contradictory to identity, confusing, or alien and dangerous. When beauty desires the beast, desire becomes complex and far from ordered and simple. Mary's repressed memories work insistently through her desire and are fanned by the scheming Hyde. Her attraction to the beast is compelling, out of her control; it is obscene and disruptive. While this may constitute a general view of human sexuality as deeply troubled, it also makes for engaging cinema. Through the return of the repressed narrative form, sexual desire is presented in sensational terms as something best kept locked under the stairs: it promotes perverse twists, is capable of subverting intentions, unknowable and uncontrollable, and full of dark, unsavoury mysteries.

Return of the repressed-based narratives in general have often been categorised by critics as either promoting a conservative message of necessary restraint or purveying a more radical anti-repressive message. In his essay 'Introduction to the American Horror film', first published in 1979 and much reprinted, Robin Wood (1984) focuses on the political ramifications of return of the repressed narratives as used within the horror genre. In some films, which he terms 'reactionary', the threat posed by the return of the repressed is contained and re-repressed, or what returns is used to punish sexual licentiousness. His examples include *Halloween* (1978) and *The Brood* (1979). While in others, termed 'progressive', such as *Night of the Living Dead* (1968) and *The Texas Chainsaw Massacre* (1974), the return of the repressed is not contained by representatives of the status quo. In these films, that which the social order has repressed returns to destroy the order from which it arose. Wood usefully points out the different guises that the return of the repressed takes in the horror film, which includes the way in which the genre treats 'the release of sexuality … as perverted, monstrous and excessive … both the perversion and the excess being the logical outcome of repression' (1984: 189). However, what Wood's either progressive or reactionary scenario elides is that most return of the repressed narratives deal precisely in the tensions between conservative and radical forces, as illustrated by the Jekyll and Hyde films. This is what shapes the ways that sex, sexuality and desire appear in such narratives and, taking this a bit further, it is one of the primary reasons why horror is such a powerful genre; it speaks to us in symbolic ways of our own internal conflicts between desire and practicality and our fear of the other (within and without) in its many guises. The articulation and interpretation of the origin of these forces may change, but in all societies and cultures people experience at a personal level the pull of conflicting rules, priorities and demands, whatever they might be named. Perhaps this idea helps to explain the attraction and persistence of the return of the repressed rhetoric as the basis for a narrative form in popular cultures from a wide variety of countries (examples can be found in Chinese, Japanese and Hindi films, particularly in supernatural tales and melodrama). Key to this idea is that subjectivity is a construct that is forged from a combination of socio-cultural and individual demands, entailing the suppression of certain behaviours and desires.

One of the guiding conditions of socialisation in the cultures of the West is the adoption of preferred attributes that are associated with a particular gender. Gender roles are, however, experienced very differently by individuals, and the construction and performance of gender has been subject to a great deal of discussion in relation to the return of the repressed in the horror film. Barbara Creed (1993) and Carol J. Clover (1992), for example, argue that many horror films trade on repressed anxieties concerning women's bodies and sexualities. Basing their theory on psychoanalytic concepts, they argue that boys and men fear the female body because it is perceived as 'castrated' (physically and symbolically), and in the nexus of the imaginary, the symbolic and the real acts as a reminder of the possibility that this could happened to them. These anxieties become repressed, but are mined to produce sensational qualities by the horror genre. Creed and Clover argue that films such as *Alien*, *The Exorcist* (1973) and *Carrie* (1976) operate on the capital produced by the female body as other. Often this involves a binary pairing of monstrousness, all teeth and dripping orifices, with a 'clean and proper' nurturing female character (*Aliens* (1986) is an example commonly used to exemplify the gendered economy of the return of the repressed used in horror; the alien being the embodiment of the 'monstrous feminine' and Ripley the good nurturing mother – although it could be argued that both are in their own ways 'good' mothers). Creed argues that the return of the repressed narratives of the horror film 'provide us with a means of understanding the dark side of the patriarchal unconscious' (1993: 166). What is often rather underplayed in her analysis is that both men and women are subject to the experience of their body and desires as 'other' and beyond conscious control, which I would argue is illustrated by *Mary Reilly*. While it may be that uncontrollable id-like forces are projected onto women in a culture in which masculinity is defined by self-control, it is also the case that men are often presented as monstrous (see Krzywinska 2001 on 'demon daddies' in horror films), as indicated by Hyde. In addition it may also prove to be the case that the revolting, unfettered, monstrous female body can be a source of retributive enjoyment for some women viewers (even if that threat is eventually staked, contained or reburied by a film's resolution).

The other important gender aspect here, which is the subject of Clover's analysis, is that because of the coding of femininity as vulnerable and in need of protection, it may prove easier for men to empathise with the plight of a female character caught up in a threatening situation. Perhaps Mary Reilly's class, gender and humanity, plus the women's film attributes of the film, makes the conflicts she experiences more available in emphathetic terms to spectators than those experienced by the aristocratic Jekyll. Similarly *Ginger Snaps'* gendered revision of the classic werewolf film promotes greater audience involvement with the terrible effects of her atavistic transformation than is present, for example, in the return to primal masculinity of films such as *Wolf*. Clover argues that a female, rather than male, 'victim' allows men to experience vicariously the pleasures of passivity and masochism that are effectively repressed or at least somewhat suppressed if men are to take up a masculine subject position. This is counterbalanced by sadistic violence, however, that is often perpetrated on female victims by primal-hyper-masculinised monsters such Mamoulian's Hyde. A dual economy affords spectators, of whatever gender, a Jekyll and Hyde-like split identification. As Steve Neale has noted, 'the identifications of the spectator are … split between the polarities of a sadistic, aggressive and controlling position and a masochistic, suffering and controlled positon' (1984: 342). Spectators can take up various positions in relation to the text, much as one would do in a dream perhaps, even where these positions are conflicting or opposed. The availability of both a passive masochistic and active sadistic economy at work in many return of the repressed narratives enables – so the theory goes – repressed aspects of the psyche, which may indeed originate from the effects of the organisation of gender, to be dramatised and indulged in a fantasy context. This approach chimes with my discomfort with Wood's excessively binaristic paradigm in which he splits return of the repressed-based films into 'bad' conservative and 'good' progressive forms. Instead what the return of the repressed narratives articulate is precisely the tension between conflicting positions and forces.

Return of the repressed narratives hinge on presenting aspects of the psyche that do not 'fit' within the civilised order (which, according to Creed, Clover and Wood, is constructed and defined by white male patriarchy). What this particular narrative form deals in is 'otherness' and difference. These might be articulated as embodying primitive appetites, the monstrous feminine or simply the non-human. In the controversial horror film *Shivers* (1975), the return of the repressed is embodied in genetically-altered parasites that are spread from person to person by sexual contact. The infestation transforms people into sexually voracious beings, which has led Robin Wood to read the film as

> single-mindedly about sexual liberation, a prospect it views with unmitigated horror … The release of sexuality is linked inseparably with the spreading of venereal disease, the scientist responsible for the experiments having seen fit … to include a VD component in his aphrodisiac parasite. (1984: 194)

However, the parasites could easily be read as symbols of greed, consumer culture (hungry mouths feature prominently), fear of being out of control, or as David Cronenberg, the film's director, has stated that the film takes the point of view of the parasite: it just wants to survive, and is not conscious of the havoc it creates for the world of the human and its values (cited in Rodley 1992: 82). If we follow Cronenberg's logic, the film dramatises the human propensity to disavow anything that threatens its narcissistic sovereignty and autonomy (this is the basis for socially-produced psychological repression according to psychoanalysis). The contamination and corruption of the *human* world has become a common trope in cinema for expressing the return of the repressed. This may be presented as an externalised supernatural evil, as in vampire films or in the malevolent primal masculine force that operates in *Fallen* (1998). In other films, the return of the repressed is presented as coming from within, as in most werewolf films, demonstrated in the Jekyll/Hyde examples, in non-genre films such as *Fight Club* (1999) and more complexly in *Being John Malkovich*. The return of the repressed may be overtly framed or interpreted as a kind of biblical or hubristic punishment for immoral or transgressive acts, as in Mary Shelley's critique of inhuman science in her novel *Frankenstein* (1831), in transgressing universal physical laws as in *Event Horizon* (1997), or punishment for colonial oppression as in *Candyman* (1992). What most of these films/novels trade on is that the social order and the process of becoming socialised produces monsters. Therefore the return of the repressed, whether it is an embodiment of primal instincts, a disease, or simply a woman doing that which is ordinarily denied her, is subversive because it articulates the tensions and struggles that are engendered by a particular hegemonic order. According to the remit of the horror genre, the return of the repressed is presented in suitably perverse and 'distorted' form, but it is not a 'compromise', as Freud originally proposed (see 'The "Uncanny"', 1990b) – far from it. Rather perverse and distorted form yields the qualities of sensationalism that horror trades upon, as well as providing an allegorical means of demonstrating and dramatising the effects of social control on minds and bodies. Return of the repressed narratives shape sex and sexual desire into monstrous and perverse forms in keeping with their gothic legacy and they are often maligned for their prurient sensationalism and tastelessness. Yet in going beyond the pale this narrative form seems to speak of certain truths about the construction of sexual desire and the effects of socialisation on the psyche.

What has emerged from my exploration of three types of narratives – proper/improper couple, circuits of desire and return of the repressed – is that narrative form, as much as genre or style, plays a primary rhetorical role that influences the rendering of representation of sex, sexuality and desire in cinema. Return of the repressed narratives, in particular, have, as noted at the start of this section, a very special and pervasive formal relationship with censorship and moral values. And, it is the institutional incarnation of censorship and its effects on the representation of sex in cinema that provides the focus of the next chapter.

Institutional Frameworks: Censorship and Regulation

$\mathcal{C}$inema's success at reaching a mass audience brought with it the attentions of those who feared that without proper regulation it could have a serious detrimental impact on public morality. In 1915 the Supreme Court in the US declared that due to its commercial status and mass appeal, cinema was not eligible to be protected by the first amendment's right to free speech. This judgement followed the institution of a number of state-based regulatory bodies that acted to regulate cinema's content over and above the National Board of Review, an industry- and interested parties-based regulatory board set up in 1909 (a similar body was set up in the UK in 1912, and in 1916 was given a government-appointed head in order to circumvent regional censorships). Clearly cinema was felt to be a powerful threat to the status quo, and commercial interests had to be bought to heel. The Supreme Court ruling, as well as the various bodies set up to standardise regulation, responded to certain high-profile reformist concerns, which in essence feared the social effects of what it deemed to be immoral ideas purveyed in cinema as entertainment. These concerns hinged on the notion that cinema should properly represent the values of the ruling classes to the masses and this extended, of course, to the representation of sex, sexuality and desire. Regulation and censorship also worked to protect the industry: in standardising criteria for censorship, it acquired a more legitimate cultural status as well as helping to insulate against potentially expensive court cases and bad publicity (a factor that continues to be the case).

Institutionalised regulation

Regulation had, and has, a profound shaping effect on film, in terms of narrative form, textual strategies such as editing conventions, as well as on the types of topics and themes dealt with in mainstream cinema. It also consolidated the encoding of topics and types of films that were outlawed by the regulatory bodies as more intensely transgressive, a factor exploited by the marketing of certain films as forbidden fruit. Since the introduction of regulation, exploitation films have traded on 'what the censors didn't want you to see'. Other films have also made capital out of the fact that censorship rulings have been lifted. A useful example of the way that censorship is used to attract interest in a film, and the way that film regulation links to wider cultural-national agendas, can be found in the case of *Ecstasy*, an Austrian/Czech co-production that told the story of a woman who leaves her husband and finds sexual fulfilment with another man. The central character, played by Hedy Lamarr, is seen walking naked in a wood, and when she has sex with her new lover it is indicated clearly by her expression that she achieves orgasm. An exploitation specialist imported the film into the US, but not before a series of high-profile run-ins with customs and censors ensued. According to Eric Schaefer, the film was eventually 'sold with such catch lines as "Suppressed Until Now! US Customs has finally released the most amazing motion picture ever produced" and "The picture the world is whispering about"' (1999: 333). He goes on to say that the film's notoriety, compounded by its exciting 'foreignness', aided box-office returns, but by the same token it was used by newspapers and critics to exemplify a difference between the morally 'clean' American film industry and degenerate European ones (1999: 334).

Across the full continuum of possibilities, cinematic sex has continued to prompt concerns about its moral influence. Since the early days of cinema to the present, screen-based sex, as a source of visual pleasure, has fuelled debate and controversy. Often such concerns are linked to basic definitions of what a 'civilised' society is and how such a society should represent itself in the public domain. Sex in some form or another has a presence in most people's lives, and therefore provides many narratives with their dramatic pulling power. The representation of sex in cinema is, however, highly 'managed' and contrived to suit the specific visual and dramatic demands of cinema in terms of both form and institution. As a result there is often a fundamental faultline between actual sexual behaviours and cinematic representation in evidence, a point made by various critics across cinema's history. Precisely because cinema is in the public arena, the representation of sex accrues an added transgressive edge. Removed from private space and the field of sensual physical contact, cinematic sex enters into the field of voyeurism, which is deemed in sexological literature to be a type of sexual perversion. In presenting what is expected to be privately intimate for mass consumption, making money out of it, and the act of making sex a spectator entertainment, the representation of sex in cinema challenges some of the basic principles that are perceived to order a civilised society. This, in conjunction with the idea that cinema has a role in setting moral standards – something that can easily be turned to apparently subversive ends, leads to the intensive activity that has occurred throughout cinema's history in the management of screen sex.

While Western attitudes to sex have certainly become more liberal and the terrain of debate may have shifted into the arena of gender politics, the increasingly explicit depiction of sex in film continues to solicit controversy (although the representation of sexual violence often takes precedence over other concerns, as reflected in the current criteria used by the British Board of Film Classification (BBFC)). Yet with the inclusion of more explicit sexual acts in mainstream cinema, the management of the regulation of sexual imagery still has a high profile in contemporary culture. The focus throughout this chapter is on the way that sex in film has been regulated, by whom and why. It asks how regulation has shaped the representation of sex in film, and proposes the idea that regulation has helped to consolidate the representation of sex as an ostensibly transgressive act. Given that the aim of this book is to map out factors that help shape the portrayal of sex in the cinema, this chapter will focus on aspects of censorship history that have often played – and still play – a fundamental role in the way that sex and sexuality appear in film. To cover every aspect of censorship over the span of a century would, of course, be impossible and beyond the scope of this study. Because the focus is mainly on Hollywood and British cinema, it is mainly American and British state, local, industry regulation that is addressed. Although there will be no sustained concentration on censorship and regulations outside these two countries, some key examples of the treatment of 'foreign' films by American and British regulatory bodies are used where they have had a significant impact on the shift in modes of representing sex and sexuality in cinema. Examples drawn from a number of films are used to show how the regulation of sexual imagery in cinema operates, not simply in terms of what could or could not be shown, but, importantly, how regulation has influenced textual aspects such narration, theme and content.

There have been many scholarly studies of the history of film censorship and most have a particular political or critical goal, and so it is worth briefly sketching out such approaches as they reveal productive disagreements and divergences about the meaning and status of the institutional regulation of cinematic sex. Annette Kuhn's instructive *Cinema, Censorship and Sexuality 1909–1925* (1988), which focuses mainly on Britain, has an overt feminist agenda, thereby addressing the gender politics of censorship. Gregory Black's comprehensive survey of Hollywood censorship in *Hollywood Censored* (1994) and *The Catholic Crusade Against the Movies 1940–1975* (1997), by contrast, looks at first glance to be a fairly neutral archive-based history. Like Frank Walsh's *Sin and Censorship* (1996), Black's works are nevertheless driven by a need to understand how and why the Catholic Church had such a significant and colonising impact on the shaping of Hollywood cinema's ethics, content and marketing strategies. The implication of Black's analysis is that the very form of classical Hollywood film was dictated by a Catholic agenda. By virtue of Hollywood's commercial success overseas, its morally loaded forms extended to other cinemas, and the formal legacy of this moral agenda can still be found in contemporary cinema. In *The Wages of Sin* (1997), however, Lea Jacobs provides a tacit critique of Black's view that Joseph Breen (who headed the Production Code Administration) and the Catholic Church were so instrumental to the shape of Hollywood's regulatory system during the 1930s. She usefully argues that the regulation of film in America cannot be accounted for by looking to one man or one group;

rather, it reflected a composite of more general concerns and values, which in themselves were under debate. Jacobs therefore emphasises the workings of culture and discourse over individuals. The particular agenda that underpins the approach of this study to the regulation and censorship of cinema is to show that a mix of forces contributes to the way that sex in cinema is shaped and given meaning. Following Jacobs and Kuhn's approach, I advocate that to simply focus on what is withheld from public view by regulation presents us with an incomplete picture. Instead, it is more useful to demonstrate how censorship and regulation work to produce narrative forms, conventions and vocabularies that have been used to represent and mediate sex, sexuality and desire. Institutional restrictions come out of a particular cultural context, and, as such, are often in some way reflective of that terrain, with all its various pressure points and faultlines.

Official censorship bodies set up to regulate what is seen on the screen are perhaps the most public and visible means by which the depiction of sex in cinema is shaped. Regulatory bodies, such as the Production Code Administration or the British Board of Film Classification do not operate in isolation, however. They fit into a network of different interests and investments, which often prove to pull in different directions. These include legal statutes, governmental policy, the economic needs of the film industry, the impact of pressure groups, the responses of the popular press to 'morality' issues, cultural and regional sensitivities which may be stitched into local power struggles, as well as the economic power of veto afforded to cinema-goers. As Kuhn has argued persuasively, any analysis of censorship must take into account all these factors, as censorship is always embedded within a melange of cultural, legal, governmental, media and industrial investments (indicated by the example of *Ecstasy*). Nevertheless, because edicts from censorship bodies respond to these competing voices, they tend to have a primary impact on the way that the film industry and its products are shaped. This can be seen in terms of marketing, genre, form, narrative, exhibition and production strategies. The ways in which sex has been, and is, treated and represented in cinema results from a complicated combination of variables. Censorship is therefore frequently contradictory and lacks consistent application; it is always the result of compromise and has regularly reflected the views of minor, yet powerful, groups.

Direct and indirect censorships

The existing academic work on censorship in the movies often makes use of a distinction between direct and indirect censorship. Direct forms may come from the government. These can be political and/or moral and are, therefore, firmly tied into the ideological perspective taken by that government. For example Islamic countries may censor films from the West for their perceived immoral representations of sexuality. With the growth of global media companies, the specific censorship rulings of individual countries entail that films are produced with an eye to conforming to the rulings of the countries films are exported to. Censorship may originate from a country's legal system, or stem from regional laws, as with the current Obscene Publications Act in Britain. This act operates legalistically to control sexually explicit images; however, what constitutes 'obscenity' is not easy to define, precisely because opinions and tastes vary. This is especially the case in culturally diverse societies. The implementation of the Obscene Publications Act in the UK has generally hinged on the notion that a film will 'corrupt and deprave' and that sexual content should be linked directly to dramatic action rather than enjoyed for its own sake. The problem with the ruling and other rulings that relate to other forms of censorship is that they often involve subjective judgements, which may include aesthetic value judgements. These all too easily become entangled with moral ideas and taste, both of which may be related to class and other factors. A good example of this is Home Secretary (at the time) Jack Straw's personal involvement with the workings of the BBFC in which he ordered a cessation of its liberalisation policy (Straw's direct involvement is strongly denied by Robert Duval from the BBFC in an interview with the *Guardian* on 1 March 2001). Yet as Julian Petley has noted, Straw has spoken of his own view of pornography as 'nasty, degenerate and worthless', and that this moral position is likely to have influenced his reaction to the BBFC's efforts to liberalise the representation of explicit sex (2000: 98, 101). There have, however, only ever been a handful of films prosecuted in Britain under the Obscene Publications Act (of which *Last Tango in Paris* was one), although more indirectly the Act has been and is still extremely influential. Under the guiding rubric of this Act, it has generally been left to the industry and classification systems to regulate film content; an expedient move that means that the courts are not log-jammed and the state or film producers do not incur the costs of lengthy court cases. Since the 1920s, in both Britain and the US, the film industry has been the primary agent in the regulation of its images of sex, desire and sexuality.

The intention behind the formation of the US-based Moving Picture Producers and Distributors Association (MPPDA) in 1922 was to allow the industry to make its own rules and regulations on film content and avoid government intervention in industry matters. In Britain the British Board of Film Censors (BBFC) was initially an industry-based group with a government-appointed head. Both Britain and the US now operate a system of classification, and no longer claim to 'censor' films; they see their role as classificatory (which may involve demanding cuts to be made if a film is to be included within a certain classification). Only if a film is deemed obscene or infringing other laws, such as blasphemy or incitement to racial hatred, is it submitted for judicial ruling.

Local authorities have been another means of direct censorship; for example London County Council banned *Frankenstein* (1931),[27] while *The Exorcist*, which was passed uncut in the UK and assigned a 'R' rating in the US, was banned by some British regional authorities, a case that also applied to *Last Tango in Paris*. Lobby groups, perhaps aided by the local or national press, might also call for the banning of certain films and may put pressure on exhibitors not to show certain films. The 'buttery buggery' scene in *Last Tango in Paris* was cut by ten seconds by the BBFC as a means of placating the Festival Light lobby group, which aimed to clean up British culture. Even after this cut, the head of this lobby group bought a private prosecution of the film under the Obscene Publications Act that was eventually dismissed (see Mathews 1994: 212–13). Lobby groups have generally been unsuccessful in their attempts to overturn the 'liberalisation' of sexual representation in cinema, yet regulatory bodies are often sensitive to their concerns, especially when they have high media profiles. Regulatory bodies therefore make judgements about general levels of what is deemed acceptable and to whom, this would include judgements about the availability of films to certain age ranges.

Another form of direct censorship might occur when a film makes the transition from big screen to little screen. This may perhaps be instituted to accord with 'watershed' regulation (the time in a television schedule after which it is deemed that more 'adult' material can be shown), or perhaps to fit a programming schedule (which may mean trimming a film to fit an allocated time slot), or it may involve cutting a film to suit the more general audience that television is likely to reach.

Indirect or hidden censorship is more likely to occur in the process of production, which can originate from a range of pressures and sources. Financial support from government or commercial sources may also be withdrawn on moral, political or financial grounds. Studios may edit films or reshoot scenes to accord with their own agendas or, as is said of the 'orgy' scene in *Eyes Wide Shut*, where sexual images were masked out by the introduction of computer graphics. In most cases this is done to tailor a given film to particular sets of classification criteria. In some cases the reason for censoring an image is more ambiguous. The blurring effect used to mask the female nude pin-ups in the sleeping quarters of the crew in *Dark Star* (1974), for example, may have been so that the film could accrue a 'lower' classification and a potential wider audience, or it may have been done to prevent a copyright suit from *Playboy* magazine. Whatever the reason was, in this case, the device served both purposes. Films may be deliberately withheld from release by their production company or distributor. The release of *The Wicker Man*, for example, was held up and complicated by a company take-over, and *Performance* (1970) was held back because distributors Warner Bros. expected a less obscure and risqué movie.

There are then many forms of regulation and censorship that may impact on the exhibition or content of a given film. And it is important to note that whether policing of film content is direct or indirect, it is often the case that censorship and issues of regulation are bound into a complex mixture of interlaced political, economic and cultural factors.

Evolution of the regulation of sexual representation

Some film historians claim that the institutionalisation of film regulation began in 1907 in both Britain and the US. In Chicago, for instance, exhibitors of films had to apply to the local police force for a permit to screen individual films; Gregory Black argues that this is the first instance of 'prior censorship' in the cinema (1994: 10). Previously films had to be reported as 'obscene' to be censored. Nonetheless morality remained of central concern and sex, and its adjuncts, were strongly implicated. Although prior to 1907 there is no specific censorship related to film content, films were subject to obscenity rulings in both Britain and the US, as well as other rulings relating to the public exhibition of films, such as the Disorderly Houses Act of 1751 in Britain. Individual complaints against particular films were often made public by newspapers, for example Guy Phelps reports that two films involving kissing, *The Kiss* (1896) and *Courtship* (1899), caused complaint and signalled the growth of concerns about the morality of showing 'sex' on screen (1975: 19). Fear of 'moral' contamination is the hallmark of American and British censorship in the Pre-Hollywood and classical Hollywood period, and represents tension between conflicting interests: within class terms, the middle-class reformers sought to police working-class pleasures, and commercial imperatives often clashed with social interest.

From 1907 there were an increasing number of regulatory bodies set up to regulate film content. Often these worked in isolation and could be town-, city-, county- or state-based. The 1917 Supreme Court ruling that cinema did not warrant first amendment 'free-speech' immunity stayed in place until 1952 and its effect has had a profound effect on the style and narrational strategies used by Hollywood cinema (with a knock-on effect in other cinemas). There is something of a consensus in film studies that this ruling was instrumental to the formal and thematic particularities of Hollywood film, and because of Hollywood's influence and global reach, these particular formations are also present in many other cinemas outside Hollywood and America.

In Britain the BBFC was set up in 1912 with the aim of 'raising' the standards of cinema (another example of morally-induced regulation). The Board also assigned classifications to films submitted to them: 'U' for 'universal' and 'A' indicating that a film was more suitable for an 'adult' audience. These were intended to be advisory only, although some counties and cities did enforce the classification by banning children from class 'A' films. No system of classification operated in America until the 1960s, a factor that proved especially significant to the anodyne shaping of Hollywood's representations of sex (with the possible exception of some films from the Pre-Code era). As well as assigning classifications, the BBFC also issued a rather long list of 'grounds for deletion', 43 in all, in 1916. The items included the following: excessive cruelty to women and infants; nudity; display of underclothing; impropriety in conduct and dress; excessively passionate love scenes; subjects dealing with white slavery; premeditated seduction of girls; prostitution and scenes set in a 'disorderly' house; indelicate sexual situations; incestuous relations; men and women in bed together. Although other rulings on the list relate to prescriptions about portrayals of religion, war and politics, the bulk of the list relate to the representation of sex, sexual activity and related issues.[28] This is evident in the case of an American film that was submitted to the BBFC in 1920. *Broken Blossoms* (1919) was granted an 'A' certificate (which was advisory only, except in certain counties or cities). Nevertheless cuts were still demanded in accordance with the 43 rules, and we might presume that they were intended to excise the violence perpetrated on the central character who is regularly beaten by her violent father, and to attenuate the implied references to incestuous sex and interracial sex. Unfortunately as no records survive about the exact nature of the cuts it is only possible to infer what they might have been from the list of reasons for deletion. Interestingly the list contains no edict against miscegenation (love or marriage between people of different races), and one cannot therefore assume that this aspect of the film was cause for deletion (a Chinese immigrant falls in love with an abused and vulnerable white woman). The rules do list a prohibition on 'themes and references relative to "race suicide"'. It is unclear if this was intended to be applied to miscegenation; any ambiguity inherent in this ruling was erased with the outlawing of images of sexual relations between white women and 'coloured' men in 1922. This was clarified, yet again, in 1928 to include relations between 'white girls and men of other races', a ruling that relates directly to Britain as a declining colonialist power (Matthews 1994: 88). Miscegenation was also the subject of concern for the American-based MPPDA.

The first advisory list used by the MPPDA was drawn up by its head, Will Hays, in 1927, and is generally know as the 'Dos, Don'ts and Be Careful' list. Previously Hays had promoted the idea that studios should introduce a 'morals' clause into stars' contracts, after a series of adultery, sex, drugs and death scandals (Black 1994: 31). Black somewhat flamboyantly claims that, as a Protestant Republican, Hays bought solid middle-class values to the industry and although his presence helped redeem cinema for the moral majority he nevertheless failed as an effective censor (ibid.), a position that Black reserves for Joseph Breen. Nonetheless, as Jacobs points out (1995: 27, 35), Hays' list already contained much of what became part of the influential Production Code. This included the prohibition of nudity and 'white slavery' as well as advocating care over the representation of sexual matters, yet despite all the 'be carefuls', only 'sexual perversion' was regarded as a firm 'don't'. Unlike Breen, Hays was not acting as a 'censor', and never intended to be. Instead, he saw his role as protecting the industry. This was to be achieved by negotiating and responding to the various demands of reformist and lobby groups, with the aim of retaining a mass film-going audience (both in and outside the US), and by promoting the need for the industry to regulate itself without legislative, state, city or governmental interference. The Production Code of 1930 comes precisely out of this strategy of mediation and compromise (yet it was not implemented strictly until 1934).

Black maintains that the Production Code was drawn up by a group of Catholic men, including Joseph Breen, who listed what was acceptable and unacceptable to show, with the intention of doing away with censorship in the future (1994: 39). What this meant was that no films would have to be cut or reworked if they stuck to the letter of the Code (although it should be noted that no 'definitive' version is extant, the one published by Thomas Doherty is, however, a good indication of the working content of the Code as used by the MPPDA (1999: 345–59). The Code was not just about outlawing certain images, as with the 43 grounds for deletion set up by the BBFC. The difference between the two systems was that the Code also made recommendations about narrative content and how things were to be portrayed, so as not to be considered immoral and incur condemnation from the very active reformist groups of the time. As Jacobs writes, 'within the process of self-regulation, the Code did not operate as a set of hard and fast rules but rather facilitated the task of anticipating public reaction to a film and established guidelines within which producers and industry censors could discuss specific problems' (1995: 35). Further, the Code pointed out that cinema hinged on spectator identification: the audience were likely to be sympathetic to known stars and therefore 'more ready to confuse actors and the character' (cited in Doherty 1999: 350). The implication is that cinema, with its particular mode of creating the suspension of disbelief and erasing the signs of production, has greater influence on viewers than any other art, and in many ways this is the underlying paradigm upon which the Code operated. This factor is instructive in the way that regulation often works, particularly in its assumptions about spectatorship and differences in the levels of sophistication in the way spectators 'read' (or interpret) films. Indeed a class difference dimension is written into the letter of the Code: 'it is difficult to produce films for only certain classes of people' (cited in Doherty 1999: 349).

Pre-Code Hollywood

Within contemporary scholarly views of Hollywood history the period between 1930 and 1934 is often known as Pre-Code Hollywood. This is a something of misnomer as the Production Code was in operation during that period, but only after 1934 was it enforced stringently. Pre-Code films are often characterised by their strikingly frank, cynical and feisty approaches and many of their themes and treatments of sexual issues disappear from view after 1934. *Red Dust* (1932) provides an excellent benchmark with which to ascertain how Hollywood's treatment of sex changed and the limits of the Code were pushed.

Set in the appropriately steamy confines of a Vietnamese rubber plantation, *Red Dust* is all about sex. Wisecracking 'good time gal', Vantine (Jean Harlow) – 'I'm a just a restless adventurist type' – strikes up a no-strings, antagonistic and fiery sexual relationship with hard-bitten, tough-talking colonist Dennis Carson (Clark Gable). The situation becomes more complex when Carson falls for the 'decent' wife of a new employee, Barbara (Mary Astor). Various factors make it clear that Carson has had sex with both women: 'it's been nice having you' he says to Vantine as she boards a boat to leave the compound. On her return from a trip up-river, Vantine attempts to manipulate herself back into lovelorn Carson's affections. She does so after Carson gets a case of 'nobility' after he is unable to tell the 'nice kid' new employee that he and his wife are going to leave together. Carson tells Barbara that she means nothing to him (a noble lie) and in return she shoots him. A moment later the jilted husband returns and quick-thinking Vantine makes double capital by saying that the shooting occurred because a drunken Carson broke into Barbara's room and she shot him 'the way any virtuous woman would with a beast like that'. Barbara gets away with her extra-marital fling and Vantine nurses Carson back to health which promotes a returned sexual interest in her. Despite the lack of punishment here, Vantine's

Pre-Code Hollywood: Jean Harlow and Clark Gable in a publicity poster for *Red Dust* (1932)

actions and 'management' of the volatile situation restores the ideology of class-based 'proper couple' ordering. Various aspects of the film, including the narrative, based as it is on a sexual triangle, the semi-nudity, adultery without punishment and the innuendo-rich dialogue, would have been untenable under the stringent enforcement of the Production Code after 1934.

One interesting aspect of the film is the women's proactive sexuality, something that is ring-fenced by punishment and moral reprehension in post-1934 Hollywood film. Vantine is a very likeable character: deliciously cheeky and inventive, tough yet tender. Although we hear that she 'ain't used to sleeping at night' there is no pathetic 'fallen woman' cliché here. Vantine is in control of herself, able to get what she wants without being a femme fatale, bitchy or vicious, and her playfulness means audiences are unlikely to read her as morally 'evil' simply because she is more interested in a good time than in marriage and maternity. Like Mae West's characters in Pre-Code films such as *She Done Him Wrong*, Vantine is precisely the kind of sexually-aware female character that was outlawed by the post-1934 Code enforcement. This demonstrates how, post-1934, the Code shapes both narrative and gender representation, particularly in relation to sexual desire. The same applies to Barbara. She may be middle-class and upstanding, signalled by her buttoned-up clothing and her need for a curtain on the makeshift shower, yet despite the trappings of respectability, she still falls for the rough charms of Carson and does not 'confess' the affair to her husband, and, in the end, her commitment to her husband is strengthened. Her 'mistake' is treated precisely as that, and not an indication of the collapse of moral values, which would demand due and dire punishment in later Code-compliant films. Like other Pre-Code films, such as *She Done Him Wrong* and *Madame Satan* (1930), the narrative of *Red Dust* is informed by the idea that sex and desire, complicated as they are, are a part of life. As Doherty notes, films from this era are more 'realistic' in terms of their content than the good (decent) versus evil (indecent) moral approach to sex used in later Hollywood films. Indeed, perhaps because of the sexual electricity sparked between Gable and Harlow, plus the way that ideals and realities are juxtaposed, the film was a box-office hit and consolidated Harlow's star persona as premier mischievous blonde bombshell.

The Code, in its pre-1934 guise, specified that a plot should never muddle morally 'good' and 'evil'; and when adultery was present in a narrative it should never be depicted as 'alluring' nor weaken 'respect for marriage'. The Code stresses that cinema has a moral responsibility, but it is recognised that sexual impropriety is often important to a plot. Therefore the Code did not forbid sexual transgression; instead it prescribes the way that it should be shown in moral and aesthetic terms. Doherty claims that *Red Dust* 'violates the Code (the triangle does not receive "careful handling")' (1999: 15) and that Gable's character 'violates propriety and the bonds of matrimony with impunity' (1999: 14). The film may contain aspects of the sensationalism that Doherty assigns to Pre-Code films, yet it is also important to note that the film is not totally unaffected by the Code, as he suggests. Carson might be slippery and fickle, but as he tells Vantine he has done a 'noble' thing by giving up his claim on the decent, yet yielding, wife of his employee. He clearly demonstrates some respect for the idealistic image of middle-class domestic bliss conjured by the cuckolded husband. In some ways Carson's nobility seems rather out of character, and can only really have been included in the film because of the need to take on board aspects of the Code. Once Barbara arrives on the scene, Carson marks his relationship with Vantine as immoral. In one scene he makes it clear that she should not come to his bed with the 'decent' woman living in the house. We could infer that this change in behaviour is in accordance with the Code's edict that 'impure love' should be marked as 'wrong'. However, this apparent compliance is somewhat slippery as Carson changes his approach to Vantine on two occasions (when Barbara arrives, Carson deems Vantine immoral and after she leaves he is happy to return to their sexual alliance). This makes Carson something of a hypocrite – something more in keeping with his general personality. His actions owe more to sexual convenience, rather than a case of demonstrating moral ideals. And, this is why Doherty is right to some extent in seeing the film as in violation of the Code, yet the Code is clearly 'at work' in shaping events. Vantine too plays her part in the restoration of the married couple: she does this artfully to help accord with the Code's edict on the need to respect marriage, but at the same time protects her own relationship with virile Carson. There is little doubt that the testy and impulsive relationship between Carson and Vantine is the chewy centre of the film, and both stars, Gable and Harlow, bring the requisite glamour and 'real life' problems around desire with which audiences are likely to identify.

The film certainly skirts close to the limits of the Code, which at that time was far more open to interpretation than after 1934. The Code points out that nudity is never permitted, in this case a pretty unambiguous statement, yet filmmakers were left an exploitable loophole to show semi-nudity, which was designated as permissible under certain conditions. In *Red Dust* semi-nudity does double duty, providing visual thrills yet also signals a key difference between Vantine's carefree nature and Barbara's middle-class decorum. In the majority of scenes, Vantine dresses in a satin bathrobe that gapes at the front, partially revealing her breasts. And in another, when she is more properly attired, she petulantly swings her legs onto a desk so that her thin skirt falls upwards to reveal her legs (such 'gratuitousness' was something that Breen expressed his intention to clean up on when he became head of the PCA). In addition much is made of the differences between the two women's approach to bathing. As soon as Barbara arrives she has curtains installed around the shower area, an indication of her often spoken-of 'decency'. Vantine refuses to use them, much to Carson's disgust, who showed no interest in curtains before Barbara's arrival. When he tells Vantine to use them she responds, all covered in soap and clearly nude, with 'what's the matter, afraid I'll shock the Duchess?' As Vantine jumps into the drinking water barrel, Carson pulls her by the hair and then plunges her under. With Barbara looking on, Vantine capitalises on the situation saying, 'Good morning, you're just in time to see the trained seal'. As well as providing visual thrills and humour, semi-nudity is used to display a clear class difference between the 'new' woman and the 'true' woman, a difference that is neatly and subversively undermined because both fall for Carson's rough sexual charms.

Semi-nudity was often seen in American films before 1934, under a number of different pretexts and, in what seems ironic now, it appears in a range of biblical films. In Cecil B. DeMille's *The Sign of the Cross* (1932), for instance, a pagan and decadent Roman Empress (Claudette Colbert) is shown taking an asses-milk bath. At one point a nipple becomes visible, thereby following in the tradition of bare-breasted women in epic depictions of classical historical subjects, such as *Ben Hur* (1925) and the Babylonian sections of Griffith's *Intolerance*. Despite the biblical theme (decadent, barbarous pagans versus virtuous Christians), the film was banned in 1934. In other genres semi-nudity is often related to women with loose morals. Like Harlow's confident sexual come-on in *Red Dust*, Ivy Pearson, the 'singer' (read: prostitute) in *Dr Jekyll and Mr Hyde* also displays quite a lot of flesh to get her man in a scene that was excised from the film in Britain and which would later be outlawed by Breen's Production Code Administration. In the documentary/adventure *Trader Horn* (1931), shot on location in Africa there are many topless black women shown, often for protracted periods and in mid-close-up. Their status as 'natives' and the documentary footage helped to justify the nudity. The shot of two young African women with breasts exposed is even framed as a point-of-view shot of a young white man at one point – he looks sheepish and the two women laugh. There is clearly a racial agenda as well as a double standard at work here. Famously in *Tarzan and his Mate* (1934), a nude Jane (Maureen O'Sullivan) swims un-derwater in (importantly) long-shot alongside Tarzan (Johnny Weissmuller). Presumably the long-shot was intended to get around the edict that complete nudity was not permitted; or perhaps it was a 'trading' device intended to ensure that Jane kept her scanty clothing in the rest of the film. As Doherty reports this was the first case that was taken to the MP-PDA jury, who upheld that it was a violation of the Code and the scene was deleted from the film (1999: 261). Semi-nudity was often not simply 'gratuitous' in these films, although it was often included on rather flimsy plot-grounds. In contrast to such fleshly displays, after 1934 even a tight dress that traced the shape of a breast was grounds for deletion and the PCA demanded that costume designs as well as scripts were vetted. All these Pre-Code films were cut or banned after 1934, and it might be said that the exertion the pressures that films like *Red Dust* and *The Sign of the Cross* put on the Code lead in part to the subsequent clamp down.

As with many Pre-Code films, innuendo was a common device used to evoke sex in a veiled form, designed to speak to an adult sexually-aware audience (innuendo was one of Breen's objects of disgust). *Red Dust* crackles with innuendo-laden witticisms between Carson and Vantine, and many are far from subtle. There are some instances that are more subtle and work not simply for lewd humour, but rather as an insight into Carson's sexual psychology. When Carson shows Barbara the processes involved in making rubber, he pours a fluid onto the rubber while stating, which I read as an analogy, that 'the rubber resents the insult and stiffens up into an indignant mass'. This carries more than a simply sexual subtext; earlier he told Barbara that he has a 'special fondness for somebody who stands up and fights back', thereby this innuendo is also a conceit in that it is a verbal encapsulation of the nature of his relationship with Vantine. At one level the film operates along the lines of the proper-couple format: Carson is clearly better matched to volatile Vantine than the often hysterical and outraged Barbara. In this the film accords with class-matching that guides the proper-couple narrative format discussed earlier.

Red Dust is an example of the way that many Pre-Code films put sex firmly on the enter-tainment agenda. To a present-day audience coming to these films after seeing Post-Code Hollywood offerings these films are likely to seem surprisingly risqué. Some are what one might expect in sexploitation cinema: the gladiatorial games scene of *The Sign of the Cross* involves skimpily-dressed, bound maidens being eaten by crocodiles, ravished by a gorilla, and Amazon women battling it out, and *Murders on the Rue Morgue* (1932) and *King Kong* (1933) have explicit references to bestiality (of which more in Part II). Others, such as *Red Dust* and *Red Headed Woman*, sparkle with Hawkesian-style tough banter alongside representa-tions that acknowledge the complexities of human sexual desire. These films should also be considered in the wider context of the Depression, that some critics have cited as the source for disillusion with authority, and which is clearly visible in many of the films of the period. Boundaries were constantly being tested and textual devices, such as innuendo, worked to make the audience complicit with the 'dissing' of the Code, a factor that concerned deeply the newly-formed and influential Catholic Legion of Decency. With the release of *The Sign of Cross*, with its pagan nudity, lesbianism and perversion, many concerned commentators argued that the industry was out of control and its products made sin fascinating. With Roosevelt's 'New Deal' (which included the expansion of federal power and sought to tackle poverty and combat cynicism) of 1933, sociological studies looking at the effects of cinema on children and the increasingly vitriolic and powerful Catholic Church, the writing was on the wall for the boundary pushers: and the captains of the film industry became increasingly worried that the government would seek to police cinema. Cinematic sex was to become, at least for a while, tamed, less vital and much more idealised.

Hollywood and the Production Code Administration

During the Pre-Code period an increasingly greater number of local authorities were banning films that were passed through the MPPDA office. Lobby groups were becoming more active, including the Catholic Legion of Decency which went so far as to have its own 'condemned' list, and there were, of course, economic stakes at risk, namely the possibility of government anti-monopoly actions. All these reasons helped persuade the studios to adopt the Code in 1930, but why was it necessary to reinforce the Code more rigorously in 1934? There is no one answer to this. At a general level the idea that movies affected behaviour was becoming more prevalent. Christian and reformist groups had been evangelising on this score for a decade at least, but now they had the support of social science in the form of the Payne Fund studies. This body sought to prove the ill-effects of cinema on public morality and their studies were reported in the press, including some film trade papers (see Black 1994: 104). The Catholic Legion of Decency also threatened to promote a Catholic boycott of the cinema (see Jacobs 1997: 19). It is now widely thought that these pressures led to the revision of regulatory practices. This included a revision of names: the Studio Relations Committee became the Production Code Administration (PCA) headed by Joseph Breen.

   The newly-formed PCA vetted costume and set designs as well as suggesting changes to scripts to make them more moral. A seal was assigned to films passed by the administration. Under Breen's direction, the PCA emphasised the importance of 'moral compensation' in a storyline. It was no longer a matter of tacking on a redemptive ending, instead the narrative and narration must take a more pervasive moral approach; no longer could it simply be left to one character to comment on the immorality of a protagonist's action, which sufficed in the Pre-Code era. This was a decisive point in the history of classical Hollywood. The PCA sought not simply to say 'no' to certain images or ideas, but to enforce a simple black and white manichean universe onto Hollywood; there must be no moral ambiguity and 'evil' (immorality, including adultery) must be compensated by 'sufficient good'. As Black has written, 'the studios soon learned that cooperation with Breen resulted in less controversy, larger markets, and less money spent on rewrites and post-production editing' (1994: 199). Black also paints a picture of Breen's attitude to the representation of sexuality in cinema as largely laced in the language of transgression and sin, believing, it seems, that illicit sex was against divine law and its 'incorrect' portrayal could corrupt spectators (1994: 208).

Because Breen used *Anna Karenina* (1935) to exemplify his approach in the PCA Annual Report of 1935, both Jacobs and Black chart the way the film's central adultery theme was handled. Jacobs points out that as a result of the 'new' approach there was a return to nineteenth-century treatment of adultery and the 'fallen woman'. Any of the sexual details of the affair are kept offscreen and the moral condemnation of the couple is articulated through the narration of the story (meaning the way that a story is articulated and framed cinematically) (Jacobs 1995: 120–31). While there is a clear condemnation of the affair in *Anna Karenina*, it is nevertheless the case that Anna's marriage is dull and her husband is, as she says, only interested in his social standing, despite his speech about the sanctity of marriage. This highlights the fact that even with careful management of a film's moral message on adultery, it is exceedingly difficult to police investments and interpretations of the action. Contemporary public response to the film did indeed vary widely; the Legion of Decency condemned the film, whereas some newspapers pronounced the film 'old-fashioned' in its approach to marriage (Black 1994: 217). Sassy women, of the likes often played by Jean Harlow and Mae West, became pale shadows of their former selves. Sex disappears into the defiles of the texts and is presented in fairly anodyne ways, often sublimated and symbolised. What emerges here is that under the PCA, regulation had a very active role in the shaping of Hollywood's thematic content and approach to sexual morality, indeed it was instrumental to the formation of classical Hollywood narrational style. And its legacy is still with us, in the proper couple-format and in the tendency to polarise sexual behaviour into good and evil. Even in a film as recently made as *Unfaithful* (2001), punishment is meted out for extra-marital sexual pleasures (discussed in Part II, 'Adultery'). Classical Hollywood cinema therefore tended to smooth problems into saccharine 'all is well with the world' endings, often in the form of a marriage or remarriage typified by comedies such as *The Philadelphia Story* and *His Girl Friday* (1940). And thus we can see how the Code in its post-1934 guise played an important role in the shaping of both narrative and the concomitant representation of sex.

'How bad can a good girl get?': exploitation and stag films

While obscenity laws meant that hard-core 'stag' films were definitively categorised as an illegitimate and illegal form, the effect of the Code was to create a category of films that were endowed with an exploitable illegitimate and risqué aura but which were legal in certain contexts (although there were some states and cities, at various times, in which they were illegal (see Schaefer 1999: 8)). This came to be known as exploitation cinema, sometimes termed 'Adults Only' cinema. Exploitation cinema was very much an American phenomenon, precisely because it was a direct product of the Code and its implementation. Eddie Muller and Daniel Faris maintain that the regulatory 'do-gooders' 'forged two lasting accomplishments: they taught all future exploitation producers how it was done, and they pioneered a thriving and lucrative fringe enterprise that made millions off the public's fearful desire for "forbidden" objects' (1996: 9). Schaefer too argues that exploitation films found a niche market precisely as a result of the 'don'ts and be careful' list and the later Code (1999: 8). Industry regulation therefore played a vital role in the shape and content of the American exploitation cinema, which Muller and Faris claim constituted around two per cent of known film production from the 1920s to the 1950s (1996: 16).[29]

Stag films have a longer history than exploitation cinema. They were shown in private spaces, and were produced and consumed in many countries. Tom Dewe Mathews notes that many were South American imports (1994: 13). Both exploitation and stag films have their own particular forms that are tailored to their legal and industrial status and their target audiences. 'Exploitation' was a term used by the industry from the late 1920s (see Schaefer 1999: 4). It describes films that lay outside the Code, and comprised mostly of low-budget pictures, some feature-length, produced mainly by 'poverty row' production companies, although some were foreign imports such as *Ecstasy* or *Naked in the Wind* (*L'Île aux femmes nues*, 1953). They were independently distributed and shown in a range of exhibition sites that included theatres not connected to the major studios. The films were marketed in exceptionally lurid ways and focused on some of the topics and themes prohibited by the PCA and the MPPDA, which proved to be instrumental to their financial viability. Exploitation pictures traded on sensationalism to attract audiences, using salacious advertising and titles, such as *Is Your Daughter Safe?* (1927), *How to Undress in Front of Your Husband* (1937) and *Test Tube Babies* (1948). These titles were often far more lurid than the actual content of the films, set to invoke a transgressive aura while managing to stay in the main on the right side of obscenity law. By contrast, stag films where mostly illegal, a status assigned because they depicted actual sex, thereby ensuring a market difference to exploitation. An early example noted by Linda Williams is *Am Abend* (c. 1910), a German film which in many ways resembles the form and content of standard fare found on the present-day hard-core video circuit. Even the earliest known stag films combined close-ups of genitals and penetration with mid-shots, thereby creating a vocabulary of shot types and patterning that are seen in most later hard-core films.[30] Stag films were exhibited in brothels or men-only clubs, which, alongside their particular formal attributes, indicate that these films were designed expressly for sexual arousal, rather than narrative satisfaction (Williams 1990: 74). The films were often amateurish and have been described as 'primitive' in form, a camera simply set up in front of the action as can be seen in the collection of antique hard-core shorts released in Britain under the title *The Good Old Naughty Days* in 2004.

Both stag and exploitation films respond to, and exploit, regulation and censorship to create interest and market difference, and the forms used by both are directly related to this aim. Most exploitation films comprise a rag-bag of Code off-cuts, sometimes showing older films that infringed the Code; many 'White Slavery' (prostitution) films come under this category, for example. It was fairly common practice for exploitation producers to splice in footage from existing films to give added spice at no cost. Often, salacious capital was made

'A good girl until she lights a reefer'; classic exploitation rhetoric to promote *The Devil's Harvest* (1942)

of films that had been produced for 'educational' purposes before the Code's implementation. This was particularly the case with 'sex hygiene' films. These had been in existence since the 1910s, and included such titles as *Damaged Goods* (1914) and *The End of the Road* (1919), which warned of the dangers of syphilis and other sexually-transmitted diseases. Others dealt with vice, focusing on the forbidden topics of drugs, prostitution (white slavery) and nudity (such as *Elysia* (1934), filmed in a large American nudist camp). The pulp fiction-style titles of many of the films where intend to signal sensationalist content, for example *Scarlet*

Youth (1928) and *Gambling with Souls* (1936). Dope movies, many of which now have cult status, such as *Human Wreckage* (1923), *Narcotic* (1933), *Marihuana* (1936) and *Devil's Harvest* (1942), drew the exploitation crowds, some with the promise of showing young women 'going wild' under the influence, all carried out under the banner of 'education'. Often these films adopted the rhetoric used in stag films to promote a movie, yet they did not in fact deliver much more than nudity, providing a further example of the way that aspects of illegitimate cinema gradually become accommodated by less *outré* cinemas.

Jungle pictures (termed 'exotic' or 'goona goonas' by the trade) often combined staged stories with documentary footage of topless African and Balinese women. *Ingagi* (1931) and *Wild Women* (aka *White Sirens of Africa/Bowanga Bowanga*, 1951) are examples, as is *Trader Horn*. Aspects of these films, albeit in more diluted form, are also present in the more well-known *King Kong* (discussed further in Part II). Vice, white slavery, nudity, sexual disease and child birth were staple themes of the exploitation picture, and many distributors and exhibitors continued to show these films under different titles to gain maximum mileage. Producers made low-budget films, which were sold to distributors who then sold the rights to exhibitors. Exploitation films were exhibited in independent theatres (often termed grindhouses) and roadshows, which operated like circuses and targeted small towns. Schaefer reports that more mainstream theatres showed exploitation pictures when the economic going was tough (1999: 120). Advertising was prominent and lobby displays common (Dwain Esper, director of the aforementioned *Narcotic*, used a mummy in one of his). 'Education' was often the central theme. Some shows had speakers on the issues raised by the film and often screenings were split into men and women only. One *Variety* reviewer wrote in 1929, 'The law allows managers to arouse curiosity, but does not permit gratification. So the boys strike a balance. It's an organised business' (cited in Schaefer 1999: 103), demonstrating the way that the promise of transgression was moulded to fit the legalistic and formal particularities of the exploitation format. Schaefer notes that 'exploitation films subverted the formal qualities of Hollywood films while carnivalising the presentation process' (1999: 134).

'Burlesque' films appeared in the 1940s and often combined striptease with stand-up comedians, as for example in *Varietease* (1954). These produced a number of female 'stars' whose names still have erotic and cult currency, such as Bettie Page, Tempest Storm and Lilli St Cyr, and some of the films they starred in are still available on video, such as *Teaserama* (1955). In some cases live striptease acts accompanied films.

European art films were also shown under the exploitation banner. *Ecstasy* is a good example of a film that carries many 'art' movie conventions, including dissolves and temporal discontinuities. Yet the image of a nude and orgasmic Hedy Lamarr was used to publicise the high-profile censure of the film by US customs, certain states and cities and the PCA. Exploiters turned censorship to its own marketing ends and as a result the film turned in high box-office returns (Schaefer 1999: 158). This import, along with others, incurred the wrath of the Legion of Decency, who used such films to promote a view of America as clean living: 'all the filthiness and perversion that has been so largely wiped out of American pictures is appearing in newly-imported films' (cited in ibid.). Other imports that incurred the wrath of the Legion of Decency and the PCA included high-budget British films *The Wicked Lady* (1945) and *The Private Life of Henry VIII* (1933) (passed without censure by the BBFC), which, by virtue of historical accuracy, depicted the King's adultery and rejection of Catholic marital values with a certain affectionate relish. The perceived threat made by European films to the morality of American society would also be a matter of concern in the 1950s. And, it was a European 'sex film' import, ...*And God Created Woman*, plus a homegrown narcotics movie, *Man with the Golden Arm* (1955), that contributed to the revision, and eventual demise, of the Code.

The Code certainly promoted the construction of a split between mainstream and exploitation film. The divisions between mainstream studio-based films, exploitation and stag films, were key to their commercial success. Although there are examples of formal trade-offs between them, it was the degree of transgression that provided the basis of their formal differences, a factor that continues to inform present-day hard-core. The exploitation style too has made its way in more mainstream cinema: John Walters' films are a good example, with films such as *Female Trouble* (1975), which pays homage to sex hygiene, vice and drugs movies, and it could be argued that is a neo-exploitation movie. Schaefer claims that 'classic' exploitation cinema finished in 1959 which coincided with the demise of the Code. It was replaced by the more explicit 'sexploitation' cinema (1999: 8–9), which, in some cases, drew on certain formal aspects found in the stag film. More than simply curiosities, exploitation and stag films provide the formal blueprint for many more recent sex films.

New demands and mainstream 'adult' cinema

The pre-war period saw some stability in terms of mainstream film production and the regulation of sexual representation. In the US and the UK, changes were made in the pre-production phase and as such very few final films were cut or not given a PCA seal of approval. The process worked for the industry as no expensive reshooting or editing had to be done. As some critics have noted, Frank Krutnik (1991) in particular, this was a time in which both American and British studio-based cinema least reflected the realities of people's lives, a 'dream factory' producing disingenuous sanitised images that promoted family values and coerced desire into straitened pathways. However, some veiled references to risqué sexual matters were present, but always in veiled and coded form. A useful example of this is the metaphoric value of the lost dinosaur tail 'bone' that is central to the narrative of the screwball comedy *Bringing Up Baby*. You do not need a very sophisticated grasp of psychoanalysis to understand its phallic symbolism. The rigours of world war brought some aspects of the Code's values into question, however, and alongside the more secure position of cinema in American and British culture, censorship/regulatory rules relaxed a little.

The war years saw an additional layer of censorship, but this related mainly to the bolstering of morale and focused on the way that the nation was represented. In the UK this was conducted by the Ministry of Information. Films were pressed into patriotic service, but images of sexuality became darker (in accordance with the 'noir' preoccupation with vice, paranoia and sexual perversions) and the Code was interpreted a little less rigidly. As such remakes of films made in the Pre-Code period appeared, such as *Waterloo Bridge* (1931; remade in 1940) and *Back Street* (1932; remade in 1941). Both films solicit sympathy for the 'transgressive' main female characters: in *Waterloo Bridge* the main character is forced into prostitution after her fiancée is reported dead in action. *Back Street* is about a woman whose life as a mistress is depicted in terms of love, loyalty, fortitude and sacrifice. During the 1940s the female audience became an important resource for the British and American film industries. This is the era of the 'woman's film': films that often had women as central protagonists whose points of view guided the organisation of narration. These films are distinguished by their engagement with women's desires and are often set in the stylistic and thematic context of noir expressionism and paranoia. Events are often bound up with hysteria, aggression and violence (see Doane 1987: ch. 5). The fall of the romantic idyll brought with it the return of the repressed, desire grows darker, gothic, and more complex, paranoia takes hold, as in *Dragonwyck*, *Rebecca*, *Wuthering Heights* (1939), *Gaslight* (1940; 1944), *Jane Eyre* (1944), *The Seventh Veil* (1946) and *Secret Beyond the Door* (1948). In Britain, Gainsborough Studios produced films that allied spectacular, often historical, settings with adultery and gender transgressions designed to thrill female audiences. Films such as *The Wicked Lady* (of which parts had to be re-shot after it came under the scrutiny of the PCA in the United States), *Blanche Fury*, *Waterloo Road* (1945), *Madonna of the Seven Moons* (1945) and the US-made *Frenchman's Creek* (1944) each depict women having illicit and exciting affairs with exotic men (typified by the gypsy looks of Stewart Grainger or the adventure-hungry yet sensitive French pirate played in *Frenchman's Creek* by Arturo de Córdova). The success of the trend is exhibited in the fact that these films were made by a number of different studios. *Brief Encounter* (1945) also dealt with adultery, but in a far more naturalistic and less 'fantasy'-based manner. In order to accord with the edict of the Code, the female protagonists in all of these films are in some way 'punished' for their extra-marital desires, but nonetheless it was the attraction of sexual transgression that proved to have audience pulling power.

The 1950s saw a progressive loosening of Code rulings. Perhaps the most important factor was that in 1952 the Supreme Court of America granted film first amendment status (see Randall 1985: 510). With several celebrated controversies over various films, including the import ...*And God Created Woman*, and a court of appeal judgement that nudity was not in itself obscene, the scene was set for a mainstream cinema that dealt more directly with sexual issues. *Cat on a Hot Tin Roof* and *Written on the Wind*, for example, focused on issues, including nymphomania and impotency, topics previously the domain of exploitation cinema, but given mainstream kudos through the presence of high-profile stars and high production values. By 1966 the Code was revised and the 'X' rating was introduced in America, and could be self-administered. America, like Britain, moved towards a regulatory system that sought to classify films rather than censor them. By the end of the decade David Friedman, a porn filmmaker and president of the Adult Film Association, argued in court for first amendment protection for the soft-core pornography. Since that time the MPPDA ratings have taken several guises, with the creation of the 'NC-17' classification being instituted in 1990 (now defunct), *Henry & June* (1990) was the first film to be given this rating. In Britain the BBFC had made certain concessions on the regulation of sex in cinema, and recent developments on the rulings on images of penetration are worth taking a look at as this means, at least potentially, the erasure of traditional divisions between legitimate and illegitimate film forms. There have been many high-profile films that have been cut or banned by various censors: some, such as *Cape Fear* (1962) which was cut in Britain because it was thought to encourage rapists (see Robertson 2000: 70), act as benchmark cases setting the agenda for a period on a certain issue.

Blurring boundaries: 'R18' and hard-core

To end this chapter on regulation, and to bring us to the cinema of the present, the focus will now fall on a particular aspect of British regulation and the recent blurring of the boundary between mainstream cinema and hard-core. Since 1986 the BBFC have deployed the 'R18' class to designate explicit sex films that can be only obtained from licensed sex shops or shown in specially-licensed cinemas. The BBFC website describes the category as follows: 'the "R18" category is a special and legally restricted classification primarily for explicit works of consenting sex between adults. Films may only be shown to adults in specially licensed cinemas, and videos may be supplied to adults only in licensed sex shops. "R18" videos may not be supplied by mail order'.[31] 'R18' is bounded by the laws on obscenity, as well as those laws which apply to the British postal service. The category rules regarding distribution also accord with the 1984 Recordings Act. Any change to this requires an act of parliament; difficulties regarding access to licensed sex shops, which are licensed by local councils who often turn down applications, are therefore outside the BBFC's domain, an issue raised by some anti-censorship groups.

The 'R18' category operates within legal rulings therefore, and the BBFC provides a list of unacceptable acts and images. At the time of writing these are: no breach of criminal law; material likely to encourage abusive sexual activity; any activity which is not consented to by all participants; no real or simulated physical harm (except where mild and consensual); no physical restraint that prevents vocalising non-consent; no penetration associated with violence; no degrading or dehumanising acts.[32] These replace the Home Office-approved lists used between 1985 and 1999 (see Petley 2000: 97), which, although they changed a little throughout the period focused mainly on what part of the bodies and sexual acts that could be seen, with particular emphasis on what was seen in close-up as opposed to long- or mid-shots. The introduction of the 'R18' category, as Julian Petley states, responded to a report written in 1979 entitled 'Report of the Committee on Obscenity and Film Censorship',

Year of decision	Total number of works	Number cut	Cut %
2005	590	7	1.2%
2004	562	5	0.9%
2003	588	11	1.9%
2002	585	20	3.4%
2001	508	14	2.8%
2000	525	12	2.3%
1999	532	19	3.6%
1998	448	14	3.1%
1997	439	16	3.6%
1996	446	21	4.7%
1995	410	27	6.6%
1994	401	21	5.2%
1993	380	37	9.7%
1992	371	28	7.5%
1991	379	47	12.4%
1990	424	45	10.6%
1989	406	59	14.5%
1988	369	54	14.6%
1987	344	36	10.5%
1986	387	44	11.4%
1985	399	72	18.0%
1984	433	72	16.6%
1983	514	123	23.9%
1982	444	97	21.8%
1981	400	69	17.3%
1980	464	75	16.2%

source: www.bbfc.org

in which it was concluded that terms such as 'obscenity' and 'deprave and corrupt' were deemed as 'having outlived their usefulness' and that sexual material should be available in specialist sex shops to over 18s (cited in Petley 2000: 94). They also recommended that no license should be needed. Looking at the post-1999 list, it is clear that violence and consensuality are of greatest concern. Images of penetration, for instance, are not used as grounds for cutting or censorship (although, in effect, it rarely occurs).

There has been a huge increase in the number of films submitted for the 'R18' catego-ry, with more films presented in 2000–01 than the sum total of previous submissions (see www.bbfc.org). What created this change? The answer lies in events that took place in 1999. A number of videos put forward in the category were refused a certificate by the BBFC, and the distributors of these films lodged an appeal to the Video Appeals Committee who then pronounced that they should be granted 'R18' status. The BBFC states that it has refused certificates on the grounds that films were potentially harmful to children, something con-sidered badly judged by the Video Appeals Committee. The BBFC's official statement on the overturning of their decision announced that films with 'similar content continues to be seized and forfeited under section three of the Obscene Publications Act. This is a matter of continuing concern to the board.' As a result the criteria for 'R18' classification was changed, enabling many European and American hard-core distributors to put forward some of their products for legal British consumption; as can be seen from the table above the trend is for fewer films submitted to the BBFC to be cut.

As a result an apparently seismic shift took place in the British censorship of explicit sex films and it still remains unclear whether the BBFC see themselves as agents of common law or if they will leave the courts to rule on blasphemy or infringements of the Obscene Publi-cations Act. Alongside the more inclusive remit of the post-1999 'R18' criteria, a concomitant change was affected on more mainstream films available to a wider potential audience. *The Idiots*, for example, included an image of penetration (albeit that this is very brief and sex is far from being the main focus of the film's narrative). This constitutes a significant incur-sion into the boundaries that previously divided illicit hard-core from mainstream cinema. It is easy to over-state the extent of liberalisation here, however, and it is still the case that the type of film, the narrative context in which it appears and the potential audience are factored into decisions on cutting images. For many years the erect penis was off limits for mainstream film (while female genitalia were permitted); however this image is no longer deemed 'obscene' and has now become more common in recent films, such as *Romance* where it is regarded by the Board as important to storyline. (The imagined practice of the BBFC applying an angle criteria to define what actually constitutes an erection has amused/ bemused many critics, particularly as the below-45° rule meant that the use of condoms in sex scenes was ruled out.) *Baise-moi* depicts a graphic non-consensual rape scene, which would not be permitted within the 'R18' category, but because it is shown in the context of a more broadly focused story, it is permitted in an '18'-rated film, also the case with the 'real' sex that appears in *The Idiots*. A ten-second cut was, however, required of *Baise-moi*, to excise a shot of a woman's vagina being penetrated by a penis in extreme close-up (sug-gesting that penetration is still subject to censorship). This sequence was shortened by the BBFC on the grounds that the shot was not integral to the story. The violent rape, however, was considered suitable viewing material because the film was probably only going to be consumed by a small audience, and without it the girls' rampage makes little sense. It also seems to the critical eye, however, that European, non-English speaking films, are permitted greater latitude in what they can show, perhaps because, again, it is assumed they will only reach a small sex-literate audience. The new rulings have certainly shifted the types of sexual acts permitted on video and film, and in effect hard-core images are becoming, under rather stringent conditions, increasingly visible within the more mainstream market, as occurred, at least to some extent, in the US during the 1970s.[33]

***

As has become clear throughout this analysis of the factors that shape the representation of sex in cinema, there are various moments in film history when the lines that divide legitimate from illegitimate cinema become blurred. A pattern of dialectical exchange has often proved to be at work; as boundaries are pushed a counter-force is often in operation, but usually a new set of boundaries become consolidated through regulation and shifts in social mores. Throughout cinema's history, and for a variety of reasons, 'transgressive' sexual imagery has become appropriated by the mainstream. Part II builds on this notion by focusing on various forms and themes in cinema that couch sex within different rhetorics of transgression.

Themes of
Transgression

Rhetorics and Forms of Transgression

*P*art I considered the ways that formal and contextual factors shape the representation of sex in cinema. Building on this, Part II makes a more specific investigation of films from a range of genres and aesthetic styles which draw upon sexual themes that in some way cross boundaries or challenge prohibitions, limits or norms. The location and formation of these boundaries are bound to the contours of a given socio-cultural landscape, with its particular pressure points, conflicting interests and investments. Within the context of this potentially dynamic environment, some sexual boundaries and limits are more stable than others, with dominant ideologies and discourses acting as fixing agents (some with more success than others). For a film to speak cogently to its intended contemporary audience about sex, sexuality and their meanings, then, contentions and conflicts around those meanings have to be implicitly or overtly in play. This is particularly the case with art-cinema films, but also appears in genre output. In whatever genre or style, the films that are most closely focused on sex and sexuality tend to put social and sexual ideals and norms under pressure. In the most extreme cases these are completely negated. The way that certain films deploy sexual desires coded culturally as forbidden to facilitate narrative disruption has already been addressed in some detail, in particular in relation to 'return of the repressed' narratives and melodramas. We have also seen how, at various points in its history, legitimate cinema has borrowed features from more risqué, outlying cinemas to inject potential 'X' appeal into flagging genres. In so doing some mainstream films have appropriated modes of expressing sex, sexuality and sexual desire that have a charged currency within the wider cultural landscape. In many cases capital is made from the inevitable contestations that arise from shifts in attitudes to sex and its representation. Legitimate cinema has, therefore, some license to go off limits if certain reverences are observed. One of the primary tasks for this second half of *Sex and the Cinema* is to assess the conditions under which different forms of sexual transgression are articulated and permitted in cinema.

In addressing films that actively interface with boundaries around what is culturally and historically defined as permissible in reality and representation, a number of key issues and contentions arise. Often such interfaces provide images, narrative and thematic tensions that touch base with the interests of a film's intended audience. These are likely to key into generational or other micro-cultural differences in attitudes towards sex, desire and sexuality. Central to the thematic interest of many films that deal with the sexual is the operation of socio-cultural processes and pressures that work to channel sexual behaviours, desires and their representation in ways that accord with dominant interests and agendas. As has been established, it is common to find that films focused on sex and sexuality draw on rhetorics of sexual repression.[34] In some this is overtly politicised, as with New Queer Cinema for example; in others it is designed to arrest attention and provide entertainment or titillation. However, the division between the two is not quite as clear as it might seem. The former group often invites interest through erotic or titillating content and the latter may raise for some viewers issues concerned with sexual politics. It is also the case that although some films deploy the indecent and obscene actively with the intention to challenge dominant norms around the meaning and propriety of sex, particularly the case with films that carry a permissive message or those seeking to court sensationalist interest, it does not mean that they set out to change anything. In fact underwriting the stability of the status quo can prove to be an important, if inadvertent, consequence of the enterprise of creating sexual sensationalism.

Many of the films discussed here represent sex in ways that could be regarded as in some way indecent or even obscene (especially if considered out of context). These labels are nonetheless notoriously slippery and increasingly difficult to define in ways that are meaningful in a general sense. There may be certain acts or ideas in the films discussed here that appear to fulfil the terms of the obscene. If this occurs it is then that a palpable experience of a boundary being overstepped is likely to be had. Due caution is required, however. The narrative and interpretative contexts within which forbidden or transgressive acts and desires appear often prove extremely important. These contexts have to be addressed if an over-simplification of the presence of sexual transgression in cinema is to be avoided. Most of the films discussed in Part II of this volume present sex, sexuality and desire as unruly in both personal and social terms, usually based on the notion that they run counter to rational or conscious intention in some way. What is of special interest here is the ways in which different sexual transgressions are formularised and conventionalised within the context of cinema. The manner in which an act or desire is lit and staged, the influence of genre, narrative structure, techniques such as innuendo, offscreen action, or strategies of disavowal built into the text, each play a role in the way that sexual transgressions are presented and rendered in accordance with cinematic values. The formal devices used to represent transgression are absolutely central to the meanings it is likely to convey to audiences. Such devices may make what would ordinarily be the object of our disgust palatable, as we will see with the way in which *King Kong* treats its theme of bestial desire. As already noted, as the object of the cinematic gaze, sex is, in itself, a challenge to the divide between private and public spheres. This provocation invokes a range of interdependent issues around spectacle and spectatorship, as well as complex relationships between morality, imagination, representation and reality, the social and the personal.

The overarching concern of this half of the book is to focus on different rhetorics of transgression that inform the representation of sex in cinema and to show what values such rhetorics convey in terms of form, sensation, spectacle and impact, as well as their relationship to social context and reception. As we shall see, these rhetorics play a primary role in shaping the forms and meanings of sex in cinema, as well as constituting and giving formal and semantic shape to what is deemed transgressive. It is common for signifiers of transgression to be invoked in the marketing of mainstream as well as more marginal films. In Hollywood, for example, even under the Production Code, *The Outlaw* (1943) was commended by Howard Hughes to the public for 'two reasons' (Jane Russell's breasts). It is also evident in the trangressive rhetoric that infuses the teaser taglines used to promote this film: 'Finally, at last, after a 3 year delay, you can see…' and 'Sensation too startling to describe'.[35] Art-cinema also often uses the provocation of transgression as a means to lure an audience. One of the posters used to advertise *Romance* showed in close-up a woman's body naked from a couple of inches below the waist to just above the knees with a hand and large red X printed as an overlay covering the pubic area (see also Lewis 2000: 207).

The X inscribes a transgressive dimension onto the image. Used only in the UK, another poster for the film proclaimed that 'Love is desolate. Romance is temporary. Sex is forever'.[36] In this instance the transgressive coding is written into the sentiments that lie behind the tagline. All these examples use advertising techniques that would be expected of films designated as exploitation or even hard-core. Transgressive rhetoric is used to signify the presence of sex constructed as that which goes beyond the expression of sanctioned romance. Large breasts or sexual experimentation, the focus of these two films, are within themselves not particularly transgressive, but they are deliberately couched within sensationalist rhetoric to pique the curiosity of potential viewers.

Part II explores the particular conditions that shape the representation of transgressive sex in cinema under five thematic subheadings: adultery, the beast within (animal transformation and bestiality), incest, sado-masochism and real sex. There are many other themes that could have appeared, but in choosing to address a limited number of categories, which cut across different genres, aesthetic styles and periods, this provides greater scope for more in-depth analysis. Each theme has a significant representation in cinema and typifies different aspects of the way that cinema represents sex and sexuality through regimes of sensationalism and rhetorics of transgression. What then is meant by the concept of transgression? Various philosophers and theorists have found the concept valuable from a number of different perspectives. Some consideration of how they comprehend and define transgression, its uses and constitution, may help in the endeavour to understand how rhetorics of transgression operate in cinema to give meaning to and energise certain aspects of sex and its presentation.

The term 'transgression' comes from the latin *trans* (across) and *gradi* (to walk) and appears to have been in common use in both France and Britain during the Medieval period in the context of breaking a command or law. The term has a strong biblical resonance in an English-speaking context, used as it was in translations of the Bible. While the term itself is not used in the Book of Genesis, prohibition, transgression and punishment are absolutely core to its message, as is also the case with the rest of the Old Testament. Genesis is remarkable for the purposes of this study as it provides a foundation narrative or 'ur-myth' that explains in imaginary and ideological terms the origin of sex, as well as related concepts such as shame, marriage, gender difference and hierarchical order. While we might dismiss this story as fable, it nonetheless still plays its hand in the way that sex and sexual difference are regarded. At the heart of the myth is the breaking of God's prohibition that Adam and Eve must not eat from the Tree of Knowledge (Genesis 2:17). Couched in the specific mythological and narrative terms of the Bible, this act of primal transgression is symbolically over-determined with a range of meanings. As noted in Part I, it provides an allegory for the shift from innocence to experience and is emblematic of free will and moral choice. It is also a narrative that explains the source of original sin and the fall of humankind from a state of grace. Man (woman, actually) challenges God's authority, and as a result, Adam and Eve are thrown out of Eden, the garden of plenty, to scratch out a bare subsistence living. Important for a cultural-archaeological or epistemological understanding of transgression, and the meanings that the myth has accrued, is that within the biblical paradigm the conception of original sin yokes sex and desire together with a challenge to God's supreme authority. Outside certain permissible limits sexual knowledge is positioned as dangerous and subversive. Within this rhetoric of temptation, rebellion, sexual difference, isolation and shame, transgression becomes defined as an affect of will and fallibility. These features play a strong hand in the ways that the condition of human existence is defined, interpreted and expressed in Western, Christianised, cultures.

Transgression has a metaphysical dimension within the creation myth of Genesis. Building perhaps on the 'free will' aspect of The Fall, transgression becomes a core notion of twentieth-century existentialist philosophical thought. Transgression was considered by some, at least in an abstract sense, as a potential means to achieve self-authenticity (a sense of being true to oneself). Charged with the authority of tradition and widespread familiarity, the myth of The Fall continues to have a place in the complex matrix of ideas that inform the way that sex and sexuality is regarded in the Christianised West. While sex may no longer in itself be seen in broad terms as inherently base, sinful or shameful in Western contemporary culture, these concepts have nonetheless provided filmmakers across cinema's history with a useful means of presenting cinematic sex as frisson-laden forbidden fruit. This is particularly the case in films that set out with a soft-core pornographic agenda, those that use a setting drawn from the historical past and films that make use of a repression/return of the repressed basis for their narratives (a regular feature of horror but surprisingly common elsewhere, as we will see).

French philosopher Georges Bataille (1897–1962) developed over a number of works and in different written registers an analysis of transgression.[37] He begins with the notion that limits and borders arise out of the formation of society and the self and are intrinsic to their shape and structure. His main focus of interest is on the way that human beings are impelled to test and transgress such man-made, but often God-ordained, limits. He argues that this rebellious process does not destroy but instead conserves and maintains the power and solidity of those limits. The integrity of a social system, and the social subject, is therefore dependent on the material experience of transgression, from which self-loathing, anguish, shame, grief, or distress are likely to arise. Such experiences are devastatingly powerful in a direct form, but still effective in a weaker mediated or ritualised form: 'the fictional nature of the novel helps us bear what, if it were real, might exceed our strength and depress us. We do well to live vicariously what we daren't live ourselves' (1991: 130). According to Bataille, we resist the roles and demands that society imposes on us, even though they play a strong role in determining who we are. The experience of such produces anxiety and also leaves a sense that something is missing, as if we are incomplete or inauthentic in someway. This is an idea also found in psychoanalysis and the work of Bataille's contemporary, Jacques Lacan (both men married the same woman, consecutively, and they moved in the same intellectual circles). The imposition of conditions from external sources on the way we live our lives means, inevitably, that those conditions are at some time or another tested out. The transgressive act can therefore be experienced as a liberating pleasure. Authority (forces of determination) and our sense of autonomy are often in conflict. Challenging external authority can provide a sense of power and control, as well as affording a sense of personal authenticity. Cinema capitalises often on the range of emotions experienced through the interplay of personal agency and repressive external forces. Such emotional dynamics lend dramatic tension, often based on Oedipal-style conflicts, and produce narrative disequilibrium/equilibrium. A sense of pleasurable relief is often experienced once the repressive bonds are thrown off or defeated (evident in some adultery and animal transformation films). Sexual power-play between characters is informed often by something similar.

Bataille claims that sex and death are the two areas of life that rupture the borders that stabilise and constitute both the self and the social order. It is for this highly disruptive reason that sex and death are couched in taboos and prohibitions. Taboos and prohibitions are social-cultural constructs but are often locked into place through reference to metaphysical agents such as God or social forces such as law or social sanctions and traditions of etiquette. Sex and death are excessive, beyond control, and therefore become the source of anxiety and mystery. Taboos, rituals, social niceties, regimes of disgust, all those ways that society has for dealing with intrusion of the sublime,[38] collect around sex and death, which in our efforts to attain mastery, we wish to contain, recuperate, deny and solve. Yet at the same time the dangerous, 'othered', qualities of sex have a deep fascination: 'The turbulence and disastrousness of sexuality are of the essence of temptation. Temptation is the desire to fall, to fail, to faint and to squander all one's reserves until there is no firm ground beneath

one's feet' (Bataille 1987: 240). And yet, like Freud, Bataille argues for the persistence of taboos in the socio-cultural arena; order, in all its meanings, will collapse without it, as would
an individual's identity. Herein is the attraction of devastation. Bataille might side in part
with excess and transgression (particularly in his novels), but he understands its seductive
dangers in a way that exceeds Catholic notions of sin. Boundaries and taboos, those markers
that contour and manage both the social order and the socialised being, come at the cost
of repression at the level of the personal, however. Sexual desires of a transgressive kind are
produced directly by the ordering regimes of the social structure and socialisation. We are
the product therefore of forces that police thoughts and actions and we are complicit with
that policing, in ourselves and how we treat and communicate with others.

This idea is nicely elaborated by reference to Freud who developed a dual model of the
ego (the part of the psyche that represents us to ourselves). The 'realist' ego mediates between the conditions of social reality and the desires of the id, whereas the 'narcissistic' ego is
far more egocentric and self-serving. This model may help in the attempt to understand the
way in which competing forces are in constant attendance at a personal level in our dealings
between desire and social demands. The appeal of cinematic sex (at least some of it) could
therefore be said to exploit that which is deemed transgressive and dangerous by providing
the viewer with a vicarious means of experiencing liberation from prohibition. Although this
is in the register of the imaginary/fantasy, engagement with what occurs on the screen is
potentially still able to produce palpable emotional states and desire. At the same time, the
norms and narratives that produce boundaries, taboos and prohibitions and which hold the
social fabric in place, making it rigid and inflexible, are reinforced and reiterated.

Bataille claims that eroticism is the product of shame (1987: 31). Both, he argues, are
by-products of humanity's emergence from the instinctual, animal world. Born of shame,
eroticism is the ultimate sign of self-consciousness. This resonates with the biblical story
of The Fall and corresponds to Freud's inquiries into the formation of the psyche in 'Totem
and Taboo' (1913) and 'Civilisation and Its Discontents' (1930). Myths like The Fall are narratives that help form the contours of a culture and, in this long-lived and widespread case, a
number of different cultures. Such stories act as a form of imagined history that set out and
symbolise social-cultural limits as well as fixing the regimes of difference that give collective meaning. While none of the myths that relate to the origins of sexual shame are true in
a scientific sense, they do suggest, however, that sex and sexuality are problematic. In the
story, shame is the product of The Fall, but what it tells us is that we find ways of narrativis-
ing and making sense of the strangeness of sex. Sex might be socially conditioned but it is
also something that exceeds the predefined roles inherited and assigned to it by the social
order. This notion of a 'wild' sexuality, connected to instincts, is one that will be examined
later, especially in the chapter that deals with animal transformation and bestial desires.
Libertarian arguments for the 'free expression of sex'[39] and many anti-censorship lobbyists
often, although by no means always, assume that sex and sexuality can be divested of its
mysterious strangeness and entanglement with power. It is implied that sex and sexuality

have a fixed content and that to remove repression would make for a prelapsarian sexual utopia. The Lacanian model has no truck with such hopeful naïveté; sexual desire depends on making the other into an object, an object of desire. We labour under the illusion that union with this (ever-changing) object of desire will make us complete. In addition, the charge of sex and desire, its *frisson*, is related directly to what has been repressed or deemed transgressive. Bataille covers similar ground from a loftier perspective. He argues that what is fundamental to the human experience is the dynamic experience of continuity and discontinuity (an idea reworked from Hegel and which mirrors Lacan's structural centralisation of lack in the workings of the psyche). Individual existence is experienced as discontinuity. We are split off from each other and from the absolute.

> We are discontinuous beings, individuals who perish in isolation in the midst of an incomprehensible adventure, but we yearn for our lost continuity. We find the state of affairs that binds us to our random and ephemeral individuality hard to bear. Along with our tormenting desire that this evanescent thing should last, there stands our obsession with a primal continuity linking us with everything there is. (Bataille 1987: 15)

The sense of this breach promotes anguish and anxiety, as well as a desire to retrieve the missing continuity. Sex promises to provide that missing continuity because it promises to dissolve the boundary between self and other. As a violation of the borders that produce the sense of a coherent self, sex is also a foretaste of death: 'the whole business of eroticism is to destroy the self-contained character of the participators as they are in their normal lives' (1987: 17). In other words, the drive to eroticism is based on our desire for the annihilation of the self through an overwhelming passion, which often means breaking the bounds of internalised and externalised repressive, 'civilising' forces. While in Freud, death has an appealing dimension in the sense that it offers respite from the pain of being a 'discontinuous being', for Bataille this same notion also lies at the heart of the sexual (1987: 15).

Against ourselves, sometimes, the blood stirs to the call of erotic transgression. It is this that is exploited by advertising for films such as *Romance* and may help to explain the common presence of sex coded in transgressive rhetorical terms in cinema. Bataille shows that sexuality is complex and contradictory. It is the product of the prohibitive fetters in which it appears to be enchained, yet it also carries a nub of something that is, enigmatically, more than that.[40] He argues that eroticism draws its transgressive power from being in violation of the law of reproduction and the work ethic. We might extend this idea as a means of analysing the way that the heterosexual matrix works (the structures that co-work to channel sexuality into heterosexual form, to which it is pertinent to add monogamy). Otherness (the otherness of sex and sexual desire of whatever type) is assigned to non-hetero sexualities as a means of rendering certain types of sex more 'normal' thereby drawing off some of its disruptive turbulence. But within the terms of Bataille's model, the strangeness of sex, desire and sexuality that certain forces seek to ameliorate is valued because it has the energising power to 'destroy the self-contained character', which is the product of social forces and indeed this strangeness is valued under certain circumstances because it has the power to 'destroy the self-contained character' (1987: 17) (a state of being that has spiritual significance in many different religious cultures). In a prosaic sense, perhaps the desire to ensure that sex and sexuality retains some of this magical strangeness goes some way towards explaining the appeal of erotic 'curiosities' in the pornographic imagination.

In their influential book *The Politics and Poetics of Transgression*, Peter Stallybrass and Allon White map transgression in terms of the operation of social hierarchies (1986: 2–3). While they use ideas derived from Bataille, their aim is to politicise overtly in the terms of cultural materialism the notion of transgression. As such, this conception of transgression moves away from Bataille's more mystical approach. They begin with the premise that for a hierarchy to exist there must be discrimination between the high (the ideal/the exalted) and the low (the base). The debased low reinforces the value of the high; the high needs the low to define itself (an idea based on Hegel's dialectics and Structuralism). They argue that this plays out through, amongst other things, the sexual body and its representation. Transgression is, in their model, an expressive act that in some respect contradicts or inverts codes and norms (1986: 17–18).[41] Therefore the low is aligned with transgression in the sense that low culture is disrespectful, does not buy into and sends up the values of the high. This idea is evident in some cinemas. In hard-core, for example, the corporeal materiality of sex is emphasised to 'prove' the realness of the sexual action and in so doing it becomes an expression of low culture. This status is reflected in colloquial terms for hard-core: smut, dirty movies, fuck films. These terms also betray that the intent to move the body is lower in the hierarchy of class and taste than the intent to move the mind (Kant defines 'Art' in accordance with the latter). Popular genres often seek to move the body and to provoke sensation: action movies seek to pump up the adrenalin of the viewer, horror seeks to engender fear, soap and melodrama seek to provoke tears. Art movies may also deploy sensationalist aspects, but they also often want to create an aesthetic, authorial vision and promote intellectual engagement; sensationalism in this context is often part of an intention to incite reflection. The rhetoric of transgression deployed by Stallybrass and White is one that emphasises the body-positive, life-affirming, value of sex as base and vulgar as well as its potential challenge to elite values. Their argument can be marshalled to sanction the presence of the obscene and the indecent in film and it will prove important to an understanding of the way that sexual transgression in film is potentially a means of troubling the status quo. While it is open to question whether cinematic representations of sex offer any sustained political challenge to dominant norms, it is evident that transgressive images and identities in cinema *do* sometimes offer alternatives to the norm and, at times, demonstrate the conditions and vested interests on which sexual ideologies and rhetorics operate. However, there are many instances of films where sexual transgression operates in narrative terms to reaffirm dominant values, following the typical narrative structure of equilibrium, disruption, equilibrium. As realised in cinema, sexual transgression may therefore carry with it a corrective or containment element, sometimes at the same time as offering a promising glimpse of something beyond the norm. In attempting to balance different forces, cinema serves often with two hands: sensationalist rips appear in the fabric of the normative, while, often, they are hastily sewn up again.

The process of becoming socialised requires individuals to internalise boundaries, which carries a psychological dimension. For Julia Kristeva (1982), a theorist who draws on psychoanalytic understandings of the process at work in the formation of the subject, socialisation means that we must learn to develop a controlled, clean and proper body. Impulses, drives, desires and even identifications that are somehow out of place in a given context have to be repressed or marginalised to enable us to function effectively in a social context. Kristeva's work on the horrors of abjection is valuable because it connects the social to the psychological, something that proves important to understanding why it is that unruly sexual transgression carries with it a complexly-charged combination of enjoyment and horror. Kristeva's essay on horror links aspects of Bataille to Mary Douglas' work on regimes of pollution and taboo (1991; first published in 1966), which she argues operate in all cultures, albeit in different ways. It is the particularities of these regimes that are constitutive of a culture.

Given that the forms and meanings of sexual transgression are directly, if sometimes inversely, linked to cultural and societal norms, what is considered as sexually transgressive is far from stable and is therefore subject to contestation and revision. The specific historical and cultural context that informs interpretation proves of central importance (particularly as Bataille and psychoanalytic understandings of transgression can appear overly generalised in socio-historical terms). It is therefore essential to address the specific narrative and stylistic context within which a representation of sexual transgression takes place: this context is often aligned to the intended message, or preferred reading, present in a given film. An act of sexual transgression in a film can be used, as already indicated, to reaffirm dominant values, as is the case in *Fatal Attraction*.[42] Here an adulterous affair leads the central male character to appreciate family values, consonant with the dominant political emphasis on family values in the US at that time. Transgressive sexual acts have a very different intended meaning, however, in the more permissive context of, for example, European exploitation cinema. In *Behind Convent Walls* (1977), sex, made all the more transgressive because it occurs within the confines of a celibate order, represents a challenge to what is seen as the 'unnatural' repressive regime under which the nuns live. These two examples represent polarised instances of negative and positive treatments of sexual transgression, which serve different rhetorical purposes in terms of form and ideological ramification. There are, however, many films that lie somewhere in between, with sexual transgression couched in more ambiguous terms (as is the case with *Last Tango in Paris* or *The Piano Teacher* (*Le Pianiste*, 2000)). The meanings of sexual transgression in cinema are therefore diverse and extremely sensitive to a gamut of textual and contextual factors. Different approaches to the representation of sex and desire encoded as in some way transgressive operate therefore within broader spheres of, for example, cultural, semantic and industrial contexts (including genre, target audience, regulation and classification).

Transgression is a highly-charged concept that has profound political, social and emotional ramifications. The evocation of sexual transgression in cinema touches on all of these areas, providing potentially exciting yet vicarious contact with the *outré*. Within academic discourse, transgression is most commonly used in relation to the breaking of certain boundaries that are part and parcel of the social-cultural order. It is also the case that the word itself has a certain sophisticated weight in that it often imbues a political, critical and subversive significance to what might otherwise be seen as simply anarchic fun, perverse, sensationalist, or a form of audience-attention seeking. Many of the films discussed below present sex and desire in ways that are not normally available to us and the ensuing pleasure that they may accrue for spectators is based precisely on the *frisson* of a 'safe', vicarious, and virtual experience of sexual transgression. A certain caution is therefore required here if we are not to adopt a fashionable, 'cool' pose of elevating the representation of, and the potential enjoyment in, the unconscionable. It is hard, for example, to see rape or child sexual abuse as something to celebrate as an unqualified, joyous breaking of boundaries. That said, address of the particular formal context of such representations is absolutely vital to understanding what such transgressions might mean and how they are positioned in ideological, ethical and cinematic terms.

Adultery: Domestic Transgressions

dultery is a term used generally to describe sexual relations outside a marriage. From a contemporary liberal perspective, with increasing divorce rates and with fewer couples getting married, the term seems somewhat outmoded. It is perhaps more common now to speak of cheating on a partner, or, more formally, having an extra-marital affair. We might expect the treatment of adultery in cinema to have altered somewhat in line with demographic change. Under the Production Code adultery had to be shown to be wrong and punished, but as we will see it is still the case that adultery is made under the sign of transgression. A quick glance at the Shorter Oxford English Dictionary (1991) reveals a colourful and dramatic definition: adultery is a 'violation of the marriage bed'; this is the rhetoric of transgression in biblical and juridical terms. Marriage, it is implied, is surrounded by an aura of delicate sanctity that can be spoiled, polluted, corrupted and adulterated. The use of such rhetoric locates marriage and adultery within the economics of purity and danger, as outlined by Mary Douglas (1991). As a contract of agreement between two people, wherein they agree to be sexually faithful to one another, the juridical, the religious and the personal all come together to formulate one of the cornerstones of Western social order. Marriage might not be undertaken by all couples yet the act of living together also constitutes a contract in financial, familial and emotional terms. Adultery might seem to belong to the domain of marriage, yet sexual infidelity can have a profound impact on those concerned directly and those close-by in relationships where couples are not married. While adultery might not appear to be 'transgressive' in the most excessive and outré form in Western cultures (it is common and hardly the equivalent of human sacrifice or murder), its emotional and personal effects might nonetheless be the nearest that many of us come, married or not, to the gut-wrenching upheaval that Bataille argues accompanies overstepping a boundary. Our sexual relationships play an important role in defining who we are, particularly within the context of the family, and changes to them can have a significant impact on the organisation of our lives and how we regard ourselves. It is not then that surprising that adultery is a common topic of interest in cinema.

Marriage is culturally defined. It has many forms and is bounded by rules and expectations specific to a given culture. It has generally been the case that marriage in Christianised cultures is regarded as a permanent bond between partners and confirmation of a sexually-exclusive relationship; both aspects enshrined within Catholic and Anglican marriage ceremonies. Over the past thirty years the status of marriage in the West has changed. It has become more secularised, the divorce rate has increased and many couples live together without getting married. Nonetheless marriage still plays an important part in our lives as individuals, even if we choose not to undertake it. According to sociologists and anthropologists, 'marriage' plays a significant role in shaping the social order. To cite one typical anthropological view, 'it organises parents and children into domestic groups in which basic roles are allocated according to age and gender. This specific institutional pattern has been heavily sanctioned in moral and legal codes' (Schwimmer 2003: 1). However, this could apply equally well to family. Stephen Heath, a psychoanalytic film theorist, makes an even stronger claim about the structural role played by marriage in society, stating that 'adultery ... is "category confusion", the slide from identity to indifference, a total indistinction of place' (cited in Doane 1987: 119). He argues that the role of wife is instrumental in keeping the gendered and social order in place. It is not clear, however, that what constitutes a wife is so very settled in contemporary society.

For some groups in the West, sex outside marriage is considered in some way wrong, either for religious, moral or tradition-based reasons. While proven or admitted adultery might form the basis for divorce in most Westernised countries, juridical or religious institutions are not sanctioned to punish offenders. By contrast, in some cultures adultery is punishable by imprisonment, physical chastisement or even death. In general terms, direct, external prohibitions on adultery are rather weak in the West, yet the contract of marriage or partnership in both emotional and social terms, particularly where there are children, is so deeply embedded in the way society is organised that it remains a strong and influential institution. It is important to note that some married couples in the West agree to have open marriages sexually and that for many couples, with or without children, marriage, in the legal sense, is not regarded as necessary for a range of different reasons. In some respects, speaking of consensual monogamy rather than marriage includes rather than excludes this increasingly large latter group and includes non-heterosexual couples. In these groups there may be an agreement of whatever kind that sex stays exclusively between the couple; if this agreement is broken, particularly if it is behind one of the partner's back, then in both cases emotional upheaval can ensue. In anthropological and sociological terms marriage and its concomitant institution, the family, helps to preserve the integrity of the patriarchal line through 'legitimacy' and, as Brian Schwimmer (2003) has said, it proscribes roles. Adultery is not inimical to all marriage systems, however; a fact that works counter to Heath's universalised argument. In many non-Western marriage systems there is a more casual approach towards sex and patrilinearity, although certain rules are still likely to be in place (see Schwimmer 2003).

Across the historical breadth and national width of cinema, adultery has proved a popular topic. Representations of adultery under the Production Code were subject to the rule of metaphysical retribution. Because adultery lends itself so well to drama, as it had done for ages past, and rather than give it up as a completely taboo topic, an unseen force (the Code) worked its morally-upright power by meting out extreme forms of punishment to those exhibiting transgressions of extra-marital desire (usually death). Mary Ann Doane, for example, argues that adulterous women, or women who were too closely connected to sex were irrecuperable (1987: 120). Since then, the treatment of adultery has in formal and thematic terms become more complex. Its transgressive status has become diluted and more ambiguous, yet as we will see punishment is still in evidence. As a theme, adultery forges connections between the fictional and real world by dealing with conflicts between desire and duty; the ideal and reality. These factors make the subjective and emotion-focused milieu of melodrama the 'home' of adultery narratives. What is at stake in most adultery-based films is the family, no matter how the adultery is staged or in what context it appears. Rogue desires are agents of disruption: making an assault on narrative equilibrium, the family and the notion that desire is stable, controllable and unified. Of all the forms of cinema-based sexual transgression that appear in Part II of this book, adultery is the one that seems most profoundly caught up in conflicts between domestic demands and desire, between fantasy and reality. Most adultery-focused films demonstrate overtly or covertly the costliness of both fidelity and infidelity, and their impact on self-identity. To use Freud's terminology, the adultery film is the site of a fundamental struggle between the principles of reality and pleasure. Or, as Justine Last (Jennifer Aniston), the central character of The Good Girl (2002), puts it: 'As a girl you see the world as giant candy store … but as a woman you are in a prison … something's locking you up.'

Given that we have already discussed adultery in relation to the Production Code, here focus is on a range of more recent films that deal with sexual unfaithfulness. Older films are referred to where relevant. Some of the films discussed here privilege a women's point of view. For some critics this in itself is a form of transgression in terms of the gender order, at least potentially. Mary Ann Doane, for example, argues that 'the cinema in general, outside the genre of the woman's picture, constructs its spectator as the generic "he" of language … [women's pictures] deal with female protagonists and often appear to allow her significant access to point of view structures and the enunciative level of the filmic discourse' (1987: 3). The Bridges of Madison County brings the voice of Francesca Johnson (Meryl Streep) back from the dead, via flashback, to speak of desires that her son and daughter had no idea that she had. In her will she asks her son and daughter to have her body cremated and the ashes sprinkled from a particular bridge. This unexpected request prompts the children to read her diaries and letters; a device that sanctions the use of voiceover and flashback. Over the course of the film we learn that middle-aged Francesca had a deeply passionate, if short in

Justine (Jennifer Aniston) dreams of a more interesting life in *The Good Girl* (2002)

physical terms, affair with a photographer, Robert Kincaid (Clint Eastwood), for whom she continued to feel passion for the rest of her life. The affair, which took place over four days when Francesca's husband and teenage children were away, is shown in retrospect, punctuated by Francesca's comments on how she felt and the experience of conflicts that occurred between her commitment to family and an intense love for Robert. Her voiceover and point of view supersede those of her children, who read about the affair from her diaries. As such, the film speaks from Francesca's point of view.

Taking the adulterous woman's perspective, and inviting the audience to identify with her transgressive sexual desires and experiences, is not, however, solely the domain of recent film. *Frenchman's Creek*, for example, takes a similar approach to *The Bridges of Madison County*, even though it was made forty years before and set in Restoration England. Dona St Columb (Joan Fontaine) seeks to escape the sexual interest of her husband's unscrupulous best friend, Lord Rockingham (Basil Rathbone), by leaving London for the tranquillity of Cornwall. There she meets a handsome French pirate, Jean Benoit Aubrey (Arturo de Córdova), with whom she falls in love and embarks on various risky adventures that incur the wrath of some pompous landowners who are her husband's long-standing friends. Jean is regarded by the landowners as a threat and they spread rumours that he and his crew are rapists; however it is clear that many of the Cornish women of the area prefer these French lovers to English ones. In a neat act of transgression born of enunciation,[43] the film places us on the side of those outside English law and authority, designated here as the side of passion and adventure. (It should be remembered this is an American film and judging by the representations of adultery discussed in this chapter it seems that in American popular culture the French are often invested with a magic sensuality.) The film is shot almost entirely from Dona's perspective; she is present in nearly every scene and parries verbally with all the men she meets, getting the better of most. Unlike the movement between flashback and the present-day used in *The Bridges of Madison County*, events take place entirely in the present tense. The former film is framed as the 'sum' of Francesca's life and her decisions. Looking back over a life is common in mid-twentieth-century women's films (resurrected with a suspense-style twist in *American Beauty* (1999)), where it often operates ideologically to show the ill effects of a 'fall' from marital grace. At the end of *Frenchman's Creek*, however, there is no real sense of closure on Dona's life, despite her adultery. While there is no voiceover or in-memoriam flashback, the film is framed with the aim of creating a link between the audience and Dona's point of view on life, her morality and desire.

Like *The Bridges of Madison County*, *The Good Girl* makes its enunciative position clear as Justine speaks directly to the viewer in voiceover at the start of the film and she is central to events. As with *The Bridges of Madison County* and *Frenchman's Creek*, it is a woman's desires and dilemmas that drive the narrative. *The Good Girl* takes a rather off-beat anti-melodramatic approach to adultery, and actively counters some of the more overblown, calorie-laden aspects that are common in adultery-based films. Nonetheless, as is the case with the other films, there is something missing from Justine's life; she is bored by her home life and her job. Very many feminist theorists and critics, from the down-to-earth criticism of Molly Haskell (1987) through to the more esoteric heights of French feminist theory, have argued that patriarchal, phallocentric cultures police women's desire and identity, and the images of such, to privilege male desire and power. Any desires or actions that are not related to child-rearing and husbandry are therefore coded as transgressive. Some adultery films take as their material the experience of thirtysomething heterosexual women who are wives, in long-term partnerships and/or mothers, and for whom romance and passion has been superseded by routine. The act of speaking such desires in a public and fictional domain is therefore important economically and socially (which might account for the standing of melodrama amongst many men as 'dross'). But it is not simply women who suffer from the constraints of domesticity and one group of adultery films focus on the constraints of marriage and monogamy in a more inclusive way.

American Beauty, *Unfaithful* and *Zandalee* (1991), three very different films in other respects, do not privilege an 'adulterous' woman's point of view (*Unfaithful* appears to do so, but halfway through the film the perspective swings to that of the jilted husband).[44] This latter group of adultery-based films share their points of view between several characters. While in the former group the spotlight falls on the sexual desires of the central women characters that arise from the constraints of their roles as wives and mothers, the latter group of films focus more intently, and in different ways, on the interpersonal context of monogamy and adultery. But what all these films have in common, no matter what their moral take, is that monogamy is presented as fragile and given the right conditions is easily put under siege. It is based on a set of rules that, if broken, can blister up into raging emotions and shatter the contours of identity, terms that resonate strongly with Bataille's concept of the experience of transgression. As an emotion-manipulating medium, film is apt to use a range of textual devices to deliver a sense of this. *Zandalee*, for example, pulls out all the stops, whereas *The Good Girl* pulls in the opposite direction: sensation is muted, 'locked up' and what might be tragic or melodramatic elsewhere becomes muted and banal.

Most adultery films have other common features that prove important to the meanings assigned to extra-marital sex. A particular narrative pattern can be traced along with some common textual conventions but, as we shall see later, the presence of such commonalities are not always consistent with the particular moral and stylistic take on adultery that each film has. *Unfaithful* opens on an external shot of a comfortable suburban home in Autumn (for which the American term 'Fall' makes more of a play on bathetic fallacy). A strong wind is blowing. A cut moves proceedings to the inside of the house where Constance Sumner (Diane Lane), her husband, Ed (Richard Gere), and her young son live. They are having breakfast, getting ready for work and school. It is intended to be mundane and familiar. Normality here is white, middle-class and economically privileged, the comforts of which underscore still further the excess of her extra-marital sexual relationship. In formal terms the opening scene constitutes narrative equilibrium. A similar opening scene, detailing domestic life, occurs when Francesca begins her narration in *The Bridges of Madison County*. However, *The Good Girl* does not focus on the kitchen as the heart of domesticity as with the previous two films. Here it is the routine of work in the not very busy store, coming home to find Phil (John C. Reilly), her husband, and his friend stoned and watching TV that constitutes equilibrium. Justine and Phil are not economically privileged and in many ways present a far less manicured picture of everyday life than the other films. What all these films have in common, however, is that equilibrium is defined by routines around family and work, which generate for the central characters boredom and lack of fulfilment.

Following the expository prologue of *Unfaithful*, Constance catches the train to New York City. The wind strengthens and while shopping for children's party goods she is blown forcefully into the body of a dark stranger carrying books. From the physical impact, they fall to the ground, with her on top of him, books and party fripperies scatter and fly every which way. Failing to get a cab for her, he invites her to his apartment to clean up a cut on her leg incurred in the 'fall'. He introduces himself, Paul Martel (Olivier Martinez), a French bookseller, apartment sitting for a friend. In terms of the narrative structure of adultery films, this is The Meeting. The circumstances of The Meeting are, however, subject to quite wide variation. They range from *Unfaithful*'s dramatic, 'blown together' meeting to rather more banal meetings, often taking place in the home or workplace. *The Good Girl*'s Justine meets Tom/Holden (Jake Gyllenhaal) in the store in which she works. *American Beauty*'s Lester Burnham (Kevin Spacey) sees the object of his desire at a school basketball game (she is one of a group of teenage cheerleaders that includes Lester's daughter). His wife, Carolyn

Burnham (Annette Bening), has known the man with whom she has an affair for some time and is his less successful business rival. Robert Kincaid pulls up outside Francesca's house to ask directions in *The Bridges of Madison County*.

In some of these films mutual desire is made apparent immediately at The Meeting, in others it takes time to build. Johnny (Nicolas Cage) walks into the kitchen where Zandalee (Erika Anderson) is cooking; he stares at her and says enigmatically 'now we know who the other is'. There is a curious intimacy about the way he regards her and his directness annoys her. He will continue to get under her skin throughout the whole film. Lester's first sight of Angela Hayes (Mena Suvari), his teenage daughter's best friend, kicks into being a luscious fantasy in which the real-life cheerleading dance morphs into an seductive show by her exclusively for him. Her striptease number ends with a shower of tactile red rose petals pouring from the top she slowly unzips. In contrast, Justine asks simply who the new boy is, a kind of low-key matter-of-fact interest that echoes the film's anti-melodramatic aesthetic. Francesca's rather girlish self-consciousness betrays her sexual interest in Kincaid, echoed in Constance's first conversation with Paul and in Lester's first conversation with the 'real' Angela. In each of these latter cases the middle-aged protagonist is placed back in the position of an awkward teenager, which raises some interesting questions about what is regarded as constituting sexual desire and to whom it properly belongs. In all instances there is at least some sense of a spark between the transgressive couple.

An especially neat use of the specific formal features of cinema is the way The Meeting appears in *Madame de…* (1953). *Madame de…* (Danielle Darrieux), a married aristocrat, meets a dashing ambassador at a party. (Her last name is never revealed, an absence signalling scandal, but importantly suggesting that the affair leaves her nameless and, in social terms, without an identity.) Through a series of continuity edits, the dancing couple whirl across time, signalled by the changes in rooms and clothes. In each shot they hold each other more tightly and the dialogue glides from the register of the trivial to that of passion. This is particularly successful in capturing cinematically the effect that infatuation has on the perception of time: nothing happens of any significance in between the moments they are together.

One particular feature of The Meeting that warrants attention is the way that the 'object of desire' is presented. The gender politics of the gaze has provided film studies with one of its central issues. Mulvey's (1975) notion that Hollywood cinema is built around women as object of the gaze has been challenged by various critics such as Steve Neale (1993) and Kenneth MacKinnon (1998), who demonstrate that men too are often presented in cinema as the object of the gaze (while acknowledging that the terms of such presentation are often different). As adultery films are focused on sexual desire, it is perhaps inevitable that characters/actors are presented for us to look at; this is part and parcel of enabling viewers to identify with the desire of the protagonist. Working with a heterosexual economy, in the films discussed here where a woman's desire is central to the narrative it is men who become the object of the gaze. The way that an actor is presented to the audience is therefore crucial to help facilitate identification with the woman protagonist's desires. The object of Constance's desire has long dark hair and a succulent French accent that drips like honey-dew from full lips. He is younger than her, but not that much younger, and dressed in what magazines might call smart Bohemian style. As with pirate Jean in *Frenchman's Creek*, he is an exotic object of desire in both looks and demeanour. He is very attentive to Constance's needs, humorous, reads poetry and is obviously interested in what she thinks. In all these films the audience is actively invited to compare the incumbent husband/wife with the object of desire. Paul is dressed, shot and lit differently from Constance's husband, who dresses conservatively and does not have the matinee idol looks of Martinez. In *The Bridges of Madison County* Robert/Clint Eastwood has dangerously sparkling blue eyes, is taller, thinner, has more hair and has much finer features than Francesca's farmer husband. He leads an unconventional life as a photojournalist, has no family and, importantly, enjoys reflective conversations which engage Francesca at a level missing from her daily life. These conversations serve to emphasise to her that life has not turned out the way she had hoped.

In *The Piano*, Ada (Holly Hunter) and Baines (Harvey Keitel) are matched as a 'proper' couple, as both pay little heed to Victorian manners and niceties. Baines is neither young nor classically handsome, yet he has an exotic air mixed with an earthy sensitivity. This is apparent the first time that Ada meets Baines and her new husband, Stewart (Sam Neill) on the beach. Stewart is dressed in a top hat and suit with waistcoat, emphasising his stiffness, while Baines wears looser, lighter clothing, complete with an artisan's straw hat. Stewart tells her 'you're small, I didn't think you'd be small', while Baines says that she 'looks tired'. This juxtaposition sets Baines up as the more perceptive and caring of the two. The tattoos on his face signify outwardly that Baines is open to Maori culture; he speaks a little Maori, respects their customs and lives among them, something likely to help endear him to a liberal audience. By contrast, Stewart holds the Maoris in contempt, yet fears them; at times his bemusement at what he regards as their lack of civilisation slides into disgust. In keeping with his insensitive disposition, Stewart is mainly oblivious to Ada's intense and passionate music; when he finally listens he is disturbed by it. The less self-conscious and more bohemian Baines finds her music captivating and erotic. As such, Baines is likely to fit with the preferred image of the target audience. This is important because it is for him that Ada chooses 'life'.

In all these examples the audience is shown in some detail what is attractive about the character set up as the object of desire. This is even the case in the most off-beat adultery film, *The Good Girl*, as the slightly gawky Tom is in conventional terms more physically attractive and lively-minded than sturdy and slow Phil. And, in the first few weeks of their meeting, Tom becomes the object of Justine's gaze. In a general sense The Meeting is what sets the narrative chain into action. In some cases desire is immediately invoked, often through point-of-view shots. The Meeting itself becomes imbued with a sense of promise and possibility. In others desire begins as an antipathy between characters, as is the case with Johnny and Zandalee.

The next progression in the narrative formula of the adultery film is The Affair. This stage is characterised by elation, furtiveness and riskiness. These emotional keys help create drama, suspense and engagement with the main character/s and have a bearing on the transgressive coding of adulterous sex in the films. Guilt and shame are added to the mix in some of the films. Constance, for example, is invigorated by a rush of energy. Buying new underwear indicates a renewed erotic interest. She falls into reverie while doing the washing up (it is this particular incident that alerts her husband to the affair) and strains to tell lies about her movements. The overwhelming, consuming nature of her involvement with Paul is seen in cinematic terms by the fact that it uses up most of the screen time in the first half of the film. Each time Constance meets Paul their sexual engagement becomes increasingly intense and experimental, fuelled in part by a sense of danger. In most adultery films there is a dramatic near miss, where the couple are almost caught in a compromising situation. This creates suspense, adding a further dimension of sensual stimulation to erotic urgency, and often helps to side the viewer emotionally with the transgressors. Here this occurs when Constance runs into neighbours outside Paul's apartment. She goes for coffee with them, phoning Paul to say where she is. He arrives and they have sex in the toilet of the café. Riskiness becomes increasingly important to the sexual frisson of their relationship, which intensifies still further the transgressive coding of adulterous sex.

The same emotional pattern of elation and furtiveness is also evident in *Frenchman's Creek* although Dona can be somewhat less furtive because her husband is absent. Nonetheless, she colludes with her servant so that she can spend a few days at sea, engaged in elemental pleasures with her amour aboard the pirate ship. Risk is also an integral part of their relationship. Dona takes part in a number of raids with the pirates, dressed as cabin boy. She finds these exhilarating and in one she saves the crew through her quick thinking and audacity. Sex is kept offscreen, merely suggested through the use of ellipses, providing therefore one of the ways in which sex is coded institutionally and textually as transgressive. This is intensified and given an added piquant danger because Dona is not just having an affair, she is collaborating with an enemy of the state in the pursuit of thrills. In the first stages of The Affair, transgressive activities are experienced in as breath-catching excitement (although not always quite so daring as in Dona's case). As Francesca's family is away and her home remote there is less furtiveness in her four-day affair with Robert, except that when a neighbour drops in unexpectedly he has to be concealed upstairs. Francesca's elation blinds her to the danger of social stigma should they be found out, however. The danger posed to her is represented by a woman who is shunned by the conservative town's people because of an affair (the majority of the film is set in the early 1960s). Robert, ever the observer of the people he meets, realises the community implications of their affair for Francesca if it were to be revealed, and because of her rather blasé approach he seeks to protect her. A further transgressive dimension is added through the film's sex scenes. They are far from being 'raunchy' and are rather less explicit than those in *Zandalee* and *Unfaithful*, but it is quite unusual in Hollywood to see tender, passionate sex between two less than young actors (Meryl Streep was in her mid-forties and Clint Eastwood in his sixties). Nonetheless, a great deal of care was taken to keep the scenes visually 'tasteful', which works to preserve the 'romance' as ideal.

In *The Piano* there is rather less emphasis in its mid-section on elation and furtiveness, yet risk becomes increasingly present. Ada is sanctioned to be in Baines' house because Stewart gave him her piano and Baines has requested lessons from her. The fact that he has had the piano tuned heralds a more intimate relationship, but this does not flourish until much later on in the film. The affair begins with a deal: piano keys are traded for, as Baines puts it, 'things I'd like to do while you play'. Feminist film scholars have debated the implications of this trade in terms of its gender politics; at the most extreme it is seen as a form rape (see Margolis 2000: 27–8). The contract does also carry aspects of the transgressive with it. It is about power and desire, and it does indeed speak of prostitution, yet Ada drives a hard bargain, exploiting his desire to gain what she desires. Later he regrets the deal, based as it is on economics, wishing instead for a more equal and romantic liaison.

Unlike the main characters in the other films, Ada did not choose to marry her husband. It was an arranged marriage. She also has a daughter from a previous relationship, so adultery in this instance does not come with the same emotional complexity for her as it does for the women protagonists of the other films. This adulterous relationship is not at first based on love and attraction, but is economic from her point of view. It is playing the piano that induces elation at first. But her dealings with Baines unlock other pleasures and interests and she even begins to explore Stewart's body in a sexual way (something he has difficulty handling, wedded as he is to a position of control and mastery). The emphasis placed on touching throughout the film has attracted critical interest, touching being a sexual mode

The culmination of the deal between Ada (Holly Hunter) and Baines (Harvey Keitel) in *The Piano* (1993)

that is not often emphasised within the visual medium of cinema. Sue Gillet (1995) argues that touching is a feminine sexual mode, while looking is the masculine equivalent: Ada and Baines are on the side of touching, while Stewart is on the side of looking. I would, how-ever, dispute Gillet's polarised claim, and regard the touching/looking dynamic of the film in rather different terms. Stewart's voyeurism introduces a more trangressive mode of sen-suality to the film. The transgressive quotient associated with voyeuristic pleasure becomes emphasised in one scene of the film as viewers are forced into complicity with Stewart's point of view as he watches Baines and Ada indulge in sensuous erotic play (he too is taking a risk here). The interplay of looks and their sexual economy becomes all the more complex when the camera pulls away to look at him looking at them. All of this heightens the general sense of risk and the way that desire has of engaging our interest in the sexual dealings of others.

The Good Girl stands out amongst the crowd in that Justine's affair with Tom is strangely empty and lacking in elation. This is reflected in the film's low-key style. While Justine acts somewhat furtively and says she feels guilt, her emotions are never acted out in hyperbolic terms. She plays with the words 'sin', 'adulteress' and 'Jezebel', but there is no overt emotional investment in them and as such her affair with Tom is not presented in overtly transgres-sive terms. They have sex, but it uses up very little screen time. Unlike many adultery films, this film is not imbued with melodramatic, formal vivacity. There is no attempt to create erotic titillation. Faint echoes of adultery film clichés are in evidence – the wind blowing, the rain on the car that stands in for tears, and in some of the rhetoric that Justine uses in her voiceover, but in the main there is a concerted attempt to make the affair real rather than a dramatically overblown fantasy. Events are not embellished by surging orchestral strings, as occurs in *Frenchman's Creek*, nor is sex staged within an art- or book-filled loft as it is in *Zandalee* or *Unfaithful*. Instead, sex takes place in the back of Justine's small car and a cheap motel room. They go out into the countryside, but it is not rendered picturesque or beautiful, the usual effect of romantic euphoria in the *mise-en-scène* of films of this kind. Rather, it is scrubby, muddy, colourless and cold, and they look bored. There is no sense of elation in the cinematic codes used, nor in Justine's attitude to Tom. Tom binds up the affair in romantic 'outsider' mythology, but ever-sceptical Justine tires of his fantasist puff when real-life events take precedence, but in going along with it to pacify him she is complicit in his suicide, which is at source a form of self-fictionalisation.

Generally, throughout The Affair the pleasure and reality principles are in conflict, but discomfort is masked in most cases by elation and the *frisson* of sexualised risk. It is only later when reality gets the upper hand that the mask of disavowal slips, something that ac-companies a change of key in the relationship (even evident in *The Good Girl*). Once The Af-fair is fully established, the drama is heightened by the introduction of either The Choice or The Crisis (both feature but the order in which they come is variable). Various events might trigger these, and they do not always occur at the end of the film. This phase is marked by tears and emotional upheaval, sometimes leading into depression and death (as is the case in *Madame De....*). In *Zandalee*, The Crisis takes the form of a face-off between husband and best friend. It occurs once Zandalee chooses to give up her addictive sexual relationship with the latter. In *Unfaithful*, Constance's choice occurs around midway through the film. But crisis comes in two waves and constitutes one half of the film. It is a combination of pity and affection for husband Ed and guilt about her illicit sexual pleasure that prompts Constance to call off the affair, a scenario that also appears in *Zandalee*. The first crisis occurs in *The Piano* when Stewart watches Baines and Ada in bed together. Following this, and after Stewart tries to rape her, he puts bars on the windows and doors to prevent Ada from going to Baines (by this stage Ada has retrieved her piano). The second crisis occurs because Ada tries to inform Baines she loves him. When Stewart finds out, he feels deeply betrayed, grabs an axe and in high gothic-style chops off Ada's right-hand forefinger. This act of symbolic castration operates as punishment for Ada's refusal to conform to Stewart's parochial Victorian values. Soon after, Ada leaves for a new life with Baines. It is only while they are on the sea, the piano balanced across the boat, that she really makes her 'choice' to live. It is a choice to live with Baines, yet it is also a much grander existential choice.

Choice is much more strongly emphasised than crisis in *The Bridges of Madison County*. Moments before her family returns home, Francesca must decide to leave for a new life with Robert or stay. She chooses to stay, and reiterates the choice when she and her husband go into town, where Robert awaits her, just in case she has changed her mind. This scene takes place in the pouring rain, making typical, melodramatic-style, use of the bathetic fallacy: the rain on the windscreen of their car shows externally the tears that Francesca must hide from her husband. It is when *American Beauty*'s Lester finally gets to the point where Angela is willing to have sex with him that he is faced with his choice. Betraying her self-consciousness and sexual naïveté, Lester realises that his passion for her was based on a self-tailored fantasy 'Angela'. He therefore chooses not to have sex with her, despite the fact that he could. Lester dies soon after making this choice, but his choice to see Angela as a real person rather than through the gauze of erotic fantasy was a good, even a redemptory, note on which his life ends. His death is not directly related to his Lolita-style fantasies, but it is possible to see one in the light of the other. Nonetheless, his choice humanises him and affirms the audience's emotional investment in his character.

In *The Good Girl* there is no crisis in highly dramatic melodramatic terms and after Justine dumps, or rather avoids, Tom, a rather unexpected crisis/choice scenario arises. Justine discovers that she is pregnant. Tom robs the store where they both work and wants Justine to run off with him. She is now faced with a real choice between her old life and a new life on the road. In the time it takes for a traffic light to turn from red to green, she decides to stay. Having earlier tried to poison Tom and attempted to get his parents to have him institutionalised (neither of which worked), Justine turns him in (prompting the store owner to call her a good girl). In keeping with the pop culture anti-hero image he wishes to convey, Tom kills himself rather than be arrested. Justine's affair creates a range of crises in her life (including being bribed into having sex with her husband's best friend). The choice that Tom offers her is far from practical and the stuff of fiction rather than one of substance. A life with slow and sturdy Phil seems therefore preferable. Because of the film's realist approach, adultery and the complexities of human and desire entanglements are drained of the high-blown rhetorics of transgression commonly found in the enflamed hyperrealism of melodrama; instead adultery is cooled in the mould of practicalities, limitations and disappointment. Within this context, idealised notions of sexual passion and romance, tasted and savoured by Dona and Francesca, are shown as nothing but fantasy, a cruel trick of desire.

In some instances The Crisis prompts the main character to assess their options; in others The Choice promotes The Crisis. Either way The Choice comes out of a conflict between differing investments. While The Meeting and even The Affair are often undertaken without much thought, often the couple being swept along by desire, it is at the point at which a choice has to be made that the transgressive effect crashes in, and it has a significant impact on identity. The choice also operates to engage more fully the viewer, inviting consideration of what they would do in such circumstances. Neil Labute's play *The Mercy Seat* (2002) works with this conventionalised aspect of the adultery format. In this drama a married man is thought to have died in the 9/11 tragedy who was in fact away from the building with his lover. The drama pivots around his decision as to whether to stay 'dead' and begin a new life or return from the dead to his old life. Labute leaves this choice open, inviting the audience to deliberate on what they would do; the answer growing out of an indvidual's particular circumstances. By contrast, most of the films addressed in this section do not leave things open, a side is taken which operates rhetorically and ideologically but is also tailored to what are considered the tastes and attitudes of the intended audience. In all the films discussed in this chapter the forms and meanings of The Affair, and particularly The Crisis and The Choice are bound very deeply into the way a given film regards adultery. While the films might ask viewers to consider a fictional choice, that choice – how it is framed for the viewer by the film – can slide easily into moral judgement. In this the treatment of The Ending is crucial.

As we have seen, a number of formal similarities emerge in the way that all these films fictionalise adultery, yet there are also some noteworthy distinctions in the ways the films approach it in moral terms. These have a bearing on how 'transgressive' adultery is deemed to be and what that 'transgression' is taken to mean. What is 'transgressive' about adultery and its representation differs from film to film. The group of films under discussion here range from those in which adultery results in an untimely fatality to those where adultery brings, in the long run, a highly beneficial and strengthening effect to at least one of the correspondents. Most adultery films can be plotted on a continuum that runs between the two.

Located at the 'death' end of the continuum, Constance's affair in *Unfaithful* leads directly to the death of Paul at the hands of her jealous husband, Ed. The fact that she had called off their affair only adds to the pathos of this crime of passion. The killing of Paul also, oddly perhaps, brings the married couple far closer together under the sign of transgression; they collude, at least for a while, to erase the affair and the death. Once the body is found, and they go through the possibilities, Ed decides because of intense feelings of guilt to turn himself in. In earlier adultery and 'fallen women' films it was more often the case that the female adulterer is killed off, as is the case with *Anna Karenina*. *Madame de…*, for example, dies because her heart is 'weak' (a broken heart), her will to live fails, and her heart finally gives out as she hears a single shot fired by her husband into the body of her lover. The long-established duel convention used in *Madame de…* becomes translated in more recent films into a less ritualised confrontation. In *Unfaithful*, Paul invites Ed into his apartment, and although it is clear that Ed is struggling with various emotions, it appears at first that they will talk the situation out. That is until Ed sees a snow-shaker that he had once given to Constance. It is the power of this signifier of love that drives him to use it to hit Paul, causing almost instant death. It is much later in the film that Constance and the audience learn that a picture of the family, all smiling, and a note expressing Ed's deep love for her, is concealed in the shaker's base.

Although *Unfaithful* has more explicit references to sex than in films made under the aegis of the Production Code, it is nonetheless the case that the events that lead up to murder indicts adultery as a danger. The family and the identities that come with that institution are put at risk, as is capitalism itself (if businessman Ed goes to prison as is likely he can no longer provide for his family or to the economy in general). Unlike *Zandalee* and *Madame de…* there is, however, no overt reference to metaphysical or religious strictures against adultery. The adulterous couple are blown together by an ill-wind at the start of their affair and Ed seems to be driven out of control on seeing the snow-shaker. But, as we will see elsewhere, it is desire, as something beyond the rational control of the protagonists, which drives them into transgressive waters. The film plays a sneaky game. It invites women viewers to identify with Constance's desire for the beautiful and interesting Paul, yet that gaze, that pleasure, is spoiled and punished by Ed's primal, uncontrollable, murderous impulse. While the film reverses the gender alignments that appeared in its directorial stable-mate *Fatal Attraction*, it is nonetheless the case that adulterous desire is figured here as an agent of chaos that threatens, but also affirms in a negative sense, the values of American middle-class society.

Out of all the films discussed here, *Zandalee* makes the most obvious claim on rhetorics of transgression through its baroque invocation of Catholic conceptions of sin and blasphemy. There are many aspects of the film that could be described as a morality play, yet it also has a more slippery and ambiguous relationship with transgression and adultery than is the case in the more 'protestant' and straight-forward *Unfaithful*. Throughout the film, events and dialogue are subject to the play of over determination, as are the positions of the characters who each bear tragic flaws. While Zandalee and Thierry (Judge Reinhold) die in the film, it is not melancholy and contrition that prevails, as in *Unfaithful*; instead there's a livid, vitalised excess at work, in terms of existential exuberance, symbolic and aestheticised displays, and in the shift from sexual ecstasy to hyperbolic grief. The film's heightened energetic emotional state moves it along the scale just a little closer to the 'positive' end of the continuum. Catholic imagery suffuses the film, supported by the New Orleans setting, and as with many adultery films, a hint of French flavour adds extra piquancy to the dish. A Catholic church provides the location for some important scenes and flag words such sin, redemption and absolution are common features of the dialogue. Johnny, Zandalee's lover, is presented as an archetypal rebel, signified visually by leather trousers, long hair plus goatee and a tattoo which he calls the 'black rose of fate'; he drinks whiskey, smokes and uses cocaine, for which he owes money. His vigorous painting style combines expressionism and action painting. While Johnny's identity is strongly marked as 'wild at heart' and in search of existential authenticity, Thierry, his childhood friend, tries to 'do the right thing', abandoning the more gentle and contemplative art of poetry to take over his dead father's business. In so doing Thierry's identity, bound deeply into being a bohemian poet, becomes fatally fragmented. He becomes uninterested in making love with his wife, and things worsen cumulatively when it emerges that his mother has been having an affair behind his father's back for years and he realises that Zandalee is having an affair with Johnny.

Zandalee's relationship with Johnny is full of conflict, however. She is never in love with him. To her he is fascinating, disgusting, so sure of himself and his desire, and in many ways is simply, in her words, a 'prick', someone to satisfy her lust in lieu of her husband. Johnny, on the other hand, regards their relationship as given. He tells her 'we're inevitable, I want to shake you naked and eat you alive, Zandalee'. It is his sexual will and the fact that he hits Zandalee's erotic sweet spot by saying her name that he 'frees' her desire. He speaks a great deal about freeing her but Zandalee does not desire to be free of Thierry; sugar sweet she is, but it is sex she requires, not to leave her much-loved husband. In practical terms, Johnny is out to steal his best friend's wife. Yet the film will not have it just in practical terms; instead, metaphysical (or should that be hysterical) forces are summoned.

The film labours to envelope proceedings in the trappings of an occulted order at the level of the diegesis; Catholic symbols litter the *mise-en-scène* and the characters' dialogue draw on ideas and terms that are associated with a Catholic worldview. Yet, following in the footsteps of *Madame de…*, it is never clear whether the deaths of Thierry and Zandalee are orchestrated by a metaphysical authority, dishing out punishment for sin, or if they are more simply a result of self-abrogation (Thierry) and coincidence (Zandalee). Both are always in play, one never cancels out the other. In terms of the psychological motivation of the characters, two opposite forces are at work: pagan fate and Christian free will (without which sin would not exist). In Johnny, as could be said of the film as a whole, these irreconcilable positions meet. The three main characters are determined, shaped, by what they believe the other to be and each are flawed. They are caught in a tangle of contradictions born of conflicting desires and demands.

Slippage between the metaphysical and psychological, as well as the tragic and the melodramatic, comes most sharply into focus in a scene that takes place in a Catholic church. Johnny's scorn for Zandalee's marriage and his disdain for authority (they both spring from the same source), find expression here as blasphemy; the ultimate religious transgression. He finds Zandalee in the church after he has failed to turn up for an assignation, a result of Thierry, his boss, letting him know that he had 'saved' Johnny from getting the sack. Thierry, who one can imagine was the weaker and more acquiescent of the two friends in childhood, is now in a position of authority with the power to 'save'. Johnny sits beside Zandalee ostentatiously smoking a cigarette. He demands that she leaves Thierry. She refuses, prompting him to shout into the echoing void 'Fuck. Shit. Well … strike me down, Lord, 'cos if you don't leave him I will make you fucking leave him'. She tries to cover his mouth, and is clearly very upset, but the blasphemy is further underscored as he pushes Zandalee against the wall of a confession booth and fucks her; her sex is his church and he thanks God after he has come. Like a tragic hero, his flaws are blindness and arrogance and from here on the diegetic path descends into greater emotional confusion and death. Viewers are invited to make a causal link between Johnny's blasphemy and the deaths that follow, but it demands a leap of faith to see the deaths of Thierry and Zandalee as the result of the transgression of divine edict.

It is of course possible to see these events in psychological terms and the fate/Christian context is used to give added meaning to the subjective workings of authority, inter-subjectivity and desire. Before Thierry dies, he and Johnny dance together, Apache-style,[45] making for a symbolic duel. This is an 'arty' moment; violence, at least at this stage, is translated into ritualised dance, but the image also displays the intimacy between the two men; an intimacy that is far from simple or straightforward. Their dance encapsulates the struggle of power and desire that drives the dramatic situation. Thierry's death is absurd and ambiguously coded. It is meaningful by virtue of its enigma. He falls off the boat, and despite being able to swim he allows himself to drown, biting Johnny when he tries to save him. In choosing to die and refusing attempts to save him, Thierry maintains a position of authority and power. Thereby some of the power he lost by failing to step successfully into his father's shoes (the business goes into liquidation) is recouped and importantly his death will prevent Johnny from stealing Zandalee (something his father failed to do in his mother's case).

Grieving the husband whom she thought had forgiven her sins (he even tells Johnny he will give her absolution), yet who has killed himself, Zandalee is in a precarious psychological position. It is now clear to her that she has had no control whatever over Thierry or Johnny and through her affair she has become an affect of their relationship. Her world and love itself have become impoverished because of her 'fall' into Johnny's bed. When Johnny comes to her house, and as he begins to make love to her, she calls out Thierry's name. Johnny seems to see at last that he cannot step into Thierry's shoes. Distressed and wearing Thierry's coat, Zandalee runs into the street chased by Johnny. A car appears, the driver calls Johnny's name. As she approaches the steps of the church, a gun fires and Zandalee is shot several times by a dealer who shouts 'You gotta make your accounts payable, man'. Zandalee dies in Johnny's arms and he carries her limp body towards the church. The deed and its tagline has a range of possible meanings. It happens at the level of the real yet invokes symbolic connotations.

Ambiguity serves this film well. Importantly it allows the film to invoke powerful and seductive rhetorics of transgression in terms of sin, absolution and redemption, yet keep their source veiled. In a Lacanian sense, the film invokes the operation of the Other.[46] It is also the case that erotic spice and symbolism are mixed to give the film 'artistic' and mythic/archetypal dimensions, much in the manner that French 'art' cinema often operates. *Zandalee* and *Unfaithful* borrow from the erotic clichés developed by earlier French films such as *Emmanuelle* and *The Story of O*, except in these latter films the otherness of desire and intrasubjectivity are realised in less dangerous terms because they take pains to say to viewers that they are to be consumed as erotic fantasies. Thierry's mother seems to sum up best *Zandalee*'s combination of desire and metaphysics: 'a touch of sin will give it *joie de vivre*' (the French term acting as an exoticising/eroticising agent). Yet *Zandalee*, like *Unfaithful*, also follows in the path of films made under the sway of the Production Code: adultery leads to directly death. *Zandalee*'s invocation of metaphysical powers within the text, as present in the older *Madame de…*, disguises the cranking of other machinery that shape the representation of adultery; the conservative ideological and institutional forces that demand blood sacrifice when the contract of monogamy is transgressed.

In contrast to the choreographed violent deaths of *Zandalee* and *Unfaithful*, which place these films at the negative end of the adultery continuum, *The Bridges of Madison County* begins with the reading of Francesca's will, who died naturally having lived a long and happy life. Here we switch poles with films that construct much more positive representations of adultery and its effects. *The Bridges of Madison County* might seem rather clichéd in certain ways but it has a number of features that shift away from the long-established convention of punishing the woman who falls from marital grace. The film allows Francesca to gain strength and fortitude from her brief sexual relationship with Robert. Even though she chooses not to go with him at the end of their four-day affair, the memory of their contact is cherished and she continues to love him. The affair brings enchantment and passion back into her predictable life. The reason behind her choice to stay with her husband and family is carefully laid out and it lies in the power of fantasy. She is clear that if she goes with Robert the romantic-magic aura she experienced will soon diminish; the everyday will prevail, differences in lifestyle preferences will occur. The relationship will turn ordinary, tarnished by the wear and tear of daily life. By staying home, Robert can continue to represent for Francesca an ideal love. Impossible in reality, yet fortifying, the affair remains as currency in the fantasy realm of possibility. Her choice to stay also affirms aspects of her identity that she values, such as being a good wife and mother, which some viewers, perhaps those in similar familial circumstances, will regard as an important condition of their identification with her desire.

When the secret of the relationship is revealed to her children, they are forced to see Francesca as a desiring woman, not just as a mother and wife. Her affair with Robert is regarded as a transgression, at least at first, by her son, but he comes to see things rather differently later. The transgression here is that Francesca's secret passion has sustained her in the roles of wife and mother as well as restoring her appetite for life. This may not seem that transgressive, particularly when compared to some of the more obviously transgressive codings of sex that appear later in this book, or if she had gone with Robert leaving behind her children. But her choice is nonetheless a subtle subversion of the marriage system; it suggests that marriage has a constraining effect on people and produces desires that cannot be fulfilled within the practical context of everyday married life. This is invoked without reference to histrionic, metaphysical punishments. While the more liberal-minded are less likely to regard Francesca's affair as anything more than a minor transgression, especially as the sex scenes are rather timid, the film nonetheless caused various American-based Christian groups to condemn it as advocating adultery.[47] In addition, the house where much of the film was shot, known locally as the 'Francesca house' and where memorabilia related to the film could be purchased, was set on fire by arsonists, possibly by those who disliked the film's positive take on adultery. Some Christians, however, welcomed Francesca's choice to sacrifice happiness to preserve the integrity of her family.[48] While the film could not be called a 'feminist' film, appeal to its intended audience lies in the fictionalised account of a woman's particular perspective on the experience of contradictions between marriage and desire. Francesca's legacy is that once her children learn about the aspects of her life hitherto hidden from them, they both go away to reassess their own relationships. Her son renews his bonds with his harassed wife, while her daughter leaves her rather indifferent husband. This is an economical ending. Francesca retains her 'good' mother status. She passes on her 'real' experiences of the split between passion and commitment, and, like her children, the audience is encouraged to assess their lives in the light of Francesca's particular choices. In a small way this subverts in liberalist terms the more usual Hollywood ethic where conservative gender and moral values are reaffirmed.

The Piano also has what might regarded as a positive ending. Ada chooses life – a life lived with Baines. This choice seems far more life-affirming than the Victorian gothic-style situation within which she found herself with Stewart within which sex and creativity were regarded as alien and transgressive. This outcome is open to an alternative interpretation, however. Ada's choice to live, to talk, might be regarded as her acceptance and willing entry into the social order, heterosexuality and 'normality'; her wildness and creativity tamed. Yet if Ada's 'will' had chosen death at the bottom of the ocean, then Jane Campion's film would have followed in the footsteps of Thomas Hardy's morbid treatment of his lovers and the conventionalised treatment of 'excess' found in classical Hollywood. For some critics and viewers this would have proved a more preferable ending than that provided by the 'normalisation' ending. Ada and Campion chose to accept the particular constraints imposed by 'life' and thereby presented a film, an ending, that the majority of women viewers were more likely to recognise and identify with. As Ada does not choose death and because adultery leads to a place where she can express her creativity, learn once more to speak and explore sexuality, I would place the film at the positive end of the continuum. Yet it is also possible to regard the film as having two endings. The image of Ada floating above her piano is memorable and Ada herself reminds viewers of this other ending to her story. It is therefore possible to see the film as having a dual ending, each set to appease different forms of feminism (radical and liberal).

Mary Ann Doane argues that in the woman's film of 1940s Hollywood, women characters that stray from the marital path are punished for their excessive desires: 'woman commits adultery, she must die' (1987: 120). The formula locates adultery as transgressive in dramatic, social and metaphysical terms. However, on closer examination, this is not always the case. *Frenchman's Creek*, for example, bucks the trend, and it bears some similarities to *The Bridges of Madison County*. As a hybrid mix of swashbuckling action and the woman's film, the film juxtaposes Dona's life as 'cabin boy' and her life as an aristocratic Lady. As a cabin boy on board Jean's pirate ship, Dona transgresses that which defines her social role: she is no longer a 'Lady', in class and gender terms. Jean and Dona are united under the banner of risk and simple enjoyment of 'natural' pleasures. Dona inadvertently kills Lord Rockingham when he threatens to do the same to her, for giving her sexual favours to the pirate and not him. She then stages a daring raid to rescue Jean from the prison where he awaits the hangman's noose, after which she makes her choice to become once again Lady Dona St Columb rather than a cabin boy. This choice is partly prompted by the recognition of how important her children are to her. Like Francesca, she nonetheless enshrines the memory of her summer of high-adventure and love under the stars to fortify her through life. The film, and Dona, therefore escaped the formula of death enforced by the Code. Perhaps the film avoided censure because of changes to public morality brought about by World War II. As with Francesca, the important factor here that is designed to keep the audience, and the MPDAA, on side is that both women choose to be 'good mothers' over their own pleasure and desire. Dona's transgressive escapade is also very clearly coded, in both a generic and costumed sense, as fantasy (much as Francesca's affair becomes the generative source of a fantasy that sustains against lack). *Frenchman's Creek* is set in the past, a past regarded as ribald and immoral (Restoration England). But while we are invited to identify with the clever, passionate and active Dona, we must also identify with the fact that her indulgence put her children in danger and her decision to bring herself into order (it was the killing of Rockingham that catalyses her decision, demonstrating perhaps how a strong experience of transgression might operate to reaffirm boundaries). Nonetheless, what lingers, after the film is over, is Dona's guileful audacity and struggle to find something sensual and real. This she does through adultery and adventure and those of us who are smitten by such romantic daring-do are left, like Francesca, with something to fantasise about.

Over the range of films discussed here one common feature that is in play is whether adultery is contextualised as lust or love. In the adultery-as-life-affirming films, it is love rather than lust that prevails; in the case of *The Bridges of Madison County* and *Frenchman's Creek* the women fall in love with men who represent for them something 'ideal'. They are sexually desirable but represent something more than this; once Dona and Francesca choose to leave these men, they become almost sanctified, raised by their absence to a higher realm as the material of fantasy. Working with the Lacanian axiom that 'there is no such thing as a sexual relation', Renata Salecl claims:

> Women redouble their partners because they can never be sure what kind of an object they are in the other's desire. Thus for a woman it is better to fantasise that there is more than one man who is emotionally interested in her. But, paradoxically, a woman might get the most assurance about her own value as an object in fantasising about a man … who never actually desires her in the first place. (2002: 97)

In this sense these two films have it both ways: Dona and Francesca, as figures with whom to identify, have the love of two men, but as viewers women can indulge in fantasising about these men who do not desire us, yet we are acquainted with the nature of their desire by virtue of that identification.

In the case of the films at the death end of the continuum, lust is not justified or sanctified by love. Rather than masters of their desire achieved through the sublimation of lust into love and fantasy through sublimating action of love and fantasy, Constance and Zandalee are victims of their sexual desire: sex indulged in for its own sake is represented in transgressive terms as addictive, like a drug (Johnny even rubs cocaine into Zandalee's genitals). This seems to hark back to Doane's notion that women who are excessively sexual are irrecoupable. *The Good Girl* appears to sit, somewhat eccentrically, between the two poles. Justine desires Tom out of boredom and then gets bored with him. Lust is not overwhelming, sex with Tom is not mind-blowingly passionate, therefore not addictive, and nor does she come to love Tom. There is no use of soft-core aesthetics to make sex exotic, titillating or passionate, which may have invited viewers to identify more closely with Justine's sexual encounters. As such, the broader context and effects of the affair are emphasised. Justine is far from being in control and events just spin off helter-skelter from her 'transgression'. She is bribed into having sex with Bubba (Tim Blake Nelson), who becomes equal to his friend, her husband, through the act, and then learns she is pregnant. It cannot be her husband's baby as it has just been confirmed by medics that he is sterile (paternity is therefore open to question). Justine is not enough of a victim to be like her sadean namesake; she does take some pleasure in her affair and dealings with Tom, but despite the fact that she is instrumental to Tom's death and dupes her husband she is no Juliette. She would have to be far more actively transgressive, lustful and in control of events to make the film slide further down to the death pole. But, yet again, and despite the film's differences to other more melodramatic adultery films, death accompanies adultery.

Throughout all these films various forces are at work which shape into conventionalised form the representation of fictional adultery. Cinematic formulas for presenting adultery have solidified over time. Adultery films may have become more explicitly sexual and adopted features that are associated with different cinemas (horror/thriller, independent, softcore), but their formal structure has remained fairly static. The representation of adultery is 'weak' transgression, at least from a liberal perspective, in the context of cinema as a whole, but it is often appended to other more heavily transgressive events or associated with broader social issues. The adultery in *Unfaithful* leads directly to murder and in *Zandalee* it is associated with archetypal rebellion, existential angst and drugs. As such both these films have a foot in the erotic thriller camp (see Williams 2005). While *The Good Girl* draws on the 'generation x' trope, which helps flag the film's status as an 'indie' film and allows the film to indulge in a combination of quirky humour and un-Hollywood realism. In all the films discussed here, adulterous relationships kick drama into action (even in *The Good Girl*), but adultery *per se* is never intended to shock or disgust the viewer (although its consequences might). It is presented in such a way to enable the viewer to identify with the dilemmas and emotions experienced by the central protagonist. This experience goes some way to assigning the viewer a subjective, rather than objective, position on the topic, whereby the frisson of transgression is made present and moral judgement becomes more complex. This can therefore sit uncomfortably with the punishment implications of a 'death' ending. Cinematic adultery operates under the sign of transgression, not because adultery in itself is beyond the pale, but because adultery is associated with the disruptive force of desire. Produced perversely by situation, 'rogue' desire is the chaotic agent that promotes adultery, drama and dissatisfaction with the status quo. Marriage is no longer regarded in such a widespread way as a necessity, but a viewer may not have to be married to identify with the protagonist/s; rather it is the recognition of an experience of an insistent desire that sits in opposition to the status quo that prevails. It is with this that we are invited to identify through an appealing character. Even in those films that have a more positive spin, the 'transgression' lies in the fact that desire itself runs the show; it might bring a life-enhancing benefit but it is still risky and beyond the control of the protagonists. Self-autonomy and self-determination are undermined; hence the invocation in some of these films of an extrinsic agent (the 'ill-wind of fate' motif and blasphemy, for example). The fact that adultery films continue to be made suggests that the topic still has cultural saliency. This lies beyond 'marriage' and extends to the ways in which we are all likely to experience a gap between what we wish for and what we have; the space between is that within which fantasy and desire work. It is this 'occult power', working alongside more tangible institutional forces, that shapes adultery as transgression.

The Beast Within: Animal Transformation and Bestiality

$\mathcal{W}$e stray now into the lair of the beast, a terrain in which the air is thick with the collective dreams of myth and fairytale and tinged with the infamy of bestiality. Crossing the human/animal divide is a theme that is regularly taken up in fiction-based cinema, suggesting that we are dealing here with a constituent frontier that requires to be reworked in accordance with shifts in a given cultural climate. When beasts show eroticised desire for humans in cinema it is figured in a variety of ways yet it is always keyed into transgression, albeit drained a little of that frisson by virtue of the presence of fictional markers. Similarly when humans become beasts it is almost always figured as either a return of the repressed, the dominance of instinctual drives and throwing off the shackles of civilisation, or as an exaggerated literal demonstration of the material 'otherness' of the body. In many cases both are in evidence. These particular approaches to the subversion of the human/animal divide provide a conventionalised formula for figuring, and containing, the sensational and dramatic potential of transgression. Bestiality of the literal type found in the most excessive forms of hard-core is not the focus of this chapter. Such films do exist and find distribution, and examples can even be found in quite early hard-core, as indicated by the nuns and dogs routine in *Devoirs de Vacances* (1920), a loop included in *The Good Old Naughty Days* collection. Real bestiality in film constitutes a very strong form of transgression and infringes most national-based obscenity laws as well as laws that protect animals from cruelty and mistreatment, however. Nothing is left to the imagination and they are exploitative in the extreme, purveyed to solicit prurient curiosity. These films capitalise on the spectacle of degradation and dehumanisation which bestiality has come through a range of discursive formations to mean. Men are rarely participants in such films (where they do its in a jokey context) and there appears to be a strong misogynist current at work. Women who participate in such acts are reduced to the status of both animal and appetite, providing visible proof of 'woman's' sexual voracity and difference. In reality those who make such films often exploit the financial desperation of women with drug habits. While bestiality in reality – particularly when it seeks to exploit – evokes disgust, it is, however, tacitly present in a range of mainstream fictions, where it is presented allegorically, metonymically or by way of suggestion but never explicitly. It is to the more acceptable presence in more mainstream and generic cinemas of animals anthropomorphised through their desire for the human and transformations from beast to human, and from human to beast, that we now turn.

Stories about humans who are turned by supernatural means into beasts are found in *The Odyssey* (c.800 BCE) as well as appearing in myths and legends of many different cultures. Trailing backwards still further into the mists of pre-history, Palaeolithic cave paintings and engravings (c.13,000–c.9,000 BCE) depict men wearing the skins of animals or merged with animals, such as those that appear in Grotte des Trois Frères in the French Pyrenees and Le Gabillou in the Dordogne (see Hutton 1997: 10, 12; Twitchell 1985: 4–6). It maybe that the making of these images is in itself a magical process enabling men to acquire characteristics of the animals whose skins they are wearing; this is interpretative speculation, however. Images of men copulating with animals are also found in later prehistorical images in Scandinavia. Although largely ignored until recently, some anthropologists and archaeologists have suggested that these images represent communion with a totemic animal-god ('the spiritual guardians of the clan or tribe' (Hutton 1997: 7)). Within 'new age' culture, these enigmatic and fragmentary remainders from the far-distant past have been interpreted as evidence of shamanistic practice, a mode of magic that works with the occulted spiritual forces of nature. Altered states of consciousness and shape-shifting are also important components of shamanism and it is through transformation to animal form that prehistory, the revival of interest in magic/alternative religions and cinema converge. In the more recent werewolf films, such as *Wolf* and *Ginger Snaps Back* (2004), for example, there is a tendency to include aspects of shamanism into the formula. Older werewolf films used other forms of folk magic or fairytale to invoke the supernatural and the primal. As occurs across a range of cinemas and other media, the pre-historic and mythic past becomes a screen onto which various fantasies about origins and othered forms of knowledge are projected (see Krzywinska 2006). Transformation from human to animal deals in divisions fundamental to definitions of the human and civilisation and it is therefore not surprising perhaps that bestial fictions often turn to the ancient past, to the primal and the mythical. As a place of nature-based magic (which would include the affinity with animals in tropes like shape-shifting), aspects of myth and the pre-historic have also been mobilised to critique the 'civilised' present. This includes 'new age' concerns over the exploitation of natural resources, the dominance of rational-based, sanctioned, knowledge and disregard for the rhythms of the earth. As such, it is talismanic magic, herbalism or love that cures or helps the victims of bestial transformation, not science.

With its roots deeply embedded in ancient stories and images, animal transformation carries certain resonant features that make it an attractive topic for cinematic treatment.

Tales of transformation invoke the stories we are likely to have heard as children, intensified because of their ancient, paganish ring. Transformation also lends itself to the more modern magics provided by cinematic special effects. As we shall see, animal transformation has a strong connection to the release of repressed desires, thereby making a claim on transgression, but like their mythical forebears these tales are often used to shore up definitions of civilisation and socialisation, particularly through the common thematic focus on the tension between personal agency and external determinant forces. Two particular Greek myths set the scene for the way in which bestial transformation and bestiality are linked to the other: desire and offence/taboo.[49] The first is the story of Lykaon, a King of Arcady. There are many versions of this story, but the gist is that he served up human meat to the god Zeus and to demonstrate the beastliness of such a heinous desecration to all men, Zeus turns Lykaon into a werewolf. Lykaon's transgression is regarded by Zeus as indicative of humanity's degeneration into barbarity and he sends a great cleansing flood that wipes out animals and humans (with the exception of a few who are saved because they build an ark). In Ovid's *Metamorphosis* (c.7AD), a series of tales about men and women transformed in shape by the Greek gods for good or ill, it is made clear that Lykaon (the name itself means 'of the wolf') is not simply transformed into a wolf but retains aspects of his human form. This is how Ovid has Zeus say what occurred:

> I with my avenging flames brought the house crashing down upon its household gods, gods worthy of such a master. Lykaon fled, terrified, until he reached the safety of the silent countryside. There he uttered howling noises, and his attempts to speak were all in vain. His clothes changed into bristling hairs, his arms to legs, and he became a wolf. His own savage nature showed in his rabid jaws, and he now directed against his flocks his innate lust for killing. He had a mania, even yet, for shedding blood. But, though he was a wolf, he retained some traces of his original shape. The greyness of his hair was the same, his face showed the same violence, his eyes gleamed as before, and he presented the same picture of ferocity. (1981: 34)

There are several ways of interpreting this particular transformation. Lykaon becomes a symbol of the move away from the earlier practice of human sacrifice. His story provides a cautionary expression of a categorical shift that helped to define classical Greece as 'civilised' (later the Romans would use human sacrifice as way of categorising other cultures as barbaric). Zeus requires only animal sacrifice in his honour, which demonstrates a metaphysically ordained difference between man and beast (transformed into a werewolf Lykaon is not one, nor the other). Lykaon's tale shows that werewolf form is both the product of a transgression against the metaphysically ordained moral order and a transgression of the factors that define 'humanity' and civilisation. That he takes the shape of a wolf is significant for our analysis of animal transformation in cinema. Marina Warner has argued that the wolf has been used in myth and fairytale as an image of uncontrolled appetite (1998:

10). Extrapolating from the cautionary tale of Lykaon – via Bataille and containment theory – she suggests that flesh-eating monsters 'vicariously represent abominations against society, civilisation and the family, yet are vehicles for expressing ideas of proper behaviour and due order' (1998: 11).

A similar cautionary tale against not respecting the law-making wishes of the gods is found in the myth of the Minotaur's origins, this time in a tale that relates more specifically to bestiality. The myth is rather condensed in Ovid but expanded elsewhere and there are many different versions. To prove his connection to the higher powers, King Minos asked the gods for a magnificent white bull to be given to him so that he could sacrifice it for their glory. It duly arrives but so beautiful is the creature that he cannot bear to sacrifice it. A more ordinary replacement is found and the bull left to enjoy the cows. As punishment, Pasipheë, the wife of Minos, is made by Zeus to lust after the bull. She has a wooden cow made which allows her to consummate her passion (see Graves 1998: 273–4). As a result Pasipheë gives birth to the Minotaur, 'the strange hybrid creature had revealed his wife's disgusting love affair to everyone' (1998: 274). As befits its monstrous status, the minotaur feeds on flesh and blood (Ovid 1981: 183). As with Lykaon, it is the transgression of a compact with the gods that is punished by the blurring of that sacred line that divides man from beast. (The bestial motif runs even deeper in this genealogical myth cluster as Minos is also the offspring of Zeus and Europa, Zeus having impregnated her in the guise of a beautiful white bull, in this case to escape the notice of his wife Hera.)

In an effort to understand the universal order of things, the place of man in that order and how he came into being, Classical Greek philosophers were preoccupied with explaining the differences between man and animals (they were not that bothered about women). These views contribute to the formulation of a discourse in which animals, and by extension desires and actions associated with animals, are used negatively to define through concepts of civilisation and rationality man's superior difference. Epicurus argued that animals were the mirror of nature and that they had no 'intelligence' (a view commonly held). Empedocles argued in more mythological terms that in the earliest times building-block components such as blood and flesh came together to form limbs, these limbs searched for their like, but often married up 'incorrectly' to form hybrid creatures (such as the Minotaur, satyrs or centaurs). Hesiod distinguished man from animals through the capacity of the former to use a concept of justice, while it was the power to reason for Pliny that made the difference. For both Hesiod and Pliny, the ability to make a moral judgement constitutes the distinction between man and beast (see Vallence 1998: 40). Classical culture is suffused with images and stories of man/beast hybrids. Lykaon and the Minotaur lust for human meat, whereas satyrs and silens, half-men half-goats, lust for sex and wine. Within classical culture animal hybrids had an ethical and category-fixing function as well as making for dramatic tales and spectacle (for example, at festivals people often dressed up as satyrs). While we should not ignore the many historical and cultural differences, it seems that in terms of epistemology and entertainment the legacy of such ideas are still present in 'bestial' cinema.

While myth is clearly imaginary and allegorical at one level, it often carries an inner truthfulness, a meaningful significance. If it did not then a particular myth would not in an oral culture survive beyond its initial telling. This is also the case for animal transformation in cinema. Many classical myths underpinned or gave meaning to religious rituals, giving support to Walter Burkert's view that myth contains 'a secondary, partial reference to something of collective importance' (cited by Bremmer 1998: 484). While the generic bestial transformation fictions of cinema do not support religious 'rituals', at least not beyond that of post-modern Hallowe'en, it would seem that ethical structures, thresholds, rites of passage, difference, otherness and what constitutes the 'human' are still being worked through fictional metamorphic and bestial formulations. The threshold that keeps the human from beastliness is one that needs, it seems, to be constantly tested and affirmed.

Before the strict implementation of the Production Code, Hollywood of the early 1930s had a strange and rather surprising preoccupation with bestiality. Apes desire beautiful young women in overt ways in *King Kong* and *Murders on the Rue Morgue*, and something similar is implied in one scene in *The Sign of the Cross*. Humans transformed into beasts or beasts transformed into humans provide another rendition of the bestiality theme in *Dr Jekyll and Mr Hyde* (considered in Part I, 'Narrative Formulas') and *Island of Lost Souls* (1933). and while these films present bestiality in different ways and attribute to it different meanings, each operates, at least to some extent, to use established rhetorics of transgression to provoke horror and/or sensationalism. These films also use techniques of implication to suggest that which could not be shown or seen in order to avoid industrial censorship or the infringement of obscenity laws.

In *The Sign of the Cross* the spectre of bestiality arises within the general context of pagan decadence. Set in Classical Rome, depraved Emperor Nero (Charles Laughton) indulges in all kinds of behaviours designated as anti-Christian. All this amoral paganism, into which lust, homosexuality, non-monogamy, torture and murder are enlisted, makes for spectacle and sensationalism and provides a context within which bestiality does not seem so anomalous. After a group of pious Christians horrified by pagan mores are caught practising their illegal faith they are condemned to die, providing entertainment for Nero's subjects in the gladiatorial arena and, in a more general sense, proof of the perverse and inhuman 'civilisation' of paganism. While most are eaten by lions and tigers, special treatment is reserved for the more attractive young women. One is tied horizontally between two posts so that her body swings close to the ground. That she wears nothing but a strategically placed flower garland adds a certain erotic coding to the scene. Four large alligators waddle towards her, punctuated by a close-up of an alligator's mouth that could easily accommodate a human body. She screams. A cutaway shot of women in the crowd follows; these women turn away from the spectacle, sufficing to show that the woman in the arena has been devoured. The range of exotic and ferocious animals that appear in the arena are paralleled with Nero and his wife, Poppea (Claudette Colbert), both know no pity and embody lust. In the next scene a further woman appears, also wearing only a garland and tied upright to a statue of a satyr, his lewd face leers over her shoulder and appears to hold her steady for the embrace of a large ape. There is more than death in this scene as a sexual connotation is in evidence by virtue of the context in which the scene appears. There are a number of reaction shots from the crowd, who appear more appalled at this woman's fate than all the other monstrous deaths that precede and follow this. As half-man half-goat, the satyr to whom she is tied provides a fairly obvious classical allusion to bestiality. Satyrs personify unfettered 'primitive' lust and drunken licentiousness in their form and their behaviour. It does not, therefore, take much of a leap of the imagination to fill in the gap with a cross-species sexual horror. Even if the satyr's symbolism is not recognised, it is likely that those contemporary viewers that had recently seen the woman-lusting apes of *Murders on the Rue Morgue*, or the following year, *King Kong*, may well have made such an assumption.

All manner of behaviours designated as perverse are present in the film, bestiality is just one. Nero and his wife Poppea represent 'degenerate' and 'inhuman' behaviours and the monstrous spectacle and sensationalism of subjecting Christians to an ignominious death in the arena had biblical precedence (the technique of negative example was also used by D. W. Griffith, but perhaps in better faith). This was enough to earn the film an outright ban in the US in 1934. Only in *Caligula* (*Caligola*, 1979), which, like *The Sign of the Cross*, tested regulatory boundaries, does something similar crop up in a film intended for the mainstream market.

Erik the ape is in the prime of his life, so says his interlocutor Dr Mirakle (Bela Lugosi), and as such he is looking for a mate. *Murders on the Rue Morgue*'s Mirakle is typical of Universal Studios' collection of mad scientists: he believes that anything is permitted to further science. Like Dr Frankenstein, his science works against god and nature, producing gothic horrors. Mirakle's science might be groundbreaking but because of its unethical status he makes a living giving lectures on evolution in a travelling show. As if in proof of this theory, he has attributes that link him with Erik. He is able to speak Erik's language and, as if springing from a folk tale, his eyebrows meet. His quest is to find a woman, a human woman and not a female ape, whose blood will mingle with Erik's. What the product of the union might be is left hanging, but enough information is present to cue some rather unsavoury imaginings. One particular scene would not look out of place in films based on the work of the Marquis de Sade. A woman, who we are led into believing is a prostitute (the term itself is avoided), is brought in from the streets and tied to a St Andrew's cross (X-shaped), first seen expressionist-style in silhouette. After a lot of screaming, which interrupts Mirakle's thought processes, she dies. Mirakle comments that despite her beauty and youth her blood is 'impure' because of her non-virtuous profession and it will not mix with Erik's. It seems the audience is expected to surmise that blood can be polluted by 'sin'. Erik has, however, chosen his preferred mate, Camille (Sidney Fox), the young and pretty fiancée of a local medical student.

Erik is clearly enamoured with Camille from their first meeting. As an indication that this is not simply a projected fancy of Mirakle's, Erik takes and caresses her bonnet. Towards the end of the film, Mirakle establishes that Camille's blood is pure and as he moves in to do some kind of procedure on her, Eric kills him and and escapes with an unconscious Camille, taking to the Parisian rooftops. Eventually he is shot and she is saved in a scaled-down version of what occurs at the end of *King Kong*, released one year later. To a lesser extent than Kong, Erik is afforded some human attributes through his desire for a pretty woman and, oddly enough, he saves her from Mirakle's scientific species-mixing ministrations, but did Erik have something more physical in mind as he carries Camille off?

It is instructive to compare Erik to Kong, mainly because it has a bearing on the way the two films render the bestiality they conjure. Eric is not humanised as fully as Kong. Despite their similarities, Erik's death is far less moving than the death of Kong. Kong's love for his 'bride', Ann Darrow (Fay Wray), is instrumental to the creation of audience empathy. Techniques to promote empathy with Kong are far more carefully established than is the case with Erik. Kong's highly animated facial features help to endow him with a large repertoire of visible emotions that humanise him and much of his screen time is taken up in protecting Ann from various monsters, which costs him injury, freedom and eventually death. In this sense he is a typical Hollywood action hero, albeit rather larger and hairier than usual. And, like most Hollywood action heroes, he protects the heroine because he desires her for his own. This is most evident in two scenes that are quite similar. In one of these Kong tickles Ann a bit and then sniffs his fingers. It is a comic moment, underlined by the way the film is scored to mimic his tickling actions, a device that might be expected more readily in a cartoon. In the other, Kong finally gets to look at his 'bride' after defeating several other monsters and begins to peel off her clothing. With its transgressive connotations, the scene was removed for the 1938 re-release of the film on PCA recommendation. This overt invocation of bestial desire is parodied in *Flesh Gordon* (1974), a campy soft-core version of the science fiction series *Flash Gordon*, flagged by its tagline 'Planet Porno Bombards Earth with Sex Rays! … Send For Flesh'. A giant-size lizard-like monster picks up Dale Ardor (Cindy Hopkins) and begins to take off her clothes, stating in laconic tones 'I just want to see your tits', thereby making the bestial dimension of the similar scene in *King Kong* even more clear.

Erik does not have Kong's charisma, however, nor does he have his spectacular, colossal stature. But Erik presents a more disturbing and enigmatic image than Kong. Kong is animated consistently using stop-frame, thereby fixing his form and placing him in the register of fantasy. By contrast, Erik is sometimes a real chimp, at others a man in a gorilla suit and when seen in silhouette killing Mirakle he adopts the form of a large baboon. Such visual inconsistencies break the rules of cinematic continuity as well as destabilising Erik's biological category. There are practical and budgetary reasons for this, of course. But, however inadvertently, Erik is a stitched-together man-beast, underlined by the fact that he is capable of rationalisation and sophisticated speech (although only Mirakle is party to this directly). As such Erik is a transgressor of the borders that define that delicately posed, and discursively policed, difference between animal and human. This is the reason that evolution finds a place in *Murders on the Rue Morgue*'s circus: evolution challenges the cross-denominational axiom that God made man in his own image. Erik's part-man status is signalled as horrific in a range of ways, partly through his desire for Camille and partly through the gasps of the diegetic audience who learn that they are related to Erik. Origin of the species acquires a strong sexual current (which is open potentially for a racist reading). In addition, the use of chiaroscuro lighting, the creepy expressionist-style circus, the odd camera angles, embed Erik and evolution theory in the perverse accoutrements of the gothic.

Like Eric, Kong rescues the girl he loves and then dies for that love. But unlike Erik, Kong is the hero of the show, even if he does kill a few people by stepping on them or throwing them off tall buildings. Kong is worshipped by natives and gawped at by New Yorkers. He is a spectacular sign of raw, primal power and virility, yet, like Ann's tough-guy boyfriend, is tamed by feminine beauty. The audience is invited to sympathise with Kong's desires and situation. His emotional state is given far greater prominence than Erik, enticing audiences to fall for his charms; necessary if his death is to be filled with pathos. *Murders on the Rue Morgue* is much less coherent than *King Kong* and has none of its action-movie verve, partly due to a huge budget difference and production time. *King Kong* has a certain charm and even carried the 'tall dark stranger' of women's fantasy as a tagline. This can be explained in part by the fact that horror films of this period tried to introduce 'romantic' elements to appeal to a female audience (see Berenstein 1996: 12, 60–87). The tagline eroticises Kong, but the film offsets the perversity of bestiality in its anthropomorphic, stop-frame, action-movie exuberance. By contrast *Murders on the Rue Morgue*, is steeped in gothic perversity; bestiality is closely allied to sadism and is messily over-determined throughout the story. Differences in genre also contribute to the uneasiness of *Murders on the Rue Morgue*, the action-adventure and animation of *King Kong* codes more sharply into the film its impossibility. Kong's cartoonish anthropomorphism provides part of the reason for the difference but it also has to do with the difference in their size. Like the gorilla in *The Sign of the Cross*, Erik is of a size whereby cross-species sex would be possible, whereas Kong's huge size makes this totally implausible. While it might be expected in a low-budget horror context, it is extremely unlikely in today's market that a blockbuster of the equivalent to *King Kong* aimed at the widest possible market would take the risk of choosing a subject that so obviously calls on bestiality (remakes aside).

Also made in the Pre-Code period, *Island of Lost Souls* begins a cycle of animal transformation films (along with *Dr Jekyll and Mr Hyde*). In *Island of Lost Souls*, Dr Moreau (Charles Laughton, again in the role of the transgressor) is a geneticist, working to speed up evolution, thereby turning animals into humans, or part-humans. As Thomas Doherty has noted, the 'ur-theme' of Pre-Code horror was 'regression and devolution' (1999: 298). With more recent interest in genetic engineering as well as a fundamental concern about the origins of civilisation, it is not perhaps surprising that this is a common theme for horror, although meanings associated with the theme have changed. Doherty goes on to state that *Island of Lost Souls* typifies the Pre-Code approach to the regression theme as the inhabitants of the island are 'reduced to a bestial state, the veneer of civilisation torn away' (ibid.). American horror of this era often plays through images of the primitive and the uncivilised as a means to establish sensational impact and bestiality fits the bill perfectly. In *Island of Lost Souls*, it is however the case that Moreau's science is working to create a 'progression' in evolutionary terms. His eugenicist aim is to turn animals into part-humans, not humans into part-animals. He struggles with the fact that 'degeneracy' occurs, a reversal of the process; in Moreau's words 'the stubborn beast-flesh creeping back'.

Moreau's efforts are not though in the service of the greater good because he enjoys playing god. He clearly finds sadistic pleasure in his manipulative work. In addition to medical experimentation, he is also interested to find out if his only female creation, Lota (Kathleen Burke), a panther turned human, will have 'human' feelings for a male visitor to the island. Indeed she falls in love with him, and although her human object of affection kisses her, he rejects her advances because of his love for another woman. Lota eventually dies saving him in a fight with another human-beast creature, Ouran (Hans Steinke). Ouran is permitted by Moreau to enter the compound and breaks into a woman visitor's bedroom. It is clear that his intent is rape (see Benshoff 1997: 54). Thwarted in this attempt, Ouran is commanded by Moreau to kill the man the visitors send to get help. But seeing Ouran break the law that Moreau had laid down, the horde of humanised animals turns on Moreau. He dies in the House of Pain, the place in which the 'manimals' underwent their excruciatingly painful transformations. The uprising of the manimals has lead some critics such as Doherty to suggest that the film provides an allegory of insurrection, a dimension that lead the film to be given a special designation in Australia: '"NEN" – not to be exhibited to natives' (1999: 311). Doherty also reports that the PCA refused a seal of approval to reissue the film in 1935. They demanded that the film be edited to cut out mention of Moreau's pleasure in being godlike and anything to do with the 'mating' of beast and human being (1999: 312).

J. P. Telotte argues that *Island of Lost Souls* follows a more general trend in science fiction cinema, wherein the body becomes the subject of science, knowable from the 'inside out' (1995: 73). However the body – associated at some deep level with an insistent strain of animal-ness – resists such applied knowledge, breaking free of its control. Moreau's victims ultimately undo his behaviourist and bodily re-programming. They rise up to take revenge on the process of socialisation that has been forced upon them by science. This is the basis of the film's body-horror: animal transformation literalises and exaggerates the material reality of the unruly, instinct-driven body. Issues of control and power, resonating through individual psychology and the social contract, are invoked in this potent bundle. Moreau's law, 'not to run on all fours, not to eat meat, not to spill blood', is intended to civilise, to keep animal instincts from the door, but suppressive forces are ultimately insufficient. In the context of *Island of Lost Souls* bestiality is a sexual perversion borne of science – the mixing of the species – and it is open to being read in terms of eugenics, social engineering and racism, each prominent in general discourse in the 1930s. Within the ancient tales of Lykaon and Minos, it is human arrogance (hubris) that invokes the wrath of the gods, which in the case of Minos is connected with bestiality. Within *Murders on the Rue Morgue* and *Island of Lost Souls* it is

Mirakle and Moreau's arrogant manipulation of the genetic basis for species laid down by Nature (or God) that leads to the perversion of cross-species sex. This moral logic redirects their science from the noble path of enlightenment to the ignoble byway of gothic science. In addition, and as is the case with *King Kong*, bestial desire for human flesh in these films is the result of the ill-treatment, capture and vivisection, of animals by humans. This arises because there is disregard for the dignity and suffering of animals.

Following the PCA's edicts on implied bestiality, the animal transformation films of the 1940s were, in the main, pruned of any reference to sexuality. The transformations of man into beast in *The Ape Man* (1943) and *The Wolf Man* (1941), both low-budget B movies, lead to blood-lust rather than sexual lust, as occurs in later animal transformation films. In the former film the scientist-turned-ape (Bela Lugosi) kills because he needs spinal fluid to return to his human form. It is implied that in becoming ape-like through scientific experimentation his moral faculty has degenerated. In the latter film, once bitten by a werewolf, Larry Talbot (Lon Chaney Jr) cannot control his transformation and in half-wolf/half-human form he is driven to murder. Talbot is no Hollywood hero. When he comes back to his home town in rural England, after a protracted stay in the US, he is full of confidence and humour. On becoming werewolf he becomes alienated, full of anguish and is led to his death at the hands of his father. This shift lends the film a pessimistic noirish sensibility. The metamorphic 'degenerating' agent is connected lightly to Eastern Europe, following a geographic association with supernaturalism used in many gothic fictions. It is a gypsy in wolf form (Bela Lugosi again) whom Talbot chases and is bitten by, but pains are taken to show that the gypsy is as much a random victim as Talbot. The 'other' intrudes on the American body from outside, from Europe, chiming, perhaps, for contemporary American viewers with their experience of the war. Being bitten was a case of being in the wrong place at the wrong time, rather than as punishment for any transgression, as with the Greek myths and the mad scientists. This arbitrariness becomes common in the diegesis of later werewolf films (being a teenager is core to becoming werewolf in a large number of films, but even in this context becoming a werewolf could, however, happen to anyone in that age range). Talbot's transformation is not based overtly on any occulted moral logic, unlike the mad scientists who bring about their own downfall through their transgressive challenge to the creationist role of God. Talbot might grow hairy on the outside at the time of the full moon, but his transformation is not connected overtly or subtly to sin or sexual desire.

In contrast, *Cat People* (1942) makes far greater and more overt links between animal transformation, sin and sex. Irena Dubrovna (Simone Simon) cannot 'kiss' her husband because she believes that this will bring out something very dangerous in her. She originates from a Serbian village (Eastern Europe is once more the origin of supernatural terrors), where, in the past, cat people lived who did not abide by the rule of God. They were brought to order by King John, but some escaped into the hills. Irena knows intuitively that sex, jealousy and anger will bring out her panther within. She becomes beast when it appears another woman has captured the interest of her husband and again when kissed by her 'it's all in the mind' psychiatrist, Dr Judd (Tom Conway). In both cases murder is intended, successful in the case of the psychiatrist, who also wounds her. But before this comes to pass, at the behest of her husband, Irena seeks psychiatric help for her 'sexual problem', which raises a number of issues about gender difference, authority and power. As Mary Ann Doane notes:

> In the woman's film, the erotic gaze becomes the medical gaze. The female body is located not so much as spectacle but as an element in the discourse of medicine, a manuscript to be read for the symptoms that betray her story, her identity. Hence the need in these films for the figure of the doctor as reader or interpreter, as the site of knowledge which dominates and controls female subjectivity. (1984: 74)

Judd tries to uncover Irena's secrets – her story, her identity – through hypnosis, but as a good Freudian believes that her fears about her true identity are products fabricated by her mind.[50] His knowledge and authority will not allow him to see the irrational as anything other than a trick played by psychological forces. As such, he fails to see the truth of her split identity. Here animal transformation again figures as alienation, this time of the woman, and of being an immigrant whose otherness will not be easily absorbed into the American cultural melting pot. Judd and her husband see Irena's otherness on their own terms as opposite to them, working with the illusory seduction of sexual complementarity. They regard Irena's 'irrationality' as an articulation of the difference of femininity. The fact is that she has a radical and uncomplementary alterity that goes far beyond gender difference. Therefore it is Alice (Jane Randolph), Irena's rival in love, who is the only one to realise the truth of Irena's fears about herself, rather than either of the sceptical men. It is the case that the panther expresses perhaps a certain imaginary 'raw' femininity, or even characterises a model of female sexuality, much as the wolf might figure an imaginary 'raw' masculinity, but becoming beast is far more than this. While pantherhood is Irena's genetic heritage, it is nonetheless a brute external force that takes full possession of her and over which she has no control. Even though the gender/national resonances are different this is much in the same vein as the hapless Talbot of *The Wolf Man*. Ambiguity is in the ascendancy: Irena is woman and beast, the beast comes from inside but is experienced as an intrusion. Like Talbot, she is victim and monster. Irena's beast cannot be tamed, domesticated, subjugated to the rule of men, through the processes of civilisation and socialisation, or therapy. Mixed with atavism, Irena's beastly heritage, triggered by the bodily stirrings of sexual desire, is shaped by the return of the repressed formula (in this I read the film as Judd reads Irena – in terms of psychological forces understood according to Freudian orthodoxy). It is here that her case differs to that of Larry Talbot. What is suppressed through socialisation returns in distorted form (the distortion might be considered as intrinsic to transformation into animal form), and with no cure, analytic or otherwise, it is only contained through Irena's death. Her death frees her husband to marry the more complementary and normal Alice (the couple are married in the sequel, *The Curse of the Cat People* (1944)). Equilibrium and order is restored.

Becoming beast may be a trope that is connected to the return of the repressed but it also has its roots in the strange materiality and uncontrollable rhythms of the flesh. Films such *I Was a Teen-age Werewolf* (1957), Hammer's *The Curse of the Werewolf* (1961) and *An American Werewolf in London* (1981) sought to address horror very directly to what had become their core audience: teens and early twentysomethings. *Buffy the Vampire Slayer* (1997–2003) continued this tradition through the character of Oz (Seth Green). These renditions mythologise the physical and mental transformations undergone by adolescent boys: appearance of extra body hair, changes in vocal register, increased sexual drive, impromptu erection, male bonding and territorialism. In one of the most sexualised werewolf films, *The Company of Wolves*, it is the Devil, lord of temptation, who stops his car to give a teenaged boy an ointment that causes chest hair to sprout. It is rather easy for fully-fledged adults to forget the 'horror' of the changes to mind and body that occur during the 'storm of puberty' (Freud, 'The Sexual Life of Human Beings', 1991b: 354). The body becomes excessive in its accelerated metamorphosis, unfamiliar and out of conscious control, providing thereby a benchmark experience on which body horror in cinema can draw. Transformation also provides an image of adolescence that 'sustains a whole array of aids to surface maintenance … pus, blood, fat and hair threaten to erupt from below, disrupting that surface and the desire it elicits' (Richards 2004: 124). The particular changes of adolescence are connected with the onset of sexuality and as M. C. Dillon notes this is often troublesome in a social sense: 'Changelings disrupt the social fabric simply by changing, becoming sexual … we send our changelings to school … to be initiated into the practices that have to be mastered to gain adult autonomy and readmission into the social order' (2000: 23). The challenges that these 'changelings' make to the social and family order are exaggerated and capitalised on in allegorical terms by many animal transformation films. This is also the case in the more recent female werewolf films, such as *The Curse* (1999) and the *Ginger Snaps* cycle (*Ginger Snaps* (2001); *Ginger Snaps Unleashed* (2004); *Ginger Snaps Back* (2004)). These films make use of the lunar-cycle aspect found in earlier male-based werewolf films. Transformation into werewolf is linked to the onset of menstruation and becoming woman. Some of the appeal of these films for women is the fact that they give symbolic expression to the bodily and hormonal particularities that are part of most girls' and women's lives, but which are generally ignored in popular media. As well as dealing in borders and thresholds, breaking the taboo on menstruation is one of the claims that these films have on transgression. Distinct from most Hollywood films, these independently-produced films also place emphasis on close relationships other than those of a romantic nature. It is the relationship between sisters Ginger and Brigitte that is of prime importance in *Ginger Snaps* and *Ginger Snaps Back*; less so in *Ginger Snaps Unleashed* where Brigitte's relationship with a psychotic younger girl proves the most important. These films trade on the ambiguous experiences of becoming adult and entering the enigmatic world of adult sexuality, it is this that calls the beast from the wild-lands to take up residence within.

Cinematic images of the werewolf are grounded in the eruption of wild, voracious and instinctual appetites consonant with physical changes in the body. In many werewolf films there is no cure, no hope of redemption; a formula that originates from expressionism and noir and which serves well the disturbing idea that bodily processes often exceed our control. *The Curse of the Werewolf*, however, brings a new rule to cinematic werewolf lore: working in accordance with the law of the cinematic complementary couple, love can prevent the change to wolf. Amongst other things, this enables the werewolf formula to allegorise some of the contradictions that are bundled into the experience of masculinity. 'Ideal' masculinity is often represented as ruggedly individual and self-sufficient, but this conflicts with the demands of social interaction and family life. In *The Curse of the Werewolf*, love is able to overcome gender difference and Leon's beast becomes tamed under its influence. The wolf within – anti-social, murderous and sexually promiscuous – must be policed, let off the leash only under the right conditions, if not then chaos reigns. This essentialist construction can be said to capitalise on the archaic and atavistic, each couched within the framework of the repressed as a means of maintaining a particular definition of masculinity. While this configuration is present and contained for some time in *The Curse of the Werewolf*, it finds its most overt articulation in *Wolf*.

Will Randall (Jack Nicholson) is a late middle-aged, meek and mild, considerate and reasonable, publisher who is prey to the ambitious appetites of a younger male colleague. But a werewolf bites Randall one cold winter's night, after his sensible Volvo hits a wolf in the dark, snowy woods. Like Seth Brundle (Jeff Goldblum) in *The Fly* (1987), the first stages of the transformation reinvigorate him with the powers of youth. His balding head sprouts new hair, libido re-surfaces and he becomes more competitive in the work place. For a time he revels in this newfound vitality, until things go out of control and Randall thinks that he has killed his estranged wife on a nightly roam around New York.

It is not just adolescents who experience the body as exceeding control: the processes of aging and illness also testify to the alterity of our own flesh. The fantasy of youthful power that underlies *Wolf* is blazingly apparent. While the aging process is given as the ostensible reason for his decline, the film also implies it is Randall's new-man credentials that have drained his sexual desire and general lust for life. The film heeds to Robert Bly's (2004, first published in 1992) clarion call to retrieve a 'back to the woods' masculinity in which it is imagined that finding the repressed wolf within allows lost vigour and esteem to be recovered. Despite Randall's total transition to wolf at the end of the film, the message is clear – the wolf within is vital if the aging man is not to slide into a passive, and, according to this logic, feminised dotage. Nicholson's wild-man star persona strengthens this message as he transforms from uncharacteristic weary submissive into his more familiar 'mad, bad and dangerous to know' guise. Despite the film's apparent yearning for a lost wolfish version of masculinity, the male body nevertheless becomes monstrously othered, rather than the blueprint of normality, and out of control. Becoming wolf entails a release from the channel-ling processes of the social contract, something the audience and the character is allowed at first to experience as pleasurable, but all too soon autonomy is lost and the experience becomes a terrifying ordeal which eventually wipes out the human.

The sense of empowerment provided by becoming wolf also plays a role in *Ginger Snaps*. When Ginger (Katherine Isabelle), the elder of the two teenaged sisters, is bitten, she becomes increasingly driven by sexual urges and her physical strength increases. A danger-ous, excessive femininity, buoyed up by animal passions and physical power, comes into being. Her new-found assertiveness does, however, degenerate after a time to complete abandonment of those characteristics that define the human (supernaturally acquired power that turns ugly is a feature that also appears in teen-witch movies *The Craft* (1996) and *Little Witches* (1996)). To begin with Ginger and her sister Brigitte (Emily Perkins) are in-separable, but as the infection takes hold they grow into rivals, in the end fighting over Sam (Kris Lemche), who helps Brigitte to make a cure from the herb wolfsbane. In the process of trying to inject Ginger, now in full wolf form, with the herb Sam is killed. In their face-off, Ginger jumps Brigitte and lands on the knife that she holds to protect herself. Like Irena and Larry, Ginger dies. Brigitte is infected, but it is left unclear whether she chooses to take the cure or instead to experience the mental, physical and sexual power her older sister felt. The latter would come at the cost of her humanity, however. Previously, Brigitte followed her sister in all things, but as Ginger grew more wolf-like Brigitte begins to develop a more individuated identity and it emerges that she is extremely resourceful. Aware of the shift in Brigitte's character, the viewer is left to speculate which of the two possible routes she will choose. In so doing thought about the nature of the sisters' close relationship is encouraged (offering a possible topic of post-film discussion).

Ginger Snaps Unleashed, the second in the series, sees an infected Brigitte fighting to keep the wolf within under her control by injecting wolfsbane. Very early in the film she is incarcerated in an addiction centre, as she exhibits all the signs of having a drug habit (she has, it is just to a drug that keeps her problem in check). Deprived of regular doses of wolfs-bane, Brigitte is in danger of becoming fully wolf and being found by the male wolf that seeks to mate with her. Ginger returns as a figment of Brigitte's imagination to comment sar-castically on the way in which the infection brings out her latent sexuality. In one scene she dreams that her all-female class perform synchronised masturbation. This is comic sexual spectacle, yet woman-centred and non-phallocratic. As well as providing a little welcome levity to what is otherwise quite a harrowing film, it is designed to keep the sexual dimen-sions of the werewolf transformation in play. Brigitte's increasingly desperate attempts to discipline her sexual thoughts and her out-of-control body are doomed to failure, but hope is at hand as a horror-comic reading younger girl, Ghost (Tatiana Maslany), knows a way out. Although her blonde hair and small frame make her look typically innocent, Ghost turns out to be a psychopath who incapacitates those she loves. In preventing her from taking the cure, Ghost engineers to keep Brigitte, now fully in wolf form, as her pet. In so doing she fulfils the beast-master fantasies that are displayed in her own comic book-style drawings. In a variety of ways Ghost is precisely the type of amoral comic-reading child that Frederic Wertham warned of so vociferously in his anti-comics campaign in the 1950s.[51] Unlike the first film, it is not turning into wolf that allegorises the disruptions of 'changeling' sexuality. Instead that not-one-thing-nor-the-other sexuality is invoked more directly in Ghost's perverse desires and actions (which do not emerge as such until the end of the film). It is she who disturbs the order of things and in withholding her access to wolfsbane, Ghost prevents Brigitte's re-entry into the normative.

Ginger is resurrected in the third film in the trilogy, *Ginger Snaps Back*. The sisters are thrown back in time to colonialist Canada of the mid-nineteenth century and there is a resumption of close interest in their sisterly relationship. The girls are largely twenty-first-century in their speech and behaviour, which through anachronism provides comic moments and also encourages viewers to see events from a twenty-first-century perspective. Ginger is again bitten and an old shaman Indian woman prophesises that one sister will kill the other if Ginger does not kill an infected boy, who we later learn is hidden at the colonialist outpost. Unlike the first film in the series, Ginger does not turn fully to wolf form towards the end of the film. Instead she remains half-human, half-wolf, looking more like a vampire than a werewolf (perhaps because the boy who infected her is killed after she turns). Ginger commands the other werewolves and rescues Brigitte from a compound full of frontiersmen, who up until that time regarded them with suspicion, mainly because they are men-less women but also because they were not attacked by werewolves on their journey through the woods. At the very end of the film Ginger and Brigitte are left together alive, Brigitte having exchanged blood with her sister. With all the white men and the potential love interest dead, they now have command over the land. The sisters are left to forge their future on their own terms; together forever. This ending could be regarded by some viewers as suggesting the possibilities of gender separatism and sisterhood, a feminist message rendered in the conventions of fairytale and contemporary horror.

In his influential essay 'Introduction to the American Horror Film' (1984), Robin Wood regards films that appear to punish sexual desire to be morally conservative. Werewolf films are classified within this group. Aspects of sexual desire and behaviour do get out of control in these films, but this does not necessarily make them conservative. Wood does not debate in sufficient detail the fact that in most cases the animal transformation format does not project anxiety onto external groups (a process termed abreaction in psychoanalysis). While the 'infection' might come ultimately from an unknown source, most werewolf films invite the audience to identify and sympathise with the character who becomes over a period of time 'othered'. As such, transformation rarely occurs until part way into a film giving time to build character. *Ginger Snaps*, for example, paints a fairly comprehensive picture of the two sisters' lives and their relationships, their fears, interests, antagonisms and daily routine. We are invited to sympathise with their various struggles. In *The Curse of the Werewolf* we learn about the birth and childhood of Leon (Oliver Reed). As Leon, Ginger and Brigitte examine

In for the kill: Ginger (Katharine Isabelle) on the turn in *Ginger Snaps* (2000)

their bodies for signs of the beast within, viewers are perhaps reminded of the unruliness of their own bodies – the discomforting fact that our own bodies are radically other, material of which we have little control and over which our fingers often hover to take its variable measure. In this lupine version of the mirror-phase, we are confronted by the rebellious, 'possessed' body, which is ordinarily elided to conserve the necessary illusion of mind/body synergy and integrity. But it is not just the alterity of the body that animal transformation calls up: it is also the otherness of sex and sexual desire. This is not in itself conservative, as Wood implies.

Ginger's bodily changes increasingly render her other and monstrous, to herself as well as to other people. This could be regarded as hyper-literalising the way that women and their bodies are figured in the heterosexual male imagination: unknowable, scary, unpredictable, uncontrollable and hysterical. But it is also possible to see Ginger's metamorphic monstrosity in another way. Bodies, desire and sex are 'strange' to us because they exceed rational control and are subject to perpetual change. The sexual body marches to the rhythm of biological drums over which we have little or no mastery. This leads to a desire for control. As Ginger says of her efforts to remain outside adult womanhood, 'you kill yourself to be different and your whole body screws you'. Given that everyone experiences bodily deviation intensely during adolescence, Ginger's plight is available potentially to all-comers. The issue here is that emphasis is placed on the female menstrual body, which could be regarded as the seat of the horror, as might also be said of earlier horror films such as *The Exorcist* and *Carrie*. However, in *Ginger Snaps* and *The Exorcist* it is an invasive force wedded to

Sex and the Cinema

'changeling' status, of which menstruation is only one component of entry into the sexual, that is the source of the horror.

Animal transformation films are therefore a quintessential form of body horror and with the presence of both male and female werewolves in popular culture this is applicable across gender. In its reflexive approach to gender and the werewolf formula, *Ginger Snaps* offers a fairytale-come-urban myth that amplifies the experience of becoming and being woman and all the strange, powerful and disturbing otherness that this brings. Added to which, the infection convention that is present in most werewolf tales (as also with vampires) becomes in a post-AIDS context a hyperbolised, allegorical means of articulating the danger of 'unprotected' sex. As figured in *Ginger Snaps* as well as a number of other werewolf films, 'infection' and the alterity of the body, sex and desire are not intended as a warning about the sinful nature of sex, as suggested by Wood's 'reactionary' (conservative) category of horror. Alterity and the sexual body might be presented within the rhetorics and conventions of horror, but it is not a punishment for sexual promiscuity nor does it affirm normative values about sex and gender; on the contrary the use of such rhetorics of monstrosity denaturalises embodiment, sex and desire.

In quite a few instances of films focused on metamorphosis it is sex or sexual desire that triggers, or is closely related to, transformation. Sexual jealousy and a kiss catalyse the transformation in *Cat People*. Adulterous sex in the woods, under the stars and bathed in firelight, triggers the transformation of the couple in *The Howling* (1981), clumsy prosthetics melting into far more coherent and graceful animation. Once bitten, never again shy, Ginger becomes ravenously lustful, whereas beforehand she showed no interest in men or sex. Leon's defeated werewolfism comes back once he begins an affair with his employer's daughter and becomes drunk on his night off. According to Wood's thesis, any image that makes sex monstrous is a form of cautionary punishment. Critics working to uncover the gender economics of horror, such as Barbara Creed (1993), have also sought to show how horror carries a conservative agenda by arguing that monstrosity in female form betrays male fear of the female body as potentially castrating and therefore frighteningly other. Both of these points of view offer something of interest but do not get to the core of the werewolf formula. It is the discomforting material fact of sex and sexual desire, the way it shapes us, drives us, changes us, that is allegorised in a formulaic way in werewolf films (an attempt perhaps to gain some kind of purchase on the material body through the process of symbolisation, but which ultimately resists it). The werewolf transformation scenario is not simply an embodiment of misogyny or a moral lesson about sex. There is something far more fundamental in play that has been missed by critics focused on horror; animal transformation in fantasy and horror expresses in generic form the experience of transformation brought about by the physical, emotional and psychological effects of sex and sexual desire.

Unlike other forms of cinema focused on sex, animal transformation demonstrates in graphic terms the insistent otherness of desire itself, operating often as an agent of transgression. As such, the thirsty desires of the werewolf are never slaked. This trope conforms to the way that various articulations of popular culture have so often formulated that which resists socialisation and/or civilisation. The werewolf formula (paralleled by various other 'manimals' – or should that be 'femimals', including cat people, ape men and some vampires) gives the endless mutability of desire and the body tangible and coherent form. In some cases this is accompanied by rules and techniques to contain and mollify it, while in others it is put to work to speak of sexual empowerment. Traditionally this applied mainly to men (often scientists) but increasingly this applies to fictional women. In Angela Carter's short story 'The Tiger Bride' (1981: 51–67), for example, the heroine finds the beast within at the end of the tale. She is released through her new animal form from the constraining fetters of femininity and civilisation, where she was merely an object of exchange between men. A similar tale is to be found with Rosalie in *The Company of Wolves*. Becoming wolf is Rosalie's choice, providing a contrast to most other werewolves in cinema who have no choice in the matter. Here the choice to become wolf is emblematic of Rosalie's entry into the mysteries of sex and sexual desire.

However, most werewolf and other animal transformation films make dramatic and narrative capital from efforts to contain and control the monster within. Restraint and containment occur in a number of ways, although few are successful to any degree. Irena, Talbot, Leon and Ginger (in the first film but not the third) fail to curb their beast within and are all killed. Their deaths provide each film's ending with a sense of tragic closure. Brigitte too struggles to discipline her unruly body. While *Ginger Snaps* proffers a cure, it turns out in the sequel that wolfsbane is simply a temporary palliative. In *The Curse of the Werewolf* Leon is offered the hope of a conditional cure: normalisation through continued love of a good woman. The romanticism of *The Curse of the Werewolf* replaces the noirish pessimism of *The Wolf Man* with a more moralised and sexualised slant. As Marina Warner puts it of Jean Cocteau's *La Belle et la Bête* (1946), the film 'represents the long-held idea that civilisation can be achieved though courtly love' (1993: 34). *The Curse of the Werewolf* also operates on the principle that being loved unconditionally will pacify the endless pacing of relentless desire and dampen down the flaming rages of the 'animal' sexual body. An illusion of romantic complementarity that will plug the gap of lack is one which, according to Lacan, we all cherish. As well as offering a mirage of hope, the love-as-cure angle of *The Curse of the Werewolf* may well have been calculated to entice a teenaged female audience who would be regarded typically as a group that are likely to be seduced by images of romantic love (primed as they are by various aspects of girl-culture).

As well as speaking of the alterity of gender, desire and sexuality, the animal transformation formula within the context of horror and fantasy has also been used to bring into play racial difference. Given that the wolf represents that which is uncivilised, it is open to be allied to the way that racial difference has been organised hierarchically in certain strains of white Western discourse. Yet while it is certainly the case that a racist dimension hovered very close to those earlier films that deal with apes, in two of the more recent werewolf films a far more overt and egalitarian approach to race is taken.

In *Ginger Snaps Back*, werewolfism is linked to colonialism, in much the same way that vampirism is linked to colonialism in the blaxploitation film *Blacula* (1972). We learn from the Indian hunter (Nathaniel Arcand) that the werewolf infection was brought to the Canadian frontier by European colonialists. Neither he nor the Indian shaman woman know how to control it, but they understand it is linked to the destiny of the land. Some of the British and French soldiers stationed at the outpost at which the sisters arrive regard the hunter with suspicion and fear, others do not (as is also the case with the sisters themselves). As the film's emblem of outmoded repression, the Reverend Gilbert (Hugh Dillon) believes that the werewolf infection is punishment for sin. He regards miscegenation as the sin that has incurred the wrath of God. The captain of the camp married an Indian woman and they had a child. She is bitten and killed and the child is the on-the-turn werewolf that infects Ginger. Not only is Reverend Gilbert racist he is also a rampant misogynist; he tries various means to kill Ginger and Brigitte, fearing their capacity to tempt into sin the other men. Because of his extremely repressive and illiberal views, his death is one that we are invited by the film to enjoy. That we are sanctioned to do so is signalled by Brigitte who tells him that she saw his death in a trance and that it pleased her. While the Reverend represents stereotypically colonialist and patriarchal values in negative terms – a character designed for the audience to hate – other aspects of the film's approach to colonialism are more nuanced in moral terms.

In its approach to the relationships between colonialism and transformation, there is an interesting contradiction. Becoming wolf operates under the sign of amoral colonialism, but when Ginger and Brigitte both become wolves at the end of the film, they break the shaman woman's prophesy that one will kill the other. They can at last be 'together forever', a phrase they use to demonstrate their solidarity in all three films, but which was not realised in the two previous films. Yet while white, patriarchal rule is broken by the solidarity of sisterhood, a high price is paid: the loss of the lives and knowledge of the Indian hunter and the shaman woman.

A rather different way of using the werewolf formula through which to speak of racial difference is found in *Underworld*. In some respects the film borrows from *Romeo and Juliet* but this is translated by way of comic-book superheroes into the rhetorics of the horror genre and it has an upbeat ending. Vampires and Lycans (werewolves) are immortal enemies. They have been at war for centuries. Before the war the Lycans acted as 'daylight guardians' of the Vampires, but were in effect their slaves. The daughter of one of the Vampire elders falls in love with a Lycan, Lucian (Michael Sheen), and is pregnant with his child. Her father, Viktor (Bill Nighy), regards the affair and their unborn child as an abomination, a betrayal of the purity of bloodlines. To him Lycans are uncivilised and fit only for slaves, he also fears that the product of a Vampire and Lycan union will be stronger than the Vampire elders and he will lose his powerful position. As such, he has his pregnant daughter killed in a spectacular and public way, which Lucian is forced to watch. This barbarous act starts the war between the races. Centuries later the Vampires are in the ascendancy. Kraven (Shane Brolly), a Vampire, claimed to have killed Lucian in battle, a falsehood engineered with Lucian to halt the war. Lucian is, however, still alive and in search of Michael Corvin (Scott Speedman), one of the human descendents of Corvinas, who had three sons: a Vampire, a Lycan and a human. Michael's blood can be mixed with that of both Lycan and Vampire. Lucian intends to become more powerful by killing the vampire elders and make Kraven the new Vampire elder. He also intends to mix his own blood with Michael's and one of the Vampire elders in order to generate the new cross-race dynasty that is so feared by Viktor. His plan is thwarted because Selene (Kate Beckinsale), seeking to protect Michael, now a werewolf after being bitten by Lucian, awakens Viktor from his ritual sleep. She does this to put an end to what she regards as Kraven's apparent betrayal of her kind. It emerges, however, that there are unsavoury facts about Viktor that have been withheld from her. She believes that Lycans killed her family; in fact they did so at Viktor's command. It also emerges that Viktor will not hesitate to kill Selene, as he did his beloved daughter, to prevent her from mixing her blood with Michael's. He tells her this directly when he learns of her love for Michael. Viktor is the keeper of the law; it is he that defines what is transgressive within Vampire culture. The situation is only resolved when Selene feeds off Michael thereby giving him the attributes of Vampire in addition to those of Lycan. Enhanced in this way he dispatches Viktor in the closing fight scene, thereby opening the way for the integration of both races and sanctioning inter-race sexual relations.

Selene and Michael become, despite their beastliness, the film's 'proper couple'. It is through their love and co-operation in a fight context that Viktor's racism is defeated (it should be noted that despite their different fantasy 'races' they are still aligned with conventional gender difference). The film uses the rhetorics and forms of horror to construct a love story across the racial divide. As such the film uncovers for thematic and narrative ends regimes of inequality and superiority. This is achieved mainly through the audience's identification with the couple's transgressive relationship. In this context, the werewolf infection becomes the means to provide an imaginary solution to the insidious effects of racial hierarchy.

Connotations of real racial-world difference are present in the way the two imaginary races are presented. The Lycans are presented as entirely male, wearing scuffed leather and with long unkempt hair they are presented as tough feral fighters. Early in the film they are gathered together around two of their number fighting in a sewer (much like a scene in *Fight Club*). The Lycans are coded in dress and behaviour as largely 'uncivilised' (Lucian often reminds them to act with more restraint and decorum). They are mainly white, but one of the strongest Lycans is black. The Vampires are both men and women and are coded as decadent aristocrats. They are far less muscular than the Lycans, dressed in elegant clothes and are seen draped languidly over velvet and gold sofas in their baroque mansion. There is one prominent black Vampire, however. He is the head of security. Yet through references to slavery, raw 'uncivilisation' and physical power, the film invites the audience to see the Lycans in terms of black history. The ways in which black cultures have been regarded in colonialist and racist literature are also resident in some of the Vampires' opinions of the Lycan clans. The Vampires are represented as self-obsessed, self-serving, decadent and almost medieval in their social structure. The two races are not, however, split into good and bad, there are good and bad in both. The inclusion of black and other racially-defined individuals in both camps prevents overly simplified one-to-one readings of Lycans and Vampires as 'black' and 'white' in racial or moral terms. Racial difference in this film is figured not in terms of the colour of the skin but along other lines. Nonetheless, power, authority and knowledge are at stake.

The film also figures 'becoming werewolf' in a way that is not found in other werewolf films. Becoming both a Lycan and a Vampire brings Michael unsurpassed physical and mental strength. His supernatural augmentation also makes him equal to Selene (equality is a core feature of the complementary couple). His transformation is not sexualised, as it is in other films, and there is far less emphasis on the subjective experience of transformation. Rather the focus is on the way that otherness becomes figured under particular power regimes, filtered as it is through the rhetorics of horror-based fantasy. Becoming Lycan in Michael's case is a 'blood' issue, related to genealogy, rather than an arbitrary occurrence as in many other werewolf films. *Underworld* is at pains to construct a well-rendered imaginary world complete with a history that contextualises transformation. As such, becoming Lycan (or Vampire) is far more 'naturalised' here than in those films where transformation comes, unexplained and unknown, out of the blue. This also alters the meaning context that prevails in the *The Wolf Man*, *Cat People* and the first two *Ginger Snaps* films: alienation and pessimism are taken out of animal transformation. As such *Underworld* becomes better suited to the mainstream context of the Hollywood blockbuster.

Animalised humans and humanised animals have been used in cinema to provide spectacle and to arouse spectators. Transgression and taboo arise from the way these films focus on sensitivities that circulate around thresholds and borders, difference and otherness, and the sexual. Bestial desire and animal transformation have become vehicles for formularising and conventionalising the transgression of social mores and epistemological categories. They are also a means of figuring the sexual in terms of the primal and the return of the repressed. This began with the representations of barbarity and horror in American films made in the Pre-Code era and their legacy can be traced through to the most recent animal transformation horror films. The werewolf myth in particular has proved exceptionally malleable and has been reworked in films such as the *Ginger Snaps* trilogy and *Underworld* to subvert the racist and gender-specific aspects of the earlier films and to explore issues around the experience of the sexual body within the particular generic vocabulary of horror. While films that deal with these themes are clearly located as horror and fantasy, they nonetheless touch on some of the most fundamental taboos and boundaries that constitute what it is to be human; one of the ways they do this is by asking what it means to become a creature of difference.

Family Relations: Incest in the Cinema

$\mathcal{T}$hroughout this chapter a range of films are examined with the aim of demonstrating how cinematic representations of incest are informed by and articulate ideas that originate within the broader arena of academic thought. To understand more fully the ways in which cinema uses rhetorics of transgression it is also the intention of this chapter to show how the context and form of cinema mediate some of the more prominent theories and under-standings of incest and incestuous desires.

Alongside the threshold that divides the animal from the human, the incest taboo has been considered by anthropologists and sociologists as a cornerstone of 'civilisation'. Claude Lévi-Strauss' structural approach to anthropology looked for the foundational structures that organise and facilitate social life. He argued that most kinship systems are based on marriage alliances between different families; with women from one group marrying into another. This arrangement serves a range of purposes, but depends on a prohibition against incest. This prohibition becomes, in Lévi-Strauss' model, the basis on which a coherent social structure rests. Anthropologists Margaret Mead and Bronislaw Malinowski working during the early to mid-twentieth century also put the incest taboo at the centre of their view of the social. It is now accepted largely within social science that prohibitions against incest are present in some form or other in all cultures. Within this structural model, it is not moral culpability that leads to prohibitions on incest; instead, incest prohibitions are intrinsic to the very definition of society and family. In some cultures the incest prohibition is designat-ed rhetorically as God-given; in Christianity and as written in the Bible, for example, incest is forbidden directly by God. As such a religious and, thereby, moral meaning of an absolute nature is often assigned to the incest prohibition. Despite the common view that the incest prohibition is universal, it is nonetheless the case that incest is a common phenomenon across cultures: if it were not and if it was 'hardwired' then a prohibition or taboo would be unnecessary.

Basing his assertion on a range of data from across a global spread of different cultures, Lloyd DeMause argues that 'it is incest itself – and not the absence of incest – that has been universal for most people in most places at most times' (1991: 2).[52] He goes on to claim that the incest taboo is not quite as universal as had been thought, finding evidence of incest in a range of cultures where certain incarnations in particular circumstances are accepted as the norm and not sanctioned against. The Muria, an ethnic group living in India, provides one of his many examples, 'who make their young children a part of their sexual activities in the family bed' (1991: 10). DeMause thereby challenges the axiom that the incest taboo is universally applied. His work provides evidence in support of the notion that sexual practice is extremely sensitive to cultural difference. In order to account for these variations, he claims that there is a link between the incest taboo and the way in which children are regarded. The incidence of incest with children is higher in cultures that 'have only recently moved beyond what I have termed the infanticidal mode of childrearing, whereby as much as half of the children born were killed by their parents, the use of children for the emotional needs of adults is far more acceptable, an attitude that fosters widespread incestuous acts along with other child abuse' (1991: 8). While DeMause challenges the universalism of the incest taboo, it nonetheless appears that his infanticide model has a certain teleological aspect: 'civilisation' becomes defined progressively in terms of the degree of strictness and success with which the incest taboo is implemented.[53]

The notion that incest is a sign of backwardness or degeneration in a straightforward sense is not one that becomes employed by most films that deal directly with incest, however. While 'in-breeding' in isolated communities is directly employed in films such as *Deliverance* (1972), most films that deal directly with incest as a central theme make of it a dramatic device that occurs behind the lace curtains of white, middle-class families. The way that DeMause correlates incest with degree of civilisation reflects a more generalised and populist view of incest, and it is this that influences the way that incest is cast in many films as dangerously perverse or even evil. In films such as *Twin Peaks: Fire Walk with Me*, *Close My Eyes* (1991) and *The War Zone* (1999) it is the dramatic juxtaposition of middle-class affluence, as a kind of bourgeois model of civilisation, with incest, indicating something that should have been repressed by the processes of civilisation, which calls for our attention. The common presence of this juxtaposition in most incest films draws on the psychoanalytic model of the repression of incestuous desires and the power struggles that precedes it, as well as more general understandings of the disruption to family and social structure caused by incest.

The teleology of DeMause's infanticide/incest correlation raises the question: if there is a progressive fall-off in instances of incest in civilised cultures, where children are valued and not regarded as commodities, why then is it a fairly common topic for fictional treatment? While the fact of such fictions suggest there is something of a problem with DeMause's thesis, there are a number of ways that such fictions are informed by notions whereby 'civilisation' (as noun and verb), and thereby socialisation, has a deep connection to the incest taboo. The idea that appetite and reason operate in conflict can be traced back to Plato through Christianity to Freudian thought (see Silverman 2000). As we have seen in the last chapter, civilisation has often been defined on the ability to manage appetite. As such, the topic of managing sexual desire and appetite plays a central role in Western philosophy, religion, myth and drama. Appetite and its management are also central to Freud's conceptualisation of subjectivity, sexuality and socialisation. The management of desire strongly informs Freud's work on incest; he argues that within the context of the social human beings are constantly assailed and shaped by competing demands to indulge or restrain desires. The popularisation of Freud's psychoanalytic ideas through literature, therapy/self-help and cinema has meant that his model of how the incest prohibition is acquired and how it informs adult sexuality is perhaps the most obvious discourse from which representations of incest in cinema draw. In part because psychoanalysis in general is focused on tangible family relationships rendered in melodramatic terms and because of the increasing numbers of people interested in therapy, the Oedipus complex as a rhetorical construct became disseminated more widely in Europe and the US than most other aspects of philosophy, with the effect that aspects of psychoanalytic ideas take up a place in cinema where they are used to create storylines and/or provide character motivation. As has already been established, psychoanalytic concepts such as repression have had a profound influence on the way cinema shapes the meaning and representation of sex and desire, as well as providing a rhetorical model that gives transgression a particular articulation. As it proves important to the representation of incest in cinema, it is necessary to outline in some detail how incest fits into Freud's understanding of sexuality and 'civilisation'.

Freud places incest and its prohibition at the centre of his view of psycho-social development. He too argued that there is a special connection between incest prohibition and civilisation: 'incest is anti-social and civilisation consists in a progressive renunciation of it' (cited in the editor's introduction to '"Civilised" Sexual Morality and Modern Nervous Illness', 1985: 30). Incestuous desires and their renunciation are considered core to the child's relationship with its carers and to the general development of the social subject. Freud uses the story of Oedipus, as outlined in Sophocles' play *Oedipus the King* (c. 425 BC), to illustrate by way of analogy the drama of incestuous desire and its suppression, which he regarded as playing out in all child/parent or child/carer relationships. In his *Introductory Lectures on Psychoanalysis* (1991b), Freud refers to the hostilities that break out in families between same-sex parents and children, either based on the parent's tendency to police their offspring or through competitiveness ('The Archaic Features and Infantilism of Dreams', 1991b: 242). These hostilities have their roots in childhood, hostilities that Freud expresses as being based on rivalry in love. As a child, a son has a strong attachment to his mother but feels that his father is 'a rival who disputes his sole possession' (1991b: 243). Reversed for the girl; her mother is regarded as an impediment to the girl's relationship to her father. This is what Freud terms the Oedipus complex and it produces for the child fantasies related to the killing or subjugation of the rival and possessing the loved parent. Although Freud points out that this is not the sum of relations with our parents, he nonetheless cautions that 'there is more danger in our under-estimating rather than over-estimating its influence and that of the developments that proceed from it' (1991b: 244). An important aspect of the Oedipus complex for the boy is the fear of castration. He fears this will be the way that the father puts a stop to his incestuous desire for the mother (1991b: 245). Fantasies of castration also relate to the way that gender difference is perceived by the boy, the visible absence of a penis in the mother (as well as women/girls in general) is seen as evidence of the imagined threat posed by the father. Subsequently, in later life, the fear and frustration associated with a loss of agency and the thwarting of desire recall earlier castration anxiety. While Freud locates castration anxiety as particular to boys and their anatomy, symbolic castration – a block on desire and agency – can be regarded as experienced by both men and women. However, Lacan suggests that castration – as a block on desire and agency – is experienced differently depending on gender because femininity is figured already as 'castrated'. Incestuous desire provides a core around which repression, castration anxiety, the 'order' of familial relations, adult sexuality, and the experience of desire and agency circulate. As such incestuous desire plays a central role in the rhetorical staging of psychoanalysis.

Expanded and reworked by Lacan, castration becomes yoked to the way that the symbolic field of language and the social structure produce for us a sense of alienation. These structures pre-exist us and predetermine the social roles that we all to some extent inhabit, often causing distress and discomfort through the threat posed to our sense of liberty, agency and autonomy. Similarly language, with its rules of categorisation and its structural function, is something that 'speaks us' rather than us speaking it. The structures into which we are born and which determine the conditions of our social being, are termed in Lacan's lexicon the big Other. The big Other and castration anxiety/fantasy are connected to roles played by the father. The imaginary father (the one of fantasy), the symbolic father (representing authority) and the real father (as a thinking, feeling, acting person in his own right) are each powerful determinants that act on us in our early lives (even if the 'real' father is not physically present). These fathers represent collectively aspects of the Oedipal scenario and the prohibition of incest (the case is rather more complex in that of girls than boys and the father's role in the implementation of the incest prohibition is a factor that proves important to the way that father/daughter incest is represented in cinema). The positions occupied by these fathers provide the child with a microcosmic experience of the way that social forces govern and influence lives before they have developed an awareness of a world beyond the domestic arena. To some extent, Lacan's model places the father as representative of a block on agency – but it is equally the case that the mother plays a prohibitive role in any child's life. However, Lacan argues that she has less access to the register of law (authority) because she is imagined as castrated. The link between castration and incest is important to the status of the latter as a taboo. It is not therefore a moral prohibition in the first instance. It is in fact grounded in the fear that incestuous desire generates through the Oedipus complex; agency and desire are subject to powerful extrinsic forces that then determine the condition and experience of both. In what is often seen as a sleight of hand on the part of the psyche, the incestuous desires that preceded the prohibition are disavowed, forgotten, repressed. The Oedipus complex hinges, therefore, on incestuous desire and its management and containment, and, according to psychoanalytic accounts, it informs our relationships with the external world and its forces.

While there is no one essay devoted to what Freud terms the Oedipus complex, the concept provides a corner-stone of psychoanalysis. Freud states in a footnote:

It has been justly said that the Oedipus complex is the nuclear complex of the neuroses, and constitutes the essential part of their content. It represents the peak of infantile sexuality, which, through its after-effects, exercises a decisive influence on the sexuality of adults. Every new arrival on this planet is faced with the task of mastering the Oedipus complex; anyone who fails to do so falls a victim of neurosis. With the progress of psychoanalytic studies the importance of the Oedipus complex has become more and more clearly evident; its recognition has become the shibboleth that distinguishes the adherents of psychoanalysis from its opponents. ('Three Essays on the Theory of Sexuality', 1977: 148 n. 1)

He speaks therefore of what is disavowed in Western culture: incest, incestuous desire and the sexual life of children.[54] What is regarded as 'normal' adult sexuality is a construction composed of various culturally determined channelling and management regimes. Learned disgust, for example, is a powerful tool for ensuring that the boundaries that define the norm are policed and 'in the course of development and education' sexual pleasure becomes narrowed to a particular set of sanctioned objects/situations; where once it was generalised it becomes focused down onto the genitals ('The Archaic Features and Infantilism of Dreams', 1991b: 245). 'Psychoanalytic researches have shown unmistakeably that the choice of an incestuous love object … is the first and invariable one'; Freud argues, therefore, that severe prohibitions are called for (1991b: 247). Within Freud's model, all sexual wishes/objects repressed through socialisation are still present in the unconscious, forgotten yet still active. In other words, there is still a desire investment in these but the status of that desire has become imbued with an added transgressive, subversive and dangerous edge. In what was to prove very controversial, Freud makes it clear that all small children have incestuous desires. These must be considered sexual but he regards childhood sexuality as qualitatively different to adult sexuality, because the former is not governed by a genital economy. Childhood sexuality is, he argues, far more diffuse and polymorphic than this. Freud did, however, recognise that abusive incest forced on children by parents, carers or siblings was a reality, experienced by many people, despite any 'prohibition' on incest.

The child's incestuous desires are fuelled by the care afforded to that child by the mother/carer. A mother's desires, unconscious or otherwise, are inscribed in some way into the way she handles and cares for her child. According to Jean Laplanche these 'signs' are carefully monitored by the child and they believe that everything she does is addressed to him/her (1989: 125–30).[55] These messages become 'enigmatic signifiers' (1989: 126) and they produce fantasies which are attempts on the part of the child to try to give meaning to these puzzling messages. The provision of milk that sustains the child's survival needs is not simply read as giving him/her life but produces a question for that child: What does the provision of this milk mean? What does it say about her desire for me? The fantasies that are produced by the child in speculative answer to the questions posed by the mother's enigmatic desire (written in to her care of the child's body) are repressed in the post-Oedipal phase, but they nevertheless inform adult sexuality. Building on these fantasies can also produce and intensify Oedipal desires. This drive to knowledge, to read the desire of the mother, is also one that dovetails quite neatly with Roland Barthes' analysis of textual and hermeneutic pleasures – formally in the way that a story reveals truths, provides answers to enigmas as well as engaging through enigma the desire to investigate, know and understand. It could therefore be said that the satisfaction provided by resolution in fictional or factual form, either in terms of puzzles solved or a situation returning to a steady state, fills a fundamental gap of knowledge experienced in relation to another person's enigmatic and unreadable desire in our early childhood. Narratives – stories – which provide meaning and make sense of phenomenon, are the basis on which social cohesion and collective identity rest. Our need for these may well stem from the particular circumstances of our early relationship with the mother (or primary carer), where we are looking for strung-together signs of love, desire and recognition. The configuration of desire in this incestuous context is echoed later in romantic love. Laplanche's focus on the figuration of sexuality through the child's incestuous relation to the mother may go some way to explaining why sex is the object of curiosity and investigation rather than just something we simply 'do'. Sex is deeply connected to our emotional and psychical lives; it plays a significant role in our identity, it is both public and secret, and is the source of much thought, speculation and discussion. It is therefore not surprising that sex is so important to our enjoyment of popular culture and that it is exploited often to attract the interest of potential audiences.

Freud argues that while the child's incestuous desires are repressed and forgotten and we fail to see the echo of them in our adult relationships, those desires nonetheless often become material for dreams and works of art: 'Disavowal applies only to real life. Narrative and dramatic works of the imagination may freely make play with the themes that arise from the disturbance of this ideal' ('The Archaic Features and Infantilism of Dreams' 1991b: 243). This idea is perhaps borne out by the fact that Oedipal narratives, wherein incestuous desire informs the action in displaced ways, are extremely common in cinema, whereas direct portrayals of incest are rather less common, but far from unknown. This does not, however, confirm that the Oedipus complex is universal or hard-wired. The Oedipus complex is itself a narrative, an analogy, used to make sense of phenomena. Its attraction is enhanced perhaps for the same reasons that many of us like 'transgressive' cinema: it lures us with the sensationalist drama of buried secrets and horrors. The concept of the repressed also has the added bonus of making us a mystery to ourselves. Most direct, rather than subtextual, narratives of incest are couched as melodramas rendered in an art or independent cinema context and can be described as relying on the drama of revelation and the transgression of the boundaries that define familial roles. All incest narratives subvert the social order by transgressing the borders that define those 'clean and proper' familial roles. In most of the films where incest provides the central focus, it promotes anguish and deep confusion for all those involved, emotionally and in terms of identity. 'Artful' context enables such films to deal with issues that are often left unspoken in reality and to avoid accusations of taste-lessness and exploitation, and thereby potential censorship, direct or indirect. Importantly, the fact that these films are 'fictions' using actors who are in fact unrelated also provides a fail-safe mechanism that might help these films to bypass personal and institutional censorship.

The Oedipus complex and the importance of prohibition for social and family structure are conceptualisations that help determine the ways that incest is defined and understood. They also provide models that influence the way that cinema represents incest. A number of film academics, including myself, claim that the Oedipal scenario informs films that on the surface do not appear to engage with transgressive articulations of sex and desire. Conflicts between heroes and father figures, who are often in the process of fighting for a female 'prize', are extremely common in popular films, for example. However, while Oedipal-style narratives are found across a range of cinemas, it is only in a fairly small range of films that incest becomes the main focus of the drama. Mother/son incest is treated explicitly and provides the narrative core of *Oedipus Rex* (*Edipo Re*, 1967) and *Bad Boy Bubby* (1993). Father/daughter incest is treated most explicitly in *The War Zone*, appears in slightly more ob-scured terms in *Twin Peaks: Fire Walk with Me* and operates subtextually in *Broken Blossoms*. The most common variety of incest found in cinema is that between sister and brother; it features in *Close My Eyes, Angels and Insects, Excalibur* (1981) and *The Cement Garden* (1993), for example. Most of these films mix melodrama with art-cinema aesthetics. Brother/sister incest also appears in the context of the mytho-historical drama; as in *Excalibur* and *La Reine Margot* (1994) although more tangentially because it appears in the broader context of dynastic power struggles.

What follows is a close analysis of films that depict brother/sister, mother/son and father/daughter incest. I aim to show how these films approach the representation and meaning of incest, how they draw on existing rhetorics of incest and transgression, how the particular style of a given film contributes to the way in which the viewer is interpolated into a particular position as regards the incest depicted and what 'conditions' sanction such transgressive representations as entertainment. In some of these films incest is depicted as abuse, and where this is the case the films present incest as a form of transgression that seeks to horrify, rather than titillate erotically, the viewer. There are, however, some examples, particularly in the case of those that focus on brother/sister incest, where representations draw on rheto-rics of transgression in a way designed to titillate. Some draw explicitly on Freudian rhetorics (particularly the mother/son-focused films); others put such ideas in play but are more implicitly present, with events available to being read through such rhetorics by the viewer. *The War Zone*, for example, can be read in the light of psychoanalytic and anthropological views of incest, which in my view lends the film a certain added richness. The rawness with which the experience of characters caught-up by sexualised power relations in the family is shown makes this film very complex emotionally, but this is ratcheted up several degrees when regarded in the light of psychoanalytic understandings of childhood desires.

Close My Eyes is intent on investigating through fiction what is transgressive about a brother and sister expressing affection sexually. The film contrasts with other films in this chapter because to some extent the transgressive status of sibling incest is underplayed and thereby questioned. Like many British films, *Close My Eyes* draws upon a certain English quirkiness to gain the attention of prospective viewers (particularly American viewers) and to some extent the incest that appears in this film is made in that mould, and it is the only film discussed here that places incest within the same formal structure used by films focused on adultery. The incest tagline plays on sensationalism which may have been considered to help the film attract press interest. As a middle-budget film it relies on plot and character interaction to engage audiences and like many other British films, and several of the films discussed in this chapter, it is a well-made drama (the combination of a sensationalist topic and signifiers of 'art' is a cunning strategy used to sanction risqué content, as has already been argued and is discussed again in greater detail in 'Real Sex', below). In this case the love affair between adult siblings, Nathalie (Saskia Reeves) and Richard (Clive Owen) is set against the backdrop of 1980s Britain (during Prime Minster Thatcher's second term of office). The pair has a somewhat tense relationship, meeting rarely and when they do one or other is late, sharpening their irritation and testing each other's toleration through sibling power-play. Importantly, their parents, now dead, had split up when the children were small, each child living with a separate parent. Other than to impart this information, the pair make no significant mention of their parents. The absence of the parents, and the siblings' estrangement, is important to the drama and proves to be a primary 'condition' for the viability of this representation of incest. The beginning of the film finds Nathalie, recently split from a boyfriend, weeping. Richard coaxes her to look positively to the future, demonstrating that he cares for her. In her grief, she kisses him on the lips. This is a 'teaser' for the audience, but also has the same function for the couple. Richard is somewhat startled by a kiss that is more sensual and intimate than would be expected from a sister, and he does not forget it.

Time passes, Richard leaves a highly-paid job and works for a charity, and is seen with a number of different women. Nathalie marries an extremely rich man, Sinclair (Alan Rickman). When the siblings meet again, Richard is intrigued by the fact that Nathalie wears the necklace that she wore when she kissed him, marking mutual sexual interest. One day Nathalie arrives, late again, at Richard's apartment. She makes sexual overtures, but then pulls away. This game of prevarication goes on for some time but eventually passion overwhelms them, only to be followed by immediate regret. Nathalie says that the incident must be forgotten. Nonetheless, the affair continues, and in a displaced echo of the Oedipus complex, this culminates in a weekend spent together in Sinclair's parents' apartment and in their bed. The siblings go barefoot, play like children and treat the whole event as a joyful game; this time spent together and the way they connect invokes childhood and pleasure in naughtiness. The way that this section of the film is figured might be considered in a psychoanalytic sense to deny the power and place of the father and his prohibition on incest. Meanwhile Sinclair begins to suspect his wife is having an affair (the source of some comedy). He later tells Richard what he believes, who becomes afraid, but is now deeply in love with Nathalie. The final crisis (mirroring the format of the adultery film) occurs when Nathalie breaks off the affair, and she and Sinclair have a going-away party. Richard's distress hits its peak and the two fight like children, rolling on the ground and nearly getting killed by a passing car. In this response, they act-out the types of behaviour that they might have indulged in if they had lived together as children. Sinclair guesses what has been happening, is rather bewildered but nonetheless thinks rationally rather than melodramatically, as the other two are inclined to do: he simply asks not to be told any details.

In the interviews that appear on the UK DVD release with the cast, which took place in 2004, 13 years after the film's initial release, Clive Owen suggests that one of the reasons that the film gained popularity on its release was the fact that incest is presented as a consensual adulterous romance, rather than as abuse or in full-blown sensationalist terms. Owen comments that the siblings' incest was largely overlooked by both himself and the audience. Why should this be so? Is this proof of the incest prohibition at work at the level of reception? In diegetic terms, the incest word is never spoken. Although emotions run extremely high towards the end of the film, there are more parallels with the standard adultery narrative than with the films discussed below. The fact that the two did not grow up together, that they do not look alike, and that there are no parents to underline their blood relation all help to keep this transgression of the incest prohibition rather low-key. Their relationship does not in truth challenge the social order or the family as there are no 'families' in the film. It is also made more palatable because audiences know that when they watch Nathalie and Richard make love, they are in fact two actors who are not related. Incest is therefore invoked in the film, but although Nathalie and Richard are brother and sister all these things work to cover over the real – in diegetic terms – nature of their relationship.

Disavowal plays a very strong role in the film; Owen's comments suggest that this is reflected in the reception of the film. The siblings often deny in dialogue and in some of their actions what they are doing. Nathalie has perhaps the most complex attitude to having sexual relations with her brother. She articulates a host of excuses about her behaviour, sometimes claiming that 'seeing' her brother cannot be in and of itself an adulterous 'affair', and it is clear that at one level the type of teasing that characterises some sibling relationships is taken by Nathalie into the register of the sexual. Childhood sibling games of power seem to have been transposed into the genital sexual economy of adulthood. Despite these games, Nathalie does however regard Richard as a brother and in this she differs from Richard. Richard falls in love with her, he blindsides the problems that their affair raises, believing that they can escape to live as man and wife. When Nathalie calls the affair off, he is devastated and reduced to hysterical behaviour. But unlike the case with most affairs, the two cannot simply go their separate ways. Their transgression is irreparably stitched into the fabric of their family, despite Sinclair's sanguinity. In overstepping the boundary and entering transgressive territory, these two experience at first elation, then confusion and anguish. In this the film borrows the structure of adultery films, which positions viewers in a familiar context and also contributes to making incest seem less transgressive and disruptive. Thereby the film skirts many of the more difficult and troubling aspects of incest. Unlike those films that present incest as abuse, desire is mutual here. The film calls on psychoanalytic understandings of incest, but through the medium of cinema invites the viewer to identify with the characters and asks them to understand the logic of their mutual attraction. Certain safety mechanisms acting as 'conditions' are therefore in place to contain this sexual transgression, which might prevent viewers from looking too closely at their own familial relationships (making the siblings estranged, for example). In addition, through the adoption of the formal attributes of the adultery film, *Close My Eyes* marks itself as imaginative speculation. Nonetheless, the adultery format in combination with incest also lends a certain subversive quality, with the viewer placed on the side of transgression and the return of that which should have been repressed.

Within the generic context of myth and fantasy, *Excalibur* has a far more perverse, and subversive, rendering of brother/sister incest, although here it is not the sole focus of the story. Unlike *Close My Eyes* and *The Cement Garden*, films that invite viewers to side with the incestuous desires of siblings that arise from mutual affection and extraordinary familial circumstances, *Excalibur* links incest to power and evil. In addition incest is used within the film as a means of subverting the patrilinear, gendered, social order. The fact that the film is set in a mythic context, and is therefore obviously fictional, means greater risks can be taken. Narrative context is extremely important for the meanings that circulate around incest here; as such some explanation of the plot is required. Early in the film, Merlin (Nicol Williamson) uses magic to allow Uther (Gabriel Byrne) to satisfy his lust for Igrayne (Katrine Boorman), who is married to the Duke of Cornwall (Corin Redgrave). While Cornwall is lying mortally wounded away from the castle, Merlin uses the 'spell of changing' to transform Uther into Cornwall's guise. He enters the castle to make love to Igrayne. The price for such magic is that Merlin gets to bring up the offspring (Arthur) of what is essentially engineered rape; as he puts it: 'what issues from your lust shall be mine'. These events are seen and understood by Morgana, then a child, the daughter of Igrayne and Cornwall. Morgana (Helen Mirren) does not appear again on screen until the day Arthur (Nigel Terry) marries Guenevere (Cherie Lunghi). Morgana's clothing, make-up and jewellery mark her out as different from the other women of the court. And, while the royal couple stand to say their marriage vows at the Christian altar, Morgana seeks to seduce Merlin with the aim of learning his magic. As Merlin tells Morgana, they are part of the old world with little place for them under the one god and the rule of men. This places them both on the side of magic and paganism. Morgana pursues her magic, learning from Merlin, stirring trouble at Arthur's court and attempting to put asunder the rule of men. It is she that causes Gawain (Liam Neeson) to accuse the Queen of adultery; the first stage in the downfall of Arthur's new order.

In her pursuit of power, Morgana is taken to Merlin's cave, where he intends to consign her to oblivion, but due to Arthur's planting the sword of power between the naked and sleeping bodies of his adulterous wife and Lancelot (Nicholas Clay), Merlin is struck down, enabling Morgana to learn the spell of changing that had previously been used to deceive her mother, and freeze Merlin in crystal, telling him 'I will find the man and give birth to a god'. Morgana goes straight away to Arthur, taking on the guise of Guenevere. Arthur kisses her and just as he reaches orgasm, she tells him she has 'conceived a son, my king … my brother' and reveals her true guise. From that point on the land and the king are in decline, Mordred (Charley Boorman/Robert Addie), the product of her incestuous deception, and Morgana gain power. Finally, Morgana is visited by Merlin, awoken by the love of Arthur, and persuades her to perform the spell of changing. She does this to show him her power, but it reduces her to a withered shell; disgusted by her (could this indicate a further form of incest?), Mordred kills her, cleanly and coldly. Mordred and Arthur, his father/uncle, do battle and, impaled on each other's, weapons they die. The land is left without a king, the Pendragon dynasty over, but so also is the link to the old magic, the old ways, where women could be as powerful as men, which Morgana sought to resurrect.

Morgana operates in the world of men; her magic disrupts their law and their prosperity, along with the gendered order that go with them. Her magic aims to put asunder the Christian patrilinear order; in robbing Arthur – her brother – of his seed, she negates and drains his power, setting up her own power-base. At the peak of his powers, Arthur was surrounded by a land in bloom, brimming with plenty; under Morgana the land is winter-bleak, dream and reality blur, and children die. The hope of the knights on the grail quest slowly fades and Arthur is in decline. Morgana uses beauty and guile to gain power in a court ruled by men. She represents evil, corruption and prevents progress, but it is also possible to read her, subversively, as an emblem of resistance to patriarchy. The obvious glee that she displays once she reveals herself to Arthur in the incestuous encounter is testimony to her desire to avenge herself against those powers that destroyed her family. As such the motives that lie behind Morgana's incestuous seduction of Arthur are very different to those of Nathalie in Close My Eyes. Morgana will not submit to giving away her son as her mother did, while she may love him he is also key to her plan to bring down the patrilinear line and make herself – like Merlin – the power behind the throne. Given this subversive witchiness that springs from prehistory and the primal where, in Freudian terms, incest is not yet subject to prohibition, it is little wonder that she must die robbed of her beauty and power at the hands of her son. It is easy to celebrate her poisonous presence at the heart of the patriarchal order precisely because in effect her actions are a form of revenge for the rape of her mother. While Close My Eyes took pains to avoid any real threat to the family or the social order so as to preserve the romance of the siblings' romance, here the intention behind incest is a rejection of the notion that women are objects of exchange through exogamous marriage. Whether or not this was intended by those who wrote and directed the film is a moot point, but once the film is regarded in the light of theories of incest (as well as with an eye to politics of gender representation), it becomes clear that Morgana works her magic to disrupt the foundation on which social scientists argue that 'civilised' social structure rests.

Oedipus Rex and *Bad Boy Bobby* are very different films stylistically and tonally, yet both are focused intently on the Oedipus myth. Both Oedipus (Franco Citti) and Bubby (Nicholas Hope) commit incest with their mothers and kill their fathers, transgressions that challenge the very definition of civilisation, but in very different circumstances and with different implications and trajectories. *Oedipus Rex* is based on Sophocles' play from which Freud took his now widely-known concept. In a range of ways is seems that the intent behind the film is to explore the play in ways that acknowledge but also go beyond Freud's use of it. While it would be difficult to stay broadly loyal to the narrative of the play without reference to those aspects that Freud uses, particularly the theme of blindness (disavowal) and the workings of occulted fate (the workings of the unconscious), the film does much to make what might be familiar strange, in keeping with art-cinema values. Hollywood-style conventions such as continuity and transparency of character are fractured, making the story rather hard to follow and therefore making events seem more enigmatic and dreamlike. The flow of the story is often interrupted by seemingly incidental, almost touristic, shots of landscape; almost as if the spirit of place supersedes the director's focus on the narrative. It is also often hard to understand Oedipus' actions because Hollywood notions of character motivation are largely ignored in an effort to come closer to the radically different worldview of ancient and classical Greeks. In so doing an acute sense of otherness is invoked that also distances the viewer, throws them off balance, so that they are not quite sure what to make of what they see. With its distancing techniques, the film avoids the graphic and sensational, which could easily be invoked given the nature of the story. Rather than the immediacy and transparency of sensationalism, easy access of meaning is withheld. The meanings of the images and events present themselves as a puzzle, but without a code to solve that puzzle. This is reflected in the way that the mother's enigmatic changeable expressions are presented to the camera/viewer (who is aligned with the point of view of the baby) near the start of the film (an echo of Laplanche's theory of the child's relation to the mother outlined earlier). This strategic and poetic 'strange-making' persists throughout the film and is illustrated best by referring to one particular scene in the film. To make sense of what takes place it is necessary to explain the events that lead to it.

As a small boy Oedipus is left in the desert to die because his royal parents, Laius (Luciano Bartoli) and Jocasta (Silvana Mangano), fear a prophecy that proclaims that he will kill his father and marry his mother. He is found and cared for as a son by neighbouring royals. When he reaches adulthood he goes to the oracle who repeats the prophecy, and, not knowing that his parents are surrogates, he fears for them and sets off on a journey. Upset and set adrift, he eventually comes to a crossroads, covering his eyes and spinning around, the path he takes he leaves to fate. On this road he encounters a chariot occupied by a king, signified by a large gold hat, accompanied by four guards. The king demands Oedipus stand aside; he refuses. After a time, Oedipus throws a rock at one of the guards and runs off in the other direction, chased by the guards, but he picks them off one by one.

During this scene spatial and temporal location is hard to follow. In some shots Oedipus runs across the screen right to left, and in others left to right. Spatial continuity is distorted. Elliptical editing also distorts the timeframe in which events happen. Facilitated by non-conventional editing that breaks the rules of continuity it appears that an occulted power, – fate – brings Oedipus back to the chariot from which he had run; whatever route he takes he is brought back to the same place. The expression of the operation of fate as it is rendered here is deeply idiomatic, only possible to accomplish in this way in cinema where space and time can be manipulated through editing regimes. Film is a medium wherein linear space and time can be spliced into and altered, offering the potential to present dream-like spatio-temporal non-logic and this capacity is used here to invoke the combined dimensions of the archaic and the unconscious as entities that fall outside history and order. What the scene demonstrates is that Oedipus has no autonomy, despite his attempts to confound the prophecy, and will end up no matter what he does killing the king, who is his real father. In Lacanian terms this expresses the principle that the letter of the unconscious always reaches its destination. Much of the detail of the death remains offscreen, just out of the viewer's line of sight, thereby mirroring Oedipus' disavowal of his truth. This also applies to the obscured ways that the sex scenes with Jocasta, his wife/mother, are filmed. Oedipus sees literally what he has done, yet does not see events in their true guise.

Blindness is absolutely central to the film's theme: Tiresias is blind but sees truth; Oedipus sees but cannot interpret, or read, the truth. The viewer is given signs without a code, actions happen offscreen and there is no chorus, as in the play, to guide their reading of the textual signs. Lingering shots of landscape, for example, are symptomatic of the veiling process of disavowal at work in the film's deeper logic. Through a psychoanalytic frame, 'blindness' can be regarded as analogous to castration (curtailing agency), disavowal (failing to see) and repression (putting out of sight). Oedipus wants to know the truth of his identity at the end of the film, yet as is evident in his speech to the Sphinx he does not wish to know the truth of himself. In this he is a deeply-split character, but he cannot see this. Truth threatens to destabilise his identity and the social/familial order, thereby challenging the Greek axiom 'know thyself'. Knowledge of the truth, desire for the truth, does not afford power; instead power is only attained by disavowal. Once the truth of his incest and parricide is revealed and Oedipus the transgressor is exiled, the plague the gods cast on the Thebans is lifted. In this context, knowledge and insight are not therefore linked to progress or power as in Enlightenment and modernist thought, instead both are tricky chimeras that promise, but can do nothing, to fill the perpetual gap of lack. Autonomy and agency are also undermined through the combined forces of fate (acting as the letter of the unconscious) and self-deception. These are hard lessons, comparable to those of Lacanian psychoanalysis.

Oedipus does not desire to kill his father or to sleep with his mother, as is the case with Freud's model in its pre-resolution phase; instead he is, as we have seen, fated to do so without being aware of what he does. Nonetheless, once he has a strong inkling that Jocasta is his mother, he practically rapes her, the transgression and confusion of identity fuelling his ardour in a kind of frenzied desperation. Through a psychoanalytic frame, invisible and incontrovertible fate becomes the workings of the unconscious: that which undermines agency. The film does not sever the connection to modern psychoanalytic thought, but it does take pains to locate the concept of fate within a mythic-archaic context which speaks through a combination of realism and metaphor. In Sophocles' play, the chorus often comments on characters' thoughts and actions, thereby giving a sense of what contemporary audiences would have made of these. There is no chorus in the film; the camera, *mise-en-scène* and sound acting together as a substitute chorus (or 'narration' as David Bordwell would term the sum of the cinematic parts used to show a story). The wordiness of the play is pared down to basics, the effect of which is to emphasise otherness and lend a stronger sense of the estranged archaic. In the play, the chorus is displeased with the way Jocasta, in particular, does not respect the rule of fate, sanctioned by the gods, when she attempts to get around the prophecy by having baby Oedipus killed. For the classical Greeks this is a play about autonomy and metaphysical predetermination; for a modern audience this is translated through a psychoanalytic frame into a conflict between autonomy and the subtle yet insistent workings of repressed unconscious desire. In pulling the threads of these together, the film is able to operate across time and culture.

The Moroccan sets used for most of the film present an arid non-European landscape, complete with mud-brick buildings. Landscape often becomes the object of the gaze in its own right; lingering shots of storks building nests high on the rooftops, for example, break up the flow of the narrative, distancing the viewer through the lure of the situational footage from the fiction. The landscape itself is, however, hostile to human life and the people who live within it are beyond Western cultural comprehension; Western viewers are unable to read the signs of an othered culture, much as the baby cannot read the signs carried by the mother's voice, body and actions. Images that connote 'civilisation' are confined to the modern scenes that book-end the film and there is no real sense of Classical Greece as a sophisticated civilisation: a place of debate, citizenry and aesthetic inquiry. Pier Paolo Pasolini often uses non-professional actors in his films, many of whom belong to tribes or people who live in ways that invoke for urbanised Westerners an archaic form of existence. As Oedipus travels through the landscape he comes across a group of men jumping up and down, in what appears to be some kind of rite-of-passage ceremony, followed by a couple wreathed in flowers in what could be a marriage ceremony. None of these people are given voices, however. Instead they provide a sense of otherness, becoming objects of the gaze because their actions and values are obscured for Western audiences. The line between documentary realism and the tourist gaze is blurred, put to work to help alienate viewers from their familiarity with the Oedipus story. Gesture also plays a significant role in the film, often operating without an index to help break the code. Gesture works hieratically often in the film, as it might do in the plays of Jean Genet or in Artaud's theatre. It invokes ancient ritual. Oedipus' body provides a language that he does not understand, cannot translate. One particular gesture is, however, recognisable and it operates in an over-determined way both structurally and symbolically.

When truth comes close, Oedipus throws his arm across his face, a gesture of horror and denial. Gestures are one of four components that Pasolini claimed are instrumental to the creation of poetic cinema; they are 'an indication of an extremely elementary stage of civilization' (1988: 169). The repetition of this gesture becomes ritualised and structural. That we can read this gesture is a concession to the viewer; it connects the past with the present, but because of its repetition and stylised form the gesture retains an alien quality that calls up both personal and social 'pre-history'.

The gesture that Oedipus uses provides a bodily means of expressing the anguish of transgression, and the gesture is connected to incest throughout the film, beginning, as Freud suggests, with the incestuous desires of early life. Here the film looks to Freud and the psychoanalytic rendering of the Oedipus complex rather than to Sophocles' play. The connection between the gesture and incest becomes clear in the two scenes set in the modern era that bookend the film. The first, set in the 1930s, shows a baby being born, then suckling at his mother's breast and listening to her voice. The child's father intrudes on these happy scenes and expresses his hatred for the child. An inter-title states his internal thought: the child has usurped him and stolen the love of his beautiful wife. After making love to her, he goes to attend the crying baby, and seizes the baby by the ankles; this action creates a visual and transitional link to Sophocles' play. Transported into the past, the baby boy is slung by his hands and feet to a pole on route to being dumped in the desert (a literal translation of Oedipus is 'swollen-footed'). Pasolini stated that the opening modern scene represents his own relationship with his father, which he clearly regards in Oedipal terms. The link between the ancient and the modern, the general and the specific, is indicated through casting: the modern father and Oedipus' father are played by the same actor as is also the case with Jocasta and the modern mother. The jealousy and rivalry is entirely on the side of the father, who expresses the conflict in sexual terms. In the closing section of the film a blinded Oedipus 'time-travels' to 1960s Italy, guided by a young boy, Angelo the Messenger (Ninetto Davoli). He returns to the place where baby-Pasolini of the opening scene suckled at his mother's breast as a place to die. The circularity connects the past and the present, the personal and the mythic. Oedipus is present in the modern world; he emblemises the particular boundaries that construct family and social relations as well as providing a figuration of twentieth-century explanations of sex and desire.

While *Oedipus Rex* spirals downward into tragedy, *Bad Boy Bubby* spirals upward through pathos and comedy to romance. *Oedipus Rex* moves towards the Oedipal crisis, whereas

Bad Boy Bubby moves in the opposite direction. *Bad Boy Bubby* is more conventionally shot and the viewer is encouraged to identify with Bubby and his journey. We are asked to see the world though his eyes, which can produce for the viewer a real sense of seeing the world and what we do in it in a different way. Bubby is the device for making what we commonly accept as 'normal' seem extremely strange. I should confess that this is also one of the most affective and involving films I have ever seen. It is about love and pity, expressing the strange conditions of being human from the position of an outsider looking in and looking to come in. The first 'act' takes place in two very basic adjoining rooms with bare, concrete walls and no natural light. Bubby and his mother (Claire Benito) are first seen as she washes a naked Bubby and then she goes on to wash herself. Bubby's actions are that of a small boy: his mother cares for him, he plays, parroting his mother's words to the cat; much of his behaviour and language is much as one might expect of a three-year-old. He has never been outside as his mother claims there is poison out there and wears a gas mask each time she leaves. As well as the grim atmosphere and the sight of an older woman with large naked breasts washing herself, it is the fact that Bubby is a full-grown man, slightly balding and quite hairy which makes the scene so striking and strange. Even more so when they are shown in bed together, she sitting astride him and he playing with her proffered breasts. 'Good boy, good Bubby', she tells him gently, contrasting with her more harsh way of policing his behaviour; good caring mother superseding bad careless mother temporarily. Their routine is interrupted one day when Bubby's father, who has been missing for 35 years, returns. Pop (Ralph Cotterill) takes Bubby's place in his mother's bed and proclaims that Bubby is a 'weirdo'. Soon after this, Bubby suffocates his parents using 'clingwrap', an act he undertakes dressed in Pop's clothes. But Bubby is an innocent transgressor and identification with him is made easily. After he kills his parents Bubby is on his own in a very aggressive and strange world, that, at first, resembles the dystopian visions of science fiction cinema, and for which he is desperately ill-equipped to deal.

In many ways the film is a psychoanalytic parable made along the lines of Melanie Klein's version of the Oedipus complex. She differs from Freud by shifting a genital economy and the Oedipus complex forward in the child's development, starting as soon as the child is born rather than between the ages of three and six. Within Klein's model the Oedipus complex is ever-present and arises throughout life. In the very early years it is related not to people but 'part objects' (such as the breast) and those are regarded as either good or bad (the good breast, for example, provides what the child needs, the bad either overfeeds or is not present when required). Objects that threaten possession of the good breast or mother are regarded by the child as hostile.[56] Rosalind Minsky provides a useful summary of the distinctions between the ways that Klein and Freud understand the role of the Oedipus complex:

> There are two poles to Klein's theory, both involving the construction of the phantasy world. The first is the self or ego's relationship, through phantasy, to the exter-

nal work of objects at first seen as the mother's breast which includes other part objects, and later as the mother is seen both as a whole and as a combined object containing the idea of the father. These objects are either idealised or denigrated through the mediation of love or hate. The second pole is the self's relationship, through phantasy, with its inner world containing instincts, impulses, bodily sensations and, most importantly, the baby's anxiety. This fundamental anxiety is the fear of being psychically annihilated by its own internalised aggression and not Freud's much later Oedipal fear of the loss of the penis (castration anxiety) by the father seen as a rival in love. Taken as a whole, Klein's work is concerned primarily with how the child copes with what it assumes as the loss of the mother when she is absent, by dividing her and the external world by means of phantasy. Significantly the breast replaces Freud's phallus as the object of most importance to the formation of the child's sexual identity. (1996: 84)

Bubby has a gift for mimicry and as things get very tough for him on the street, he adopts Pop's aggressive persona as a means of defence; this operates in Kleinian terms to preserve Bubby as 'good'; but Pop also threatens to overwhelm Bubby. Bubby only remerges intact when he is coaxed out by Angel (Carmel Johnson) who, as her name implies, represents the 'good' mother. His ear for sound and music is a strong feature of the narrative and the film's soundscape is carefully constructed from Bubby's point-of-hearing; there is no non-diegetic music. He is deeply affected by music, emotionally; melodic sounds are soothing and comforting, while discordant sounds are loud and jarring. Sound can be regarded in the light of the two different registers of his mother's voice (one soothing and praising, the other harsh and scolding) and it is very clearly split into good and bad in the film.

Bubby is an 'idiot savant' made in the mode of foundling Kasper in *The Enigma of Kasper Hauser* (*Jeder für sich und Gott gegen alle*, 1974), yet who has the endearing features of that other savant orphan-boy, *Edward Sissorhands* (1990). Bubby has not yet learned the context-bound dynamics of social etiquette and does not realise that he cannot fondle any breast that takes his fancy. On encountering a pair of irresistible large breasts he reaches out to touch them, breaking the invisible boundary of personal space and sending their owner screaming for the police. Other women to whom he had done this previously had simply removed his hand as they might do a curious child, but because he is dressed up and in a posh restaurant he appears to be an adult.

This act lands him in jail at one point. Sat in a cell, playing at being Pop, he is assailed by the scratchy discordant sound of bagpipes, designed it seems to annoy the prisoners. The noise drives Bubby to ask for a change of cell, the new one is a 'dirty' cell, covered in excrement, in which resides a naked man, also covered in excrement. The man rapes Bubby repeatedly, the camera closes in on Bubby's face and his silent tears, showing the violent movement of his body as it is pounded at by the man. This could be regarded in the light of Freud's concept of the anal stage in the trajectory of psychosexual development but it is only the rape and excrement that connects to this as Bubby takes no pleasure in any aspect of what occurs and his sexuality is already locked into a genital and heterosexual economy. It is also a form of punishment for his impulsive sexualised and incest-based action, for which he is subjugated to the desire of the man. But Bubby's morality is more complex than this punishment equation; his morality is increasingly sophisticated. He is told and he understands that murder has a transgressive status (after he clingwraps Angel's bigoted parents at her request). This is not the crude, mechanistic morality he learned from his mother and father, and through his experiences he begins to understand the operation of personal boundaries, which means that when he meets Angel he asks if he can see and hold her breasts, rather than simply grabbing them.

Bubby is also a member of a rock band. He concocts a montage of the sounds he has heard, reproduced perfectly on stage (parallels can be drawn with early 'Nick Cave and the Bad Seeds', an Australian band who gained a cult following). In other words, through his art, Bubby transforms his damaging and traumatic experiences into symbolic form, providing a form of catharsis for him as well as the diegetic and non-diegetic audience members who take to his performance. Through the transformational power of art, his romantic relationship with Angel and his contact with her profoundly disabled charges, for whom he has a close and sympathetic affinity, he develops a stronger sense of identity and agency. Angel is key to this: she is the 'good' object in Bubby's life that makes the real world seem more comfortable. The film ends with an aerial shot of Bubby and his and Angel's child playing in a lush green garden in the middle of an industrial area; Angel sits to one side playing with a cat, providing an expression of couple complementarity (Bubby has several important relationships with cats).

There is something profoundly moving and human about this film. It sides with those who are, for one reason or another, marginalised socially. It is very rare to find a film that deals with disability so boldly and humanely. Rachael (Rachael Huddy), for example, with her cruelly twisted, uncontrollable and painfully thin body, and inability to articulate speech, is afforded, through Bubby's ability to hear what she says, sexual desire. The viewer is urged to sympathise with the effects of her disability, the rejection and loneliness that goes with it. The film also reveals the processes that produce what appears to be 'normal' social functioning, what is needed in Kleinian terms for that to happen (good internal objects to counter the bad), but it also shows the 'normal' to be something that needs to be strived for, that demands work and is not therefore natural or hard-wired. The film positions the viewer in sympathy with Bubby; his transgressions are made fully understandable given his circumstances. We are encouraged to laugh at some of Bubby's social blunders, partly in the light of identification but also potentially so that one can see how laughter betrays the way that behaviour is policed at a social level. The movement from dark claustrophobic basement to bright garden is not presented as being simply a matter of escaping the sphere of the mother, something present in many rite-of-passage films; it is very clear that Angel carries many of the characteristics of the mother, and we even see her in the act of becoming one (watched by the whole band!). Angel might have allowed Bubby to kill her horrible parents but in so doing, in Kleinan logic, the ideal of the good parents is preserved for their own relationship. To Bubby she is the good breast/mother/lover, and to her Bubby is the good father, that Pop and her father were not.

While Bubby is on a trajectory to some semblance of normality – learning to be a 'clean and proper' social subject – his journey is in some respects a lesson to the viewer. The film uses Bubby's pre-social point of view to demonstrate the contradictions, cruelties, peculiarities and idiosyncrasies of the social order. Incest and parricide are far from sensationalised in the film. But the explicit way in which mother/son incest is presented to the viewer in such an unidealised form is important to the film's strongly psychoanalytic project to reveal the foundational role played by incestuous desires in the processes of socialisation, in the construction of identity and in the development of sexuality. The gap in age between Bubby and his mother is far wider than that between Jocasta and Oedipus in *Oedipus Rex*. This is important to the transgressive impact of the mother/son relationship on the viewer. The opening scene of *Bad Boy Bubby* provides a far sharper emotional jolt than is the case with *Oedipus Rex*. Yet that shock is not simply for its own sake; it is designed to disorient the viewer in a range of ways as well as engage them emotionally in ways that *Oedipus Rex* avoids through its distancing techniques. Both Bubby and Oedipus are complicit in the incest with their mothers, yet Bubby is able to go on to other relationships. In neither case is incest presented as abusive in overt terms. In both cases it concerns adults and not children; a factor that admits incest to legitimate cinema and makes it a suitable subject for entertainment. The fact that Bubby is both child and adult provides a means of disavowing the possibility of incestuous child abuse although, more so than *Oedipus Rex*, it certainly has a presence in the margins of the film. In both cases psychoanalytical concepts are deliberately called upon in their portrayal of incest and familial relationships.

In the case of father/daughter incest in legitimate cinema it is far more common for such relationships to be shown in an abusive context. It has been noted by a range of feminist critics that cinema often defines femininity through the terms of being a victim in need of rescue. In the case of father/daughter incest film, the power balance is tipped almost entirely to that of the father and there is far less of a sense of enjoyment and complicity in this relationship than is the case with mother/son incest as discussed above. *Broken Blossoms* presents a relationship between father and daughter in terms of abuse and cruelty (the mother is dead and there are no siblings). Battling Burrows (Donald Crisp) is a brutish prize fighter, a womaniser and mostly drunk, described in an inter-title as a 'gorilla' of a man. His daughter, Lucy (Lillian Gish), is terrified of him and his violence: an inter-title proclaims 'When she is not serving as a punching bag to relieve the Battler's feelings, the bruised little body can be seen creeping around the docks of Limehouse'. It would be easy to take his abuse at face value as simply violence, but certain features stand out that enable viewers to infer the possibility of incest. There is only one single bed in their dwelling which suggests they sleep in the same bed. It is possible that this is a product of the economics of staging the film and it may not have been regarded by contemporary audiences as remarkable, given that it was common for those living in poverty to share beds in the era in which the film is set. Nonetheless there are a number of other signs that imply incest. In an early scene, Lucy accidentally spills stew on her father's hand, he accuses her of doing it deliberately and despite her pitiful pleading walks to the bed and from under the mattress pulls a short leather whip and beats her with it.

Later, once he brings her home from Cheung's (Richard Barthelmess) house, where she was recuperating after the last beating, her father again threatens her with the whip, this time waiving its phallus-shaped handle in her face. She hides in a cupboard, the door of which he attacks with a small axe and drags her to the bed where he whips her to death, her innocence underscored as she clutches a doll. It may seem a rather crude Freudian interpretation, but the phallic objects and the violent whippings that take place on or next to the bed have an obvious sexual connotation. Two smaller clues might also be read as testimony to sexual as well as physical abuse. When Lucy lies on Cheung's divan recovering from her injuries, an anomalous shot appears: Cheung's face looms in at the camera (currently acting as Lucy's point-of-view). It is hard to read his features (following the 'inscrutable' Chinese stereotype), but the next shot shows her horror at what now emerges as sexual intent. The sexual nature of this intent is made transparent by an inter-title that explains that despite urges to the contrary he keeps his love for her 'pure'. How else would Lucy, who signifies in her dress, framing and actions childlike innocence, understand his intent as sexual in nature if she had not already encountered sexual attention, which is unlikely given her circumstances to have come from anyone else but her father. Later, Burrows comes to Cheung's shop to retrieve Lucy from what he regards as a sexual liaison with a foreigner which disgraces his honour. The looming close-up is repeated, but this time with Burrows in the frame. His face is full of hatred, but the repetition of the shot, with Lucy in bed, places him as sexual aggressor.

Prostitution, rape, murder and miscegenation are all invoked quite directly in *Broken Blossoms*, but incest, that crime that subverts the notion and identity of 'family', is veiled. Yet it lurks off-frame and it is up to the viewer to infer more than what is actually seen. The incest interpretation also accords with the film's intense picture of abuse and with D. W. Griffith's notion that women need protection from the brutality of men. While incest might lurk only in the fuzzy space of interpretation, given that incest is subject to the cloaking devices of family role and is subject to disavowal, there is a certain logic to the way it might be regarded as lurking at the margins of the film. And if we buy this, then the next question is why it is that murder and violence are acceptable subjects to be shown overtly but incest is not? Disavowal seems the most obvious answer. In *Twin Peaks: Fire Walk with Me* and *The War Zone*, where father/daughter incest is central to their narratives, the trajectory goes from disavowal to devastating revelation.

In both films teenage daughters are abused sexually by their fathers. In *Twin Peaks: Fire Walk with Me*, Laura Palmer (Sheryl Lee) has somehow duped herself into believing that the man who visits her bed at night was not her father but Bob (Frank Silva). While in *The War Zone*, Jessie (Lara Belmont) is fully aware of what is happening to her. In both cases it is implied that these incestuous relationships have gone on for many years. Laura was 12 years old when it began, and given that Dad (Ray Winstone) begins to sexually abuse Jessie's baby sister it seems possible that he has been abusing Jessie since she was young.[57] Both Jessie and Laura spend much of their time in tears, confused by competing emotions and motivations. They are torn apart by guilt and shame, an ambiguous position that straddles powerlessness and the power their bodies have over their fathers. In a psychoanalytic sense their guilt is produced by the fact that they believe they have achieved their Oedipal wish to replace the mother, but this comes at a huge cost. Incestuous desire places both girls on the borderline: their roles in the family and the broader social arena are no longer clear to them and each one becomes self-destructive. Laura knows she is going to be consumed by the 'fire' and her self-loathing and misery lead her to sustained drug-use and prostitution; incest makes all her relationships seem false and hollow. Jessie practices self-mutilation in her self-hatred and her relationships with others are also superficial. Neither have the help of their mothers, who are seemingly blinded to the unconscionable acts taking place in what appears from the outside to be happy and prosperous families.

The War Zone is in many ways a plainly-told drama. It deals with an 'ordinary' family who viewers are meant to take as 'real'. It is well-acted, in a naturalistic style. The scenes of family life are characterised by long silences and mundane routine, helping to lend a greater sense of reality. With little diegetic music and with a limited number of locations, the film is in many ways more like a television drama. While the film deals with a 'gritty' issue in the tradition of well-made British drama, it does not resort to the hand-held camera work that has become synonymous with 'realism' in recent years. Instead the film is classically and unobtrusively shot. The majority of the film is set in rural Devon in early spring. This is not picturesque holiday Devon, however, but muddy, wet, cold and inhospitable. There is no warmth or comfort in the film's colour palette. The house the family of four (Mum and Dad, Jessie aged 18 and Tom, 15) have recently moved into is an isolated and old-fashioned farmhouse. There are few technological comforts. The only concession is the telephone, located in the hallway, on which Dad seems to spend most of his time. But there is no television, computer or radio, which increases the sense of isolation. There is no living fire burning in the grate that might introduce a sense of warmth; instead gas heaters are present with cold blue flames, and boxes remain unpacked in the bedrooms. This house is not yet a home and the sense of isolation and coldness seen outside is present inside. Stuck in the past and bearing no obvious relationship to 'civilisation' (the house is not located spatially in relation to a town or a shop or even a made-up road), the house emblemises in a subtle way the immobility that accompanies incest and anguish. The weighty secret of incest anchors Jess to the family; she can never escape or form outside relationships while the abuse continues. Unlike the abusive father of *Twin Peaks: Fire Walk With Me*, Leland Palmer (Ray Wise), Dad seems not to suffer anguish over his deeds, instead he seems to be concerned with keeping the family close to him; this is what seems to motivate his need to sexually control, and thereby cleave to him, the female members of his family.

After the soap-style adrenaline of the opening, where the family crash on their way to taking in-labour Mum (Tilda Swinton) to hospital, causing her to give birth at the roadside, the family appears to be quite ordinary. Tom (Freddie Cunliffe), rather than Jessie, provides the main point of entry into the film. Sullen and miserable because of their move from London, he has none of his usual distractions to take him away from domestic life. One day Tom sees his sister and father doing something sexual through the bathroom window. As we do not see what he sees, it is not clear if he has imagined this. He begins to watch family-life more closely and challenges his sister, who responds in a hostile way. It begins to appear that Tom has become obsessed, in an aggressive way, with his sister's sex life. He blames her for attracting his father's sexual interest. But, after staging a situation where he watches his father and sister in an old concrete lookout post, he realises that Jessie is not to blame and nor is she complicit. Dad forces her to have sex with him and she cries throughout the ordeal. Dad also penetrates her anally, perhaps as a means of separating what he does with his daughter from what he does with Mum. Jessie asks why he cannot do it the way he 'does it with Mum'; a comment spoken from the place of Oedipal rivalry with the same-sex parent. He also kisses her body several times once he has finished, perhaps thinking to make some kind of reparation for his act and lessening the sense that he has abused her. The lookout-post incest scene is also important from Tom's point of view; he sees far more than he wishes to. In this, his position is linked directly to the viewer of the film: curiosity flounders in the face of the 'reality' of the unconscionable. He then throws the camera that filmed what he has seen into the sea. This is an act that mimics disavowal, but he cannot now forget what he has seen.

Later in the film, the fact that Tom has seen what his father does to Jessie means he is able to read the blood in his baby sister's nappy as confirmation of the appalling fact that his father has been abusing the baby. He warns his mother and returns home from the hospital, where Mum is with the baby, having the baby's anal bleeding investigated. Banned from the hospital, and on returning home, Dad yells abuse at Tom, threatening him, accusing him of lying. Dad never admits what has been happening even when Jessie accuses him. He says she is also lying. Tom stabs him, on the marital bed. The ending is ambiguous, it is unclear if Dad is dead and it is left to speculation whether Tom and Jessie seek sexual solace with each other (as occurs in the novel on which the film is loosely based). There are indications, however, that this will not happen as it is fairly clear that Tom's experience has afforded him a concrete sense of the incest prohibition.

The seriousness with which incest is dealt with in the film is underlined by the fact that the director, Tim Roth, has stated that he experienced something similar when young. He also chose to re-work quite significantly in the light of his own experiences Philip Roth's novel, wherein it is Jessie who entices her father to have sex with her, to place greater emphasis on abuse. He may well have feared that the original narrative might be seen as providing a 'well, she wanted it' narrative that could act to sanction incest and sexual abuse (something that would be regarded negatively by regulators, as well as critics, perhaps). While the film has been praised for its realistic picture of incest, a subject that is rarely tackled because of its sensitivities, from a gender perspective, all the women are victims in this film, thereby according with the over-worked position of women as victims in cinema generally. It is Tom that puts an end to his Dad's activities and in so doing it could be said that Tom is fulfilling his own Oedipal desire. Despite its focus on the rawness and psychological ramifications of incest, it is an Oedipal logic seen from the place of the boy that finds voice in a number of ways in this film (not perhaps surprising given the experience and gender of the director and screenwriter).

Twin Peaks: Fire Walk with Me has a much more complex structure and deliberately renders events in enigmatic terms designed to tantalise the viewer. Broadly speaking there are two registers that operate across the film: the world of everyday reality and a 'liminal' other which might be described as a kind of collective dreamworld or unconscious that operates outside the rational, but which influences the plane of the everyday in obscure ways. This structure allows the film to inflect the seemingly familiar with a deep sense of otherness. It does so through surreal imagery and arguably it is more dreamlike and has greater visual impact than the invocation of 'otherness' through the 'archaic' in *Oedipus Rex*. Most of Lynch's films entice viewers to interpret events that are rendered deliberately enigmatic. But unlike the practice of most films, Lynch does not provide the viewer with the means to unlock the hermeneutic code. The effect of this is an open text where various solutions are hinted at but never fully confirmed. Despite the openness of the text, the Oedipus situation can often be detected in operation in the way that the film realises incest, except that here we are asked to identify with the subjective confusions experienced by a girl.

Laura and her father, Leland, are deeply connected with the othered realm, of which they are broadly unaware (Laura has some sense of it towards the end). Boundaries of all kinds are ruptured throughout the film and nothing is what it seems. Characters experience each other as capricious and opaque, each locked on to a tune only they can hear. On the surface Laura is an archetypal high-school prom queen: blonde, pretty and privileged, but there is a darker side. She is heavily into cocaine, mixing it with other drugs and alcohol, stringing along two boyfriends, alternating between being sweet and loving, bitter and estranged. As a mark of her desperation and self-devaluation she prostitutes herself in the local club. Perhaps all these things are connected to the fact that Bob/Leland has been 'banging her since she was 12'. The splitting of her character and her indulgence in sensual pleasures provide her with a form of insulation against depression, subjugation and the duplicity of her home life.

Leland is also deeply split: he is a caring father, regrets his sexual abuse of Laura, yet he is consumed by rage and lust at various points throughout the film; although it is not expressly indicated, it is suggested that he is possessed demonically by Bob who impels him to commit the worst crimes. Bob might simply be a means of symbolising in visual terms the return of repressed urges. We see Bob in the Red Lodge, a liminal place peopled by strange beings and having no clear geographic link to Twin Peaks, the town. The Red Lodge has an extremely artificial appearance; within its walls speech is always distorted and everything looks staged. All of which can be equated with psychoanalytic notions of the unconscious, the place were repressed desires including incestuous ones reside; the Red Lodge is in a sense the place where repressed desires are 'put into scene'. Bob appears here without Laura's or Leland's presence, so it is unclear if Bob is Laura's invention to protect herself from the earth-shattering truth or has an independent existence. Lynch has said that he only cast Frank Silva in the role of demon-Bob when he saw him on set working in a technical capacity. Previously it must be assumed that he intended Ray Wise to play the role of Bob as well as Leland. In using a different actor to play Bob and Leland, Lynch dusts over the tracks of the split father; putting viewers off the scent, perhaps, of the way in which the imaginary father is split here between good and bad incarnations (much as occurs with the mother in Melanie Klein's work). Silva's rugged and unkempt appearance, the fact that he only screams (with one exception when he hoarsely whispers to Laura the enigmatic line 'fire walk with me'), with the camera often entering his mouth to show a waggling epiglottis echoing vulvic and phallic shapes in one succinct, all-encompassing and fleshy image, comes in total to represent something primal, barbaric and demonic. Bob's out-of-place presence in the Palmer's middle-class home emphasises his wild and uncivilised status. Bob begins as Laura and Leland's defence mechanism protecting them against the horror of incest, a protection that diminishes as we move closer to Laura's death and accordingly Bob's status becomes increasingly unclear.

Throughout the film most of the main characters are in a state of disavowal, motivated-forgetting protects them from devastation, fragmentation or alienation. James (James Marshall), the more morally upright of Laura's two boyfriends, sticks to his illusory belief that they are in love, despite her taunting and ill-treatment; but as Laura says to James 'you do not know me'. Laura's mother cannot act, despite the fact that she has some inkling as to what is taking place between her daughter and husband – all she can do is smoke incessantly, blowing into place a symbolic smoke-screen of disavowal. In many ways the film finds novel ways to explore psychical defences against alienation, the radical alterity of desire and lack of agency, but ultimately it shows that these are illusions that cover up the fragmented and conflicted nature of subjectivity. Along its psychologically convoluted path *Twin Peaks: Fire Walk with Me* exposes the barbarous aspects of family life that are hidden behind the barrier of the front door, as well as debunking the myth of romantic complementarity. Laura dies at the hands of Leland and Bob; as she is being killed we see from her perspective a point-of-view shot where the image of her killer alternates between the two images of Leland and Bob, eventually merging into one (which consolidates the split-father reading). Following her death at the hands of her demon-father, Laura meets in the Red Lodge an angel that disappeared from a picture on her bedroom wall sometime earlier. This Angel might be regarded as an image of redemption, or the good mother, except for the

Angel's truly kitsch rendering, and the fact that Laura is shown laughing at it for longer than is comfortable, suggests that the Angel is just an illusion. Loaded with conflicting signifiers the scene's meaning is shrouded, like much of the film, in mystery and is open to a number of possible meanings. Incest in *Twin Peaks: Fire Walk with Me* is not a fantasy; it is diegetically real and has real and horrific effects on Laura. Incest is also but one way that the film creates a picture of 'humanity' that resonates with Lacan's unblinking view of the cloaking tissue of falsehoods and self-deception that allow the subject to function, to have a sense of agency and coherence and which colours our relationships with other people. Unlike *The War Zone*, where the name of the film itself seems to refer to the hostilities of male Oedipus complex and where only the women retain the status of victims, Laura and Leland are both victims caught in a web of deceit and duplicity.

Despite their differences, *Broken Blossoms*, *The War Zone* and *Twin Peaks: Fire Walk with Me* locate father/daughter incest in far more disturbing and abusive terms than those films that focus on mother/son incest or sister/brother incest. In the latter groups, incest serves a range of aesthetic, dramatic and thematic purposes and is subject to a wide spectrum of emotional tones. These range from the elevation of family melodrama to high art in *Oedipus Rex* to the pathos-turned-comedy-turned-romance of *Bad Boy Bubby*; from adulterous romance in *Close My Eyes* to high fantasy and magic in *Excalibur*. It should be noted that same-sex incest is completely disregarded by these films and I know of no films that dramatise this variation of incest, which suggests that the psychoanalytic model, focused as it is on cross-gender hostilities and desire, is in play. The abusive context given to father/daughter incest in cinema also chimes with the psychoanalytic view of the father. The father figure is regarded as the keeper of moral order and is representative of power and authority, which makes his transgression of the incest prohibition all the more disruptive, and thereby it is shown as such within cinema. This logic only makes sense within a culture where families and other key social structures are organised along patriarchal and patrilinear lines. Freud's protracted deliberations on the 'family romance' uncover what he regards as the node that connects together civilisation, family structure and the incest prohibition. In 'Moses and Monotheism' (1939) Freud describes what he terms the 'primal father':

> The strong male was lord and father of the entire horde and unrestricted in his power, which he exercised with violence. All the females were his property – wives and daughters of his own horde and some, perhaps, robbed from other hordes. The lot of his sons was a hard one: if they roused the father's jealousy they were killed or castrated or driven out … The expelled brothers … united to overpower their father, and, as was the custom in those days devoured him raw. (1990: 324–5).

I will not read Freud's rhetoric as pre-historic truth or as universal but it works as an analogy that demonstrates how the incest prohibition is connected to the way in which civilisation is defined. Alongside the differences between those films that focus on mother/son and father/daughter incest, Freud's sensationalist rhetoric also shows that 'civilisation' is defined on patriarchal lines, which is underpinned by exogamous kinship systems and the protection of the family as a discrete and identifiable unit. Battling Burrows, Dad and Leland Palmer each carry with them aspects of Freud's 'primal father'. Each father transgresses the Oedipal contract in that they act as if they have sovereign rights over their daughters and are therefore sanctioned to take over control of their daughters' sexual choices. Perhaps this is the logical outcome of a social structure where the real father adopts a position of absolute authority, and it might explain the necessity for a strong prohibition against father/daughter incest. In support of this, Battling Burrows and Dad are challenged and killed by 'sons', and not their daughters, who remain victims; two of three daughters in the films analysed here are killed by their fathers (Lucy and Laura), those that commit incest in the mother/son and sister/brother films do not die (except for the witch Morgana). While the death of these fathers at hands of 'sons' might fulfil an Oedipal wish and give structural logic to a dramatic narrative, it also suggests that the Freudian promise that such an act (gendered very specifically as father-son rivalry) puts into place the 'proper' functioning of the prohibition is also fulfilled. This confirms that Freudian, as well as structuralist and social anthropological, understandings of transgression and taboo are central to the ways that cinema realises incest as a subject for fictional entertainment, and particularly in the way that psychological and situational repercussions of incest are understood.

Bondage, Domination and Sado-Masochism

$\mathcal{T}$he stinging kiss of leather on taut skin, breath coming in urgent gasps, the body straining at the pull of fiendishly tight ropes. From moustache-twirling villains and track-bound maidens, through the various incarnations of Fu Manchu's diabolical tortures, to the modish practices of *Preaching to the Perverted*, bondage, torment and torture have provided filmmakers with an effective source of sexualised sensationalism. Bondage, domination and sado-masochism (BDSM) have been used in some films and in various ways to explore evil and the darker aspects of desire, sexuality, power and relationships. Sometimes BDSM im-agery is used for comic value, either through bawdiness or parody, or to demonstrate and make capital from the playful and performance elements of sexuality. At other times such imagery is clothed in the dark accoutrements of gothic melodrama, while the most extreme use of all is found in those films that address sexualised violence with serious intent.

Films focused on BDSM key into conceptualisations of the sexual as having some kind of dangerous component. This might be related to the idea that BDSM endangers the bound-aries that secure identity and society, or because it is couched in sexological definitions of perversion, or because it invokes psychoanalytic notions that sexual desire is a force that exceeds conscious control. And, furthermore, because BDSM foregrounds the performa-tive, role-playing aspects of sexual relations. Because of these rhetorical frameworks, the portrayal of sex in cinema does not get more controversial and spectacular than when it involves bondage, domination and submission, sadism and masochism. This is especially the case in films where BDSM is presented in ways that go beyond their clichéd representa-tion in popular formats. Many representations of sex in cinema contain some form of power relations. The task here, however, is to focus on films that take as their central theme bond-age, domination and sado-masochism as sexual practices and to examine the conditions that are at work in many of the films discussed to ensure that BDSM-style fictional activities are legitimised. Our journey through these realms will take us through a number of genres: comedy, melodrama, animation, biopic, horror, fantasy and romance. In addition to these are art, sexploitation and sex films, some of which have pushed the boundaries of what forms of eroticised violence are sanctioned as acceptable for audiences. Because there are so many films that focus on or refer to sado-masochism and bondage, I will limit my examples mainly to films that relate to the figure or work of the Marquis de Sade. These films demonstrate the ways in which bondage, domination and sado-masochism are tailored to a cinematic medium, although as we shall see a surprising diversity of styles, intentions and meanings are in play. As with many of the other films and topics addressed in Part II of this book, context proves all important to the meanings assigned. It is one of the main contentions of this chapter to show that despite a wide variety of investments and styles, it is nonetheless the case that cinematic BDSM is laced in heady and seductive rhetorics of transgression, some of which draw on theories of sexuality and desire from philosophy, psychoanalysis and sociology.

What is sado-masochism? I will avoid giving a glib one-line answer to this, and, as such, no dictionary definition will be provided. This is because the meaning of the term has undergone various shifts and its definition continues to be very sensitive to who is making it and in what context. It is necessary to be aware of the medical/scientific definitions of sadism and masochism (some are outlined below). Medical definitions of sado-masochism are forged from an objective perspective; they tend to pathologise and dissect those practices rather than providing an understanding of how they are experienced and interpreted in the context of contemporary BDSM culture. As such, if you were to ask a practitioner of consensual sado-masochism how they define BDSM the likely reply would be something to the effect that it is erotic play, possibly of an exploratory nature, based on the interaction between the roles of dominant and submissive. Pat Califia, a prominent practitioner and champion of consensual sado-masochism, uses the term to mean 'sensual rituals and games' (1994: 3). However, it may appear to the casual inexperienced observer that sado-masochistic games are abusive if the 'consensual play' angle is not understood. As Laurence O'Toole notes, 'S/M sex and S/M porn can be difficult to read if you're not familiar with the codes and forms' (1999: 47). There are then certain protocols that are used in contemporary consensual sado-masochistic culture. These frame the way that 'scenes' of domination and submission are played out (the term 'scene' places emphasis on the play and theatrical aspects of BDSM).

Many films featuring sado-masochism (S/M) are based in and marked overtly as fantasy, and are intended to be consumed as such. This is one of the reasons for their often theatricalised melodramatic or campy nature. Practitioners of S/M have recounted how some of their sexual fantasies and the scenes they play out are derived from film. Scenarios derived from films or literature that might appear to be abusive may be used in actual practice, but through consensuality they are framed as a form of play. As Philip Miller and Molly Devon point out, consensual sado-masochism is a co-joining of 'tears and laughter, fear and love, intimidation and caring, bondage and liberation' (1995: v). It is this framework that for practitioners crucially distinguishes contemporary consensual sado-masochistic practice from sexual violence and abuse. The goal of much BDSM practice is to intensify and extend the sensual experience of sex. It is sometimes the case that in the pursuit of intensification and experimentation boundaries are broken to the detriment of the players; safe words and agreements are designed to prevent this as far as possible. O'Toole also centralises consensuality in his understanding of contemporary BDSM: 'it is because S/M sex is a complex, ritualised sexual performance between adults, a carefully negotiated manipulation of power relations, that issues of consent are so vital' (1999: 47). Playing at and with boundaries is what makes BDSM exciting for many players and many do so happily and without ever considering what occurs as abusive. In the fictional/fantasy-context cinema, however, greater licence is afforded.

It is important to note that indulging in the fictional fantasies of Sade or other such work is related to, but distinct from, what people do in the consensual sado-masochistic scene. Within some cinematic contexts BDSM is clearly marked as fiction/fantasy through the use of clearly signified generic contexts and conventions (assuming that a viewer is conversant with those codes). In other formats that take a more realist approach, the status of BDSM becomes more ambiguous. As such, regulatory bodies have to take account of the fact that films representing sado-masochism, bondage or domination may be misunderstood as representing 'real' practices rather than theatrical constructions. Often there is a concern that such films could encourage viewers to take pleasure in watching sexualised violence and might provide fuel for copy-cat sexual abuse. The BBFC has stated the following:

> The BBFC Guidelines for Classifying Films and Videos identify sexually violent material as potentially harmful. The Guidelines explain that the Board is stricter with scenes of sexual violence on video than film, because of their potential to be played over and over at home. Sexual violence may only be shown providing the scenes do not offer sexual thrills.[59]

Because of rulings such as this, film-based representations of sado-masochism are closely scrutinised; freedom is balanced against social responsibility. However, in providing a kind of social protection against anarchic forces, the BBFC's statement also guards against a certain kind of media 'illiteracy'. In general, it is in production companies and filmmakers' interests to ensure that their products do not incur censorship. Often this means framing representations of S/M and bondage in certain ways. Those producers that do not accord with regulatory legislation simply duck out of the system and do not present their work to the more stringent classificatory bodies, as occurs with the majority of the hard-core industry. The regulation of sado-masochism in cinema demonstrates that it is understood diversely and contextually and that erotic imagery involving power-play connects with broader social issues around violence, gender and sexual identity. In recognition of the ways in which bondage, domination and sado-masochism occupies a rather difficult position in terms of boundary-testing, various community bodies have attempted to sanction against abusive play, drawing up guidelines and boundaries to aid the process. These guidelines also have a role to play in defining contemporary BDSM practise. The American-based National Leather Association state that sado-masochistic play should be 'safe, sane and consensual' (a similar statement is often found in literature on the practice of BDSM, particularly manuals). The aim here is to distinguish good, contractually-based practice (where limits are agreed by participants) from abuse. But this does not mean that in a consensual-play context scenes owing a debt to fictional non-consensual BDSM are rendered taboo.

Many practitioners prefer the more gentle terms 'B&D' or 'kink' to the more pathologised and rather extreme sado-masochism, but not all; some use S/M interchangeably with BDSM providing a more inclusive nomenclature. So, even for practitioners, there are different uses, nuances and understandings of the term. In contrast to the consensual and play aspect that is foregrounded by those sympathetic to the practice of sado-masochism within the context of BDSM culture, are the clinical-based definitions. Many of these come out of the scientific study of sex in the late nineteenth century, which define sado-masochism in terms of a 'perversion' of 'normal' sexuality and sexual practice. Clinical definitions of sado-masochism use heterosexual copulation within a marital context as a benchmark for what is taken to be 'normal' sexual behaviour. It is here that the values of the dominant order can be seen to be at work in medical discourse; particular social and moral values are affirmed through the pathologisation. There are, however, diverse uses of medicalised terms, which stem from different value systems, interpretational investments and contexts. Changing sexual values, some of which are derived from shifts in the way that sexuality is thought about, have also had an impact on the different ways in which the term is used. As such, it is useful to see how the term 'sado-masochism' has been used and how its meanings have evolved in accordance with different agendas and investments. What has remained constant in both the clinical context and within various practitioners' definitions, however, is that the practice of sado-masochism carries a transgressive kudos; it can even be said that its practice in some cases depends on that kudos for its erotic impact. Nonetheless, the meanings of sado-masochism as a form of transgression are subject to different types of investments. Films that represent sexual sado-masochism trade on its transgressive coding to solicit erotic and sensationalist interest from across a range of possible viewers, some of whom might identify themselves with BDSM as a practice related to sexual identity, and some of whom might not.

Richard von Krafft-Ebing bought the terms 'sadism' and 'masochism' to the public arena in *Psychopathia Sexualis* in 1886.[60] As Roy Porter and Mikulas Teich have noted, this text created a 'bestiary of sexual transgressions', composed as it is of case histories that aimed to divide 'healthy' sex from 'degenerate' sex (1994: 15). Initially his project to categorise perverse acts was an attempt to formulate clinical definitions that could be used in courts of law. Yet in the course of collecting case histories, and attempting to cure people of 'perversions', Krafft-Ebing came to the conclusion that sadism and masochism are psychologically-based and are extreme versions of everyday behaviour (see Hauser 1994: 211). Krafft-Ebing's neologism 'sadomasochism' yokes together particular but very different sexual proclivities described by two writers, the Marquis de Sade (Donatien-Alphonse de Sade) (1740–1814) and

Leopold von Sacher Masoch (1836–95). De Sade's work often involves extreme situations of torture and violence, often inflicted by men and women on the innocent (as in *Justine, or Good Conduct Well Chastised* (1791)). Deleuze writes that Sacher-Masoch was much given to being dominated: 'he enjoyed pretending to be a bear or a bandit and having himself pursued, tied up and subjected to punishments, humiliations and even acute physical pain by an opulent fur-clad woman with a whip; he was given to dressing up as a servant, making use of all kinds of fetishes and disguises, placing advertisements in newspapers, signing contracts with women in his life and if need be prostituting them' (1991: 10). Alongside a number of other novels and short stories authored by Sacher Masoch, *Venus in Furs* (1870) is based on similar themes. The reason that Krafft-Ebing enshrines these two writers in his categorisation of sexual perversion is because he found that some of the people on whom he based case studies referred to the works of these two writers when describing their own sexual fantasies and actions.

Krafft-Ebing conceived of masochism as the opposite of sadism; making for an odd form of complementarity (for which he has been criticised by Deleuze (1991), who sees the two as entirely different and certainly not polar opposites[61]). Masochism describes the practice of gaining erotic pleasure from having pain inflicted on one or being subjugated to the sexual will of another; sadism describes the practice of gaining pleasure from inflicting pain and dominating others, both in a sexualised context. Krafft-Ebing discovered that these sexual economies where very often linked to fantasy and that in most cases they involved very specific scenarios that involved some form of fetishism. As such, sado-masochism was regarded as a psychological phenomenon, rather than a physiological one. This aspect of his work influenced other sexual science works on sado-masochist practices, including that of Freud, and his terms are now in common use. As Vern L. Bullough, Dwight and Joan Dixon claim, Krafft-Ebing's concepts have 'become part of modern sexology as well as popular culture' (1994: 48).

Havelock Ellis (1859–1939) wrote many books on the psychology and sociology of sex and made use of Krafft-Ebing's categories of sexual perversion. Importantly he observed that sado-masochism was often practised within loving relationships, which went a step further towards de-pathologisation. Ellis locates sado-masochism within everyday sexual relations, rather than as aberrant practice. But perhaps this observation was brought about because of the way that Krafft-Ebing's terms became part of popular discourse, providing a means to speak of different aspects of sexual experience. In partial support of this idea, many sexological works became bestsellers and were consumed as a form of pornography or were even used as sexual manuals. Renate Hauser notes that in an attempt to prevent such use, Krafft-Ebing wrote up some of the more risqué case studies in Latin (1994: 212). Some sexological literature also ran into problems with the law; a volume of Ellis' work was deemed obscene and banned by a British court. What is remarkable about the otherwise rather careful approach to naming perversions is that Krafft-Ebing's work rarely attempts to theorise the origins of his categories of 'perversion' (his word). Freud's work, which certainly owes a debt to Krafft-Ebing, went far further towards building an expansive theory of sexuality in which, in different ways, sadistic and masochistic sexual desires play a significant part.

Freud's work is based on the idea that our minds are not entirely our own; we are haunted by the ghosts of repressed sexual ideas, which arise through the process of socialisation. As has already been noted, Freud argues that if we are to live in a 'civilised' society certain aggressive and sexual desires and thoughts have to be managed; deemed unacceptable they are kept from consciousness or repressed. Mark Edmundson has suggested that the Freudian psyche 'begins to look like a sadomasochistic dungeon, with the cruel superego tormenting the hapless ego' (1999: 128). Within Freud's 'gothic' model of the sexual psyche, masochism is the result of a persecutory superego (a part of the psyche that oversees, judges and censors the ego). A child's sadistic impulses (which are non-sexual) are censored, leading to feelings of guilt and shame. These impulses are therefore turned in on the self, leading to masochism – self-harm that was originally desired to be inflicted on others. (This conception is put into play in *Secretary* (2002); it is how E. Edward Gray (James Spader) understands the reasons why Lee (Maggie Gyllenhaal) cuts herself; this insight and how it is managed 'cures' her and puts her submissive and masochistic tendencies to more playful and positive uses.) Through the Oedipus complex and other interpersonal contexts, masochistic and sadistic impulses become charged with sexual energy and where they are not realised they are likely to be indulged in through fantasy or transmuted into symbolic forms such as jokes. Sadism, in its sexual sense, is the 'turning round' of masochism, projected outward rather than inward. The composite term 'sado-masochism' is used in psychoanalysis to describe how any individual relates to themselves, others and authority. Masochistic and sadistic traits are integral to the psyche, connected as they are to our relations to the external world, including other people and to the emotional implications of conflicts between reality and pleasure principles; in a given situation one or the other might prevail.

Within Freud's model we are therefore all inherently sado-masochists. This idea may help to explain why the practice of BDSM carries with it a transgressive kudos. BDSM articulates overtly what is otherwise repressed, disavowed or covered over about the dimensions of sex and power that operate in inter-personal relationships. For Freud, sado-masochism is not therefore merely defined by a specific type of sexual practise involving whips, leather, domination and submission (although all of these might be invested with sexual energy), it is something far less localised. According to Freud, all our relationships are based on shifting positions of domination and submission. The economics of sado-masochism are built into the way we become socialised into 'clean and proper' individuals, which necessarily involves 'self-punishment' as a form of self-management wherein personal and social factors have to be balanced (Laplanche & Pontalis 1988: 401). Within this definition, theatricalised sado-masochism, as it is articulated in many films and in the BDSM community, is a symbolic, ritualised and eroticised expression of the darker currents that underlie our experience of human interaction. For some, 'acting out' such otherwise buried experiences in a safe context not only imbues sex with greater intensity but it also acts a form of therapy. The therapeutic dimension of BDSM is exhibited in films that deal with it as practise that defines identity and where it is seen in the light of positive personal benefits: *Secretary*, *Preaching to the Perverted* and *Exit to Eden* (1994) for example.

While Freud's view is an attractive one, particularly for those who practice BDSM, there are a number of drawbacks to his definition of sado-masochism. The slinky universalism of Freud's model is somewhat blinkered to the way that sexuality and sexual practice are the products of culturally-produced and historically-grounded discourse. This argument is developed by Michel Foucault in his three-volume work *The History of Sexuality*. It should also be noted that there are physiological reasons why some forms of pain produce pleasure. As Keith Kendrick says, 'endorphins are similar to morphine and produce pleasurable euphoric feelings (this 'high' is often experienced by those undertaking physical exercise that exhausts muscles)'.[62] Despite such problems, Freud's 'gothic dungeon' model of sexuality is one that attracts the 'pornographic' and cinematic imagination: working as it often does to bring an electric *frisson* to the representation of sex and sexual desire. This should not be too surprising if we follow the view that sexual desire is largely connected to the workings of the imagination.

Freud's model has been lauded as challenging sexological approaches that used sado-masochism as illustrative of the difference between 'normal' or 'natural' and 'abnormal' or 'unnatural' sexualities (see Bristow 1997: 68). This is clear in Freud's important statement that 'no healthy person, it appears, can fail to make some addition that might be called perverse to the normal sexual aim; and the universality of this finding is in itself enough to show how inappropriate it is to use the word perversion as a term of reproach' ('Three Essays on the Theory of Sexuality', 1977: 74). Freud points out that the value of Krafft-Ebing's term sado-masochism is that it not only encompasses the idea of the pleasures of giving and receiving pain, but also those of domination, humiliation and subjection (1977: 70–1). He argues that sadism only becomes a 'perversion' proper when 'satisfaction is entirely conditional on the humiliation and maltreatment of a subject' (1977: 71). Similarly masochism is only a 'perversion' when mental and physical suffering is the sole aim of a person's sexual behaviour. This threshold should be questioned, however. Even if masochism is the guiding principle of a person's sexuality, it should not be pathologised in all cases. It is a matter of degree and how it is self-managed; this is the pro-BDSM message convincingly delivered by *Secretary*. Even more problematically, Freud also links the active stance of sadism and the passive stance of masochism to over-simplified, polarised notions of sexual and gender difference. Sadism is, he claims, a fundamental component of male sexuality, which is aggressive 'by nature'. As such the cultural role played in the construction of gender is diluted and an inflexible concept of sexuality emerges (somewhat undermining the potential of an inbuilt polymorphous perversity). The longevity of such a binary paradigm of sexual difference is dependent on having people believe that gender attributes are biologically, and not socially, fixed. Many BDSM practitioners play with such pre-determined and overly conventionalised ideas about gender, often with the intention of subverting or parodying them, perhaps to intensify the transgressive voltage of a sexual 'scene'. Gender roles are often played with as a means to an end. Working with the material experience of gender and its borders by using the differences between lived realities and the ideals of society is often used to increase the emotional impact of a scene. The 'queering' of sexuality in the widest sense is something that many practitioners of BDSM value, politically as well as personally. Evidence of this is found across the historical length and stylistic breadth of films focused on S/M or BDSM. Pre-Code horror films, for example, often twist the gender alignments of sadistic villains, with perversion of every kind being deployed to signify 'evil'. In later films gender-play is far more overtly made and is often intrinsic to a given film's transgressive status. In some instances gender-play is designed to appeal across the board to both the straight, bi-sexual and gay BDSM community.

The literary works of de Sade, alongside the clinically-based works of Krafft-Ebing and Freud, have also helped shape the vocabulary of sado-masochism as a sub-cultural practice as well as an epistemological entity (the one would not exist without the other). There are, though, very different intentions behind de Sade's work than that of the other two. De Sade's work uses extreme sadistic practises in a fictional context to shock and titillate. His work was a forum for the formulation of libertarian views designed to challenge the values of the social order in which he lived (both pre- and post-French Revolution). Spending 27 years behind bars, as a result in the first instance of his sexual adventures and later for what was considered to be the moral insanity of his writing, de Sade wrote most of his work in prison. While he regarded fiction as a means of living out his desires and politicising that desire, Krafft-Ebing and Freud worked from a clinical perspective, seeking to understand the nature of sexuality and, ultimately, to cure those who found that their 'perversions' interfered too considerably with their lives and relationships. In their different ways de Sade, Krafft-Ebing and Freud challenged hetero-normative notions of sexuality. In bringing 'perverse' sexual practises into the public arena, these figures have significantly informed the various ways in which sado-masochism is articulated and represented in contemporary culture. In addition they have all added in various ways to the rhetorics of transgression that enfold, encode and energise BDSM.

There is a significant difference between the interpretational contexts that define practitioners' and clinicians' understandings of sado-masochism. These can be, and often are, set against one another, yet they do feed off and into one another. Importantly, however, the two frameworks speak from different places. Practitioners formulate their understanding from the place of pleasure, a kind of *ars erotica* (Foucault 1984: 57), which is derived from practice and experience, and is therefore based on subjective, sensual and emotional logics. Clinicians formulate their understanding by articulating knowledge from an abstract, scientific and objective point of view, which Foucault terms *scientia sexualis*. This is not grounded in the experience of 'doing'. The two positions do conjoin in some instances, mainly where practitioners are engaged in writing and reflecting on what they do (in writing academic books and self-help guides, conversations in internet chat rooms, and so on). It is important to note the difference between objective and subjective positions, though, especially when thinking about the diverse meanings that are attached to these different perspectives.

Don Miesen, one of the founding members of the Janus Society based in San Francisco, is one such practitioner. He makes a similar distinction between the two different approaches through a consideration of the connections between the aesthetic angle of consensual sado-masochism and art. In so doing, he illustrates nicely how a practitioner's view, embedded as it is in the sensory and emotional experience of BDSM, differs from a scientific approach:

> Whenever we think what makes eroticism good, we naturally think in terms of anticipation, excitement, tension, relaxation, rhythm, style, surprise, sensations, textures, delicacy, power, imagery, relief, fulfilment, and so on. These are the analytic terms of the arts (and of the performing arts, at that). They are not the analytical terms of theology, medicine, science, ethics, nor politics – though all of these have claimed sexuality for their domain.[63]

The aesthetic component of BDSM is important to contemporary practice and is largely ignored by clinicians. It is this component that bonds BDSM to the experience of cinema, as mentioned previously, as well as its cinematic representation. BDSM scenes are often set up using the types of *mise-en-scène* and characters that are found in gothic horror films (which in turn are derived from the gothic novel). Sado-masochism turns sex into a dramatic and carefully-staged scenario. Cinema trades very often on spectacle as a means of attracting audiences and the theatre of sado-masochism is well-suited to visual display. Sado-masochism also invites art cinema's interest as it involves staging sensationally the ambiguities of desire, transgression, sexual politics and the spectacle of the body and psyche *in extremis*. Certainly many films from across the range present sado-masochism as 'perverse', mixing the classic definition with that which is edgy and cool, capitalising thereby on that coding to mark erotic content as extraordinary and sensation-rich. This is supported by the way that many films are niche-marketed (for example, video distribution companies such as Redemption specialise in re-releasing older films with a cultish sado-masochistic flavour). The film industry exploits the perverse kudos of sado-masochism to attract audiences, which keeps in circulation the idea that sado-masochism is abnormal. This works to preserve its transgressive status and thereby, perhaps, its appeal. It is sado-masochism's *outré* eroticism that attracts many practitioners to its pleasures (a means of spicing up sex lives with a hint of danger or power-play). While continued adherence to the notion that BDSM is perverse is conservative, it is nonetheless the case that many BDSM-focused films raise tantalising, challenging and possibly discomforting questions about the nature of sexuality, the definition of identity and gender roles. Cinematic representations of BDSM, as with representations of sex and desire in general, do, as we shall see, interlace clinical models of perversity with more radical takes on what constitutes and defines human sexuality and desire. In many respects perverse status provides the grounds for the challenge to the sexual status quo.

Before addressing BDSM films directly it is valuable to note that concepts of sadism and masochism have often been used to theorise the experience of cinema. Analysis of the power relations built into regimes of looking, identification and objectification provide the basis for a sexualised theory of spectatorship. In 'Visual Pleasure and Narrative Cinema' (1975), Laura Mulvey theorises, using Lacanian concepts, the way in which Hollywood films orient viewers into sadistic and voyeuristic positions in relation to onscreen female bodies, which are designed as passive objects for the consuming gaze and to be done to by male characters. She argues that women spectators either have to take up the viewing/identification position of the male sadist or align themselves masochistically with the women on the screen. By contrast, Kaja Silverman (1981) argues that identifying masochistically with characters in cinema is one of its major pleasures, as does Gaylyn Studlar (1985). These film theorists use psychoanalytic theory to aid their thinking about the way that films engage viewers in terms of a sadistic or masochistic economy.

Steven Shaviro (1993), goes further than Silverman and Studlar, arguing that cinema's essential pleasure is the fact that the spectator is 'done to' by the film's textual order. He looks to French theorist Gilles Deleuze to support his supposition. Shaviro uses Deleuze's work as a means to relocate thinking about spectatorial masochism away from psychoanalytic models of sexuality, because of their tendency to anchor sexuality in the Oedipal triangle and to append desire negatively always to lack. While critics have often assumed that spectators identify with sadistic acts, this is by far from the whole picture. The spectatorial position is precisely defined as one where no action can be taken; viewers are carefully interpolated into a given position by textual strategies that locate the viewer within a film's diegesis (this placement can be rejected or resisted but if it is then different pleasures and unpleasures than those that are intended by the film's construction are likely to be gained). Through the combined effects of aural and visual regimes the spectator becomes subject to emotional manipulation. Shock, surprise, hope, trepidation, suspense, anticipation, relief through resolution, as well as affective investments in characters, are goals commonly sought by the ways a film's textual/formal features orchestrate the emotional ride that is watching a film. It is the careful construction of a sensual and sensation-based journey that many viewers regard as constituting the major pleasure of cinema. While this might not be masochism in a clinical, full-blown, sense, it bears a strong resemblance to the erotic experience of a submissive taken on a sensual journey in an orchestrated consensual sexual encounter. That is not to say, however, that sadistic pleasures are not indulged at times, yet these too are likely to be part of a larger, dynamic emotion-generating scheme, wherein sadistic and masochistic investments operate relatively.

Cinematic images of S/M and BDSM can be grouped into a number of categories, which provides an overview of the scope and generic diversity of such representations:

– *Backdrop BDSM*: those films that bring in S/M or bondage as a titillating backdrop to a story focused elsewhere or as part of a detective scenario (*Barbarella* (1968); *Maîtresse* (1973); *Sherlock Holmes and the Case of the Silk Stocking* (2004)).

– *BDSM subculture*: those that focus on the contemporary BDSM community as a subculture, (*Preaching to the Perverted*; *Exit to Eden*; *Secretary*). These films are located diegetically in the 'real' world and often deal, lightly, with identity politics. They often have a persuasive element in that BDSM is presented positively. BDSM practise is couched within the context of love and a central heterosexual romance, to which comedy might be added in an effort not to scare-off a more general audience.

– *Fantasy BDSM*: those that present BDSM overtly as an erotic fantasy; often using soft-core aesthetics and the rite of passage/initiation narrative format (discussed in Part I) (*Emmanuelle*, *The Story of O*; *Gwendoline* (1984)).

– *High-art BDSM*: those that combine 'high' art and BDSM imagery, often in short-film format (*Marat/Sade* (1967); *Mano Destra* (1986); *Marquis* (1989); *The Attendant* (1992)). As well as experimenting with the artistic and philosophical potential of cinema, these films tend to have a subversive intent, either socially or formally. Some use S/M imagery to speak of sexual identities and desires other than heterosexual, while others are engaged with high-art themes such as satire and political economy.

– *Political BDSM*: those that use BDSM imagery and themes to comment on broader power relations or politics (*The Night Porter* (*Il Portiere di Notte*, 1974); *Salo, or 120 Days at Sodom* (*Salò o le 120 giornate di Sodoma*, 1976)). These films actively set out to disturb the erotic gaze by aligning sex and desire with the power afforded by Nazi rule; transgression is put to this service.

– *Horror/sexploitation BDSM*: those that use sadistic imagery within a horror or sexploitation context (*The Whip and the Body* (*Le Frusta e il Corpo*, 1963); *Deadly Sanctuary* (aka *Marquis de Sade: Justine*, 1969); *House of Whipcord* (1974, UK)). These films are designed for maximum sensationalism, sometimes skirting on the edge of legitimacy because the line between nastiness and titillation is blurred. Arguably, some of these films adopt aesthetic and formal values that are often used to define experimental and art-cinema.

– *Hard-core BDSM*: those films that present BDSM practise within a hard-core sex context and which exist outside legitimate means of distribution in the UK and the US (*Latex*; *Kinkorama 14* (circa late 1980s); *L'initiation d'Anna* (circa late 1980s)). *Latex* is one of the rare examples of a hard-core film that can be said to exhibit art-cinema attributes. At the other end of the production value spectrum are the point-the-camera-and-shoot 'amateur' BDSM videos made for private consumption or swaps. Hard-core BDSM films show explicitly forms of BDSM that other legitimated films only suggest. This category extends into internet services where live BDSM can be viewed. Some hard-core films not focused intently on BDSM sex will include a BDSM scene for variety, while others cater for very specialist tastes.

These categories listed above also reflect in fairly broad terms how BDSM activities are regarded more generally: from harmless, consensual erotic fun, through to manifestations of deeply psychopathic behaviour that feeds on non-consensuality. It is to the films focused on de Sade and his work that we now turn.

What is most notable about the very many films that reference de Sade is that they regularly dilute the extreme situations of taboo-breaking and sexual torture present in his stories. This is in part related to cinema's censorship regimes. Films of a more populist nature that represent de Sade directly also tend to make him into a sympathetic, loveable-rogue figure who struggles with authority and his own contradictions. Working against the back-drop of the French Revolution, de Sade's writings are characterised by his view that only a truly radical transition would make an equal society and it is clear that he does not believe this is achievable given the egoistic and exploitative 'nature' of humankind. The watchword of his work is extremism; everything is made outrageously excessive. De Sade's stories do not depict an imaginary sexual plenitude, however. Instead there is vigorous straining to go beyond all limits, hence the emphasis on repetition, excessive proportions and numerous-ness. Sex and pleasure are defined as excess rather than as luxuriance and comfort; Thana-tos rather than Eros holds dominion. Most of his characters end up dead after being caught in an endless chain of non-consensual domination and submission; this is how de Sade sees the social contract. In his work sex is always connected with the exercise of power: sexual freedom always entails the exploitation of others. This is one of the features of de Sade's work that has attracted modern intellectual interest. In linking power so explicitly with sex, his work falls outside the orbit of the utopian sexual plenitude found in most pornography; instead his stories present sex brutally and in the raw, without the warming glow of eroti-cism and romance. Cold, hard-edged descriptions of physical acts that end in death and torture characterise his tales; they are bawdy yet deeply, cruelly satirical. As Angela Carter noted, 'for de Sade, all tenderness is false, a deceit, a trap; all pleasure contains within itself the seeds of atrocities; all beds are minefields' (1979: 25). For the libertines of de Sade's work, sexual enjoyment means the rejection of humanity and compassion; whereas the virtuous are never afforded either pleasure or comfort. The eponymous character of the novel *Jus-tine, or Good Conduct Well Chastised*, for example, after going through the most desperate set of trials to keep her virtue intact, is killed by a bolt of lightning once it appears she may have found salvation. There is no attempt in Sade's work to psychologise his characters; they have little inner life and motivations. Within the sadean world, sadism, domination and bondage are taken to extremes. These become articulations of a will to power and mastery (the same for virtuous Justine as well as vicious Juliette) and are presented by de Sade as an allegory of the human condition.

The nihilistic aspects of de Sade's work appear to be tempered by satirical mischievous-ness and bawdiness; in fact, their beguiling presence makes for an even darker vision of human nature. In many of the films based on de Sade's novels the pitch-dark quality of his work is markedly attenuated, however. Only *Salo*, a film banned in the UK until recently, and some of Jess Franco's exploitation films get close to the spirit of de Sade. His works attack humanism, religion and the social order in intense ways, and this is often achieved through his peculiar and unforgiving brand of comedy. De Sade's social critique has appealed to luminaries of twentieth-century French philosophy (such Georges Bataille, Simone de Beauvoir and Roland Barthes), who have elevated de Sade's reputation within the intellectual community. These writers often stress that he uses a pornographic mode as a means of uncovering the contradictions of his social order (in which medieval-style punishment, torture and legalised murder are tools of the state). Angela Carter reads his work in a feminist context, arguing that he advocated 'rights of free sexuality for women' (1979: 36) and that he did not fight shy of indicting his own misogynistic sexual fantasies as the product of his social and gender positioning. Again these are aspects of his work which only rarely appear in films that focus on him or reference his writing. As we will see, de Sade's name is often used to lend a film a transgressive kudos, yet there are many absences and reconfigurations in the way films represent him and his work. What is perhaps remarkable is that de Sade continues to speak in his idiosyncratic way and from the dungeons of eighteenth-century France to the present era. This is due in part to the perpetuation of his name in the general use of the term sado-masochism, but also because his outrageous, pornographic discourses on power, consumption and desire still have relevance in the cultural landscape we currently inhabit.

There are many films, particularly early melodramas, that could be seen as 'sadean' at a surface level due to their polarised and caricatured portrayal of villains and victims, vice and virtue. *Broken Blossoms* for example, presents Battling Burrows as a kind of sadean villain, his daughter a kind of Justine figure. Several of Griffith's innocents end up sacrificed on the altar of sexual brutality. Yet the film is far from sadean in its moral message: the innocent and suffering Justines of the world must be protected from exploitation and violation by the 'stronger' sex; in fact this is just the type of moral parable that de Sade's work satirised. The moral occult of many such films, particularly those made after the implementation of the Production Code, operates so that the more extreme the villainy and vice the stronger the subsequent punishment. These films use such polarisations to support rather than assault conventional notions of good and evil, quite different therefore from de Sade's diabolical intent. It was, however, not until the so-called permissive era of the 1960s and early 1970s that the first flush of films based overtly on de Sade and his work emerged. These appeared, at least in part, because of the more lenient approach to censorship and regulation in the United States and Britain in which 'artistic intent' gave greater license to depict more risqué sexual imagery in cinema. In the bubbling cauldron of 1960s counter-culture there was a growing investment in libertarianism. De Sade was an obvious choice of figurehead for those people railing against what was seen as repressive and paternalistic state legislation and censorship. The pot was stirred more vigorously by the increasing backlash against the liberalisation of culture, typified by groups such as the 'Festival of Light' campaigners, spear-headed by Mary Whitehouse in Britain.[64] A clear split emerged between liberals and pro-censorship groups, along largely generational lines. De Sade's run in with the forces of repression made him a fitting icon for the hedonism of the new liberalism (along with that other notorious advocate of licentiousness: Aleister Crowley). These high-profile fault lines placed sex at the centre of the conflict. Alongside the re-publication of his work, coincident with the student uprising of 1968 in Paris, it becomes clear why films began to emerge under the banner of de Sade's name.

De Sade-based films of this period fall into two categories: 'philosophic' de Sade and 'physical' de Sade; although a few use aspects of each. The former group focuses on ideas and the latter on the practise of S/M or bondage and domination in various forms intended to quicken the pulses of the audience. Peter Brook's *Marat/Sade* (1967) focuses almost entirely on de Sade's political views, which are juxtaposed with those of Jean Paul Marat (a prominent figure in the French Revolution who advocated violence against moderates).[65] The film asks expressly that the viewer judge between their two views of revolution, focusing on the two men's doubts and existential anxieties. There is no direct representation of sex or sexual torture, marking the film off from others that use aspects of de Sade and his work to titillate viewers with sado-sexual imagery. The film flies its 1960s art-movie colours high by denying the viewer establishing shots, staging events as a play in a single physical space and making its stage-craft plain. The theatrical origins are left intact, creating a claustrophobic and artificial atmosphere, and there is no attempt to create a fully cinematic remediation of the stage-play. De Sade is not 'psychologised' or made roguishly lovable, as is the case with some of the other films that focus on him. *Marat/Sade* draws directly on the reappraisal of de Sade in twentieth-century French philosophy and the film's diegetic debate is grounded in dialogue about the viability and ethics of revolution prevalent in late 1960s radical circles. What characterises this rendition of de Sade is his super seriousness; libertinage is presented as an abstract, philosophical concept rather than material practise, as it becomes in de Sade's novels. He is an advocate of anarchy and critical of the fact that the revolution made little qualitative difference to the social order of France in the 1790s. Little mention is made of his stories and the way his ideas are filtered through an excessive 'pornographic' imagination. The film draws on aspects of Maurice Blanchot's (1991) essay on de Sade, written in 1949. Blanchot argues that de Sade's philosophy of extreme egotism is one which is marked by 'negation' (the reduction of something to nothing). God and the law are reviled as making of the individual nothing; men are reviled for having constructed God to reduce their own importance. De Sade's libertines seek to reduce both their victims and God to naught. They are above the law in their pursuit of absolute pleasure and their 'cruel passions'. Blanchot also argues that de Sade's libertines express his notion that the mark of true libertinage is the ability to transform pain into pleasure; the pain of others as well as any pain experienced by the libertines (1991: 57). However, *Marat/Sade* to some extent divests de Sade of his power by rendering his views so very abstract. The film assumes a knowledgeable audience and has no truck with realising de Sade's imagined world of massive members, outrageous tortures and black masses in cinematic terms.

Other films take a less philosophical and more popular-style biographical approach to de Sade. In some cases this lends a credibility not sought by soft-core and hard-core films based on his work. *De Sade* (1969), *Marquis* (1989), *Markisinnan de Sade* (1992), *Marquis de Sade: Intimate Tales of the Dark Prince* (1996), *Sade* (2000) and *Quills* (2000) each focus on the life of de Sade. A number of films emerged in Europe during the 1960s and 1970s, plus a few later ones, that use his stories as the basis for films that attracted a rather different niche audience than that of the philosophical focus of *Marat/Sade*. Some include him within the fictional scene (*Deadly Sanctuary* for example), thereby providing an acknowledgement of the way we are likely to come to know de Sade through his fiction. Many of these films are soft-core or sexploitation offerings that use the 'physical' aspects of de Sade and his writing to lend the representation of sex a transgressive vigour. There have been many: *Vice and Virtue* (1963), *Juliette de Sade* (1969), *Justine de Sade* (1972); *La Marquise von Porno* (1977), *Cruel Passion* (1977) and *Justine: The Seduction of an Innocent* (1996) to name but a few.

As an adaptation of the de Sade's novel *Justine*, *Cruel Passion* is a vaselined-focus lavish costume drama, typical of soft-core sex films designed for adult mass market consumption during the 1970s. As a means of ensuring widespread appeal many of the events depicted in the novel are omitted and those that are included are altered quite significantly. In comparison to the more faithful *Justine de Sade*, the film seems rather coy and seeks through various elisions to make de Sade's fiction more palatable for a mainstream audience. The way both films render the sadean world is our focus here; the way they feed on some of the transgressive caché offered by the name 'de Sade' but also clean-up on the more difficult aspects of the novel so that censorship issues do not arise and to ensure the widest possible market. In both films Justine is presented as a beautiful innocent, who, unlike her sister Juliette, is anxious to remain virtuous no matter what the circumstance even if it incurs mortal peril; she undergoes a range of assaults on her person from those from whom she seeks help. In a major departure from the novel and as a means of truncating the number of predicaments that Justine's virtue gets her in, *Cruel Passion* sees Juliette's aristocratic and handsome lover, Lord Carlisle (Martin Potter), set out to rescue Justine (Koo Stark). As it turns out, Justine saves him from robbers, only for him to rape her. Both are killed soon after by the robbers, after they rape Justine. In this the film conflates for economic reasons several characters and events, a truncation that enables many of the scenes of sexual torture that novel-Justine undergoes to be left out. In addition, a romance is added that lends a softer erotic dimension. Lord Carlisle, Juliette's complementary lover, is a swashbuckling romantic hero for much of the film rather than a full-blown sadean libertine. In a further departure from the novel, the opening of *Cruel Passion* signals the film's entry into soft-core territory. Juliette (Lydia Lisle) and Justine are pupils, dressed as novice nuns, at a convent. Juliette is full of contempt for the nuns, but amuses herself by taunting and then seducing one of the nuns, providing the first sex scene of the film in the manner of 'nunsploitation' films. By contrast, Justine swallows wholesale messages about lust leading to the fires of Hell and is horrified by the lack of chastity and piety in the convent. These scenes present efficiently the situation in which the girls find themselves, as well as establishing character. They also provide in their differences a means by which the audience is offered a choice between the sisters. This goes someway to inviting the audience into the film. However, *Cruel Passion* does not live up to its name; the film turns away, through its tendency towards softness, from the harsh, contradictory and satirical sadean world.

The popularity of *Justine* – the novel – as a subject for cinematic remediation can be explained because of her quest to remain sexually innocent. As she tries to protect her virtue from those who would take it, the viewer is afforded the position of siding with Justine's plight, yet, at the same time, sadistic fantasies can be indulged. This ambivalence lends itself well to the majority of regulatory rulings that govern mainstream cinema, as dominant ideologies of virtue and good deeds are seen to be upheld if the story is rendered without satire. De Sade was intent on showing that virtue is not all it seems in moral terms, however; but *Cruel Passion* never truly invites the viewer to question Justine's fixed and self-endangering morality. The watered-down libertines who do express the absurdity of prizing chastity are presented in cliché gothic terms as evil; ciphers who spout weasel words which are simply designed to justify their pleasure. A more open invitation to read virtue complexly is made in *Justine de Sade* – due in part to the fact that a larger number of predicaments which ensue from Justine's adherence to her virtue are present. It becomes plain through the use of repetition that the path of virtue is one that is chosen not simply for reasons of godliness. As in the novel, Justine (Alice Arno) tells each of the people that she meets of her devotion to virtue and chastity, and of the abuse and exploitation that she has suffered. Her story always begins with 'I am but a poor orphan girl…'. After hearing/reading this a few times it strikes as rather hollow in its ritualised form, as if she is playing a role. Rather than soliciting compassion, however, her story seems to incite her listeners to libertinage. Her virtue feeds their will to sexual power – this happens frequently, but Justine does not amend her way of greeting strangers and continues to repeat these words. One of the strange things about de Sade's work is that he provides a point of identification that is on the surface reliant on pity, yet what also emerges is that Justine's adherence to piety is a form of arrogance and self-proving, a kind of self-serving pleasure, providing a parallel with the libertine. Unlike *Cruel Passion*, *Justine de Sade* goes some way towards a transgressive subversion of the typical polarised distinction between good and evil. But perhaps because Justine acts as the viewer's entry-point into the film world, which conventionally entails sympathy for a character's viewpoint/situation, this aspect is rather underplayed. Both films are sold ostensibly as erotic and bawdy dramas designed to titillate rather than challenge conventional conceptions of morality, yet *Justine de Sade* takes a few steps further into de Sade's morally ambiguous and idiosyncratic world.

Cruel Passion makes satire into melodrama by rendering most of Justine's assailants as inarticulate oafs. By depicting her attackers as simply bad and immoral people the brutal treatment of Justine is sanctioned morally. There is no real sense that they are either victims of social circumstance or libertines of the extreme type found in *Justine de Sade* or the novel. In the novel, La Dubois is a dashing beautiful robber woman who believes that the heartlessness of the rich sanctions the poor to rob them. She seeks to convert Justine to her ways and Justine is more swayed by her arguments than any of the others put to her throughout her travails. In *Cruel Passion*, La Dubois is presented as an old and physically unattractive woman, and renamed Mrs Bonny, therefore obeying the Hollywood convention that bad women, at least those not presented as femme fatales, should reflect physically their moral disposition (see Krzywinska 2000b: 117–56). *Cruel Passion* also side-steps de Sade's interventions on gender inequality made through the character of La Dubois. Mrs Bonny is presented as an inarticulate old woman rather than one who is able to express eloquently, and reflect upon, the way in which class and gender inequality operate. La Dubois is also de-sexualised and her depiction in the film demonstrates the way that the explicitly pornographic aspects of the novel are negated. The scene in the novel where the male robbers decide to preserve Justine's potentially lucrative virginity by copulating with an unwilling La Dubois, then ejaculate onto Justine's body and in her mouth, are missing from *Cruel Passion*. Yet the scene is present in the more risqué *Justine de Sade*, which under the more liberal regulations of France was able to present explicitly some of the types of sexual activities found in de Sade's work. *Justine de Sade* is not designed for the hard-core market, however. Lace cuffs, trees and monks habits are all used to cover male genitals and purported acts of penetration. To an extent this detracts from the very physical and anatomically-detailed expression of outrageous sex and exaggerated physical proportions, particularly 'non-natural' anal sex, found in de Sade's work.

Cruel Passion selects and recasts events from the early part of the novel with the effect of diluting the political and satirical angles of de Sade's work; as such the transgressive and critical flavour is significantly diminished. There is no mention of the cruel homosexual man that Justine falls in love with, who eventually sets his dogs on her, nor any mention of the monastery in the woods in which women are in the sexual service of a group of monks. The counterfeiter who engages the good Justine to aid him in his pursuit of hanging himself to the point of orgasm is also missing. All these are present in the more faithful *Justine de Sade*, however. *Cruel Passion* delivers a condensed version of the early part of the novel, yet it adds certain elements as a means of preventing those viewers in search of easy sexual thrills from being disturbed too greatly. These are mainly provided by the decadent scenes in the brothel, in which Justine's more pragmatic sister, Juliette, goes to earn her living (the film does not show that Juliette's rise to fortune is achieved in femme fatale-style by a number of seductions and murders). To lighten the tale, romantic love makes an entry into the sadean world between Juliette and her Lord, while this is somewhat undermined by that fact that he rapes Justine – an event strategically placed at the end of the film; he is nonetheless presented as a largely sympathetic character. Although the ending to *Cruel Passion* is somewhat bleak, with Justine raped and thrown for dead in a lake (rather less satirical than being killed by 'god' in the form of a lightning strike as in the novel and *Justine de Sade*), the film goes a long way to make events more palatable and visually/erotically interesting. The more perverse desires and acts are left out of the proceedings.

Justine (Alice Arno) arrives at the monastery in *Justine de Sade* (1972)

Perhaps the greatest sin committed by *Cruel Passion* is that it takes at face value what de Sade intended as satire. As such, the film becomes a bodice-ripping costume melodrama with some added nudity, as is also the case to a slightly lesser extent with *Justine de Sade*. While this angle is certainly present in de Sade's work; it is never just this. Leaving aside the nudity and more frank approach to the representation of sex, the only substantial difference between *Cruel Passion* and some of the gothic costume melodramas of the 1940s (*Blanche Fury*, *The Wicked Lady*, *Dragonwyck*, *Madonna of the Seven Moons*), or novels such as the *Angelique* series (written during the 1950s by a husband and wife team and set at the court of Louis XIV), is that Justine's rape and death occur because of her devotion to virtue, while those that commit outrageous acts for power and pleasure are afforded at least some happiness, if short-lived. De Sade made self-congratulatory mention of this structural reversal on the more usual moral formula in the preface to the 1791 edition of the novel *Justine*. In gothic melodramas of the 1940s bad girls (the Juliettes), such as *The Wicked Lady*'s Barbara Worth (Margaret Lockwood), are punished by death, while virtuous Justines generally prosper in the end. This moral structure was reinforced by the Production Code in Hollywood. Although resembling aspects of earlier gothic melodramas, *Cruel Passion* was not bound to such stringent rulings. We do not, however, see much of bad-girl Juliette's mode of progress on the road to prosperity. As befits the film's adherence to the soft-core sexual initiation and self-discovery narrative formula, Juliette is represented as sexually curious, eager to learn new sexual techniques and we last see her being 'rescued' from a sadist's beating and from prostitution generally by her Lordly lover. Unlike the novel, *Cruel Passion* does not have Juliette pledge herself to the convent in penitence when she finally meets her sister, chained and on her way to the gallows. Juliette's conversion is based on her guilt that she has committed so many real crimes, but it is the good Justine who is condemned to hang (in the novel this is presented in such a heavy-handed way that it becomes extremely disingenuous and is full of obvious satirical intent).

Juliette has a valuable presence in both films (as is the case with the novel). In using her sexual assets and her wits to gain power, she demonstrates that femininity is not 'naturally' masochistic; as might be inferred if de Sade's Justine was not juxtaposed with libertine women. However, in both films and the novel, Justine is never a willing participant in sado-masochistic scenes. Justine does not gain sexual satisfaction in her trials, and is not therefore a sexual masochist, but she does gain something from her trials: a strong, sustaining sense of moral pride. There is, however, a rather different approach to Justine's resistance in the two films. *Justine de Sade* is closer to de Sade's work in that Justine quite clearly gains a sense of pride and authenticity from what has happened to her (she also likes to recount her history). Without the libertines she would not be what she is; and nor would the 'true' libertines be what they are. Justine's resistance provides erotic drama and spectacle in both films, but *Cruel Passion* does not enter fully into the issues of identity afforded by an odd mutuality between libertine and virtuousness present in both the novel and *Justine de Sade*. *Cruel Passion* makes it all too easy to identify with Justine. She is presented as too young, naïve and innocent. She is only ever a victim, and never over-achieves her role to make it a satire on gothic moral parables. Koo Stark's Justine never solicits our interest in the use of virtuousness as a form of will to power. Her physical presence and the absence of protracted cruel travails masks the irony that brands de Sade's Justine with such ambiguity. In this sense the film cleans-up the complexity of the novel in order to render Justine's plight more erotic and less morally problematic. *Justine de Sade* is a far more faithful rendition in that it does not seek to shy away from the wordiness and intellectual engagement of de Sade's work nor from the sexual cruelty to which Justine is subjected. Like de Sade's novel this film bemuses the borders that ordinarily keep pornography and art apart.

Spanish director Jess Franco has made many films focused on the life and work of de Sade. Franco's films do not invite the viewer into de Sade's world as genially as is the case with *Justine de Sade*, but in films such as *Deadly Sanctuary*, *Necronomicon/Succubus* (1968), and *Eugenie* (1970) there is a strong attempt to capture something of the essence of de Sade. Some of Franco's work is directly based on de Sade's stories and many of his others carry sadean-style themes. In many respects Franco's numerous films typify 'euro-sleaze' (low-budget, sexploitation cinema), which suits well the sexual sensationalism component of de Sade's work. European-style horror and bizarre sexual fantasies are mixed with an art-cinema eye to visual and auditory style, all this in conjunction with a kind of perverse Brechtian dimension that withholds from viewers the comforts of identifying and sympathising with the main protagonists. Psychological realism, with rounded characters who are designed to represent the viewer in the film world, is not the aim of Franco's cinema, something shared with de Sade's novels. What the films lack, however, is de Sade's combination of playful bawdiness and biting satire. Yet Franco's films do defy generic categorisation, spanning across various modes, as occurs in de Sade's work. There are often several different versions of particular films made by Franco designed for different markets, some of which have hard-core content.

Franco's films are very different from many of the soft-focus soft-core renderings of de Sade's work. Rather than inviting the viewer into a world where misfortune and sexual plenitude co-exist in an often clichéd manner, Franco's films tend to alienate, although not exactly in the same manner as de Sade. Storylines are often fragmented and hard to follow. The films resemble feverish dreams which skit about from place to place. *Necronomicon/ Succubus* is a useful example. Lorna Green (Janine Reynaud) plays a dominatrix in an S/M-based play only to find that she is inveigled into that role in reality. She enters into a spiralled world where reality and fantasy are constantly blurred. It emerges that she may have been 'possessed' and is the victim of a larger conspiracy, perhaps supernatural, which ends in her death. There is little invitation to identify or sympathise with her; she is the object of the gaze, a cruel gaze. Although some scenes are clearly intended to titillate, the viewer is mostly likely left in a state of confusion about the intention of the film, unsure whether to align themselves with the gaze of the camera or not. In this sense the film is sadean. It uses the frame of pornography, yet never allows us to luxuriate in sex without the intrusion of outrageous violence. Sexual pleasure is located as a power game, manifesting in a sense of isolation rather than expressing intimacy or complementarity. As with many of Franco's films the intention is to disturb the viewer by blurring the lines that differentiate performance, fantasy and the real, as well as art and exploitation cinemas. Franco's films therefore provide what is required of what might be called, accurately, sadean cinema.

Deadly Sanctuary never obtained a classification in the UK, but was released in the US and mainland Europe. Here Franco tells the story of Justine, and, like *Justine de Sade*, it is in essence faithful to the tale, rendered in sadean mode with all its inverted polarities and furious contradictions that hover around desire, sex and morality. The styles of the two films are quite different, however. *Justine de Sade* is far more conventional, with little emphasis on camera technique or lighting effects. By contrast, in *Deadly Sanctuary* authorship is strongly imprinted on the content and style of the film, as is also the case with de Sade's work. Justine's travails are punctuated and book-ended by the narrator, de Sade (Klaus Kinski[66]). His presence neatly replicates the way that de Sade's authorial voice is very strongly present in his writing though direct address. The framing presence of de Sade operates in a number of ways: it locates the story of Justine as a creation of a specific imagination produced under a very particular circumstance; it provides a useful means of differentiating the film from other more mainstream costume dramas, reminding viewers that de Sade was in the business of writing to subvert and highlight the moral contradictions and hypocrisies of his time; and it foregrounds the concept of authorship, something that is reflected in the striking cinematic formal strategies that bring a strong auteurish quality to the film.

In the film's prologue de Sade is brought to his castle dungeon, leaving the light of day for a darkened, interior space of a windowless cell that resembles a theatrical 'black box'. His tormented mental state is constructed visually through the use of staccato zooms that often end in out-of-focus shots and close camera work which precludes a view of the entire space. These cinematic techniques fragment and dehumanise de Sade's physical appearance. In addition, undifferentiated inky blackness is broken by the whiteness of de Sade's powdered wig and pools of light are abstracted by the shadows of the prison bars. The collective effect is of a claustrophobic yet boundless space that deprives the senses and stirs the imagination to fill the void. As Justine's story unfolds, springing from de Sade's imagination, his presence is insisted upon through a number of devices: the narrator's voiceover; the return to him writing in the cell at the end of 'chapters'; and the use of his image in one particular scene in which he is murdered by Juliette. The superimpositions of de Sade's image onto the scene in which Justine is held captive and tortured by four priests devoted to the pursuit of libertinage calls for attention. This particular scene is the most perverse and sadistic scene in the film and perhaps to legitimate its inclusion for audiences and regulatory bodies it is granted the film's best-known star, Jack Palance. Justine is tortured with skin-puncturing pins and then tied to a cross. As she slips in and out of consciousness, de Sade's hunched and transparent figure haunts the scene, frantically writing as if to catch up with the intense flow of his fantasy. This marks the scene as a product of his imagination, acting therefore as a useful device to help the film avoid censure, especially given the realism of the skin-puncturing. In marrying the two locations together de Sade is located within the context Franco's particular cinematic style. Franco does not resort to the black mass imagery of *Justine de Sade* (where Justine is placed naked on an altar, the host placed on her sex and each of the four then have sex with her), but the layering of images and the *mise-en-scène* construct a very cinematic scene that works to intensify the film's depiction of sado-masochism as a form of transgression.

Alongside *Deadly Sanctuary*, a number of films have been made that focus on de Sade himself where he is presented in a largely sympathetic yet darkly attractive way. *Marquis de Sade: Intimate Tales of the Dark Prince* presents de Sade (Nick Mancuso) as a roguish, swashbuckling anti-hero; a red-blooded, flamboyant and slightly ridiculous epicurean, whose pleasures are curtailed by his incarceration in the Bastille, facilitated by his outraged mother-in-law. He escapes prison with the help of Justine, a young women searching for her sister Juliette, who is hiding in de Sade's country chateau. He is presented as a Three Musketeers-style hero, making this rendition the apotheosis of the 'physical' de Sades. He rescues Juliette (with whom he is in love) from the sadistic intentions of the local judge, police chief and priest; the very people who imprisoned him, denounced his writings and who provided the blueprints for his characters. This dramatic device is not intended to be overtly political, however. Instead, it manufactures an action movie-style de Sade, a fighter for justice and liberty who rescues the day. This is not entirely fictionally grounded: de Sade did indeed make a carefully planned and daring escape from prison when incarcerated in

Sardinia (he even left notes for his jailers). This is a de Sade made to be admired much in the manner of a character played by Errol Flynn.

However, the darker side of de Sade is also in evidence. The inclusion of references to vampirism invokes the monstrosity of de Sade while retaining a certain seductive allure. The eponymous 'dark prince' is a name usually reserved for Dracula and also used in *Interview With the Vampire* for Lestat (in both Anne Rice's novel (1976) and Neil Jordan's film (1994)). At one point Mancuso's de Sade bites into his arm letting blood flow into his mouth (referring back to the bloodletting Count who appears towards the end of the novel *Justine* and who appears in *Justine de Sade*). The connection between Sade and vampirism as rendered here follows a recent trend in vampire fictions, evidenced by films, novels and television series such as *Interview with the Vampire*, *Dracula*, *The Vampire Lestat* (1985), *Buffy the Vampire Slayer* (1997–2003) and *Angel* (1999–2004). In each of these texts, vampires are presented as glamorous anti-heroes and who often engage in bondage and domination-style sex. This development was initiated by Anne Rice, with a little help from Byron and Milton.[67] In the world that Rice creates vampires have to negotiate a kind of rise to sadean existence when they are bestowed with the 'dark gift'. They do not die easily; a concept that de Sade explores in his novels. As Blanchot notes, de Sade's libertines state that they prefer victims who do not die, who can suffer endlessly, so that the libertine can gain greater pleasure (1991: 56). In the film of *Interview with the Vampire*, the character Lestat (Tom Cruise) has many sadean characteristics. He and Louis (Brad Pitt) appear in the early part of the film as eighteenth-century aristocrats, in the French style. Lestat frequents upper-class parties to hunt for victims and relishes the pleasure of the kill as well as his inhuman strengths and immortality. Human beings are playthings for his pleasure; their blood an intoxicating delight.[68] As seen through the eyes of Louis, Lestat is a sadean libertine, played against Louis as a virtuous Justine. Louis hates having to kill to live and drinks rats' blood to stay alive; because of this Lestat regards Louis as going against his 'killer nature', much in the same way that the libertines regard Justine's insistence on chastity. Like Lestat or Spike in *Buffy the Vampire Slayer*, Mancuso's de Sade is a charming blood-drinking bad boy and these credentials allow him to become an object of fascination and desire, a means by which the sadean world can become, without too much trouble, the fuel of fantasy. But unlike de Sade's most 'successful' libertines, and to underpin their potential appeal, the vampire anti-hero and Mancuso's de Sade retain certain vulnerabilities, little sparks of humanity that light up against amorality, to lure us into identifying with or desiring them.

The melodramatic frame of *Marquis de Sade: Intimate Tales of the Dark Prince*, its pristine costumes, comic moments and Mancuso's Grand Guignol performance, indicates that this portrayal is not to be taken too seriously. This de Sade is a man of action and bawdiness, a populist figure rather than the intellectual de Sade of *Marat/Sade*. As with many other films, de Sade's reputation is used to infuse a smoky-salty flavour to what would otherwise be an action-based sex-romp. Oddly enough it is possible to see both these sides of de Sade in his writing and contrariness; it is the juxtaposition of playfulness set against sexual violence and negation that makes him such a pliable yet enigmatic figure. Perhaps it is this that has made de Sade the subject of so many differently-pitched films and which lends BDSM culture and cinema such an important and iconic figure.

Perhaps the most surreal entry into the library of de Sade-based films is the mixed media *Marquis*. Masked actors are used in the main body of a film that elaborates on his life in the Bastille. Animation is also used to bring the (impossible) stories the Marquis (voiced by François Marthouret) writes to cinematic life. Diegetic reality is divided from de Sade's imaginings through the use of live action, but the actors each wear animal masks and display other animal attributes. The combination of the human and the animal has a strange-making effect, providing visual novelty and used to connote character type, but also resonates with de Sade's notion that human behaviour is driven by 'Nature' (by which he seems to have meant what might be called 'fundamental drives or instincts' in twentieth-century thought). The Marquis (as he is named) is a rather gentle doe-eyed spaniel who has been imprisoned in the Bastille because he had defecated on a crucifix. Residing in the Marquis' trousers is Colin (voiced by Valérie Kling – a woman), an oversized talking penis (with a mechanically-animated face), who constitutes a separate, although physically attached, consciousness. In a literal rendition of the mind/body split that has preoccupied aspects of European philosophy since it was raised by René Descartes in the seventeenth century, Colin and the Marquis often have conflicting desires and argue about which of them is in charge. This resonates with modern psychoanalytic understandings of sex and desire, where unconscious desires of a sexual nature undermine and distort language and rationality. As Colin demonstrates to the Marquis, it is him that influences the Marquis' ideas. One of the ways in which they pass time is putting on plays: Colin appears in what only can be described as a 'lap-theatre', the Marquis acting as director and audience.

As well as tapping into a range of pop-culture and philosophical engagements, this surreal rendition of the 'split subject' provides a visual representation of the odd and seemingly oppositional mixture of intellectual observation and pornographic intent found in de Sade's work. Colin and the Marquis become, inadvertently, embroiled in the politics of the prison. The powers-that-be use the Marquis to explain away Justine's politically sensitive pregnancy (she says she had been raped by the King of France, and was definitely raped by the rat-gaoler). She dies after giving birth to a baby who comes out of the womb wearing an iron mask (corroborating her royal connection story). The prison-Priest, a sheep, sells the Marquis' stories as his own, profiting greatly from the revenue due to the popularity of the novels. The Marquis' works are published under the pseudonym 'de Sade'. Juliette ('a filly'), meanwhile, spearheads the French Revolution but to gain access to those held in the Bastille, she becomes dominatrix to the masochistic cockerel who runs the Bastille. She stages a daring rescue of one of the Bastille inmates who she believes is important to the Revolution, who is incarcerated in a punishment dungeon with the Marquis. While the object of the rescue operation dies, the Marquis and Colin escape with Juliette. She is shot, however. Enamoured by Juliette's beauty and daring, Colin kisses the dead Juliette; miraculously she is resurrected. Soon after this, Colin leaves the Marquis to his writing, choosing to go off with Juliette to fuel her revolutionary fire. The Marquis is left to the abstract world of the imagination, while Colin embraces what he loves most: action.

While the film is certainly a quirky oddity in its muppet-style version of de Sade's life, it nonetheless broaches some of its more complex aspects. The mixture of real actors, masks and animation blur a whole range of conventional distinctions. Although the film bears superficial similarities to a children's film, it nonetheless deals with themes that are commonly subject to rhetorics of transgression: revolution, sexuality and power. The result, like de Sade's work, uses pathos, bawdiness and irony to produce comic satire. Those in the pay of institutionalised repression are the most heavily ridiculed (the cockerel, the rat and the sheep-priest). But no one is entirely free of exaggeration and/or derision, including Justine, Juliette, and the revolutionaries. As such this film is very much in the spirit of de Sade's work.

The use of animation and modelling allows a greater measure of physical fantasy than would be permitted in a live-action context. The use of stop-frame and plasticene models acts modally to mark these scenes as fantasy (for example, a coffin being placed into the earth becomes an image of coitus as the earth sprouts open legs and the coffin is rammed in and out). Animation provides a texture that visually articulates the peculiarities of the pornographic imagination. Alongside the use of models, animation also permits representations of de Sade's work that if presented though live-action would likely have found censure at the time of the film's release. Images of erect penises and penetration are found throughout the film, but only in a mode that is obviously not 'real'. Colin, for example, is perpetually tumescent. The gaoler-rat is seen wandering around with a lobster still placed in his arse after he has been duped into thinking that he had been sodomised by Colin. Colin has sex with a crack in the wall (resulting, understandably, in an injury to his head). In animation, a battering ram and a coffin penetrate the gap between huge female legs. Sexual torture is evident as well as ejaculation. Juliette brands with a white-hot iron the cockerel in their S/M games. Justine's udders are milked so vigorously by the gaoler-rat as a form of torture that her milk turns to blood as it spurts into a bucket (she has udders and human breasts causing some confusion to the gaoler-rat). Many of these images would have presented subjects for excision under the particular rulings of the BBFC in the UK at the time of the film's release, for example, if they had not been overtly coded by the modal attributes of animation and the use of animal costumes as fantastical.

Out of all the films discussed in this chapter, *Marquis* has the most cutting satirical edge, as well as having the most explicit sexual content. The transformation of people into animals lessens the more 'pornographic' and violent aspects of his work, yet the mixing of species also lends an even greater sense of perversity, as well demonstrating the sadean view of Nature. Animation enables the boundaries, which a range of critical thinkers throughout the last century have argued constitute sex and desire, to be revealed more explicitly than would be possible in a live-action context. The virtual nature of animation also reveals that levels of photorealism are core to the way that juridical and other institutional bodies adjudge obscenity.

Unlike *Marquis*, which has so far only reached a limited audience and has (sadly) not had a video or DVD release in the UK, *Quills* reached a far larger audience. The presence of several Hollywood stars certainly aided in creating a film that invited an audience beyond that established for cult or art cinema. De Sade would not appear to be the obvious subject for a Hollywood blockbuster. The transgressive qualities of his work had to be made more palatable if the film was to reach and entertain a mainstream audience. Geoffrey Rush came to public attention after his performance in the commercially and critically successful *Shine* (1996), for which he received an Academy Award for best actor (plus a range of other accolades). With a reputation as an actor of stature, Rush brought an established artistic credibility to the role. He plays de Sade as a mischievous but largely benign law-breaker who is mis-read by the powers-that-be and a victim of circumstance. This de Sade is a man to be pitied, a hapless, if impish, tragic-comedian, tailored to the sensibilities of a modern liberal audience. *Quills'* representation of de Sade is very different from the demonic-killer who possesses the purchaser of his skull in the appropriately named horror film *The Skull* (1965), or from the aloof intellectual of *Marat/Sade*. De Sade's arch-nemesis, the sadistic Dr Antoine Royer-Collard (Michael Caine), who appears as a perverse, cruel and repressive villain from a gothic novel, also works in relative terms to moderate de Sade's infamy. The choice of Kate Winslet for Madeleine le Clerc, the object of de Sade's affections, is also calculated to soften our regard for him. Her role is informed intertextually by that which she played in *Titanic*, where her character acts as the voice of equality and throws off the shackles of upper-class snobbery. The centralisation of Winslet-as-Madeleine in the narrative invites viewers to identify with her and her fascination for de Sade and his writings (which were outlawed in France until the mid-1960s). The presence of these stars helps to position the film in the mainstream. To legitimise the subject matter still further, actors who have appeared in British productions of Shakespeare's plays appear as minor characters.

Various means are used to humanise de Sade. His acerbic humour, vulnerability and the way he is portrayed as having a modern sensibility to sex and hypocrisy, each contribute to making him a congenial and sympathetic character. In accordance with the humanising principle that guides the film, his stories appear in two different ways. Some are heard in extracts told by Madeleine, delivered in titillating mode to an appreciative diegetic audience. Others are acted out by the inmates of the asylum in which de Sade is kept as dramas to entertain patrons. Only the hypocrite villains of the film disapprove of work that is presented here simply as entertaining bawdiness. Some of these tales relate to events in the asylum. As with many of the films that focus on de Sade, fact and fiction are mixed. As the film draws to a close, his tongue is cut out and he is confined to an *oubliette* where he can only write on its walls in his own shit. After deliberately swallowing a crucifix proffered for his succour and salvation, he dies in the arms of the well-intentioned yet misguided and sexually repressed young Abbe (Joaquin Phoenix). This violent end is a complete fantasy in factual terms as de Sade lived, albeit in various prison and asylum institutions, until he was 74. Nonetheless this fiction provides a neat rhetorical device that reinforces his independence and atheism (which a modern audience is likely to regard as not too shocking, even understandable). Before his death Sade confesses a warm love and grievous pity for the murdered Madeleine, once again emphasising his humanity and thereby ignoring the cynicism found in his work about human relationships. What we are left with is a picture of martyrdom to the cause of liberal humanism.

The film's rather partial and liberalised (rather than libertarian in the sadean mode) view of de Sade as an unconventional victim of the repressive social order is indebted as much to *One Flew over the Cuckoo's Nest* (1975) as Brook's *Marat/Sade* or de Sade's own work. In humanising and siding the audience with a lovable de Sade, the film seeks to normalise him and the sexualised violence of his stories. His work is made accessible as titillation rather than as an affront to the values he regarded as poisonous to radical liberty, which involved, in theory at least, the pursuit of murder as the proving ground of the will to pleasure. The costume drama setting and the gentrification of de Sade hides from view that which attracted the interest of twentieth-century thinkers who looked to his work as a way of articulating the complex and dark dimensions of sexuality and power. In addition, the film was not designed for the niche consumption of the BDSM community and it therefore places more emphasis on character than on BDSM-style scene-building. But it is possible to regard this film as under the influence of the 'playful' mode of BDSM advocated by various practitioner-positive literatures; could the success of this film indicate that the transgressive coding of BDSM is diminishing?

Made in 1976, Pasolini's *Salo, or 120 Days of Sodom (Salò o le 120 giornate di Sodoma)* works entirely in reverse to those films which for various reasons seek to humanise de Sade. Watching *Salo* is for many viewers an ordeal, moving very far away from the entertainment values of *Marquis de Sade*, *Marquis* or *Quills*. It comes therefore with a reputation and was banned in the UK until 2000. Reading through the many user comments film posted on the *Salo* pages at www.imdb.com, it becomes clear that viewers' reactions to the film are highly polarised. Some see the film as the ultimate statement of de Sade's satanic challenge, rendered in cinematic terms, a film that makes an important contribution to art cinema and to an understanding of the ways in which objectification operates in the fields of sexual and political economy. Others see it as pointlessly disgusting and outrageous, a film that sought notoriety through its gratuitous display of the unconscionable. *Salo* is based on de Sade's longest novel *120 Days of Sodom*, which charts the torture of a group of girls and boys by four libertines in a house that exists outside of the reach of justice or authority. It is a highly repetitive read; descriptions themselves are tortuous and as the body count mounts relentlessly, it is likely that the reader will give up. There is no Justine or Juliette as a central character with whom we are invited to go on a journey. Pasolini intended *Salo* to be the first of a trilogy of films focused on death, the aim of which was to balance against the trilogy of life films that he had made previously (*The Decameron (Il Decameron*, 1971), *The Canterbury*

Tales (*Racconi di Canterbury*, 1972) and *Arabian Nights* (1974)). The other films were never made because Pasolini was murdered soon after the completion of *Salo* (a factor that also added to the film's notoriety).

Pasolini trades on the eighteenth-century contemporary setting of de Sade's work for Nazi Italy, bringing a more recent historical and political dimension, through which Pasolini lived, to the horrors of the tale. The film is structured into four parts, each named to invoke Dante's plan of the circles of Hell. A great deal of the film is shot in *tableau vivant* format, keeping the viewer at a distance from events.[69] Each scene becomes more transgressive and taboo-breaking and there is no satire or levity brought to these depictions. Pasolini eschews the bawdiness of de Sade's work, which had played a strong, positive and carnivalesque role in Pasolini's trilogy of life films. As with de Sade's work, contradiction becomes a device that reveals the fault lines of ideology and humanity. Pasolini translates such contradiction into his own idiom and for the medium of cinema. Most notably, repetition and stasis are central to the film, making it boring to watch because nothing much, at least on one level, seems to happen. Where there is some form of 'action', however, it is deeply repellent. The combination of boredom and repulsion makes watching the film a difficult experience (many report giving up after a while).

Stylistically the film also brings together two very different registers that relate specifically to the context of cinema as a medium. Aspects of realism and documentary feature, yet these sit in sharp contrast with the precise and obviously artificial choreography of each scene. This combination lends the film a very particular visual and auditory style. As with de Sade's work, stylistic affectation can provide the reader/viewer with something tangible to hide behind. It can be focused on in a manner that means that the events depicted are not quite fully engaged with, they can be disavowed but only if an active and deliberate attempt is made. Observing this defensive manoeuvre in oneself while viewing a film which disturbs is strange yet instructive. It demonstrates one of the ways that many of us defend ourselves from images which could potentially overwhelm us with horror, which might contaminate our sense of agency and belief in human values such as justice and moral reward; the danger of Pasolini's film and de Sade's work is that what is used to define the human – humanity – crumbles to dust. Rather than the energetic contempt of overt satire, which through comedy and bawdiness reasserts something of the human in de Sade's work, it is his tendency to nihilism and negation that Pasolini emphasises in *Salo* so effectively and disturbingly. Even if the viewer is able to actively disavow what they are seeing by focusing intently on the aesthetic glossiness of the carefully-staged images, the capacity of human beings to negate human values is still glaringly apparent.

The intended meanings of *Salo* are not entirely clear, however. Some argue that Pasolini turned to de Sade as a means of commenting on the emptiness of the 1968 student 'revolution' in Paris, which he regarded as nothing to do with the working class and fuelled by bourgeois values and liberalism. Other commentators on the film regard it more directly as demonstrating the operating principles of Nazism and capitalism: the exploitation of the many for the pleasures of the few. It is also plausible to argue that the film's stylised tableaux freeze life and because the viewer is left out of the action, through the lack of conventional devices that would ordinarily invite the viewer to identify with a particular character or to become sexually aroused, the film becomes in and of itself an articulation of anti-human-ism. It is the apparent aloofness of the film's approach that seems to disturb many viewers. Unlike de Sade's satirical use of clichéd bawdiness, mawkishness and hypocrisy, this film of-fers little more than superficial choreography to soften its impact. In its bleak indictment of inhumanity and objectification, *Salo* is perhaps one of the most deeply transgressive films that it is currently possible to see legitimately in Europe. This is not transgression made in the mode of joyous liberation from repression. Instead, it is designed to disgust, to freeze rather than ignite. It is possible that the film's coldness and cruelty is designed to urge the viewer to long for sex in the context of love, consensuality and mutual respect. The effect the film had on me, at least, was the intense presence of a desire for the comforts of com-passion and tenderness to rush into fill the perilous void.

As such, this film makes very clear the necessary function of certain boundaries that po-lice the outrageous inclinations born of sex, power and desire in order to preserve the social contract. This raises an unanswerable question: was it really Pasolini's intention to position the audience as liberal humanists? What is clear is that the film is certainly not intended to be consumed as a form of uncomplicated eroticism. As rendered in *Salo*, sadism is divorced from the cosy world of consensual BDSM and masochism is completely, and rightly, absent. Instead, the film impels its viewers to ask some fundamental and extremely vexed questions about sexual objectification and power. And, in asking those questions *Salo* operates in a manner very close to de Sade. It is this, plus the lack of imagery designed to titillate, that legitimates the film in art and regulatory terms.

Switching into a very different key, themes of sado-masochism and bondage are com-monly used in cinema to explore in an erotic way aspects of sexual desire and practise that are not fulfilled by 'vanilla' or ordinary sex. A number of more recently-made films do not follow the sadean pathway and instead show BDSM practices in a consensual and erotic context. *Mano Destra* (1986) is a short black-and-white lesbian BDSM film made by Cleo Ubelemann that was shown in art cinemas in the late 1980s and early 1990s. It is a kind of bondage poem, elegantly shot. The intention behind the shot design, and the way this ties into the patterns of the acoustic field, is to align the viewer with the place of the diegetic submissive (it might be suggested that the film chimes, therefore, with the argument that the masochistic position is intrinsic to the experience of being a viewer). In one section the sounds of a large gathering of people are heard, accompanied by an image of a submissive tied up, gagged and unable to move. The viewer is offered no reverse-shot or cutaway to show visually what is going on outside the submissive's allotted space. The diegetic juxta-position between public and private in the auditory and visual fields lends a greater sense of the vulnerability of the submissive; it is as if she will be exposed to the crowds that ap-pear to be milling around off-screen. This goes beyond the diegesis, however, because the submissive is indeed exposed publicly by the camera: a private scene has through cinema become public, the frame of representation broken, thereby. The use of off-screen sound, the status of which is never confirmed visually, also heightens the viewer's sensitivity to auditory cues. A strong sense of anticipation prevails throughout the film, as befits the experience of a submissive in the hands of a competent dominant. There is no actual sex in the film. Instead, the accoutrements of bondage and the textured surfaces become erotically charged, the fetishism of which is emphasised by the use of crisp monochrome. But, breaking the seamlessness and timelessness of the scene, at one point during the film the dominant is shown rubbing the shoulders of the submissive. The inclusion of this scene throws all the other events, images and sounds into relief: it makes clear that the rituals and games played out in the rest of the film are held within the context of another type of relationship, characterised by care and tenderness. Nonetheless, the film's intention is to invoke for the viewer a strong sense of charged expectation, placing them on the side of the submissive waiting for her mistress to return. As we watch the bound submissive and hear the sound of high heels coming ever closer, the guiding enigma of the film arises: what will happen when the wearer of those heels arrives? This we never see; it is left for the viewer to dream-up, or even act-out, what might possibly ensue. *Mano Destra* can be regarded in the broader context of films made by women during the 1980s and 1990s that used art-cinema tactics to explore economies of sexuality that were not present in a direct way in mainstream cinema (which seemed particularly conservative during the 1980s). This was a risky film in the context of 1980s feminism as, for some feminists, the idea that sexual relationships are based on a form of power-play, no matter how consensual, was regarded as mirroring patriarchal economies of sex.

Another short film aimed at the BDSM community is *The Attendant* (1992), a film that takes for its subject the S/M fantasies of a gay gallery attendant based on the homoeroticism of the classical pictures in his charge. The film found some success on the art-cinema circuit mainly because of the increasing prominence of gay culture and growth of interest in BDSM during the late 1980s and early 1990s. In general, BDSM became the focus for those exploring sexual identity, and it attracted people with a range of preferences – straight, gay, lesbian or bi. For some, the practise of BDSM became a means of developing an identity that challenged the status quo and the BDSM community grew with the publication of dedicated magazines (such as *Skin Two*), books, clubs and clothing, followed later by websites and MUDs (early chat rooms). BDSM became more than a sexual practise; it became a sub-culture. This status was consolidated by collective concern about the judicial status of BDSM, and in particular the case often called 'Operation Spanner'.

In December 1990 a group of gay men were given substantial prison sentences by a British court for engaging in consensual S/M on the basis that they inflicted on one another 'actual bodily harm'. The prosecution was brought by the police after a videotape recording of a group S/M session was viewed after a house raid. The police believed that the tape showed someone being murdered and that this was a 'snuff' video. Having established that this was not the case and that those involved were consensual participants, the judge pro-claimed that under British law a person cannot agree to be assaulted. In the context of the Spanner case this seems absurd, but this particular law was intended to protect people in the event of domestic violence (a woman for example might be persuaded by her husband or feel obliged to say that she agreed to be assaulted). Because the ruling applied poten-tially to anyone no matter what their sexual orientation, the BDSM community – which was somewhat split into straight, gay and lesbian groups – rallied round to protest. Oddly, this afforded some people who practised BDSM a greater sense of community because it was clear that with the precedent set by the Spanner case judge that consensual S/M was now a transgression of the law.[70] S/M films made for mainstream distribution after the Span-ner case, such as *Exit to Eden* (a Hollywood-based based on the S/M fantasy novel by Anne Rice but altered quite significantly to attract a mainstream audience) and *Preaching to the Perverted*, sought to humanise the BDSM community and its practises. In the former film, comedy is used to invite non-practitioners into the film and the story and characters are designed to demonstrate the positive values of the practise.

The romantic comedy *Secretary* illustrates beautifully a humanist and positive approach to representing BDSM and the conditions for making it so. Lee Holloway has a history of cutting herself as a means of lessening the emotional pain that appears to be connected to her relationship with an alcoholic father. After a spell in an institution she elects to find a job, choosing after some deliberation to be a secretary. Her extremely playful nature is quick-ly established as she rehearses in her bedroom what she will say at interview. She clearly enjoys this as a kind of 'dressing up' activity. At her real interview it is clear that her new boss, E. Edward Grey, is quite eccentric and although very precise in his ways is not quite in control of himself. He begins to test her, setting her more and more outrageous tasks, which she does with gusto. A regime of spanking ensues when she makes some typing mis-takes (genuine mistakes to begin with, deliberately made later). These sessions cease after a while, much to her disappointment. She seeks solace in Pete (Jeremy Davies), nice-enough, similarly aged, but sexually unadventurous and focused rather too intently on fornication than erotic games. She nearly marries him, but on realising that she loves E. Edward at the eleventh hour, Lee goes to him in her wedding dress and declares herself. He asks her to sit at a desk with her hands flat upon it and her feet on the floor. This is her trial of love. As she sits there, Pete comes by and she tells him to go; in her imagination everyone she knows comes by and tellingly her imaginary father gives her permission to live her life in whatever way makes her happy. Having proved her love, E. Edward and Lee marry, having established that they can play together in whatever way they wish.

Lee and E. Edward's games invest eroticism in the everyday and it is clear that in focusing their idiosyncrasies into these shared games both benefit, emotionally and psychologically. In fact, their games are the condition of their successful socialisation. She stops self-harm-ing, begins to understand the nature of her desires, and becomes far more confident and powerful. He no longer denies the nature of his sexuality and has found someone to share it

Office games: Lee (Maggie Gyllenhaal) goes beyond the usual secretarial duties in *Secretary* (2002)

with. As Lee shows she loves him he too becomes tender and loving. Their complementary relationship opens up a world of joy and pleasure to them. The humanism of the film's approach is based in part on the fact that the two central characters are so well-acted, making them easy to identify with despite the quirks that might be off-putting to some viewers, and on the delicate balance achieved between comedy and satire, romance and eroticism, fantasy and reality. *Secretary* might not present sado-masochism as searing transgression, as is the case in many of the films discussed in this chapter. But it nonetheless demonstrates that sexuality is far from simple and that erotic play which hovers at the border of transgression within a consensual context can prove, against de Sade, to be the apotheosis of romantic love. This independently-produced film has proved a commercial success and it reflects shifts in attitudes to sexuality and desire. The film rests on a raft of ideas drawn from across twentieth-century thought and culture: philosophies of desire, psychoanalysis, sexology and BDSM manuals. BDSM still retains something of a transgressive and subcultural flavour, and it can still be tethered to a challenge to the status quo. But, as *Secretary* and *Quills* show, under certain circumstances, especially when romance and life-affirming values are in play, BDSM can appeal beyond a niche audience. Although these films work with the increasing legitimation and acceptance of BDSM in contemporary culture, as part of a general trend in which sexual identity is regarded and aired through the media more diversely, they nonetheless trade on images and topics charged with transgressive kudos that hitherto were the preserve of outlying and marginal cinemas.

Sex and the Cinema

Real Sex

𝒥n real life sexual desires and behaviours are assigned status and meaning through the conditions, circumstances and contexts in which they appear. Whether they are legitimate and sanctioned or transgressive depends on the particular configuration of these factors. In addition, context is extremely important to the way that those desires and behaviours are experienced: expressing love and affection; exciting; naughty; mildly to extremely transgressive; a form of escape; physical release; as a form of interpersonal power-play; testing one's own physical and psychological boundaries; as an expression of fear; disgusting; violent; gentle; ecstatic; comforting; disappointing. Real sex is therefore a complex business and in some cinemas it appears as such while in others it is divested of its complications. The meaning and status of cinematic sex is also context-dependent, which includes the formal devices used in its representation. The appearance of real sex, as opposed to simulated sex, in cinema is coded rhetorically in transgressive terms, largely because 'real' sex, often authenticated by images of ejaculation and penetration, is a primary factor that distinguishes hard-core from other legitimated cinemas. As such the conditions and context of real sex as it appears in legitimate cinema have a significant role to play in the way that it is received and understood. My aim here is to show that the spectacle of real sex in recent art cinema is subject to a number of textual and contextual qualifications that legitimise its presence and mark such films off from low-brow hard-core. In so doing I revisit some of the issues and films that appeared in Part I.

The hard-core film industry has successfully exploited the spectacle of real sex to carve out a market difference from other forms of cinema. Regulation, distribution and generic form have combined to lend hard-core its aesthetic and market specificity. But with the recent appearance of erect penises and vaginal penetration in certain films classified in Britain as '18', there appears to be a challenge to clear divisions between what have been previously categorised as 'legitimate' and 'illegitimate' cinemas. European art films such as

The Idiots, Romance, Intimacy and *The Piano Teacher* each make use of images that have defined hard-core. The inclusion of such imagery represents a significant gear-change in the representation of sex in the legitimate cinema. In looking to hard-core to win audience attention, European art cinema appears to be using the attraction of real sex to compete with the sensation-inducing spectacle of Hollywood's high-octane special effects-laden blockbusters. With the increasing liberalism of the institutional regulation of cinema, the gradual legitimisation of the hard-core industry due in part to its economic success, and with easily accessible sexually explicit images available on the largely unregulated Internet, the stage is set for European art cinema to include the type of explicit sexual imagery that has hitherto been the preserve of hard-core. (While hard-core imagery has not been regulated in all countries, the regulatory regimes of Britain and America tend to set the agenda for what is included in films that seek a broad international audience.)

The introduction of explicit hard-core imagery is a new addition to legitimate cinema, but when seen against the broader backdrop of cinema, the appropriation of certain sexually-charged images from illegitimate sex-based cinemas is by no means a new phenomenon. My aim throughout this chapter is to put this gear-change into the extended context of cinema history and to discuss the formal presentation of real sex in these recent films with a particular focus on the rhetorical regimes of value and sexual transgression, the aesthetic frameworks and the distinctions between high and low culture that these films put into play. That cinema trades often on the spectacle of sex is one of the core observations of this book. What continues to change, however, is the economic environment in which cinema is produced, distributed and consumed, as well as the cultural frameworks that shape representations of sex and the way they are regarded and regulated. One significant distinction that has had currency across cinema's history is the common practice of dividing, often along generic lines, the psychological and emotional aspects of sex from the physical. Both provide spectacle of different types. The former in many cases places importance on character study, narrative and dramatic tension, while the latter places greater emphasis on the sensationalist effect of portraying sexual acts of whatever type. Bringing the two together has often enabled films to adopt the spectacle of sex in a more acceptable context, an occurrence found at various points in cinema's history. The representation of sex in either psychological or physical terms has proved consistently, and marketablely, controversial. Many films dealing with aspects of sexual authenticity as a source of spectacle have tested and, in some cases, been instrumental in shifting regulatory boundaries, something often exploited actively to attract the curiosity of potential spectators.

In Part I, I argued that throughout cinema's 'psychosexual' history, various regimes of dialectical exchange between legitimate and illegitimate cinemas are in evidence. Consideration of such dynamic trading provides a key to understanding how the recent inclusion of 'real' sex in legitimate cinema fits into a broader historical, industrial and rhetorical/aesthetic context. As has already been noted in Part I, a common strategy found across the history of cinema is the use of an established, sanctioned discourse or generic form with

Sex and the Cinema

which to frame the inclusion of publicity-garnering risqué sexual imagery. Often such inclusions have been justified under the ethical rubric of the negative example; a device used, as we have seen, in D. W. Griffith's *Intolerance* and in Cecil B. DeMille's *The Sign of the Cross*. Sexual spectacle is offered in both films. Bare-breasted harem women appear in the former. In the latter it is found in the lesbian seduction performed in the form of an exotic dance, the sight of Claudette Colbert's 'real' breasts and the voluptuous carnal desires that prompt her character to corrupt the good Christian hero, as well as the bestiality and violence seen in the gladiatorial arena, discussed above. Although banned under the Production Code the year following its release (and likely contributing to the decision to impose the Code more stringently), the film was a box-office success, not unaided by the controversy that it fuelled in the American press (see Black 1994: 65–9; Walsh 1996: 78–80). For many critics and state censors it was the purported biblical context that sanctioned the inclusion of decadent 'pagan' images (pagan being synonymous at that time with unbridled lust and amorality), thereby the film was able to 'get away with scenes that would be eliminated in secular context' (Walsh 1996: 52). After 1933 the double-dealing technique of the negative example became a staple of exploitation cinema. Luridly-titled films such as *Slaves in Bondage* (aka *Crusade Against the Rackets*, 1937) and *The Wages of Sin* (1938) focused on issues such as white slavery, sexual disease, birth control and drug use to facilitate salacious content. American exploitation cinema of the 1930s through to the early 1950s afforded a forum for the type of sensationalist sexual images excised by the Production Code, occupying a place between legitimate and illegitimate/hard-core cinemas. Films made under the banner of exploitation often promised more than they delivered but evaded state obscenity rulings by eschewing the explicit imagery found in hard-core stag films. These films traded on transgression and sensationalism to draw their audience, much as *The Sign of the Cross* sought its audience under the more inclusive Pre-Code era.

The Sign of the Cross used an established genre (the biblical drama) through which to frame and justify the presence of its *outré* sexual themes and images. This type of formal hybridisation is also evidenced at several critical junctures in cinema history, occurring often when regulatory bodies were under pressure to change in accordance with shifting cultural values and the industry was in the throes of economic crisis. 1950s 'adult' melodrama and 1970s soft-core art and comedy films, for example, adopted a strategy of marrying risqué sexual imagery to an industrially recognised genre (Hunt 1998: 114). With the weakening of the Production Code in the 1950s, American mainstream cinema reintroduced psychosexually-inclined 'adult' themes. These were in part a response to the box-office success of foreign 'sex' imports in America (such as ...*And God Created Woman*), some of which were immune from MPPDA regulation, as well as responding to the threat posed to cinema by television. More explicitly-oriented images and topics were reintroduced to the mainstream screen through the established generic framework of melodrama, a factor that is important to the general acceptance of racier themes (as in *Written on the Wind*, *A Streetcar Named Desire* and *Cat on a Hot Tin Roof*). The focus on the perceived realities of psychosexual problems, rather than anodyne romance, was intended to attract potential adult audiences by offering topics that would not be permitted on family-oriented television.

The sexual health of America was high on the agenda during this period, sparked in part by the publication and mass consumption of sexological studies (Kinsey, for example). While these dramas of desire had little in the way of overt sexual imagery, they nonetheless touched base with real sexual issues that were taboo for mainstream American cinema since the introduction of the Production Code and only found previously in the particular, and lurid, context of non-MPPDA-regulated exploitation cinema. Extra-marital affairs, conflicts between personal desire and family values, rape, nymphomania and impotency were therefore groundbreaking and exciting topics in the context of 1950s legitimate American cinema. The psychological emphasis as well as the high-gloss style of such films set them apart from exploitation and hard-core cinemas. 'Adult' melodramas had a connection nonetheless to exploitation cinema, which regularly took sexual problems as an ostensibly socially relevant mask for bringing titillating images to the screen. The strongly-marked psychosexual focus of such films, couched in the generic rhetorics of melodrama, bears considerable similarity to the way in which images of real sex have been contextualised and legitimised in later 'art' films. These include those that appeared in the 1970s, such as *Emmanuelle* and *Last Tango in Paris*, as well as the more recent flush of art cinema films, such as *Intimacy*, *The Piano Teacher* and *Romance* that bear images only found hitherto in hard-core.

Emmanuelle and *Last Tango in Paris* marry the psychological and the physical to construct narratives that place sex within the artfully existentialist context of identity formation and the meaning (or its lack) of being. In *Emmanuelle* sex is rendered as a means of 'coming' to power and achieving an authentic, fulfilled state of being. *Last Tango in Paris* focuses on a character that regards sex as a means of achieving existential authenticity but ultimately fails to find it. Both films contemplate the notion that shame and repression are bourgeois affectations that impinge on personal freedom and expression. These thematic and narrative components, borrowed from melodrama, French philosophy and pop radicalism help to distinguish the films from the episodic what-you-see-is-what-you-get form of hard-core. Combining dramas of transgressive desire with artful cinematography furnishes the spectacle of sex with the rhetoric of high cultural value. This marriage places the films within the culturally-sanctioned domain of 'art': an argument that also applies to the more recent flush of art cinema films (although *Baise-moi*, with its exploitation/New York underground colouring, is arguably an exception).

The sexual initiation narrative of *Emmanuelle* sets it apart from hard-core. Its soft-focus aesthetic, exotic Eastern location and psychological framework locate the 'real' elements of the actors' sexual performance in a fantasy and melodramatic context. Alongside its bondage/domination-oriented stable-mate *The Story of O*, *Emmanuelle* is a sexual fairytale. Both films are couched as erotic fantasy, laced with improbable scenarios and a lot of dressing up. These velvety coming-to-sexual-womanhood tales of sexual adventuring were designed to maximise their market potential by capturing the attention of the *Cosmopolitan*-reading 'where's your G-spot?' female audience. The slick photography and semi-mystical approach to female sexuality set them apart from the starkly edgy verité style of the New York underground (Warhol's films for example) and hard-core; the spectacle of 'real' sex is located thereby in two very different aesthetic registers. While *Emmanuelle* posits sexual authenticity within the modal context of languorous fantasy, *Last Tango in Paris* makes its claims on sexual authenticity through a combination of philosophical pretension, pessimism and realism. As discussed in relation to sexual initiation narratives in Part I, *Last Tango in Paris*'s director, Bernando Bertolucci, has explained in interview that the core intention behind the film was to explore in cinematic terms the 'present of fucking' (cited in Mellen 1974: 131). Along with Brando's improvisations and method acting, it is very much a 'performer' film. By virtue of such self-reflexive frames, sexual performance is deeply over-determined and laden with ambiguous coding and resonance; requisite values to claim the film as art cinema. *Last Tango in Paris* actively keeps the viewer at a distance from the proceedings: there is no invitation to regard events as erotic fantasy, as with the opening narrated section of *The Story of O* (indicated by the fairytale timelessness of the opening words 'One day O's lover…'). *Last Tango in Paris* sells its sex as spectacle, but this comes with efforts to keep the spectator at one remove from the 'present of fucking', a coldness echoed by its soft version of a realist aesthetic and the thematic focus on alienation and the insularity of human relationships. Nonetheless, physical sex provides the two central characters with a temporary respite from the complexities of their lives, although the sex in which they indulge themselves is still couched in a matrix of interlaced yet conflicting psychological investments. The core meaning of sex is obscured for the characters: the physical and the psychological slide past each other without much interaction, creating a sense of fragmentation rather than symbiotic plenitude.

As the narrative of *Last Tango in Paris* develops, temporary sexual satisfactions give way to a deeper pessimism about the viability of the couple's relationship. Under the aegis of Lacan's axiom 'There is no such thing as a sexual relationship' ('Il n'y a pas de rapport sexuel', 1991: 134), the film uses the same despondent themes that frame and sanction the use of real sex in *Intimacy*, *The Piano Teacher* and *Romance*. By being placed in a psychosexual context, the spectacle of 'real' sex is given an emotional and philosophical colouring very different from the more superficial and immediate spectacle of the real found in hard-core. The inclusion of a psychosexual dimension, borrowed in part from melodrama, makes the designation of the 'real' a relative and complex affair, an aspect that is underlined in the way such films play reflexively at the interface between the body-mechanics of sexual performance and its staging for cinema. Sensationalism is thereby tempered by the invocation of the way in which transgressive desire – that which exceeds rational control – has been regarded as a core and agonistic component of the human condition. The recent representation of real sex in legitimate cinema trades in a qualified way on a transgressive kudos, albeit that the nature of transgression differs within individual cases and depending in part on their cinematic heritage. With the home video success of sex-based art films such as *Last*

Tango in Paris or *Betty Blue*, it is not surprising that studios such as Studio-Canal looked to real sex as a way of increasing the relatively small market for its art cinema products. The hard-core video industry had an estimated global annual turnover of US$4 billion in the mid-1990s, testifying to widespread interest in explicit sexual material that cinema could potentially exploit (O'Toole 1999: 351). While *Intimacy* and *The Piano Teacher* took quite small returns at the box office in Britain, they nonetheless attracted a great deal of press coverage, mainly because they contained sexual images that had not previously been seen in legitimate cinema in Britain. Although there are national differences in the way sex and its representation are regarded, the inclusion of real sex in legitimate cinema pushes at regulatory and generic boundaries.

While simulated sex acknowledges normative 'appropriateness' of purpose, the act of putting real sex on camera disturbs normative rhetorics of sex as an intimate and private affair. When characters have 'real' sex on screen, spectators are to some extent taken out of the frame of fictional representation, focus shifting perhaps from character to actor. A modal ambiguity is created between the real and fiction. In *Intimacy* it is Mark Rylance, the actor, as well as Jay, the character, that has an erection. Actively exploiting such disruptions to the distinction between fact and fiction further allows narrative-based films such as *The Idiots*, *The Piano Teacher* and *Intimacy* to explore the complex role that performance plays in the protagonists' lives, as well as sexuality and sexual relationships in general. As with *Last Tango in Paris*, what each have in common is that these fictions are conducted through real (sexual) bodies, underlined by the centralisation of 'real' sexual activity and nakedness as well as the aesthetic context of realism and the quest by director and performers for authentic performance. (This also calls to mind responses to the realistically-coded sex scene in *Don't Look Now*, discussed in Part I.) With the attenuation of devices that might help to mark performance off from the real, the modal positioning of these texts becomes unstable – in other words the frame of representation is splintered if not broken. The inherent ambiguity of staging real sex for the screen becomes an overt thematic impetus that focuses on the convolutions of existential matters. The use of psychologically-based narratives within which to frame 'real' sex in such films also works against the way that hard-core isolates sexual sensation from the wider and messy ramifications of interpersonal relationships. *Last Tango in Paris*, *Intimacy*, *The Piano Teacher* and *Romance*, for example, place real sex in a thematic psychological minefield of reflections, refractions, misconnections, social, personal and interpersonal contradictions and transgressions, that are rarely present in the comparably untroubled sexual spaces of hard-core (Michael Ninn's artful hard-core excepted). With such historical, contextual, aesthetic and performative factors in mind, we can move on to a closer analysis of the specific attributes and ambiguities of the use of 'real' sex in recent art cinema films, focusing specifically on *The Piano Teacher* and *Intimacy*.

Both films acknowledge, in different ways, the place hard-core has in contemporary culture and the way its particular formal devices have played a role in shaping the mediation of 'real' sex. *The Piano Teacher* address very directly the place of sexual imagery the-

Mark Rylance and Kelly Fox have real sex as their characters in *Intimacy* (2000)

matically, and alongside *Intimacy* borrows and reframes formal elements from hard-core. *Intimacy* opens with a scene that bears formal comparison to hard-core, but with some significant differences. The scene borrows from the 'stranger sex' format: a narrative device that has often been deployed in hard-core because it tends to sideline complex emotional connections in favour of carnal pleasure without obligation. The context is an unkempt London flat inhabited by a thirtysomething man, who we first see stretched out sleeping on a sofa, mimicking and gender-inverting the languid female nude odalisques of nine-teenth- and early twentieth-century painting. A hand-held camera follows as he opens the door onto a thirtysomething woman. Cursory greetings are exchanged, with no courtly flirtation, emphasising self-consciousness and establishing that they do not appear to know each other well. Clothes are discarded awkwardly, without recourse to the mannered style of striptease, and they fuck urgently on the debris-strewn floor. The pace of editing speeds up, fragmenting the coupling and isolating each of the protagonists. Hand-held camerawork and a short depth of field without skin-enhancing lighting effects intensify the impression of immediacy and presence given to this explicit brief encounter. These are the types of devices we might expect from hard-core or from verité: the two styles coming together under the illusion of unmediated realism. Unlike hard-core, the sexual encounter is not staged rhythmically through various 'acts' or positions and there is no cum-shot, al-though the spectator is left in little doubt that penetration has occurred. As with hard-core, the sexual performance of the actors is highlighted in this scene, with all other aspects in abeyance. There is no non-diegetic music and ambient close-miking is used to enhance the intimate presence and texture of the couple's breathing and the sounds of skin moving across skin.

The sum of these strategies gives the sense that the camera is following, rather than orchestrating, a real rather than fabricated and choreographed event; going, as it were, with the action. These are techniques often used in hard-core to encode sex as authentic in audio-visual and performative terms, particularly in the low-budget 'authentic' end of hard-core rather than silicone-enhanced spectacle of higher-budget offerings. Even if some of the typical shot patternings of hard-core are missing (there are no close-ups of genitals for example), the whole emphasis of this episodic scene is focused on fleshly connection and sexual performance. But such a comparison with hard-core must also be considered against the broader structure of the film's narrative.

The opening scene acts as a kind of enigma posed to the viewer about the nature of the connection between the couple: Who are they? How are they connected? What repercussions might this sexual encounter have? These are questions that are unlikely to arise with any insistence in watching a hard-core film. The scene compares with the stylistic resonances of on-the-fly techniques used in some forms of art cinema (verité and Dogme 95 for example) but resonates equally with the style of raw low-budget hard-core European films, as opposed to the slicker, suntanned, more continuity-shot style of 'mom and pop' American hard-core. However, as the film progresses, the performance of real sex is placed within the narrative frame of emotional ramification, which lends the film's real-sex thematic an artful and melodramatic justification. This is a strategy present in most of the sex-focused art films mentioned here. The spectacular pleasure of watching real sex in this context comes at a price: the spectator is narratively cued and cajoled into making an emotional, empathic and speculative investment in the two characters. In hard-core the spectator is rarely interpolated in such ways: it is the pleasure and sensation of the participants that we are invited to identify with rather than the psychological complexities and conflicts of a central, carefully-wrought fictional character.

With its smooth unobtrusive camerawork and seamless editing, *The Piano Teacher* differs from the circumstantial style of hard-core. But there is one particular formal device in common with hard-core: the use of real time in a number of key scenes. The first of these is a ten-minute sex scene, the one scene in the film which operates most like that which might be expected of a hard-core production. Unlike hard-core, the scene has no orgasmic climax, however. The withholding of orgasm, a condition for sex insisted on by the title character Erika Kohut (Isabelle Hubert), as well as the partially out-of-frame act of fellatio, plays with both spectators' and the male character's expectation of a climactic resolution to earlier sexual tension between the pair. Real sex lurks at the margins of the scene thematically and literally. This is in keeping with the film's focus on the lead character's pathologised confusion between sexual fantasy and reality (reiterating that outworn spectacle of the sexually-repressed hysterical woman, which is given a far more refreshing and reflexive treatment in *Romance*). Like *Last Tango in Paris* and *Intimacy*, the film addresses sex in a psychosexual context, and each centralises the failure of interpersonal communication. In *The Piano Teacher*, however, the failed communication involves a misunderstanding about the status of the central character's masochistic fantasies, which she and her male pupil take, in different ways, all too literally.

Sex and the Cinema

A contention central to the argument here, as well as to the analysis of the representation of sex in cinema more generally, is that the conventions of hard-core provide a benchmark coding for 'real' sex in art cinema. Such films treat these conventions in self-reflexive ways, however, to raise questions about the status of fantasy, spectacle and the real. The direct representation of real sex in *The Piano Teacher* comes not in the central character's performance, as it does in *Intimacy*, but through the inclusion of a short section of a hard-core video that Erika views in a porn shop video-booth. The video includes many of the audio-visual codes of immediacy and authenticity that are regularly seen in such films. The graininess of the video image, the jerky camerawork and the close-up of a woman fellating a man – intensified by being blown up to fit the widescreen cinematic frame – are juxtaposed against the rich celluloid texture of the rest of the film. This may appear to make the video seem more 'real' in conventional audio-visual terms, but when viewed in the context of the diegetic real difficulties that Erika experiences in her own sexual encounters, it comes to represent something ideal, unattainable, enigmatic and very unreal. This is best illustrated by the fact that Erika's attempt at fellatio, seen previously as the source of pleasure in the hard-core video, ends abruptly with her throwing up. Not what might be expected to happen in the choreographed, unimpeded ecstasies of hard-core's pornotopian world.

The real of sex means, therefore, something very different in the diegesis of *The Piano Teacher*, as is also the case with *Romance* and *Intimacy*. The spectacle of hard-core's unconditional 'real' sex that Erika views in the pay-per-view booth at the video shop is juxtaposed with the painful reality of Erika's fraught relationship with her younger male pupil. The spectator is left with the question as to what exactly constitutes real sex: Erika's excruciating attempts to act out her masochistic fantasies, misunderstood by the object of her desire, or the pornotopian hard-core sex she sees in the booth. As in *Last Tango in Paris*, *Intimacy* and *Romance*, real sex between real people is a messy alienating business, worlds away from the formalised images of sexual ecstasy found in hard-core. In *The Piano Teacher*, the inherent spectacle of hard-core sex is drained of its power to signify the real.

Following the circular path instituted by Max Ophüls in melodramas such as *La Ronde* and *Letter From an Unknown Woman*, recent art films such as *Intimacy*, *Romance*, *Eyes Wide Shut* and *The Piano Teacher* are intently focused on the convoluted circuitry of sexual desire and the interlacing of performance, fantasy and the real. This provides a narrative context within which explicit imagery occurs, constituting an important modal difference from hard-core and having a significant impact on the meaning of the spectacle of real sex. Sexual sensationalism is shifted into the melodramatic register of psychological conflict and tension, whereas hard-core emphasises the physical mechanics and rhythms of sexual performance. Psychological dimensions are only present in hard-core when they add something to the spectacular and sensational intent of representing 'real' sex (although psychological aspects are more common in soft-core and the relatively few examples of hard-core that have 'artistic' pretensions). Unlike hard-core, explicit art cinema is centred on complex characterisation, and in some senses this distinction reiterates well-established rhetorical differences between pornography and eroticism that have often been deployed to demarcate boundaries between legitimate and illegitimate texts.[71]

In different ways, the more recent examples frame sex in terms of established art values. The cinematic representation of real sex, it seems, is sanctioned only on the conditions that certain signifiers of 'art' are present. The excision of the penetration scene in *Baise-moi* by British censors appears to be related to the fact that the film has far fewer conventional signifiers of 'art' than others of the current trend. Both *Intimacy* and *The Piano Teacher* make very direct appeals to 'art' within their storylines: drama in the former and classical music in the later. *The Piano Teacher*, for example, sandwiches the hard-core video that Erika sees at the porn store between two pieces of high-brow classical music. The music that is part of Erika's mental furniture becomes temporarily masked out by the overwhelming effect of watching the video. An 'artful' tension between high and low culture comes to the fore. The use of classical music contributes to the way the film constructs a high-cultural context for the inclusion of low-culture hard-core.

The presence of explicit imagery in these sex-based art films has a resonantly ambiguous – and therefore 'artful' – status; titillation is rendered more complex than it is in hard-core. Through the rhetorical frame of psychological realism, sex and desire become a source of dramatic and existential enigma. This reaches beyond the frame to the spectator, who is not left in the dark simply to enjoy at the level of spectacle and sensation. In hard-core the presence of a diegetic spectator often works to make spectators more comfortable in their voyeurism, implying that they are not alone in their voyeuristic pleasure. This is not the case in recent art-cinema films such as *The Piano Teacher* and *Requiem for a Dream* (2000). In *Requiem for a Dream*, Marion Silver (Jennifer Connelly) trades sex for heroin, culminating in a scene in which she has sex with another woman surrounded by well-dressed men. This is the type of scene that might be found in any number of hard-core films, but here it is contextualised by binding the scene into a wider narrative arc that focuses on the effects of addiction. *Romance*, too, seeks to destabilise untroubled titillation through its focus on Marie's sexual experiences, from which she learns that 'you can't have a face when a cunt tags along'. As already stated in Part I, the film stages graphically the Madonna/whore binary in one fantasy scene. A number of women lie on benches and are bisected by a barrier that prevents visual access from either side. On one side of the barrier – a clean, clinical-looking area – their faces are stroked by men; on the other – sleazy and dark – men fuck the women's lower halves. As with the decadent sex-party scene in *Eyes Wide Shut* (which would not look amiss in *The Story of O*), the scenario could be lifted from one of the more elaborate hard-core films. But, rather than being presented simply as erotic spectacles, both scenes invite the spectator to contemplate the muddled relationships between sex, desire and power. When we watch Erika watching the hard-core action, watch her delve into a bin to fish out and sniff 'used' tissues, we are not invited to immerse ourselves in the hard-core images she sees. Their presence is fractured and interrupted by the protracted reaction shots and the narrative context. As explained above, within the frame of the narrative, *The Piano Teacher* positions hard-core sex as an unattainable manufactured fantasy. Unlike hard-core, these films foreground the cultural construction of sex, desire and gender; their conflicts, contradictions and pressures. Images of real sex are intentionally titillating, yet spectators are also invited to consider the nature of such excitement, a claim to the type of artistic value also likely to placate censors.

Films such as *Intimacy*, *Romance* and *The Piano Teacher* invoke the immersive sensationalism of hard-core; but, unlike hard-core, these films frame 'real' sex in terms of issues such as identity politics, power and the blurred relationships between reality and fantasy, the ideal and the actual. The presence of such elements prevent the viewer from enjoying these films as simply erotic spectacle. Often striking chords with the psychological realism of melodrama, which locates the physical within the psychological, these films contemplate the complexity of sex and sexual desire in a way that differs substantially from hard-core. Fiction therefore plays a far stronger role in the way that real sex is contextualised in art cinema than in hard-core. Rather than buying into overly simplified distinctions between authenticity and performance (a distinction markedly visible in most hard-core), it is the awkward slippage between the two that provides art films with their major thematic and philosophical focus. In framing sex this way, such films are sanctioned as more culturally and artfully valuable than the low-culture bump-and-grind, one-purpose goal of hard-core. They provide commentaries on the spectacle-based commodification of sexual performance in contemporary culture and, unlike exploitation and hard-core, treat sex within the familiar and culturally established generic context of the well-made drama. What they also demonstrate is that established hierarchal regimes of 'good' taste are still in operation in the circuit between production and regulation. Representations of sex and desire couched in the rhetoric of transgression but framed by aesthetic dexterity and psychological complexity warrant the label 'art'. These purport to stir the intellect rather than, as is the case with most hard-core, providing salacious and sleazy entertainment, seeking to stir the body and call the mind down into the sensuous depths of the pornographic imagination.

Coda: Economies of Desire

In our journey through the varied terrains of sex in the cinema it becomes clear that cinematic mediations of sex and desire are shaped by a host of factors; some are cultural, some related to industry and market, while others are aesthetic and formal. While the meanings of sex and desire in cinema are various, their representation is informed by a range of epistemologies, formal conventions, theories and rhetorics. It is also apparent that the way in which an individual film portrays sex and desire serves a rhetorical purpose in its own right.

As has been identified in a number of contexts, cinematic sex acts to some degree as a gauge for measuring historically specific pressures that shape the meanings and practises of sex, desire and sexuality in real life. This may include what is left unseen or unspoken, as much as what appears. The representation of sex in the cinema shifts in accordance with cultural attitudes and even at times plays, through the rhetorical dimension of representation, a promotional role in the production of such shifts. While cinema is mainly driven to produce commercially viable entertainment, it also contributes to the prevailing contemporary socio-cultural climate, its ideals and dispositions. Films can often open up new sexual vistas for viewers and contribute to ensuring that sex and desire are regarded in multiple ways. This is regardless of whether a film focuses on adultery, coming-out stories or sexual close encounters of the hard-core kind. Through the cross-current of exchanges between representation and culture, sex in the cinema has an important role in the formation of dominant attitudes to sexuality, as well as promoting particular sexual identities either by positive or negative example. Even as it might exploit minority positions as a source of spectacle and salacious seduction, cinema plays an important cultural role in the way that sex and desire are understood in a general sense.

Representations of sex and sexual desire in cinema are often the product of a complex interchange between inter-cultural forces. Different forms of sex in cinema may be mapped in direct relation to the way that those intra-cultural forces regard the functions and meanings of sex and desire. Throughout cinema history, for example, a line has often been drawn between sexual content designed and deemed suitable for mainstream consumption and that which operates either apparently or actually outside regulation. Various films from both camps have tested lines of general acceptability over the course of cinema's history. These lines are never fixed for long, however; as is evident in the case of films like *Intolerance*, *Red Dust*, *The Sign of the Cross*, *…And God Created Woman*, *Last Tango in Paris*, *Ai No Corrida*, *Caligula*, *Romance*, *Baise-moi* and, oddly perhaps given the age of the short films collected here, *The Good Old Naughty Days*. The borderline status of these films, which in some cases marry established legitimate forms with aspects borrowed from illegitimate sources, demonstrates how a dialectical process of exchange often operates to effect changes to what is deemed as acceptable for mass consumption. In addition, these boundary-testing films demonstrate how the regulation of cinema is often under pressure to mediate changing social attitudes into its processes.

Of all the influences that prevail on cinematic mediations of sex and desire, it is transgression that proves to be a significant guiding factor; it is extremely common for films to couch sex and desire in rhetorics of transgression. While these might prove important in attracting the attention of a target audience, the particular way that transgression is coded has an in-built moral and value-laden perspective (what this is differs quite widely, however). Sexual transgression often provides a catalyst for dramatic action, as occurs in films focused on sexual desires directed outside a sanctioned situation. Sexual transgression provides the basis for films that focus on the way that desire and the body exceed our control; this is given spectacular form within the special effects-laden contexts of horror and fantasy, evident in those films that focus on animal transformation. One of the reasons that lines of acceptability are so often tested is that many films work to render sex as 'forbidden fruit', and as such employ rhetorical devices that are redolent with transgressive caché, although often this is counter-balanced by devices that attempt to sidestep norms by taking the moral high ground or through the reiteration of conventions such as the heterosexual complementary couple. The seductive qualities of forbidden fruit is perhaps why so many films discussed in this book refer to notions of sin and temptation, or make use of psychoanalytic ideas such as repression, the return of the repressed, or desire as radically other. Cinema's very form also calls on transgression in that sex is made the object of the gaze; sex becomes a public entertainment which infringes on the commonly-held value that sex should be a private affair, hence scrutiny from regulatory, reformist or other bodies, and the presence of 'conditions' that govern the legitimate or illegitimate status of a film. Many representations of sex on screen work to draw viewers' interest by making of sex an invitation and mystery; working with people's curiosity about sex has proved to be a commercially lucrative strategy throughout cinema's history. Concepts such as sin, repression and transgression work well within this model as a sensationalising agenda; as one of the characters in *Zandalee* points out 'a touch of sin brings *joie de vivre*'. But, although cinema objectifies sex as inherent to the process of turning it into audio-visual entertainment, seeing cinematic sex solely in terms objectification does not accurately represent the multifaceted experiences that watching cinematic sex brings.

The meaning and emotional register of representations of sex and desire are extremely sensitive to the textual and aesthetic context in which they appear. This includes dramatic, narrative, narrational, generic, stylistic and interpolative context. Most fictional films encourage the viewer to engage emotionally with the experience of characters. It is emotional engagement facilitated by the strategies employed by a text which generates involvement that extends beyond the undeniable pleasure of looking. The promotion of a broader cognitive, physical and emotional engagement with a film often proves important in distinguishing hard-core from more legitimated images of sex. Such engagement proves to be an important 'condition' under which sexual transgression is made permissible as a form of public entertainment, and although lines between illegitimate hard-core and legitimate cinema are becoming more blurred it is still nonetheless the case that in Britain, the US and Australia textual context is all-important in making sex accord with regulation. This is clearly a condition for the legitimate presence of real sex in art cinema, as I have shown. These divisions and set conditions might seem to some arbitrary, morally conservative, or based on an outmoded notion of entertainment as a form of public service. It certainly seems odd that in liberal cultures, and given its massive revenue generation, that hard-core is still illegitimate fare. But as we have seen, transgressive status works well for the industry, and, given that hard-core footage was mainly distributed via mail order and is now increasingly distributed via the unregulated Internet, there is no longer any real concern about distribution; outlying status may have been regarded previously by the industry as an obstacle to consumer access rather than an enticement to purchase and look at that which has been forbidden.

What emerges from researching for and writing this book is that it is highly problematic from a number of perspectives to regard the sensationalist dimension that accompanies sex in most cinemas in an entirely negative light. Sensationalism is often used in cinema – not just sex-based cinema – to engage viewers emotionally and physically, and the energies invoked by sensationalism and transgressive coding compensates, to some extent, for cinema's missing dimension of tactility (music also provides such compensation). Sensationalism and transgression do not function therefore just as marketing ploys. As we have seen, values that signify 'art' are often used to authorise sensationalist, transgressive and explicit representations of sex outside hard-core and sexploitation. They do so based on judicial and marketing factors, but also in terms of hierarchies of taste and cultural value; often art films marry sensationalism and transgression with reflexivity, engagement with complex issues and the exploration of psychological and aesthetic form. Intellectual engagements and high production values are often regarded – by regulators, pundits and critics – as more worthwhile than films that seek to engage viewers at the level of the emotional, and even more so at the level of the physical. As such, films that set out with the aim of engaging viewers erotically are often considered to be valueless. It is often the case that greater value is placed on those films that focus on the psychological complexities of sex in serious and non-symbolic ways. But it is often those films that are made for niche audiences and in less-than-good-taste that present the greatest challenge to the palliative rhetorics of romance, sex and desire found mainstream cinemas. Where cinema generally also has a case to answer is the way it often sets viewers impossible expectations of real-life sex and desire. But this does not entail a call for 'truth' in cinematic representations: wild fantastical fictions also have their value. Utopian visions of sexual plenitude, for example, can highlight, in an inverse way, the problems with realities and conflicts of interests at a personal or social level. What remains in the mind, after watching a host of films focused on sex, is that cinemas of all types are intent often on capturing the transformative nature of sex and sexual desire, in its many guises. What also emerges is that sex and desire lie at the very heart of the way that identity, society, family and civilisation are experienced, classified and defined; sex is mythologised, narrativised, elevated, debased, but it never loses its power to fascinate.

Notes

1　'Rhetoric' is a useful term and appears frequently throughout this book. I follow Brian Sutton-Smith's definition of rhetoric as 'a persuasive discourse, or implicit narrative, wittingly or unwittingly adopted by members of an affiliation to persuade others of the veracity or worthwhileness of their beliefs. In a sense, whenever identification is made with a belief or a cause or a science or an ideology, that identification reveals itself by the words that are spoken about it, by the clothes and insignia worn to celebrate it, by the allegiances adopted to sustain it, and by the hard work and scholarly devotion to it, as well as by the theories that are woven into it' (2001: 8).

2　'Sexuality' is a term that encompasses the host of feelings, desires, longings and fantasies of a sexual nature that inform our relationships with others, that constitute our sexual identity, and which are related to – but not the same as – the act of sex.

3　'Exploitation cinema' has been described as films that 'typically sacrifice traditional notions of artistic merit for the sensational display of some topic about which the audience may be curious, or have some prurient interest'; http://en.wikipedia.org/wiki/Exploitation_film. Accessed 14 February 2005. See Schaefer 1999 and Muller & Faris 1996 for more extensive accounts of exploitation cinemas.

4　I am grateful to Linda Ruth Williams for this suggestion, personal communication August 2005.

5　What is defined as 'hard-core' is of course subject to change but broadly speaking it describes films that are focused solely on sexual acts of an explicit nature and where the sexual acts are real rather than simulated.

6　For a discussion of early stag films see Williams 1990: 58–92.

7　See Klinger 1994 for an in-depth analysis of 1950s 'adult melodramas'.

8　'Remediation' refers to a process by which an idea developed originally in one media context is used in another.

9   For an extended discussion and introduction to 'New Queer Cinema' see Michele Aaron (ed.) (2004) *New Queer Cinema: A Critical Reader*, Edinburgh: Edinburgh Univeresity Press, and Robin Griffiths (2006) *New Queer Cinema: Beyond the Celluloid Closet*, London: Wallflower Press.

10   The Book of Genesis describes in mythical terms the way in which the first man and first woman were cast out of the Garden of Eden or paradise (Genesis 3:23). In transgressing God's one rule (Genesis 3:3) by eating the forbidden fruit Adam and Eve experience nakedness as shame (Genesis 3:7–11) and at God's command Eve was henceforth to be ruled over by Adam (Genesis 4:16). As well as establishing a gendered order, the myth conflates entry into the knowledge of good and evil with sexuality. Ironically it is the biblical association of sex and shame that lends many cinematic representations of sex their transgressive appeal.

11   The term 'homosocial' is used to describe the organisation of inter-male relationships under heterosexuality and patriarchy, a concept developed by Eve Kosofsky Sedgwick (1992) to help explore the effect of homophobia on society and sexuality.

12   See Evans & Gamman 1995 for a useful overview.

13   For a discussion of the way that fairytale and horror films often present witchy seductive beauty as a mask for an ugly soul see Krzywinska 2000a.

14   http://www.etonline.com/celebrity/a3279.htm. Accessed 9 February 2002.

15   Ibid.

16   See Jacobs 1995 for a detailed account.

17   See Lacan's essays 'In You More Than You' (1987) and 'Encore' (1998).

18   The film was banned in Ireland but received '18' ratings in most countries; http://www.imdb.com. Accessed 21 June 2002.

19   This binary is not simply identified by modern feminist theorists of gender. It has a presence in literature and in the gothic novel *The Monk* (first published in 1796). The villain of the piece, the eponymous Monk, says 'What charms me, when ideal and considered as a superior Being, would disgust me, become Woman and tainted with all the failings of Mortality' (Matthew Lewis cited in Clemens 1999: 74). This view of women is echoed in a non-religious context by the husband in *Romance*.

20   See Lewis 2000 for more on the reception and the self-imposed 'X'-rated classification of *Romance* in the US.

21   See Krzywinska 1998a, 1998b and 1999 for discussions of these films.

22   'Circle' is derived from the latin *circulus* denoting a circus ring or circle. An etymological factor that, coincidentally or not, has a resonance within many of Schnitzler's stories and plays as well as the iconography of *La Ronde* and *Lola Montès* (1955).

23   http://www.bbfc.co.uk. Accessed 13 June 2002.

24   See Jean-Francois Lyotard's *Libidinal Economy* (1993) in which he argues that all exchange is based on pleasure and desire; Jacques Lacan's emphasis on the notion that desire is radically other and endlessly deferred; Gilles Deleuze and Felix Guattari's *Anti-*

Oedipus (1984) in which it is argued that we are all 'desiring machines', desire operating mechanically beyond our control.

25 Defining 'soft-core' is not particularly easy, tied as it is to more subjective differentiations between of erotica and pornography, as Linda Ruth Williams points out. Differentiation 'generally rests on subjective judgements of personal disgust or arousal, making one person's soft another person's hard' (2005: 39). She goes on to suggest that '"Soft" is often understood as mainstream material distributed with an 'R' or 'NC' rating in the US or with a '15' or '18' certification in the UK, whilst "hard" is that which is obtainable only in sex outlets in the US and UK, though much hard-core which can legally be rented or bought in the US still remains beyond the pale of even the 'R-18' certificate in the UK, and is thus illegal' (ibid.). These definitions therefore hinge on the legality and regulatory rating of sex-based films. Williams goes on to suggest that a key difference also lies in the fact that hard-core 'primarily features real sex performed by porn actors, whilst soft-core ... shows simulated sex performed by movie actors' (ibid.). This definition hinges on the conditions of performance in the production of a film. For a further discussion of soft-core, its history and definitions, see Andrews 2004; for a useful analysis of the development of the sexual melodrama, see Williams 2005: 390–5.

26 Jean Laplanche and Jean-Bertrand Pontalis define repression as 'an operation, whereby the subject attempts to repel, or to confine to the unconscious, representations (thoughts, images, memories) which are bound to an instinct. Repression occurs when to satisfy an instinct – though likely to be pleasurable in itself – would incur the risk of provoking unpleasure because of other requirements' (1988: 390). They define the 'return of the repressed' as 'a process whereby what has been repressed – though never abolished by repression – tends to re-appear, and succeeds in doing so in a distorted fashion in the form of a compromise' (1988: 389).

27 http://www.bfi.co.uk/website. Accessed 14 June 2002.

28 For the full list and related information see http://www.bbfc.co.uk under 'guidelines'.

29 It should be noted that is hard to ascertain how many exploitation films where actually made in this period as there are few records in existence, due mainly to the transient nature of exploitation film production.

30 See Williams 1990 for a comprehensive analysis of early stag films.

31 http://www.bbfc.org. Accessed 16 June 2005.

32 For a very useful account of the wider influences, especially radical feminist calls for the censorship of sexual imagery, that played a role in shaping current regulation, see Williams 2002.

33 See Lewis 2000 for an extensive account of the regulatory and classificatory situation in the US in the early 1970s, and of the ways in which the American film industry was saved from financial crisis by the imposition of classifications that outlawed 'foreign' sex films from the mainstream.

34 See footnote 1, above, for a definition of rhetorics.

35 http://www.imdb.com/title/tt0036241/tagline. Accessed 9 September 2004.

36 http://www.imdb.com/title/tt0194314/posters. Accessed 4 January 2005.

37 See *The History of Eroticism* (*L'Histoire de l'erotisme*, 1976) and *Sovereignty* (*Le Souverainete*, 1976), both published in *The Accursed Share* (1991); essays such as those published in *Visions of Excess: Selected Writings 1927–39* (1985); novels such as *Story of the Eye* (*Histoire de l'oeil*, 1979) and *Blue of Noon* (*Le bleu du ciel*, 1988).

38 Meaning, in this context, that which lends a sense of awe, of being insignificant in the broader scheme of things.

39 Found for example in the writings of Herbert Marcuse (*Eros and Civilisation*, 1969) and Wilhem Reich (*The Function of the Orgasm*, 1961; *The Sexual Revolution: Towards a Self Governing Character Structure*, 1970). For a sustained discussion of these texts see Jeffrey Weeks' (1985) *Sexuality and Its Discontents*, Chapter 7 'Dangerous Desires'.

40 See Jenks 2003 for a useful account of Bataille's ideas and how they key in to anthropological conceptions of transgression, particularly Mary Douglas' work on pollution found in her book *Purity and Danger* (1991).

41 Their model of transgression echoes in some respects Bataille's work on transgression, particularly in *Eroticism* (1975), yet Bataille focuses more intently on the way that eroticism is in itself a challenge to the order of work as well as exploring the links between eroticism and the annihilation of the self.

42 See Faludi 1992 for a sustained analysis of the conservatism of *Fatal Attraction*.

43 'Enunciation': the place from which a film speaks; its point of view.

44 Linda Ruth Williams (2005) explores *Zandalee* and *Unfaithful* as erotic thrillers; she provides a slightly different perspective, therefore, on the way that adultery is figured in terms of the rhetorics of transgression.

45 A dance-style developed in Paris of the 1880s, characterised by mock fighting.

46 The Other – spelled with a capital O in a Lacanian context – designates that over which we have no control but which has power over us. In the context of cinema this might be regarded as offscreen forces that orchestrate events according to a hidden moral order; this might be attributable, in diegetic terms, to God or to the forces at work in cinema as an institution.

47 http://www.probe.org/docs/adultery.html. Accessed 5 November 2004.

48 http://www.theparson.net/madison.html. Accessed 5 November 2004.

49 'Other' defined in this context as 'that which is not me', or 'that which I do not recognise as me'.

50 See Paul 2004 for a useful analysis of the film and its representation of psychoanalysis.

51 See Barker 1984 for a fuller explanation.

52 See 'The Universality of Incest' at http://www.geocities.com/kidhistory/incestd.htm. Accessed 2 December 2004.

53 'Teleology': an explanation of a phenomenon in terms of ends or final causes, as if that phenomenon fits into some pre-planned overarching design or scheme.

54 'Disavow': to repudiate or disclaim the knowledge of something.

55 See Van Haute 1995 for a helpful overview of Laplanche's work.

56 See Klein's 'A Study in Envy and Gratitude' in *The Selected Melanie Klein* (1991) for a more in-depth account. For a useful commentary on this article and on the importance of Klein's work see Minsky 1996: 78–109.

57 Jessie and Tom's parents are never referred to as anything else other than Mum and Dad. The film is shot from the point of view of the children, which goes some way to explaining this, but in addition it emphasises the fact that families apportion roles and that with these roles comes a predefined and socially-sanctioned set of boundaries and responsibilities.

58 For more on the role of the primal father in cinema see Krzywinska 2000b (especially chapter two, 'Demon Daddies').

59 BBFC statement made on their refusal to issue a certificate for the video release of *Straw Dogs* in 1999. The video release was approved in 2002.

60 For an informative essay that seeks to reassess the significance of Krafft-Ebing's sexological writings see Hauser 1994.

61 In acknowledgement of Deleuze's criticism of the conflation of the two terms I use a hyphen as a means of breaking up the composite term.

62 http://www.soj.org/articles/whysm.html. Accessed 20 November 2004.

63 http://www.soj.org/miesen.html. Accessed 31 July 01. The original version of this essay was written in the 1970s and then revised by him in 1981. It was originally published as 'A View of Sadomasochism – The Adult Sex Game'.

64 See Hunt 1999 (chapter two) for a useful overview of 1970s 'permissive' Britain.

65 The film was also released under the appropriately wordy title *The Persecution and Assassination of Jean-Paul Marat as Performed by the Inmates of the Asylum of Charenton Under the Direction of the Marquis de Sade*.

66 A rather apt bit of casting as Kinski has a reputation as a sexual athlete, which he capitalises on in his autobiography.

67 Under various pseudonyms, Anne Rice authored a range of S/M fantasy novels, including *Exit to Eden* (1985).

68 Lestat savours the blood of the evil-doer, but Louis is unaware that there is in fact a moral logic to his enjoyment; this is not present in the film or the novel on which the film is based because both are written from Louis' point of view (Louis prefers to regard Lestat as amoral).

69 '*Tableau vivant*': literally 'living picture'; 'a scene presented on stage by costumed actors who remain silent and motionless as if in a picture'; http://education.yahoo.com/reference/dictionary/entry/tableau%20vivant. Accessed 13 January 2005.

70 For a detailed history of Operation Spanner see http://www.spannertrust.org/documents/spannerhistory.asp. Accessed 4 January 2005.

71 See Sontag 1983 for a discussion of distinctions between pornography and eroticism.

Filmography

…And God Created Woman (*Et Dieu … créa la femme*, Roger Vadim, 1956, France/Italy)

À ma soeur! (Catherine Breillat, 2001, France/Italy)

Ai No Corrida (*Empire of the Senses*, Nagisa Oshima, 1976, Japan/France)

Alien (Ridley Scott, 1979, UK)

Aliens (James Cameron, 1986, US/UK)

All That Heaven Allows (Douglas Sirk, 1955, US)

Amelie (Le Fabuleux destin d'Amélie Poulain, Jean-Pierre Jeunet, 2001, France/Germany)

American Beauty (Sam Mendes, 1999, US)

American in Paris, An (Vincente Minelli, 1952, US)

American Pie (Paul Weitz, 1999, US)

American Pie 2 (James B. Rogers, 2001, US)

American Werewolf in London, An (John Landis, 1981, US/UK)

Angel (Joss Whedon, 1999-2004, US)

Angels and Insects (Philip Haas, 1995, US/UK)

Anna Karenina (Clarence Brown, 1935, US)

Ape Man, The (William Beaudine, 1943, US)

Arabian Nights (*Il fiore delle mille e una notte*, Pier Paolo Pasolini, 1974, Italy/France)

Attendant, The (Isaac Julien, 1992, UK)

Baby Doll (Elia Kazan, 1956, US)

Back Street (John M. Stahl, 1932, US)

Back Street (Robert Stevenson, 1941, US)

Bad Boy Bubby (Rolf de Heer, Australia/Itlay, 1993)

Baise-moi (Virginie Despentes, Coralie, 2000, France)

Barberella (Roger Vadim, 1968, Italy/France)

Behind Convent Walls (*Interno di un Convento*, Walerian Borowczyk, 1977, Italy)

Being John Malkovich (Spike Jonze, 1999, US)

Bell, Book and Candle (Richard Quine, 1958, US)

Belle et la bête, La (Jean Cocteau, 1946, France)

Ben Hur (Fred Niblo, 1925, US)

Betty Blue (*37°2 le matin*, Jean-Jacques Beineix, 1986, France)

Bilitis (David Hamilton, 1977, France)

Birth of a Nation, The (D. W. Griffith, 1915, US)

Blacula (William Crain, 1972, US)

Blade Runner (Ridley Scott, 1982, US)

Blanche Fury (Marc Allégret, 1947, UK)

Brandon Teena Story, The (Susan Muska, Gréta Olafsdóttir,1998, US)

Bridges of Madison Country, The (Clint Eastwood, 1995, US)

Brief Encounter (David Lean, 1945, UK)

Bringing Up Baby (Howard Hawks, 1938, US)

Broken Blossoms (D. W. Griffith, 1919, US)

Bronx Tale, A (Robert De Niro, 1993, US)

Brood, The (David Cronenberg, 1979, Canada)

Brotherhood of the Wolf (*Le Pacte de Loups*, Christophe Gans, 2001, France/Germany/Italy)

Buffy the Vampire Slayer (Joss Whedon, 1997–2003, US)

Caligula (*Caligola*, Tinto Brass and Bob Guccione, 1979, US/Italy)

Candyman (Bernard Rose, 1992, US)

Canterbury Tales, The (*Racconi di Canterbury*, Pier Paolo Pasolini, 1972, Italy/France)

Cape Fear (J. Lee Thompson, 1962, UK)

Carrie (Brian De Palma, 1976, US)

Cat on a Hot Tin Roof (Richard Brooks, 1958, US)

Cat People (Jacques Tourneur, 1942, US)

Cat People (Paul Schrader, 1982, US)

Cathy Come Home (Ken Loach, 1966, UK)

Cement Garden, The (Andrew Birkin, 1993, France/Germany/UK)

Close My Eyes (Stephen Poliakoff, 1991, UK)

Company of Wolves, The (Neil Jordan, 1984, US)

Conan the Barbarian (John Milius, 1982, US)

Confessions of a Window Cleaner (Val Guest, 1974, UK)

Conspirators of Pleasure (*Spiklenci Slasti*, Jan Svankmajer, 1996, Czech Rep./Switzerland/UK)

Courtship (1899, UK)

Craft, The (Andrew Fleming, 1996, US)

Cruel Passion (Chris Boger, 1977, UK)

Curse, The (Jacqueline Garry, 1999, US)

Curse of the Cat People, The (Robert Wise and Gunther von Fritsch, 1944, US)

Curse of the Werewolf, The (Terence Fisher, 1961, UK)

Damaged Goods (Tom Ricketts and Richard Bennett, 1914, US)

Dangerous Liaisons (Stephen Frears, 1988, US/UK)

Dark Star (John Carpenter, 1974, US)

De Sade (Cy Endfield, 1969, US/Germany)

Deadly Sanctuary (aka *Marquis de Sade: Justine*, Jess Franco, 1969, Italy/West Germany)

Decameron, The (*Il Decameron*, Pier Paolo Pasolini, 1971, Italy/France/West Germany),

Deep Throat (Gerard Damiano, 1972, US)

Deliverance (John Boorman, 1972, US)

Demolition Man (Marco Brambilla, 1993, US)

Devil's Harvest (Ray Test, 1942, US)

Don't Look Now (Nicolas Roeg, 1973, Italy/UK)

Double Indemnity (Billy Wilder, 1944, US)

Dr Jekyll and Mr Hyde (Rouben Mamoulian, 1931, US)

Dr Jekyll and Sister Hyde (Roy Ward Baker, 1971, UK)

Dracula (Francis Ford Coppola, 1992, US)

Dragonwyck (Joseph L. Mankiewicz, 1946, US)

Ecstasy (*Extase*, Gustav Machatý, 1932/33, Czechoslovakia/Austria)

Edward Scissorhands (Tim Burton, 1990, US)

Elysia (director unknown, 1934, US)

Emmanuelle (Just Jaeckin, 1974, US)

End of the Road, The (Edward H. Griffth, 1919, US)

Enigma of Kasper Hauser, The (*Jeder für sich und Gott gegen alle*, Werner Herzog, 1974, West Germany)

Erotika (*Erotikon*, Gustav Machatý, 1920, Czechoslovakia)

Eugenie (Jess Franco, 1970, Spain/West Germany/Italy/France/US)

Event Horizon (Paul W. S. Anderson, 1997, US)

Evil Dead II (Sam Raimi, 1987, US)

Excalibur (John Boorman, US/UK, 1981)

Exit to Eden (Garry Marshall, 1994, US)

Exorcist, The (William Friedkin, 1973, US)

Eyes Wide Shut (Stanley Kubrick, 1999, US/UK)

Fall of the House of Usher, The (Roger Corman, 1960, US)

Fallen (Gregory Hoblit, 1998, US)

Fatal Attraction (Adrian Lyne, 1987, US)

Fear Eats the Soul (*Angst Essen Seele Auf*, Rainer Werner Fassbinder, 1974, West Germany)

Female Trouble (John Walters, 1975, US)

Fight Club (David Fincher, 1999, US)

Flash Gordon (Mike Hodges, 1982, US)

Flesh Gordon (Michael Benveniste and Howard Ziehm, 1974, US)

Fly, The (David Cronenberg, 1986, US)

Forbidden Planet (Fred M. Wilcox, 1956, US)

Frankenstein (James Whale, 1931, US)

Frenchman's Creek (Mitchell Leisen, 1944, US)

From Here to Eternity (Fred Zinnemann, 1953, US)

Gambling With Souls (Elmer Clifton, 1936, US)

Gaslight (Thorold Dickinson, 1940, UK)

Gaslight (George Cukor, 1945, US)

Ginger Snaps (John Fawcett, 2001, Canada)

Ginger Snaps Back (Grant Harvey, 2004, Canada)

Ginger Snaps Unleashed (Brett Sullivan, 2004, Canada)

Go Fish (Rose Troche, 1994, US)

Good Girl, The (Miguel Arteta, 2002, US/Germany/Netherlands)

Good Old Naughty Days, The (*Polissons et Galipettes,* compiled by Michel Reilhac, 2002, France)

Gwendoline (Just Jaeckin, 1984, France)

Halloween (John Carpenter, 1978, US)

Hellish Love (*Seidan botan-dôrô,* Chusei Sone, 1972, Japan)

Henry & June (Philip Kaufman, 1990, US)

His Girl Friday (Howard Hawks, 1940, US)

House of Whipcord (Pete Walker, 1974, UK)

How to Undress in Front of Your Husband (Dwain Esper, 1937, US)

Howling, The (Joe Dante, 1981, US)

Human Wreckage (John Griffith Wray, 1923, US)

Hunger, The (Tony Scott, 1983, UK)

Idiots, The (*Idioterne,* Lars von Trier, 1998, Denmark/Sweden/France/Netherlands/Italy)

I Married a Witch (René Clair, 1942, US)

Imitation of Life (John M. Stahl, 1934, US)

Imitation of Life (Douglas Sirk, 1959, US)

Ingagi (William Campbell, 1931, US)

Interview With the Vampire (Neil Jordan, 1994, US)

Intimacy (Patrice Chéreau, 2000, UK/France/Germany/Spain)

Intolerance: Love's Struggle Through the Ages (D. W. Griffith, 1916, US)

Is Your Daughter Safe? (Louis King and Leon Lee, 1927, US)

Island of Lost Souls (Erle C. Kenton, 1933, US)

I was a Teen-age Werewolf (Gene Fowler Jr, 1957, US)

Jane Eyre (Robert Stevenson, 1944, US)

Juliette de Sade (Lorenzo Sabitini, 1969, Sweden)

Justine de Sade (Claude Pierson, 1972, France/Italy/Canada)

Justine: The Seduction of an Innocent (Lev L. Spiro, 1996, France/Ireland/Netherlands)

Kill Bill: Vol. 1 (Quentin Tarantino, 2003, UK)

Kill Bill: Vol. 2 (Quentin Tarantino, 2004, UK)

King Kong (Merian C. Cooper and Ernest B. Schoedsack, 1933, US)

Kiss, The (director unknown, 1896, US)

Last Tango in Paris (*Ultimo tango a Parigi*, Bernardo Bertolucci, 1972, Italy/France)

Latex (Michael Ninn, 1995, US)

Letter from an Unknown Woman (Max Ophüls, 1948, US)

Little Witches (Jane Simpson, 1996, US)

Lola Montès (Max Ophüls, 1955, France/West Germany)

Love and Death on Long Island (Richard Kwietniowski, 1997, UK/Canada)

Madame de… (Max Ophüls, 1953, France/Italy)

Madame Satan (Cecil B. DeMille, 1930, US)

Madame X (Sam Wood and Gustav Machatý, 1937, US)

Madonna of the Seven Moons (Arthur Crabtree, 1945, UK)

Maidens in Uniform (*Mädchen in Uniform*, Leontine Sagan, 1931, Germany)

Maîtresse (Barbet Schroeder, 1973, France)

Mano Destra (Cleo Uebelmann, 1986, Switzerland)

Man with the Golden Arm, The (Otto Preminger, 1955, US)

Marat/Sade (Peter Brook, 1967, UK)

Marihuana (Dwain Esper, 1936, US)

Markisinnan de Sade (Ingmar Bergman, 1992, Sweden)

Marquis (Henri Xhonneux, 1989, Belgium/France)

Marquis de Sade (director unknown, 1996, Russia/US)

Marquis de Sade: Intimate Tales of the Dark Prince (Gywneth Gibby, 1997, US)

Marquise von Porno, La (director unknown, 1977, France)

Mary Reilly (Stephen Frears, 1996, US)

Matrix, The (Andy and Larry Wachowski, 1999, US)

Mermaids (Richard Benjamin, 1990, US)

Mildred Pierce (Michael Curtiz, 1945, US)

Milling the Militants (Percy Stow, 1913, UK)

Moulin Rouge (Baz Luhrmann, 2001, Australia/US)

Mummy, The (Karl Freund, 1932, US)

Murders on the Rue Morgue (Robert Florey, 1932, US)

Naked in the Wind (*L'Île aux femmes nues*, Henry LePage, 1953, France)

Narcotic (Dwain Esper/Vival Sodar't, 1933, US)

Necronomicon/Succubus (Jess Franco, 1968, West Germany)

New Wave Hookers (Dark Brothers, 1985, US)

Night of the Living Dead (George Romero, 1968, US)

Night Porter, The (*Il Portiere di Notte*, Liliana Cavani, 1974, Italy/US)

9 Songs (Michael Winterbottom, 2004, UK)

9½ Weeks (Adrian Lyne, 1986, US)

Now, Voyager (Irving Rapper, 1942, US)

Oedipus Rex (*Edipo Re*, Pier Paolo Pasolini, 1967, Italy/Morocco)

One Flew Over the Cuckoo's Nest (Milos Forman, 1975, US)

Out of the Past (aka *Build My Gallows High*, Jacques Tourneur, 1947, US)

Outlaw, The (Howard Hughes and Howard Hawks, 1943, US)

Peeping Tom (Michael Powell, 1959, UK)

Performance (Donald Cammel and Nicolas Roeg, 1970, UK)

Philadelphia Story, The (George Cukor, 1940, US)

Piano Teacher, The (*Le Pianiste*, Michael Haneke, 2000, France/Austria)

Piano, The (Jane Campion, 1993, Australia/New Zealand/France)

Pillow Talk (Michael Gordon, 1959, US)

Platinum Blonde (Frank Capra, 1931, US)

Preaching to the Perverted (Stuart Urban, 1997, UK)

Pretty Woman (Garry Marshall, 1990, US)

Princess Mononoke (*Mononoke-hime*, Hayao Miyazaki, 1997, Japan)

Private Life of Henry VIII, The (Alexander Korda, 1933, UK)

Punky Girls (c. 1995, director unknown, Holland/Germany)

Quills (Philip Kaufman, 2000, US/Germany/UK)

Raiders of the Lost Ark (Steven Spielberg, 1981, US)

Rambone the Destroyer (William Whett, 1985, US)

Rear Window (Alfred Hitchcock, 1954, US)

Rebecca (Alfred Hitchcock, 1940, US)

Reckless Moment, The (Max Ophüls, 1949, US)

Red Dust (Victor Fleming, 1932, US)

Red-Headed Woman (Jack Conway, 1932, US)

Reine Margot, La (Patrice Chereau, 1994, France/Italy/Germany)

Requiem for a Dream (Darren Aronofsky, 2000, US)

Roman Holiday (William Wyler, 1953, US)

Romance (Catherine Breillat, 1999, France)

Romeo + Juliet (Baz Lurhmann, 1996, US)

Rope (Alfred Hitchcock, 1948, US)

Sade (Benoit Jacquot, 2000, France)

Salo, 120 Days at Sodom (*Salo o le 120 giornate di Sodoma*, Pier Paolo Pasolini, 1976, Italy/France)

Scarlet Street (Fritz Lang, 1945, US)

Scarlet Youth (William Hughes Curran, 1928, US)

Scarlett Empress, The (Josef von Sternberg, 1934, US)

Secretary (Steven Shainberg, 2002, US)

Secret Beyond the Door (Fritz Lang, 1948, US)

Secrets of a Chambermaid (Eve Libertine, 1997, US)

Seventh Veil, The (Compton Bennett, 1946, UK)

Sexy Beast (Jonathan Glazer, 2000, Spain/UK)

She Done Him Wrong (Lowell Sherman, 1933, US)

Sherlock Holmes and the Case of the Silk Stocking (Simon Cellan Jones, 2004, UK)

Shine (Scott Hicks, 1996, Australia)

Shivers (David Cronenberg, 1975, Canada)

Sign of the Cross, The (Cecil B. DeMille, 1932, US)

Sin of Madelon Claudet, The (Edgar Selwyn, 1931, US)

Skull, The (Freddie Francis, 1965, UK)

Slaves in Bondage (aka *Crusade Against the Rackets*, Elmer Clifton, 1937, US)

Solaris (*Solyaris*, Andrei Tarkovsky, 1972, Soviet Union)

Solaris (Steven Soderbergh, 2003, US)

Son of Ali Baba, The (Kurt Neumann, 1952, US)

Starship Troopers (Paul Verhoeven, 1997, US)

Stealing Beauty (Bernardo Bertolucci, 1996, Italy/France/UK)

Stella Dallas (King Vidor, 1937, US)

Story of O, The (*Histoire d'O*, Just Jaeckin, 1975, France/West Germany)

Streetcar Named Desire, A (Elia Kazan, 1951, US)

Summer with Monica (*Summaren Med Monika*, Ingmar Bergman, 1953, Sweden)

Swoon (Tom Kalin, 1992, US)

Tarzan and his Mate (Cedric Gibbons, 1934, US)

Teaserama (Irving Klaw, 1955, US)

Test Tube Babies (W. Merle Connell, 1948, US)

Texas Chainsaw Massacre, The (Tobe Hooper, 1974, US)

Thelma and Louise (Ridley Scott, 1991, US)

Titanic (James Cameron, 1997, US)

Tomb of Ligeia, The (Roger Corman, 1965, UK)

Top Gun (Tony Scott, 1986, US)

Trader Horn (W. S. Van Dyke, 1931, US)

Twin Peaks: Fire Walk with Me (David Lynch, 1992, France/US)

Underworld (Len Wiseman, 2003, US/Germany/Hungary/UK)

Unfaithful (Adrian Lyne, 2001, US/Germany/France)

Varietease (Irving Claw, 1954, US)

Vera Drake (Mike Leigh, 2004, UK/France/New Zealand)

Vice and Virtue (*La Vice et la Vertu*, Roger Vadim, 1963, France/Italy)

Virgin (*36 fillette*, Catherine Breillat, 1988, France)

Wages of Sin, The (Herman E. Webber, 1938, US)

War Zone, The (Tim Roth, 1999, Italy/UK)

Waterloo Bridge (Mervyn LeRoy, 1940, US)

Waterloo Road (Sidney Gilliat, 1945, US)

Way Down East (D. W. Griffith, 1920, US)

West Side Story (Jerome Robbins and Robert Wise, 1961, US)

What Can I do With a Male Nude (Ron Peck, 1975, UK)

Whip and the Body, The (Le Frusta e il Corpo, Mario Bava, 1963, Italy/France)

Wicked Lady, The (Leslie Arliss, 1945, UK)

Wicker Man, The (Robin Hardy, 1973, UK)

Wild Women (aka *White Sirens of Africa/Bowanga Bowanga,* Norman Dawn, 1951, US)

Wolf (Mike Nichols, 1992, US)

Wolf Man, The (George Waggner, 1941, US)

Written on the Wind (Douglas Sirk, 1958, US)

Wuthering Heights (William Wyler, 1939, US)

You've Got Mail (Nora Ephron, 1998, US)

Zandalee (Sam Pilsbury, 1991, US)

Bibliography

Aaron, Michele (ed.) (2004) *New Queer Cinema: A Critical Reader*. Edinburgh: Edinburgh University Press.

Altman, Rick (1984) 'A Semantic/Syntactic Approach to Film Genre', *Cinema Journal*, 23, 3, 6–18.

Andrews, David (2004) 'Convention and Ideology in the Contemporary Softcore Feature: The Sexual Architecture of *House of Love*', *The Journal of Popular Culture*, 38, 1, 5–33.

Barker, Martin (1984) *A Haunt of Fears: The Strange History of the British Horror Comics Campaign*. London: Pluto Press.

Bataille, Georges (1987) *Eroticism*. Trans. Mary Dalwood. London: Marion Boyars.

____ (1991) *The Accursed Share, Volumes II & III*. Trans. Robert Hurley. New York: Zone Books.

Benshoff, Harry (1997) *Monsters in the Closet: Homosexuality and the Horror Film*. Manchester: Manchester University Press.

Berenstein, Rhona, J. (1996) *Attack of the Leading Ladies: Gender, Sexuality and Spectatorship in Classic Horror Cinema*. New York: Columbia University Press.

Black, Gregory. D. (1994) *Hollywood Censored: Morality Codes, Catholics, and the Movies*. Cambridge, New York and Melbourne: Cambridge University Press.

____ (1997) *The Catholic Crusade Against the Movies 1940–1975*. Cambridge, New York and Melbourne: Cambridge University Press.

Blanchot, Maurice (1991) *'Sade' in Three Complete Novels: Justine, Philosophy and the Bedroom, Eugenie de Franval*. London: Arrow Books.

Bly, Robert (2004) *Iron John: A Book about Men* (second edition). Cambridge, MA: DeCapo Press.

Bogle, Donald (1991) *Toms, Coons, Mulattoes, Mammies and Bucks: An Interpretative History of Blacks in American Film* (second edition). New York: Continuum.

Bordwell, David (1991) *Making Meaning: Inference and Rhetoric in the Interpretation of Cinema*. Cambridge and London: Harvard University Press.

Bremmer, Jan (1998) 'Mythology', in Simon Hornblower and Anthony Spawforth (eds) *The Oxford Companion to Classical Civilisation*. Oxford and New York: Oxford University Press.

Bristow, Joseph (1997) *Sexuality*. London and New York: Routledge.

Bullough, Vern L., Dwight Dixon and Joan Dixon (1994) 'Sadism, Masochism and History, or When is Behaviour Sado-Masochistic?', in Roy Porter and Mikulas Teich (eds) *Sexual Knowledge, Sexual Science: The History of Attitudes to Sexuality*. Cambridge: Cambridge University Press.

Burston, Paul (1995) 'Just a Gigolo? Narcissism, Nellyism and the New Man Theme', in Paul Burston and Colin Richardson (eds) *A Queer Romance: Lesbians, Gay Men and Popular Culture*. London and New York: Routledge.

Califia, Pat (1994) *Public Sex: The Culture of Radical Sex*. Pittsburg: Cleis.

Carter, Angela (1979) *The Sadeian Woman: An Exercise in Cultural History*. London: Virago.

____ (1981) *The Bloody Chamber*. Harmondsworth: Penguin.

Clemens, Valdine (1999) *The Return of the Repressed: Gothic Horror From The Castle of Otranto to Alien*. New York: State University of New York Press.

Clover, Carol, J. (1992) *Men, Women and Chainsaws: Gender in the Modern Horror Film*. London: British Film Institute.

Comfort, Alex (2002) *The Joy of Sex: Revised and Updated for the 21st Century*. New York, London, Toronto and Sydney: Pocket Books.

Creed, Barbara (1993) *The Monstrous-Feminine: Film, Feminism, Psychoanalysis*. New York and London: Routledge.

De Lauretis, Teresa (1991) 'Queer Theory: Lesbian and Gay Sexualities: An Introduction', *differences: a journal of feminist cultural studies*, 3, 2, iii–xvii.

Deleuze, Gilles and Leopold von Sacher-Masoch (1991) *Masochism*. New York: Zone Books.

Dillon, M. C. (2000) 'Aletheia, Poiesis, and Eros: Truth and Untruth in the Poetic Construction of Love' in Hugh J. Silverman (ed.) *Philosophy and Desire*. New York and London: Routledge.

Doane, Mary Ann (1984) 'The Woman's Film: Possession and Address', in Mary Ann Doane, Patricia Mellencamp and Linda Williams (eds) *Re-Vision: Essays in Feminist Film Criticism*. New York: University Publications of America/American Film Institute.

____ (1987) *Desire to Desire: The Women's Film of the 1940s*. Basingstoke: Macmillan.

Doherty, Thomas (1999) *Pre-Code Hollywood: Sex, Immorality and Insurrection in American Cinema 1930–34*. New York: Columbia University Press.

Douglas, Mary (1991) *Purity and Danger: An Analysis of the Concepts of Pollution and Taboo*. London: Routledge.

Dyer, Richard (1992) *Only Entertainment*. London and New York: Routledge.

Edmundson, Mark (1999) *Nightmare on Main Street: Angels, Sadomasochism and the Culture of the Gothic*. Cambridge, MA and London: Harvard University Press.

Evans, Caroline and Lorraine Gamman (1995) 'The Gaze Revisited, or Reviewing Queer Viewing', in Paul Burston and Colin Richardson (eds) *A Queer Romance: Lesbians, Gay Men and Popular Culture*. London and New York: Routledge.

Faludi, Susan (1992) *Backlash: The Undeclared War Against Women*. London: Chatto and Windus.

Frayling, Christopher (1996) 'Jekyll and Hyde', in Kim Newman (ed.) *The BFI Companion of Horror*. London: Cassell/British Film Institute.

Freud, Sigmund (1977) *On Sexuality*. Translated under the editorship of James Strachey. Volume compiled by Angela Richards. London: Pelican.

— 'Three Essays on the Theory of Sexuality' [1905]

— 'Family Romances' [1909]

— 'The Dissolution of the Oedipus Complex' [1924]

_____ (1985) *Civilisation, Society and Religion, Group Psychology, Civilisation and Its Discontents*. Translated under the editorship of James Strachey. Volume edited by Albert Dickson. Harmondsworth: Penguin.

— '"Civilised" Sexual Morality and Modern Nervous Illness' [1908]

— 'Civilisation and Its Discontents' [1930]

_____ (1990a) *The Origins of Religion*. Translated under the editorship of James Strachey. Edited by Albert Dickson. Harmondsworth: Penguin.

— 'Totem and Taboo' [1913]

— 'Moses and Monotheism' [1939]

_____ (1990b) *Art and Literature*. Translated under the editorship of James Strachey. Edited by Albert Dickson. Harmondsworth: Penguin.

— 'The "Uncanny"' [1919]

_____ (1991a) *On Metapsychology*. Translated under the editorship of James Strachey. Volume compiled by Angela Richards. Harmondsworth: Penguin.

— 'On Narcissism: An Introduction' [1914]

— 'Repression' [1915]

_____ (1991b) *Introductory Letters on Psychoanalysis*. Translated under the editorship of James Strachey. Edited by James Strachey and Angela Richards. Harmondsworth: Penguin.

— 'The Archaic Features and Infantilism of Dreams' [1916]

— 'The Sexual Life of Human Beings' [1917]

Foucault, Michel (1984) *The History of Sexuality: An Introduction*. Translated by Robert Hurley. London: Peregrine.

Gilman, Sander L. (1994) 'Sigmund Freud and the Sexologists: A Second Reading', in Roy Porter and Mikulas Teich (eds) *Sexual Knowledge, Sexual Science: The History of Attitudes to Sexuality*. Cambridge: Cambridge University Press.

Gillet, Sue (1995) 'Lips and Fingers; Jane Campion's *The Piano*', *Screen*, 36, 3, 272–89.

Gledhill, Christine (1992a) 'Between Melodrama and Realism: Anthony Asquith's *Underground* and King Vidor's *The Crowd*', in Jane Gaines (ed.) *Classical Hollywood Narrative:*

The Paradigm Wars. Durham and London: Duke University Press.

____ (1992b) 'Pleasurable negotiations', in Francis Bonner (ed.) *Imagining Women: Cultural Representation and Gender*. Cambridge: Polity Press/Open University.

____ (1994) 'Image and Voice: Approaches to Marxist-Feminist Film Criticism', in Diane Carson, Linda Dittmar and Janice Welsch (eds) *Multiple Voices in Feminist Film Criticism*. Minnesota: University of Minnesota Press.

Graves, Robert (1998) *Greek Myths*. London: The Folio Society.

Harvey, Sylvia (1978) 'Women's Place: The Absent Family in Film Noir', in Ann Kaplan (ed.) *Women in Film Noir*. London: British Film Institute.

Haskell, Molly (1987) *From Reverence to Rape: The Treatment of Women in the Movies* (second edition). Chicago: University of Chicago Press.

Hauser, Renate (1994) 'Krafft-Ebing's psychological understanding of sexual behaviour', in Roy Porter and Mikulas Teich (eds) *Sexual Knowledge, Sexual Science: The History of Attitudes to Sexuality*. Cambridge: Cambridge University Press.

Hayward, Susan (2000) *Cinema Studies: The Key Concepts* (second edition). London and New York: Routledge.

Hunt, Leon (1998) *British Low Culture: From Safari Suits to Sexploitation*. London and New York: Routledge.

Hutton, Ronald (1997) *The Pagan Religions of the Ancient British Isles: Their Nature and Legacy*. Oxford: Blackwell.

Jacobs, Lea (1995) *The Wages of Sin: Censorship and the Fallen Woman Film 1928–1942*. Berkeley, Los Angeles and London: California University Press.

Jenks, Chris (2003) *Transgression*. New York and London: Routledge.

King, Geoff (2002) *Film Comedy*. London: Wallflower Press.

Kinsey, Alfred C., Wardell B. Pomeroy and Clyde E. Martin (1948) *Sexual Behaviour in the Male Human*. Philadelphia: WB Saunders.

____ (1953) *Sexual Behaviour in the Female Human*. Philadelphia: WB Saunders.

Klein, Melanie (1991) 'Early Stages of the Oedipus Conflict', in Juliet Mitchell (ed.) *The Selected Melanie Klein*. Harmondsworth: Penguin.

Klinger, Barbara (1994) *Melodrama and Meaning: History, Culture and the Films of Douglas Sirk*. Bloomington and Indianapolis: Indiana University Press.

Kolker, Robert (1999) *Film, Form and Culture*. Boston and London: McGraw Hill.

Krafft-Ebing, Richard (1997) *Psychopathia Sexualis: The Case Histories*. Edited and trans. Domino Falls. London: Velvet Press.

Kristeva, Julia (1982) *Powers of Horror: An Essay in Abjection*. New York: Columbia University Press.

Krutnik, Frank (1991) *In a Lonely Street: Film Noir, Genre, Masculinity*. London and New York: Routledge.

Krzywinska, Tanya (1998a) 'Dissidence and Authenticity in Dyke Porn and Actuality TV', in Mike Wayne (ed.) *Dissident Voices: The Politics of Television and Cultural Change*. London:

Pluto Press.

_____ (1998b) 'Masquerading the Phallus: Laughter and the Phallus/Penis Analogue in Explicit Sex Films', *Diatribe*, 8, 15–23.

_____ (1999) 'Cicciolina: Transgression and Abjection in Explicit Sex films', in Michele Aaron (ed.) *The Body's Perilous Pleasures*. Edinburgh University Press.

_____ (2000a) 'The Dynamics of Squirting', in Graeme Harper and Xavier Mendik (eds) *Unruly Pleasures: Cult Cinema and Its Critics*. London: FAB Press.

_____ (2000b) *A Skin for Dancing In: Possession, Witchcraft and Voodoo in Cinema*. Trowbridge: Flicks Books.

_____ (2006) 'Lurking Beneath the Skin: British pagan landscapes in popular cinema', in Robert Fish (ed.) *Cinematic Countrysides*. Manchester: Manchester University Press.

Kuhn, Annette (1988) *Cinema, Censorship and Sexuality 1909–1925*. London and New York: Routledge.

Lacan, Jacques (1982) 'God and the Jouissance of The Woman: A Love Letter', in Juliet Mitchell and Jacqueline Rose (eds) *Feminine Sexuality: Jacques Lacan & The Ecole Freudienne*. Trans. Jacqueline Rose. Basingstoke: Macmillan.

_____ (1987) 'In You More than You', in *The Four Fundamental Concepts of Psychoanalysis*. Harmondsworth: Penguin.

_____ (1991) *Le Seminaire, Livre XVII. L'envres de la Psychoanalyse. 1969–1970*. Edited by Jacque Alain-Miller. Paris: Seuil.

_____ (1998) 'Encore', in *On Feminine Sexuality, The Limits of Love and Knowledge 1972–1973 – Encore: Seminar of Jacques Lacan Book XX*. Edited by Jacques-Alain Miller. Trans. Bruce Fink. New York and London: W. W. Norton.

Laplanche, Jean (1989) *New Foundations for Psychoanalysis*. Oxford: Blackwell.

Laplanche, Jean and Jean-Bertrand Pontalis (1988) *The Language of Psychoanalysis*. Trans. Donald Nicholson-Smith. London: The Institute of Psychoanalysis/Karnac Books.

Laqueur, Thomas (1990) *Making Sex: Body and Gender from the Greeks to Freud*. Cambridge, MA and London: Harvard University Press.

Lev, Peter (2000) *American Films of the 70s: Conflicting Visions*. Austin: Texas University Press.

Lewis, Jon (2000) *Hollywood v. Hard Core: How the Struggle over Censorship Saved the Modern Film Industry*. New York and London: New York University Press.

MacKinnon, Kenneth (1998) *Uneasy Pleasures: The Male as Erotic Object*. Madison: Fairleigh Dickinson University Press.

Margolis, Harriet (ed.) (2000) *Jane Campion's The Piano*. Cambridge: Cambridge University Press.

Mathews, Tom Dewe (1994) *Censored: The History of Film Censorship in Britain*. London: Chatto and Windus.

Mellen, Joan (1974) *Women and their Sexuality in Film*. London: Davis-Poynter.

Miller, Philip and Molly Devon (1995) *Screw the Roses, Send Me the Thorns*. Fairfield: Mystic Rose.

Minsky, Rosalind (1996) 'Klein: Phantasy and the Mother', in Rosalind Minsky (ed.) *Psycho-analysis and Gender*. London: Routledge.

Muller, Eddie and Daniel Faris (1996) *Grindhouse: The Forbidden World of Adults Only Cinema*. New York: St Martin's Griffin.

Mulvey, Laura (1975) 'Visual Pleasure and Narrative Cinema', *Screen*, 16, 3, 6–18.

Neale, Steve (1984) '*Halloween*: Suspense, Aggression and the Look', in Barry Keith Grant (ed.) *Planks of Reason: Essays on the Horror Film*. Metuchen and London: Scarecrow Press.

____ (1993) 'Masculinity as Spectacle', in Steven Cohan and Ina Rae Hark (eds) *Screening the Male: Exploring Masculinity in Hollywood Cinema*. London and New York: Routledge.

____ (2000) *Genre and Hollywood*. London and New York: Routledge.

Newitz, Annalee (1995) 'A Lower-Class, Sexy Monster: American Liberalism in Mamoulian's *Dr Jekyll and Mr Hyde*', *Bright Lights Film Journal*, 15, 12–17.

O'Toole, Laurence (1999) *Pornocopia: Porn, Sex, Technology and Desire*. London: Serpent's Tail.

Ovid (1981) *Metamorphoses*. Trans. Mary M. Innes. Harmondsworth: Penguin.

Paul, William (2004) 'What Does Dr. Judd Want? Transformation, Transference and the Problem of Irony', in Steven Jay Schneider (ed.) *Horror Film and Psychoanalysis: Freud's Worst Nightmare*. Cambridge: Cambridge University Press.

Pasolini, Pier Paolo (1988) *Heretical Empiricism*. Edited by Louise K. Barnett. Trans. by Ben Lawton and Louise K. Barnett. Bloomington: Indiana University Press.

Petley, Julian (2000) 'The Censor and the State: Or Why Horny Catbabe Matters', *Journal of Popular British Cinema*, 3, 93–103.

Phelps, Guy (1975) *Film Censorship*. London: Gollancz.

Porter, Roy and Mikulas Teich (1994) 'Introduction', in Roy Porter and Mikulas Teich (eds) *Sexual Knowledge, Sexual Science: The History of Attitudes to Sexuality*. Cambridge: Cambridge University Press.

Randall, Richard S. (1985) 'Censorship: from *The Miracle* to *Deep Throat*', in Tino Balio (ed.) *The American Film Industry* (second edition). Madison and London: University of Wisconsin Press.

Reich, Wilhem (1961) The Function of the Orgasm. New York: Ferrar, Strauss & Giroux.

____ (1970) The Sexual Revolution. Towards a Self-Governing Character Structure. New York: Ferrar, Strauss & Giroux.

Rich, B. Ruby (1993) 'Homo Pomo: The New Queer Cinema', in Pam Cook and Philip Dodd (eds) *Women and Film: A Sight and Sound Reader*. London: Scarlet Press.

Richards, Chris (2004) 'What are We? Sex, Adolescence and Intimacy in *Buffy the Vampire Slayer*', *Continuum: Journal of Media and Cultural Studies*, 18, 1, 121–37.

Robertson, James C. (2000) 'Unspeakable Acts: The BBFC and *Cape Fear* (1962)', in Julian Petley and Ian Conrich (eds) *Journal of Popular Culture: Forbidden British Cinema*, 3, 69–76.

Rodley, Chris (ed.) (1992) *Cronenberg on Cronenberg*. London, Boston: Faber and Faber.

Salecl, Renata (2002) 'Love Anxieties', in Suzanne Barnard and Bruce Fink (eds) *Reading Semi-*

nar XX: Lacan's Major Work on Love, Knowledge, and Feminine Sexuality. New York: State University of New York Press.

Schaefer, Eric (1999) "Bold! Shocking! Daring! True!": A History of Exploitation Films, 1919–1959. Durham and London: Duke University Press.

Schaeffer, Neil (2000) The Marquis de Sade: A Life. Cambridge, Massachusetts: Harvard University Press.

Schwimmer, Brian (2003) 'Defining Marriage' www.umanitoba.ca/faculties/arts/anthropology/tutor/marriage/defining.html. Accessed 20 October 2004.

Sedgwick, Eve Kosofsky (1992) English Literature and Male Homosexual Desire (second edition) New York: Columbia University Press.

Shaviro, Steven (1993) The Cinematic Body. Minneapolis and London: University of Minnesota Press.

Showalter, Elaine (1992) Sexual Anarchy. London: Virago.

Silverman, Hugh (2000) 'Twentieth-Century Desire and the Histories of Philosophy', in Hugh Silverman (ed.) Philosophy and Desire. New York and London: Routledge.

Silverman, Kaja (1981) 'Masochism and Subjectivity', Framework, 12, 5, 2–9.

_____ (1992) 'Histoire d'O: The Construction of a Female Subject', in Carole S Vance (ed.) Pleasure and Danger: Exploring Female Sexuality. London: Pandora Press.

Simmon, Scott (1993) The Films of D. W. Griffith. Cambridge: Cambridge University Press.

Skal, David. J. (1998) Screams of Reason: Mad Science and Modern Culture. New York and London: W. W. Norton.

Sontag, Susan (1983) A Susan Sontag Reader. London: Penguin.

Stallybrass, Peter and Allon White (1986) The Politics and Poetics of Transgression. London: Methuen.

Stanton, Domna C. (ed.) (1992) Discourses of Sexuality: From Aristotle to AIDS. Michigan: University of Michigan Press.

Studlar, Gaylyn (1985) 'Masochism and the Perverse Pleasures of Cinema', in Bill Nichols (ed.) Movies and Methods, Volume II. Berkeley, Los Angeles and London: University of California Press.

Sutton-Smith, Brian (2001) The Ambiguity of Play. Boston: Harvard University Press.

Telotte, J. P. (1995) Replications: A Robotic History of the Science Fiction Film. Urbana and Chicago: University of Illinois Press.

Twitchell, James B. (1985) Dreadful Pleasures: An Anatomy of Modern Horror. Oxford and New York: Oxford University Press.

Vallence, J. T. (1998) 'Knowledge about Animals', in Simon Hornblower and Anthony Spawforth (eds) The Oxford Companion to Classical Civilisation. Oxford and New York: Oxford University Press.

Van Haute, Phillipe (1995) 'Fatal Attraction: Jean Laplanche on Sexuality, Subjectivity and Singularity', Radical Philosophy, 73, 5–12.

Vardac, Nicholas A. (1991) 'Realism and Romance: D. W. Griffith', in Marcia Landy (ed.) Imitations of Life: A Reader on Film and Television Melodrama. Detroit: Wayne State University Press.

Walsh, Frank (1996) Sin and Censorship: The Catholic Church and the Motion Picture Industry. New Haven and New York: Yale University Press.

Warner, Marina (1993) 'The Uses of Enchantment', in Duncan Petrie (ed.) Cinema and the Realms of Enchantment. London: British Film Institute.

Warner, Marina (1998) No Go the Bogeyman: Scaring, Lulling and Making Mock. London: Chatto and Windus.

Weeks, Jeffrey (1985) Sexuality and its Discontents. London and New York: Routledge.

Williams, Linda (1990) Hard Core. London: Pandora Press.

Williams, Linda Ruth (2002) 'Sex and Censoriousness: Pornography and Censorship in Britain', in Adam Briggs and Paul Cobley (eds) The Media: An Introduction (second edition). London: Longman.

_____ (2005) The Erotic Thriller in Contemporary Cinema. Edinburgh: Edinburgh University Press.

Wood, Robin (1984) 'An Introduction to the American Horror Film', in Barry Keith Grant (ed.) Planks of Reason: Essays on the Horror Film. Metuchen and London: Scarecrow Press.

Wright Wexman, Virginia (1988) 'Horrors of the Body: Hollywood's discourse on beauty and Rouben Mamoulian's Dr Jekyll and Mr Hyde', in William Veeder and Gordon Hirsch (eds) Dr Jekyll and Mr Hyde After One Hundred Years. Chicago: University of Chicago Press.

_____ (1993) Creating the Couple: Love, Marriage and Hollywood Performance. Princeton: Princeton University Press.

Žižek, Slavoj (1991) Looking Awry: An Introduction to Jacques Lacan through Popular Culture. Cambridge, MA and London: MIT Press.

Sex and the Cinema

Index

index